MW01008681

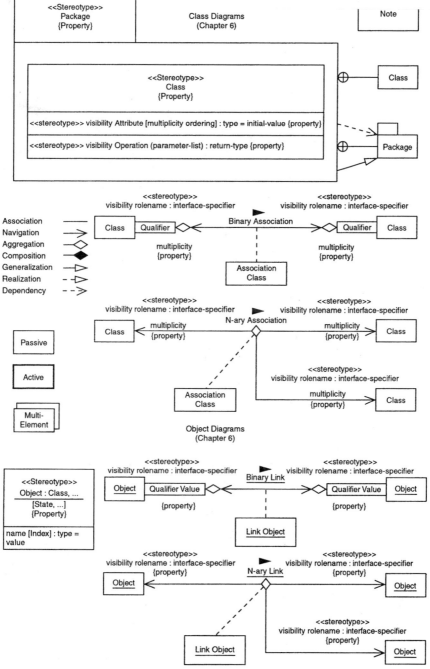

Class Diagrams
(Chapter 6)

<<Stereotype>>
Package
{Property}

<<Stereotype>>
Class
{Property}

<<stereotype>> visibility Attribute [multiplicity ordering] : type = initial-value {property}

<<stereotype>> visibility Operation (parameter-list) : return-type {property}

Class

Package

Association
Navigation
Aggregation
Composition
Generalization
Realization
Dependency

<<stereotype>>
visibility rolename : interface-specifier

<<stereotype>>
visibility rolename : interface-specifier

Binary Association

Class | Qualifier

Qualifier | Class

multiplicity
{property}

multiplicity
{property}

Association
Class

<<stereotype>>
visibility rolename : interface-specifier

<<stereotype>>
visibility rolename : interface-specifier

N-ary Association

Class

Class

multiplicity
{property}

multiplicity
{property}

<<stereotype>>
visibility rolename : interface-specifier

Passive

Active

Multi-
Element

Association
Class

multiplicity
{property}

Class

Object Diagrams
(Chapter 6)

<<Stereotype>>
Object : Class, ...
[State, ...]
{Property}

name [Index] : type =
value

<<stereotype>>
visibility rolename : interface-specifier

<<stereotype>>
visibility rolename : interface-specifier

Binary Link

Object | Qualifier Value

Qualifier Value | Object

{property}

{property}

Link Object

<<stereotype>>
visibility rolename : interface-specifier
{property}

<<stereotype>>
visibility rolename : interface-specifier
{property}

N-ary Link

Object

Object

<<stereotype>>
visibility rolename : interface-specifier
{property}

Link Object

Object

GUIDE TO
APPLYING THE UML

Springer

New York
Berlin
Heidelberg
Hong Kong
London
Milan
Paris
Tokyo

Sinan Si Alhir

GUIDE TO APPLYING THE UML

With 241 Illustrations

 Springer

Sinan Si Alhir
Consultant
salhir@earthlink.net

Library of Congress Cataloging-in-Publication Data
Alhir, Sinan Si.
        Guide to applying the UML / Sinan Si Alhir.
            p. cm.
        Includes bibliographical references and index.
        ISBN 0-387-95209-8 (alk. paper)
            1. Application software—Development.   2. UML
(computer science)   I. Title.
QA76.76.D47 A423   2002   2002019557
005.1'17—dc21

ISBN 0-387-95209-8   Printed on acid-free paper.

Printed in the United States of America.

9 8 7 6 5 4 3 2 1   SPIN 10791069

www.springer-ny.com

Springer-Verlag   New York Berlin Heidelberg
A member of BertelsmanSpringer Science+Business Media GmbH

This book is dedicated to
my father, Saad, and my mother, Rabab,
my brothers, Ghazwan and Phillip,
my wife, Milad,
and last, but surely never least,
my daughter, Nora.

I will not forget any of you,
and I only ask that you please remember me.

Contents

Preface .... *xiii*

1. **Introduction to the Unified Modeling Language (UML)** *1*
   1.1. What is the Unified Modeling Language (UML)? *1*
   1.2. The Unified Modeling Language (UML) and Process
        or Methodology *3*
   1.3. History of the Unified Modeling Language (UML) *5*
   1.4. Effectively and Successfully Applying the Unified
        Modeling Language (UML) *9*

2. **Modeling** *12*
   2.1. Languages *12*
        2.1.1. Alphabets *13*
        2.1.2. Words *13*
        2.1.3. Sentences *14*
        2.1.4. Paragraphs *14*
        2.1.5. Sections *17*
        2.1.6. Documents *18*
        2.1.7. Other Elements *18*
   2.2. Systems and Contexts *23*
        2.2.1. Domains or Spaces *23*
        2.2.2. Systems *23*
        2.2.3. Architectures *24*
        2.2.4. Models *26*
        2.2.5. Architectural Views *30*
        2.2.6. Diagrams *31*
   2.3. Modeling Mechanisms *33*
        2.3.1. Perspectives *34*
        2.3.2. Levels of Abstraction *36*
        2.3.3. Dichotomies *37*
        2.3.4. Extension Mechanisms *38*

2.4. Processes and Methodologies *39*
    2.4.1. Development Cycles and Phases *40*
    2.4.2. Iteration Cycles and Phases *42*
    2.4.3. Iteration Phase Details *44*
    2.4.4. Heuristics *46*
2.5. The Value of Processes and Methodologies *52*
    2.5.1. The Quesion *52*
    2.5.2. Fine Cuisine and Systems Development *53*
    2.5.3. The Roadmap *56*
    2.5.4. The Answer *59*

3. Object Orientation *61*
3.1. Principles of Object Orientation *61*
    3.1.1. Abstraction *61*
    3.1.2. Encapsulation *63*
    3.1.3. Generalization *65*
    3.1.4. Polymorphism *66*
3.2. Structural (Static) Concepts *66*
    3.2.1. Class and Object Diagrams *66*
    3.2.2. Use-Case Diagrams *87*
    3.2.3. Component Diagrams *90*
    3.2.4. Deployment Diagrams *91*
3.3. Behavioral (Dynamic) Concepts *93*
    3.3.1. Sequence and Collaboration Diagrams *95*
    3.3.2. State Diagrams *104*
    3.3.3. Activity Diagrams *108*
3.4. Object-Oriented Systems *111*
    3.4.1. Packages *112*
    3.4.2. Templates *114*
    3.4.3. Patterns and Frameworks *115*
    3.4.4. Systems *117*

4. The Roadmap *123*
4.1. The Unified Modeling Language (UML) Sentence *124*
    4.1.1. Collaborating and Interacting Systems *124*
    4.1.2. Services *124*
    4.1.3. Service Realizations *126*
    4.1.4. The Unified Modeling Language (UML)
        Sentence *128*
4.2. The Roadmap Space *130*
    4.2.1. Perspectives and Levels of Abstraction *130*
    4.2.2. Cartesian Product *130*
    4.2.3. The Roadmap Space *132*

4.3. The General Roadmap 135
    4.3.1. Perspectives and Levels of Abstraction 135
    4.3.2. Process Disciplines 137
    4.3.3. The General Roadmap 138
4.4. Detailed and Notational Roadmap 140
    4.4.1. Conceptual Elements 140
    4.4.2. Mechanisms 144
    4.4.3. The Roadmap 146
    4.4.4. A Roadmap Example 154
4.5. Applying the Roadmap 182
    4.5.1. Heavyweight and Lightweight Approaches 183
    4.5.2. Heuristics 184

5. Use-Case (User) Modeling 186
5.1. Use-Case Diagrams 186
    5.1.1. Actors 186
    5.1.2. Use Cases 188
    5.1.3. Actor Relationships 194
    5.1.4. Use-Case Relationships 196
5.2. Applying Use-Case Diagrams 205
    5.2.1. The Construct 206
    5.2.2. Requirements 208
    5.2.3. Unification 211

6. Structural (Static) Modeling 212
6.1. Class Diagrams 212
    6.1.1. Classifiers 212
    6.1.2. Relationships 231
6.2. Object Diagrams 247
    6.2.1. Classifier Instances 247
    6.2.2. Relationship Instances 251
6.3. Applying Class and Object Diagrams 252
    6.3.1. Conceptual Elements 253
    6.3.2. Mechanisms 254
    6.3.3. The Construct 254
    6.3.4. Analysis 257
    6.3.5. Design 262
    6.3.6. Validation 270
    6.3.7. Unification 276

7. Behavioral (Dynamic) Modeling 277
7.1. Sequence Diagrams 277
    7.1.1. Classifier Roles 279
    7.1.2. Interactions 280

7.1.3.   Lifelines 283
7.1.4.   Activations 286
7.1.5.   Messages and Stimuli 286
7.2.   Collaboration Diagrams 289
7.2.1.   Association Roles 290
7.2.2.   Collaborations 292
7.2.3.   Messages and Stimuli 294
7.2.4.   Behavioral Organization 300
7.3.   Statechart Diagrams 307
7.3.1.   States 307
7.3.2.   Transitions 310
7.3.3.   Submachines 315
7.4.   Activity Diagrams 316
7.4.1.   Action States 316
7.4.2.   Swimlanes 318
7.4.3.   Flows 318
7.5.   Applying Sequence, Collaboration, Statechart,
       and Activity Diagrams 320
7.5.1.   Sequence Diagrams 321
7.5.2.   Collaboration Diagrams 321
7.5.3.   State Diagrams 322
7.5.4.   Activity Diagrams 325

8. **Component (Implementation) Modeling** 326
8.1.   Component Diagrams 326
8.1.1.   Artifacts 327
8.1.2.   Components 328
8.1.3.   Component Relationships 331
8.2.   Applying Component Diagrams 332
8.2.1.   The Construct 332
8.2.2.   Implementation 333
8.2.3.   Unification 334

9. **Deployment (Environment) Modeling** 335
9.1.   Deployment Diagrams 335
9.1.1.   Nodes 336
9.1.2.   Node Relationships 336
9.2.   Applying Deployment Diagrams 339
9.2.1.   The Construct 340
9.2.2.   Deployment 340
9.2.3.   Unification 341

10. Extension Mechanisms *343*
   10.1. Architecture of the Unified Modeling
         Language (UML) *343*
         10.1.1. The Four-Layer Metamodeling Architecture *344*
         10.1.2. The Unified Modeling Language (UML)
                  Metamodel *348*
   10.2. Stereotypes *350*
         10.2.1. Declaration *350*
         10.2.2. Application *354*
   10.3. Properties *358*
         10.3.1. Constraints *358*
         10.3.2. Tag Definitions and Tagged Values *359*
   10.4. Profiles *361*

11. The Object Constraint Language (OCL) *364*
   11.1. What is the Object Constraint Language (OCL)? *364*
   11.2. Expressions *365*
         11.2.1. Invariants *366*
         11.2.2. Preconditions and Postconditions *367*
         11.2.3. Package Statements *369*
         11.2.4. Let Expressions and Definition Constraints *370*
   11.3. Properties *370*
         11.3.1. Classifiers and Instances *373*
         11.3.2. Associations and Links *374*
         11.3.3. Classifier and Instance-Scoped Properties *375*
   11.4. The Standard Object Constraint Language
         (OCL) Types *376*
         11.4.1. Basic Types *377*
         11.4.2. Collection Types *381*
   11.5. The Standard Object Constraint Language
         (OCL) Package *389*

References *391*

Index *395*

Preface

The great philosopher Ludwig Wittgenstein once said, "The limits of your language are the limits of your world." Within the world of systems engineering—a discipline bound by an elegant universe we often call reality, wherein two dimensions, time and space, establish the landscape for the intertwining dance of change and complexity—what language ought people and teams, processes, tools, and technologies leverage to establish a culture capable of reaching its common goals and vision in providing more value (functionality and quality), in less time to market, and with a lower cost? Could the answer to this question be the Unified Modeling Language (UML)? And if the answer is the UML, how ought it be effectively and successfully applied and leveraged?

Overview

Guide to Applying the UML offers a practical tool-, process-, and technology-independent roadmap for effectively and successfully applying the UML.

The Unified Modeling Language (UML) is an evolutionary general-purpose, broadly applicable, tool-supported, and industry-standardized modeling language for specifying, visualizing, constructing, and documenting the artifacts of a system-intensive process.

The UML was originally conceived by and evolved primarily from Rational Software Corporation and three of the most prominent methodologists, the "Three Amigos," Grady Booch, James Rumbaugh, and Ivar Jacobson. The UML emerged as a standard from the Object Management Group (OMG) and Rational Software Corporation to unify the information systems and technology industry's best engineering practices as a collection of modeling techniques.

The UML may be applied to different types of systems (software and non-software), domains (business versus software), and methods or processes. The UML enables and promotes (but does not require nor mandate) a use-case-driven, architecture-centric, iterative and incremental, and risk-confronting process that is object oriented and component based. However, the UML does not prescribe any particular system development approach. Rather, it is very flexible and customizable to fit any approach.

With the advent of the UML and its flexibility to support various types of processes or methodologies, various approaches have been applied to leverage the UML, including applying no methodology, heavyweight methodologies, and lightweight methodologies with varying degrees of success. Alternatively, the type of information truly required to apply the UML effectively and successfully and capitalize on all it has to offer may be captured in a roadmap.

GOALS

This book bridges the gap between tutorials and reference works by demonstrating how all of the elements of the UML fit together holistically and cohesively, and bridges the gap between the UML and process using a roadmap, offering a cost-conscious alternative to heavyweight methodologies such as the Three Amigos' Unified Process (UP) process framework that involves a fairly significant number of rules and practices and a maturity-conscious alternative to lightweight or "Agile," "Empirical," or "Emergent" methodologies such as the Three Extremoes—Kent Beck, Ward Cunningham, and Ron Jeffries—eXtreme Programming (XP) practices that involve very few rules and practices.

This book does not present any particular process, but focuses on a roadmap that emphasizes what ought to be addressed when applying the UML, including the decision points (or critical points within an effort at which decisions must be made) and their relationships. A methodology specifically addresses various process elements, including who does what activities on what work products, including when, how, why, and where such activities should be done. A roadmap addresses the decision points and their relationships, providing a framework for a methodology. The roadmap may be scaled to be as lightweight or heavyweight as necessary to enable organizations to succeed in applying the UML. Any specific process or methodology may be seen as a traversal through the roadmap.

This book offers rules of usage and principles of composition; style guidelines, practical real-world examples; and a tool-, process-, and technology-independent roadmap for effectively and successfully applying the UML, where the essential principles for composing UML models are collated around the UML constructs, and an essential approach for applying the UML collated as a tool-, process-, and technology-independent roadmap.

This book is unique because one can use it to be introduced to the UML, and to understand how to apply the UML to real-world projects without prematurely adopting a specific process. Furthermore, this book complements existing books on the UML by virtue of its approach.

AUDIENCE

This book is for managers, practitioners (engineers), and anyone interested in effectively and successfully applying the UML.

For managers and professionals responsible for managing the execution of projects, this book provides a broad understanding of how the UML is used, enabling managers to make more informed decisions regarding the execution of projects. The roadmap may be leveraged as a higher-level abstraction of an organization's actual process to better understand the options in executing projects. The roadmap may be leveraged as a framework in which to effectively and successfully apply the UML without being prematurely forced into adopting a process.

For practitioners (engineers) and professionals responsible for executing the various activities associated with projects, this book provides detailed examples applying the UML, enabling engineers to make more informed decisions when modeling via the UML across the lifecycle. The rules of usage and principles of composition, style guidelines, and practical real-world examples may be used to understand how to create better conceptualization, specification, and implementation models.

And for both managers and practitioners (engineers), the roadmap demonstrates how the elements of the UML are related and how the UML supports traceability and scales to support the system development lifecycle process.

This book may be used for learning (novice level) and effectively and successfully applying (intermediate to advanced level) the UML. No specific prior knowledge or skills are assumed; however, familiarity with object-oriented concepts may be of benefit.

You, the reader, are invited to undertake the journey herein to discover the roadmap and all its value. However, be forewarned that the journey demands the courage to focus, reflect, introspect, and engage in multifaceted and intricate contemplation of what we do, how we do it, and why we do it. Throughout the journey, you will gradually and progressively absorb the value of the roadmap. After all, in all things, it is not simply the destination that matters nor simply the speed with which we reach the destination, but the balance between focus, purpose, journey, destination, and speed tempered with our objectives that makes it all worthwhile.

APPROACH

The question of how lightweight or heavyweight ought a process should be can best be answered if we address an even more fundamental question: What is the value of a process or methodology, independent of its weight, and why would one process or methodology be more suitable than another? Various tactics attempting to reconcile or debate heavyweight approaches and lightweight approaches miss the opportunity to address this fundamental question regarding the value of a process or methodology, and often result in a cultural war for the heart and soul of process. These factions tend to underestimate the impact of language—a language establishes the boundaries of thought and behavior, a process establishes behavior within that boundary, and tools establish the automation of behavior within that boundary. The roadmap establishes a continuum in which the best approach, independent of its weight, can be derived and applied. This approach avoids over engineering process elements similar to heavyweight processes and avoids under engineering process elements similar to lightweight processes, but provides a practical roadmap that leverages the UML to facilitate effectiveness and success.

   I have always been a "consultant"—a byproduct of a historical time when one could not be called a consultant unless one had two or more Ph.D.'s establishing foundational academic credentials and three or more decades of industrial experience establishing pragmatic credentials.

   As a consultant, before I engage clients, I often ask them, What is the value of a consultant? Is it the knowledge they contribute to a project? If so, realize that a consultant is not—at one extreme—prolifically omniscient. Is it the work they can perform on a project? If so, realize that a consultant is not—at another extreme—pragmatically a "contractor." Perhaps the answer lies in-between these extremes; the value of a consultant is in the questions they ask that force us to seek answers and ask more questions, the options they provide by virtue of their knowledge and experience, the work they perform in pursuit of an option, and the human mentorship they provide. Similarly, this book and the roadmap herein does not contain all of the answers, but it does provide a framework for: asking and answering questions; identifying, evaluating, and selecting options; and considering the ramifications of specific choices.

   I am often queried by clients as to how I am able to work with diverse organizations and teams using different methodologies while remaining coherent and cognizant of providing value. To which I reply—the roadmap. The roadmap is not an esoteric, theoretical, or contrived "thing"; rather it is a very pragmatic, applied, timeless, and valued asset enabling practitioners to apply the UML effectively and successfully with any process, tool, and technology. In working with diverse communities of practitioners, where each community has its own unique culture involving processes, tools, and technologies, I have been able to communicate the roadmap dynamically to practitioners via the Socratic method. The Socratic method is a dialectic (converse or discourse) method in which a teacher guides a pupil into recognizing a true conclusion by progressively questioning the pupil, rather than simply indicating that the conclusion is true, until the pupil reaches the conclusion. After practitioners recognize that they already know this, as a community, they are empowered to leverage the roadmap in adopting a process or methodology, evolving their adopted process or methodology, and generally unifying, optimizing, and simplifying their approach to effectively and successfully meeting their objectives and vision. Furthermore, any modeling language other than the UML may be applied within the roadmap provided that there are corresponding concepts.

In addition, I am often queried by clients as to how practical I am—especially after reading much of my work, they perceive my approach as pedantic. To which I reply, "very practical." Many actually don't believe it until they experience working with me! Likewise, one may argue that the roadmap is too "ideal" and not practical at all. However, it is only ideal in as far as it allows us to focus our practices and practically apply the roadmap on actual projects. If it weren't for ideals, our practices would become incidental! Consider the results if we only did what is expedient or easy! Doing what is practical is not synonymous with doing what is easy and doing what is ideal is not synonymous with doing what is difficult; rather, what is easy is perhaps doing only what is practical or what is ideal alone, but what is most difficult and valued is doing what is practical in a specific context and not simply in a vacuum—that is, applying what is ideal practically while focusing and balancing the forces between what is real and what is ideal. It is a shame that too many people believe that being ideal is contrary to being practical—as success is truly a measure of practically applying what is ideal in a real context to real situations, a lesson I was taught long ago which is only reinforced each and every day of my professional and personal life. Likewise, it is a shame that too many people choose to sacrifice what is ideal over what is real in the face of adversity and challenges rather than endure and evolve what is real toward what is ideal. The proof herein is all of the pragmatic information surrounding the roadmap! After people work with me, they often conclude that not only am I contextual, but even situational yet strategic since every situation, even within the same context, is unique—and my focus is not to be process- or roadmap-oriented, but strategically results-oriented.

The UML is significantly more than a standard or another modeling language. It is a "paradigm," "philosophy," "revolution," and "evolution" of how we approach problem solving and systems. It is often said that the English language is the world's "universal language"; and now it is virtually certain that the UML will be the information systems and technology world's "universal language."

This book does not contain any source code because focus is given to the modeling language and the roadmap independent of any translation to a specific implementation. Rather than show you how to translate a system to a specific implementation, I show you how to apply the UML effectively and successfully.

This book, just like every other book ever written, is a snapshot of thoughts in time. If you discover errors in the text, please let me know. The UML will most likely have evolved since the writing of this book; however, this book captures the roadmap that is quintessential (not simply essential, as what is essential is necessary and fundamental, but what is quintessential is the essence and ideal) to applying the UML effectively and successfully. Therefore, the book should remain valuable to you. Readers who would like to contact me to ask questions or to discuss this book, the roadmap, the UML, object orientation, or other related topics are very welcome to do so at the e-mail address salhir@earthlink.net or to visit my World Wide Web site home page at http://home.earthlink.net/~salhir.

ORGANIZATION AND CONTENT

This book consists of 11 chapters. Some content is minimally repeated and significantly elaborated in multiple chapters so that when using this book on a project, you can immediately access a specific chapter independent of the other chapters and have all the related information readily accessible to you.

The first three chapters focus on introducing the UML, modeling, and object orientation.

- Chapter 1, Introduction to the Unified Modeling Language (UML), introduces the goals, scope, and history of the UML, and considers its relation to process and how to apply the UML effectively and successfully. Read this chapter if you want to understand the need for language and process.
- Chapter 2, Modeling, introduces modeling languages, systems, various mechanisms that enable us to produce better models of systems, and considers how modeling relates to process and methodology. Read this chapter if you want to understand how the roadmap addresses the cultural war between heavyweight and lightweight processes for the heart and soul of process.
- Chapter 3, Object Orientation, introduces the principles of object orientation, the foundational concepts that enable us to model system, and how to communicate these concepts using the UML. Read this

chapter if you want to gain a detailed tutorial overview of the UML notation.

The next overview chapter focuses on the roadmap, and the five detailed chapters following it focus on the various UML modeling techniques and how they are used within the roadmap. The overview chapter is a launching point into the detailed chapters. Each detailed chapter is organized into two sections: the first section elaborates on the UML modeling techniques presented in Chapter 3 with various essential rules, principles, and style guidelines using examples; and the second section discusses how the UML modeling techniques are used within the context of the roadmap presented in Chapter 4. Essential rules address "what is . . ." questions concerning the UML modeling elements, essential principles address "what is . . ." questions concerning UML models, and essential style guidelines address "how to . . ." questions concerning the UML modeling elements. Read the overview chapter if you want to gain an overview of the roadmap. Read the detailed chapters if you want to gain more depth in understanding the UML notation and the roadmap. These chapters do not contain all of the answers, but provide a framework for asking and answering questions; identifying, evaluating, and selecting options; and considering the ramifications of specific choices. If you are new to the UML and are interested in more detail than provided in Chapter 3, you may consider reading the portions of Chapters 5–9 focusing on the UML modeling techniques before reading Chapter 4, and then returning to the detailed chapters to focus on how the UML modeling techniques are used within the context of the roadmap.

- Chapter 4, The Roadmap, provides an overview of the roadmap. The roadmap is derived by exploring the UML sentence, establishing a roadmap space, defining a general roadmap, elaborating a detailed roadmap, and specifying a notational roadmap—conglomerating the contents of Chapters 2 and 3. Use this overview chapter as a launching point into the detailed Chapters 5, 6, 7, 8, and 9.
- Chapter 5, Use-Case (User) Modeling, focuses on use-case diagrams and modeling the functional dimension of a system—what functionality the system provides to its users—captured in a conceptualization model.
- Chapter 6, Structural (Static) Modeling, focuses on class and object diagrams and modeling the structural or static dimension of a system—what elements and their relationships constitute a system—captured in a specification model.
- Chapter 7, Behavioral (Dynamic) Modeling, focuses on sequence, collaboration, state, and activity diagrams and modeling the behavioral or dynamic dimension of a system—how the elements that col-

laborate to constitute a system interact to provide the functionality of the system—captured in a specification model.

- Chapter 8, Component (Implementation) Modeling, focuses on component diagrams and modeling the implementation dimension of a system—how a system is implemented—captured in an implementation model.
- Chapter 9, Deployment (Environment) Modeling, focuses on deployment diagrams and modeling the environment dimension of a system—how the implementation or implemented system resides in its environment—captured in an implementation model.

The last two chapters focus on introducing the UML's extension mechanisms and the Object Constraint Language (OCL), a constraint language for the UML.

- Chapter 10, Extension Mechanisms, introduces the UML's extension mechanisms. Read this chapter if you want to gain an introductory understanding of how to extend the UML.
- Chapter 11, The Object Constraint Language (OCL), introduces the OCL. Read this chapter if you want to gain an introductory understanding of how to use the OCL.

A minimal reference section is provided to notable resources on the World Wide Web and various books. Visit the World Wide Web resources for links to other resources, including methodologies and processes, tools, and technologies that leverage and implement the UML.

ACKNOWLEDGMENTS

There are a number of individuals who made this work possible, specifically those who had to live with me, who demonstrated an abundance of encouragement, patience, understanding, and had to sacrifice a part of themselves to make this endeavor real.

I thank God for making everything possible, and I thank my family for what has been, is, and will be: My father Saad and mother Rabab, for planting and nurturing the seed that has germinated to become my world; my brothers Ghazwan and Phillip, for being pivotal agents of change in my world; my wife Milad, for being a constant source of companionship in my world; and last, but surely never least, my daughter Nora, who continuously enables my adaptation and evolution by forcing me to learn the truths I failed to learn from my own childhood and by forcing me to reexamine and evaluate the "truths" I have learned.

I would also like to thank my mentors, Dr. Carl V. Page and Dr. George C. Stockman, for their continued and everlasting "presence" in my world by teaching me that the ideal, theoretical, and abstract realm of computer science and the real, practical, and concrete realm of a computer professional are not disjoint, but intersect to establish a foundation for good solutions to complex real-world problems.

I would also like to thank the many practitioners leveraging my first book *UML in Nutshell* (O'Reilly & Associates, 1998) from across the world for their support and continued acknowledgement of its value.

I would also like to thank the staff at Springer-Verlag for their work in bringing this book to life and the many reviewers for their feedback.

I will not forget any of you, and I only ask that you please remember me.

Sinan Si Alhir

CHAPTER 1

Introduction to the Unified Modeling Language (UML)

This chapter introduces the Unified Modeling Language (UML), including its goals and scope, its relation to process and methodology, its history, and how to apply the UML effectively and successfully. Our goal, in this chapter, is to understand the need for language and process.

1.1.   What is the Unified Modeling Language (UML)?

Systems development involves various challenges. We attempt to solve complex and constantly changing problems with solutions involving complex and constantly changing technologies while continuously focusing on providing more functionality, in less time, with a lower cost, and more quality. Furthermore, the business processes and requirements these systems automate may span multiple organizations and cultures utilizing various technologies. The more complexity we attempt to address, the more we change, and the more we change, the more complexity we breed—it is a vicious circle that involves the simultaneous evolution of these problems and solutions which could easily result in chaos. With so much complexity and change, it is not feasible for a single individual to develop such systems, but it requires a team effort where people and teams, processes, tools, and technologies establish a culture focused toward a common goal and vision. To succeed as a team, we need a common language that allows us to communicate and collaborate on problems and solutions and take a common approach for achieving our objectives while managing complexity and change. Without such a foundation, how do we even begin to address the challenges?

The UML is a language for specifying, visualizing, constructing, and documenting the artifacts of a system-intensive process. As a language, the UML is a means for communication. It allows us to communicate about a subject, the system under discussion, including its surrounding environment or context. Regarding modeling, the UML focuses on a subject via the formulation of a model of the subject and its context. A model captures a set of ideas or abstractions about the subject, including essential information required for understanding the subject while excluding any irrelevant or incidental information that may hinder our understanding. This technique of focusing on essential information rather than incidental information is called abstraction. By modeling, we can better manage the complexity involved in working with systems. Regarding unification, the UML emerged from the Object Management Group (OMG) and Rational Software Corporation to unify the information systems and technology industry's best engineering practices. By unifying the industry, we can leverage techniques the industry has empirically found viable.

Regarding specification, we can use the UML to communicate "what" is required of a system, and "how" a system will satisfy its requirements. Regarding visualizing systems, we can use the UML to communicate visually, capitalizing on the adage that "a picture is worth and completes a thousand words," enabling us to view systems using our mind's eye for detecting patterns. Regarding constructing systems, we can use the UML to guide our construction of the physical system, similar to a "blueprint." Regarding documenting systems, we can use the UML to document our knowledge of the system throughout the system development lifecycle process rather than treat documentation as a cumbersome afterthought. The UML facilitates specifying, visualizing, understanding, and documenting a problem; capturing, communicating, and leveraging knowledge in solving the problem; and specifying, visualizing, constructing, and documenting the solution.

The UML is an evolutionary general-purpose, broadly applicable, tool-supported, and industry-standardized modeling language. As an evolutionary modeling language, the UML was originally conceived by and evolved primarily from Rational Software Corporation and three of the most prominent methodologists—the Three Amigos, Grady Booch, James Rumbaugh, and Ivar Jacobson—and incorporated the object-oriented community's consensus on core modeling concepts. As a general-purpose modeling language, the UML may be used throughout the system development lifecycle process. As a broadly applicable modeling language, the UML may be applied to different types of systems (software and non-software), domains (business versus software), and methods or processes. As a tool-supported language, the UML is supported by various vendors and tools. As an industry-standardized modeling language, the UML is not a proprietary and closed language, but an open and fully extensible industry-recognized language that is supported by various organizations constituting the UML Partners Consortium and the OMG.

The goals of the UML were to be a ready-to-use expressive visual modeling language that is simple, more precise than natural language, extensible, and implementation- and process-independent. If the UML were too complex, it would not be approachable and would not be widely adopted and used. If the UML were imprecise, it would retract from its purpose of enabling communication. If the UML were closed and not extensible, it would only address known needs and not be evolvable to address needs that have not yet been discovered. If the UML were implementation-dependent or process-dependent, it would be very limited rather than being general-purpose and broadly applicable.

The scope of the UML encompasses fusing the concepts of three of the most prominent methodologies—Grady Booch's '93 method, James Rumbaugh's Object Modeling Technique (OMT), and Ivar Jacobson's Object-Oriented Software Engineering (OOSE) method—at the modeling language level while incorporating the object-oriented community's consensus on core modeling concepts. Furthermore, the UML is not a visual programming language, a tool or repository specification, or a method or process.

1.2. The Unified Modeling Language (UML) and Process or Methodology

The UML enables and promotes (but does not require nor mandate) a use-case-driven, architecture-centric, iterative and incremental, and risk-confronting process that is object oriented and component based. However, the UML does not prescribe any particular system development approach. Rather, it is very flexible and customizable to fit any approach.

An iterative and incremental process involves a stepwise approach to developing a system. Each step or iteration, which is made of more smaller steps, involves working on part of the overall system, perhaps in parallel, and each increment involves developing more of the system over time. Iterations are not ad hoc, but consist of a semi-ordered collection of activities or steps that constitute an approach, have a beginning and end, are planned, have evaluation criteria, require resources, and aim to produce something demonstrable that will provide feedback in guiding future iterations. Feedback makes iterations quite empirical. By using an iterative and incremental approach, we can better manage the complexity of a system as it evolves and better incorporate requirement and technology changes and discover and reveal unknowns over time while validating against the requirement and leveraging feedback each step in the overall evolution of the system. Within an iterative approach, some rework to evolve or refine the system gradually is anticipated, but it should not be the majority of the work within an iteration; that is, there should be additive results due to the gradual refinement of the system. Fundamentally, when people use the word *iterative,* they actually mean "iterative, incremental, and parallel." It is iterative in that it repeats some sequence of steps, incremental in that it is not simply rework from previous iterations, but actually evolves a system additively, and parallel in that steps may be performed in parallel or concurrently within an iteration. Likewise, regression testing is even more heightened in an iterative approach since each successive iteration must ensure that it evolves rather than introduce anomalies in the work of previous iterations. Use cases drive iterations, iterations focus on architecture, architecture guides use cases, and iterations confront risk.

A use case is generally an observable and testable "chunk," or unit, of functionality, expressed as an interaction between a system and users of the system and includes variants or alternatives of the functionality, which captures what the system is to do in providing results and value to its users. A "use case" is a "case of use" where a user uses a system. A behavior sequence is generally an individual sequence of actions and interactions from the basic or normal and variant or alternative sequences of interaction. A scenario is generally a specific instance of a use case, a specific usage of the system and subset of the functionality of a use case. A use case is a collection of individual behavior sequences and a scenario is the execution of one explicit behavior sequence (which may be composed of multiple smaller behavior sequences of actions and interactions); and wherever a use case or collection of behavior sequences may be used, an individual behavior sequence may be used, or a specific scenario may be used. For example, a login use case may have the following behavior sequences: normal behavior sequence where the user enters their user identification name and password, exceptional behavior sequence where the user enters an invalid identification name or password, exceptional behavior sequence where the network or security server is not available, and so forth. A specific scenario is the execution of an individual behavior sequence which itself might be composed of multiple smaller behavior sequences of actions and interactions. For example, Si entering the password "password", which is the wrong password, is a specific scenario of the individual behavior sequence involving the user entering an invalid identification name or password. A use-case-driven approach uses use cases (or behavior sequences or scenarios for further granularity) to drive iterations. Everything that occurs within an iteration addresses the use cases that drive the iteration. By using a use-case-driven approach, we can better ensure that iterations are driven by the requirements as they change over time.

Architecture involves the elements that collaborate to constitute a system and how these elements interact to provide the overall functionality of the system, within any other constraints related to the system. An architecture-centric or architecture-first approach focuses on the architecture of the system throughout iterations. Everything that occurs within an iteration focuses on evolving the system to address the use cases that drive the iteration. By using an architecture-centric approach, we can better ensure that iterations focus on managing the complexity of the system as it changes over time, and results in a more resilient system. Furthermore, an architecture-centric approach allows us to focus on building elements of the system in parallel, consider buy versus build decisions, and reuse existing elements.

Risks are obstacles to success, including human, business, technological risks, any concerns or issues, anything unknown, and so forth. A risk-confronting approach involves confronting the highest risks over time rather than deferring the highest risks until a later time. That is, the use cases selected to drive a given iteration are based on the highest business risks they mitigate, highest technical risks they mitigate, how much of the architecture they impact and demonstrate or exercise, and how much of the architecture they stress, especially any delicate points of the architecture. Such use cases are often called architecturally significant use cases. By using a risk-confronting approach, challenges can be addressed early and directly rather than later, where it may be too late for dealing with the challenges as the consequences may be too debilitating and significantly impact an effort or significant monetary investments in the effort are already lost.

The object-oriented paradigm focuses on constructing reusable units and encompasses conceptualization and specification concepts, while the component-based paradigm focuses on the assembly of reusable units and encompasses specification and realization concepts, both of which are based on the principles of abstraction, encapsulation, generalization, and polymorphism.

1.3.   History of the Unified Modeling Language (UML)

The history of the UML may be viewed in terms of five distinct time periods, Fragmentation, Unification, Standardization, Revision, and Industrialization, as summarized in Figure 1.1.

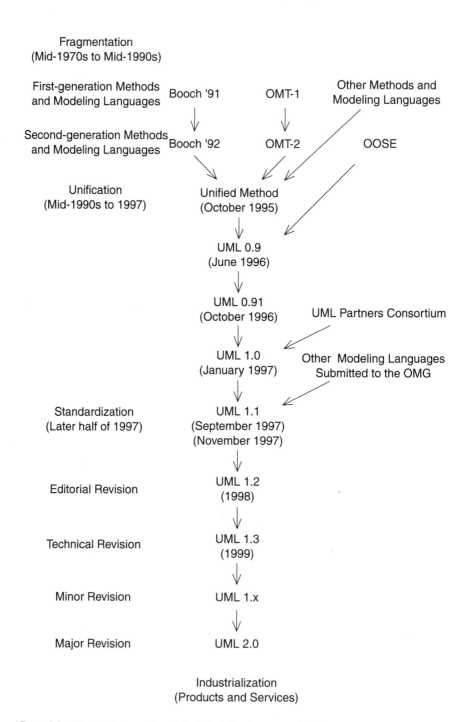

FIGURE 1.1.   The Evolution of the Unified Modeling Language (UML).

During the Fragmentation period, between the mid-1970s and the mid-1990s, organizations began to understand the value of software, and techniques for controlling and automating the production and maintenance of software were sought in order to increase organizational competitiveness. Between the mid-1970s and the late 1980s, various techniques and methods began to emerge, and object-oriented modeling languages began to appear. Between 1989 and 1994 the number of modeling languages and methods increased from less than 10 to more than 50. These became known as first-generation methods. Because practitioners had trouble finding satisfaction in using any one modeling language, "method wars" perpetuated. There was no clearly leading modeling language, but many similar modeling languages with minor differences in overall expressive power. They all shared a set of commonly accepted concepts, but expressed them differently. Lack of agreement discouraged new users from applying modeling languages due to the cost of learning many different modeling languages and equally discouraged new vendors from entering the object-oriented tools market due to the cost of supporting many different modeling languages. During the mid-1990s, as users sought after a broadly supported general-purpose modeling language, new iterations of first-generation methods began to appear incorporating each other's techniques. These became known as second-generation methods.

The following prominent methods emerged: Grady Booch's '93 method (from Booch '91); James Rumbaugh's Object Modeling Technique 2 (OMT–2) method (from OMT-1); and Ivar Jacobson's Object-Oriented Software Engineering (OOSE) method. Grady Booch's work had involved the use of Ada and the application of data abstraction and information hiding with an emphasis on iterative software development and software architecture. Grady Booch's Booch method, a design and construction oriented approach supporting excellent expressiveness for engineering-intensive systems, is expressed in his book *Object-Oriented Analysis and Design*. James Rumbaugh's work had involved various topics surrounding research and development within the context of complex algorithms and data structures. Jim Rumbaugh's OMT method, an analysis oriented approach supporting excellent expressiveness for data-intensive systems, was co-authored with Mike Blaha, Bill Premerlani, Fred Eddy, and Bill Lorensen and is expressed in their book *Object-Oriented Modeling and Design*. Ivar Jacobson's work had involved the application of object-orientation to the context of business reengineering and the industrialization of software development. He is often known as the father of use cases. Ivar Jacobson's Object-Oriented Software Engineering (OOSE) method, a use-case oriented approach supporting excellent expressiveness for business engineering and requirements analysis, is expressed in his book *Object-Oriented Software Engineering: A Use Case Driven Approach*.

During the Unification period, between the mid-1990s and 1997, these three methodologists became known as the Three Amigos due to their unification efforts. In October of 1994, Jim Rumbaugh joined Grady Booch with Rational Software Corporation in order to unify their methods. In October of 1995, they released version 0.8 of the Unified Method (as the UML was then called). In the Fall of 1995, Ivar Jacobson and his Objectory company joined Rational Software Corporation to merge his method. The Three Amigos released version 0.9 of the UML in June of 1996, version 0.91 in October of 1996, and invited, received, and incorporated feedback from the general community.

During 1996, as organizations began to see the strategic nature of the UML, the Object Management Group's (OMG) Object Analysis and Design Task Force issued a Request for Proposal (RFP) regarding establishing standards for tools that support object-oriented analysis and design; it was aimed at defining semantics and a metamodel standard for object-oriented technology. The OMG's request provided the catalyst for organizations to join forces and jointly respond.

In January of 1997, Rational Software Corporation formed the UML Partners Consortium that included Rational Software Corporation; Microsoft Corporation; Hewlett-Packard Company; Oracle Corporation; Sterling Software; MCI Systemhouse Corporation; Unisys Corporation; ICON Computing; IntelliCorp; i-Logix; IBM Corporation; Digital Equipment Corporation; Texas Instruments; and Electronic Data Systems Corporation. The UML Partners collaborated and released a well defined, expressive, powerful, and generally applicable version 1.0 of the UML that was submitted to the OMG as an initial RFP response. Other organizations also submitted separate RFP responses to the OMG, including ObjecTime Limited, Platinum Technology Incorporated, Ptech Incorporated, Taskon A/S, Reich Technologies, and Softeam.

During the Standardization period, starting in the later half of 1997, the others who submitted responses to the OMG joined the UML Partners to contribute their ideas. The UML Partners collaborated and released a more clear and updated version 1.1 of the UML that was submitted to the OMG as a revised RFP response for consideration and adoption as a standard in September of 1997. On November 17, 1997, the UML was adopted by the OMG, and added to the list of OMG Adopted Technologies. The OMG then assumed responsibility for further development of the UML.

During the Revision period, after adoption of the UML 1.1, the OMG charted a revision task force (RTF) to accept comments from the public and to make revisions to the UML. The UML underwent a minor editorial revision to become UML 1.2; a minor technical revision to become

UML 1.3, which was released in June 1999; a minor technical revision to become UML 1.4, which was released in February 2001; and a minor technical revision to become UML 1.4 with Action Semantics, which was released in January 2002. The UML 1.4 with Action Semantics elaborates the semantics of actions and procedures; specifically, it defines the semantics of action languages, languages for executing modeled actions and procedures, but does not define their syntax. A model of an action or procedure is known as an action model. The OMG is in the process of minor revisions to establish UML 1.x (potentially 1.4x or 1.5) and a major revision to establish UML 2.0, focusing on extensibility, language architecture, model management, and action language semantics to make the UML more expressive and precise.

During the Industrialization period, the OMG is proposing the UML specification for international standardization as a Publicly Available Specification (PAS) via the International Organization for Standardization (ISO). The UML will remain readily available and evolving while vendors will continue to embrace the UML and provide products and services to promote and support the use of the UML.

The UML is defined in the OMG's UML Specification document, including a UML Summary that introduces the language, UML Semantics (called the "inside" view) that defines the meaning of all UML elements, UML Notation Guide (called the "outside" view) that defines the notation or visual representation of all UML elements, UML Example Profiles that defines the UML Profile for Software Development Processes and the UML Profile for Business Modeling extensions to the UML, UML Model Interchange that defines how UML models may be interchanged using XML Metadata Interchange (XMI) and CORBA IDL, the Object Constraint Language (OCL) Specification that defines a constraint language for the UML, and two appendixes, including the Glossary and UML Standard Elements. The whole specification may be obtained from Rational Software Corporation or the Object Management Group via the World-Wide-Web.

1.4. *Effectively and Successfully Applying the Unified Modeling Language (UML)*

The UML may be applied with various types of processes or methodologies.

Organizations who are not attracted to process or methodology often attempt to adopt the UML based on the misinformation that the UML is a process. Because the UML is a "language" and not a process, these organizations struggle and many finally abandon their efforts on the basis that the UML is insufficient for their needs.

Organizations who are attracted to heavyweight processes or methodologies often attempt to adopt the UML via the adoption of heavyweight methodologies such as those comparable to the Unified Process (UP) process framework in order to leverage the UML fully. As a process framework, the UP does not define a specific process, but defines a class of processes where a specific process, called a process instance, may be instantiated as a subset of all of the constructs within the framework itself. The UP represents the merging of the Three Amigos' distinct methodologies. Heavyweight methodologies involve a fairly significant number of rules and practices. However, many such organizations often under estimate the necessary resources required in adopting a heavyweight methodology and many finally abandon their adoption on the basis that the process and the UML are too costly or complex to adopt.

Organizations who are attracted to lightweight processes or methodologies often attempt to adopt the UML via the adoption of lightweight methodologies such as those comparable to eXtreme Programming (XP) practices in order to fully leverage the UML. As a collection of practices, XP does not define a specific process, but defines a collection of practices or guidelines that establish a foundation for a specific process. XP was developed by the Three Extremoes, Kent Beck, Ward Cunningham, and Ron Jeffries. Lightweight methodologies involve very few rules and practices. However, many such organizations often underestimate the need for organizational, cultural, and personnel maturity in adopting a lightweight methodology and many finally abandon their adoption on the basis that the UML is too rigorous for a lightweight methodology. Lightweight processes or methodologies have also been termed "Agile," "Empirical," or "Emergent" methodologies.

Ironically, most organizations who do have the organizational, cultural, and personnel maturity for succeeding with a lightweight process are more attracted to heavyweight processes; and most organizations who do not have the organizational, cultural, and personnel maturity for succeeding with a lightweight process are not attracted to heavyweight processes. Furthermore, most organizations don't accurately estimate the necessary resources required for succeeding with a lightweight or heavyweight process, and those organizations who do accurately estimate the necessary resources are not always prepared to make such a commitment.

Organizations need not explicitly consider adopting lightweight or heavyweight processes in order to leverage the UML fully. Alternatively, the type of information truly required to apply the UML effectively and successfully and capitalize on all it has to offer must provide a cost-conscious alternative to heavyweight processes and a maturity-conscious alternative to lightweight processes—fundamentally, this is the type of information captured in a roadmap.

A tool-, process-, and technology-independent roadmap that is specifically derived from the UML offers a practical approach to the effective and successful application of the UML. A roadmap does not prescribe any particular process, but focuses on emphasizing what ought to be addressed when applying the UML, including the decision points (or critical points within an effort at which decisions must be made) and their relationships. A methodology or process specifically addresses or suggests who does what activities on what work products, including when, how, why, and where such activities should be done. A roadmap addresses the decision points and their relationships, providing a framework for a process or methodology. Any methodology or process framework may be perceived as complementary information to the roadmap, indicating or suggesting who does what activities on what work products, including when, how, why, and where such activities should be done; and any specific process may be perceived as a traversal through the roadmap.

For those organizations who wish to adopt a specific process, the roadmap may be viewed as a higher-level abstraction of their actual process, and for those organizations who don't have a specific process, the roadmap facilitates a framework in which to start applying the UML while still exploring their options in terms of processes rather than prematurely committing to a specific process. Organizations may utilize the roadmap to establish the best potential process fitting their situation, where the roadmap may be scaled to be as lightweight or heavyweight as necessary to enable organizations to succeed in applying the UML. A roadmap is not a replacement for a process, but highlights what ought to be addressed when applying the UML, including the decision points and their relationships, consequently providing a cost-conscious alternative to heavyweight processes and a maturity-conscious alternative to lightweight processes to applying the UML effectively and successfully.

CHAPTER 2

Modeling

This chapter introduces modeling, including the use of modeling languages, how to model systems, various mechanisms that enable us to produce better models of systems, and how modeling relates to process and methodology. Our goal, in this chapter, is to understand how the roadmap addresses the cultural war between heavyweight and lightweight processes for the heart and soul of process.

2.1. Languages

A language is a means to express and communicate information. There are three parts to a language, its semantics, syntax, and guidelines. The semantics of a language define concepts and their meanings. The syntax of a language defines a notation for rendering the concepts. The guidelines of a language define rules and idioms of usage for working with the syntax and semantics of the language. Underlying a language and the processes that utilize the language is a foundation consisting of fundamental principles or axioms. The fundamental principles of a language involve essential and "universally" accepted concepts upon which the language is established, the language's means, and facilitate some goals and scope to which the language applies, the language's ends. That is, a language is created for a reason or purpose and applies toward achieving that purpose. To understand and apply a language, such as the UML, one must understand the language's semantics, syntax, and guidelines in the context of the means and ends of the language. The means of the UML include concepts from the object-oriented paradigm and component-based paradigm, and the ends of the UML involve modeling systems within the context of processes.

For example, the language of arithmetic has various defined concepts: the Arabic numerals and the addition, subtraction, multiplication, and division operators. Each of these concepts has a syntactical depiction: 0, 1, 2, 3, 4, 5, 6, 7, 8, 9, + for addition, − for subtraction, × for multiplication, and ÷ for division. The guidelines for this language are the rules of arithmetic. The means of arithmetic are the notions of numbers and operators, and the ends of this language are expressing quantities.

2.1.1. ALPHABETS

A language has an alphabet, the primitive parts of the language (letters, characters, signs, and marks). The alphabet of the UML includes symbol fragments and string characters.

2.1.2. WORDS

A language groups letters from its alphabet to form words, the fundamental units of meaning in the language. The UML words include concepts, relationships between concepts, and other information. The words of a language establish the vocabulary of the language, the rules governing how these words are combined establishes the grammar of the language, and the meaning of the words establishes the semantics of the language. Concepts are depicted as vertices or nodes including icons and two-dimensional symbols that may contain other elements. Relationships are depicted as arcs or paths made of a series of line segments connecting nodes. Other information is depicted as strings or sequences of characters attached to nodes or paths.

Figure 2.1 shows a collection of concepts (Person, Car, Engine, Door, and Tire) and relationships (Own and Has). Concepts are depicted as solid-outline rectangles, and paths are depicted as solid lines. Each ele-

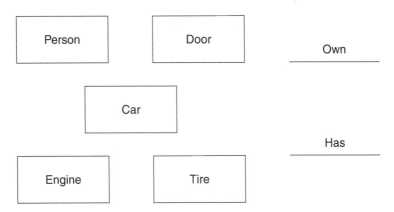

FIGURE 2.1.   Concepts and relationships.

ment has a unique identifier or name, called its selector or qualifier, in the context in which it is defined, known as its namespace.

2.1.3.   SENTENCES

A language groups words to form sentences, grammatical units of meaning containing a subject and a predicate or expression, where the predicate or expression expresses something about the subject. UML sentences are graphs or diagram fragments. Concepts and relationships are connected to depict sentences.

Figure 2.2 shows that a person owns any number of cars and a car may have any number of owners, and Figure 2.3 shows that a car has any number of engines, tires, and doors.

2.1.4.   PARAGRAPHS

A language groups sentences to form paragraphs, units of thought containing grammatical units of meaning about a subject. UML paragraphs are graphs or diagrams. Furthermore, not all elements need to be depicted on a single diagram, but only those that are relevant to the purpose of the diagram.

Figure 2.4 shows how the two sentences above may be combined to

FIGURE 2.2.   A person owns any number of cars and a car may have any number of owners.

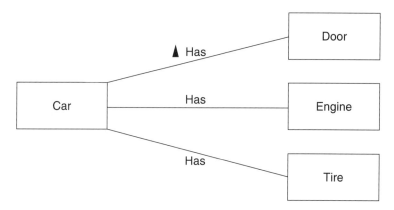

FIGURE 2.3.   A car has any number of engines, tires, and doors.

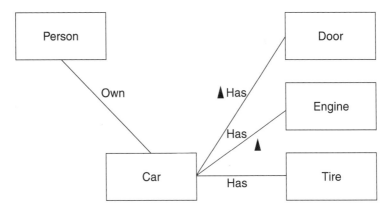

FIGURE 2.4. A person owns a car, and a car has any number of engines, tires, and doors.

form a paragraph. The visual location of elements does not have any impact on the meaning of the sentences so long as symbols are not nested inside one another. For example, the person and car are depicted on the horizontal axis in Figure 2.3 and on the vertical axis in Figure 2.4.

Figure 2.5 shows a more constrained paragraph, indicating that a car may have only 1 owner, 2 or 4 doors, 4 tires, and only 1 engine; and given a person, one can identify the person's car, but given a car, one cannot identity the car's owner, specified via the arrow, called a navigation arrow. Such information, including the number of owners, doors, and tires, is context dependent and may differ based on the specific context. For example, one may easily use the constraints that a car may have 1 or more owners, 1 to 5 doors, and a number other than 1 for the number

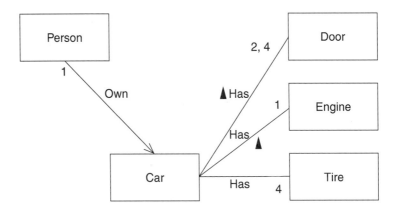

FIGURE 2.5. A car has only 1 owner, 2 or 4 doors, 4 tires, and only 1 engine; and given a person, once can identify the person's car, but given a car, one cannot identify the car's owner.

of engines. These added characteristics are often called notational adornments since they adorn or decorate the modeling element to which they are attached and provide more semantics or meaning associated with the modeling element.

Diagrams may represent specific or general sentences. The diagrams above represent general sentences since they involve general concepts. A specific concept is depicted using the same symbol as its general concept and is labeled with a name followed by a colon followed by the name of its general concept fully underlined; both names are optional and the colon is only present if the general concept is specified. A specific relationship is depicted as a path and may be labeled with the name of its general relationship fully underlined. The name is usually read from left to right and top to bottom, otherwise the name may have a small black solid triangle next to it called a name-direction arrow, where the point of the triangle indicates the direction in which to read the name, but the arrow is purely descriptive and has no semantics associated with it. Figure 2.6 shows that Si, who is a person, owns a car that has 2 doors, 4 tires, and 1 engine.

Diagrams may represent the elements or concepts that statically collaborate to constitute a system, as we have already depicted using the

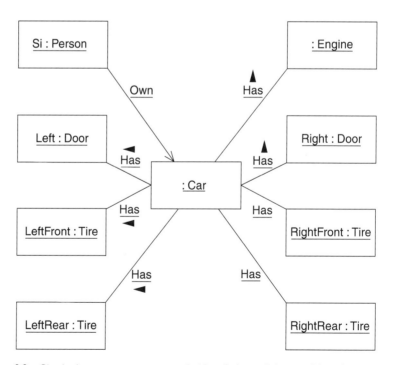

FIGURE 2.6.   Si, who is a person, owns a car that has 2 doors, 4 tires, and 1 engine.

figures above, or how these elements or concepts dynamically interact using specific or general sentences. A collaboration involves related elements working together. An interaction involves messages and stimuli being communicated between elements and elements reacting to certain messages and stimuli. A message or stimulus is depicted as a labeled arrow placed near a relationship, where the direction of the arrow indicates who is sending and receiving the message or stimulus and the label indicates the sequence number in which the message or stimulus is sent followed by a colon followed by the message or stimulus being communicated. Figure 2.7 shows how a person may generically collaborate and interact with a car, and Figure 2.8 shows how Si may specifically collaborate and interact with a specific car.

2.1.5.   SECTIONS

Paragraphs are grouped to form sections, organized units of thought. As the UML is only a language, it does not explicitly prescribe any particular set of paragraphs to use. However, a process that applies the UML would

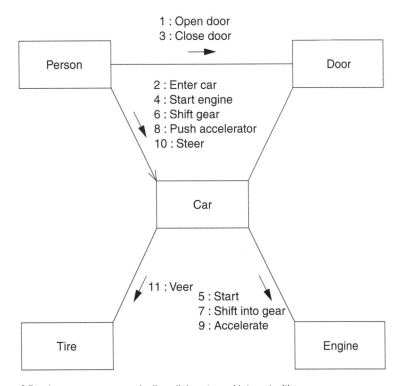

FIGURE 2.7.   A person may generically collaborate and interact with a car.

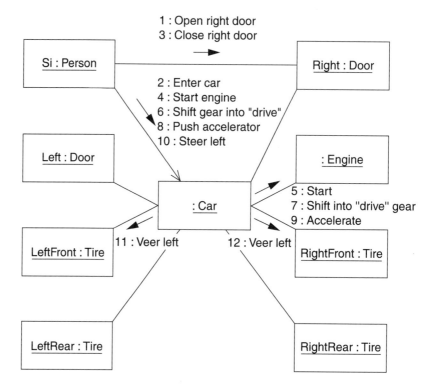

FIGURE 2.8.   Si may specifically collaborate and interact with a specific car.

recommend a set of sections to use. Such sections are often called architectural views.

2.1.6.   DOCUMENTS

Sections are grouped to form documents, organized units of knowledge. As the UML is only a language, it does not explicitly prescribe any particular set of sections to use. However, a process that applies the UML would recommend the overall organization of such UML documents. Such documents are often called models.

2.1.7.   OTHER ELEMENTS

Languages also contain other elements that are purely notational, allow for organizing documents, and extending the language.

A note is a notational item containing textual information, similar to a comment in programming. A note is depicted as a rectangle with a bent upper right corner. A note may be attached to zero or more elements by dashed lines.

Figure 2.9 shows various notes. Notice that a crossing of paths may optionally be shown with a small semicircular jog by one of the paths to indicate that the paths do not intersect or connect. Also notice that when several paths of the same kind connect to a single element, the paths connected to the element may be combined into a single path with branches into several paths, similar to a tree.

Because we may manipulate many concepts at any one time, the UML allows us to group concepts together using packages. A package is a general means for grouping elements and organizing information, similar to a file, folder, or subdirectory in using a computer. A package may contain concepts, relationships, and nested packages. A package is de-

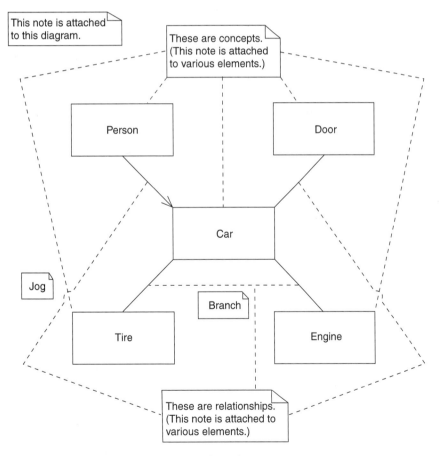

FIGURE 2.9.   Various notes showing textual information.

picted as a large rectangle with a small rectangle or "tab" attached to the left side of the top of the large rectangle. The package essentially defines a namespace and owns its contents, and each element inside a package must have a unique name. The contents of the package may be depicted inside the large rectangle, in which case the name of the package is depicted in the small tab, otherwise the name of the package may be depicted in the large rectangle if the contents are suppressed.

To reference elements within a package, a pathname or dependency may be used. A pathname is a series of names linked together and separated by a double colon (::) delimiter where the chaining together of package names and the element name starting from the root of the system or from some other point selects the element. By default, an element shown within a package is assumed to be defined within that package, and a reference to an element defined in another package is shown using a pathname to the element. A dependency is a relationship between elements indicating that one element uses or depends on another element. A dependency is depicted as a dashed arrow from the dependent element to the independent element. A dependency between packages indicates that one or more elements contained in the dependent package use the contents of the independent package. A dependency may be stereotyped, or marked with a text string keywords enclosed in guillemets («») or double-angle brackets, with the "use" keyword to indicate that one element requires the presence of another element for its correct functioning. A stereotype is used to indicate some more-specific meaning associated with the element. A dependency may be stereotyped with another keyword to indicate the exact nature of the dependency, but this is often evident from the context in which the dependency is used. Note that a dependency may be traversed in either direction, and the direction of the arrow does not limit traversal but only indicates the dependent and independent elements. A package may have branching lines to contained elements that are depicted outside of the package with a plus sign (+) within a circle drawn at the end attached to the container, called tree notation using an "anchor" icon.

Figure 2.10 shows one package for housing concepts relating to a person and one package for housing concepts relating to a car, where the person package depends on and uses the car package due to the navigation arrow as shown in Figure 2.5. The person package contains the person concept, shown using the plus sign notation. The car package shows its contents inside the large rectangle.

Furthermore, the UML is very flexible in allowing us to classify (brand) or mark elements and attach arbitrary information to elements. Elements are marked using stereotypes depicted as text string keywords enclosed in guillemets («») or double-angle brackets preceding or above the name of the element, and the elements is said to be stereotyped.

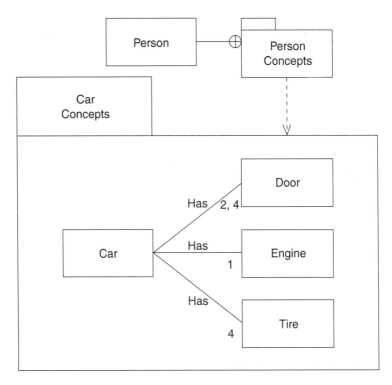

FIGURE 2.10.   A package for housing concepts relating to a person, which depends on a package housing concepts relating to a car.

When an element is stereotyped, it is marked to have a more-specific meaning. Multiple stereotypes may be applied to an element depicted vertically one below the other or preceding each other. A user-defined icon may also be used to signify a stereotype. The guillemets and the stereotype icon may be depicted simultaneously, however only one is required. When multiple stereotypes are used for an element, the icons are omitted. Information is captured using properties. A property is attached to an element and consists of property strings or property specifications representing the constraints and characteristics of the element depicted as a comma-delimited list of text strings inside a pair of braces ({}) succeeding or below the name of the element. The text strings may be expressed in any natural or computer language or be tagged values. A constraint is a property string that is a semantic condition that must be maintained as true for the element. A tagged value is a property string that is a characteristic of an element expressed as a keyword-value pair depicted using the keyword followed by an equal sign followed by its value. For properties associated with two symbols or paths, the property is shown as a dashed arrow from one element to the other element labeled by the property, where the direction of the arrow may be relevant to the property. For properties associated with three or more symbols, the property with braces is placed in a note symbol and attached to each of the symbols by a dashed line. For properties associated with three or more paths, the properties may be attached to a dashed line crossing all of the paths. Notes may be used with properties where a note has a stereotype, the "constraint" keyword or a more specific stereotype or its contents may be placed inside a pair of braces ({}), to indicate that it is a constraint and its contents are part of the model, otherwise the note is just part of a diagram.

Figure 2.11 shows that a person has been marked as an animate concept and that a car has been marked as an inanimate concept, and each element has various properties. Figure 2.12 shows Si and his car using stereotypes and properties.

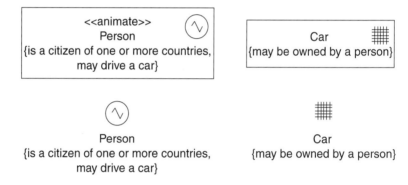

FIGURE 2.11.   A person is an animate concept and a car is an inanimate concept.

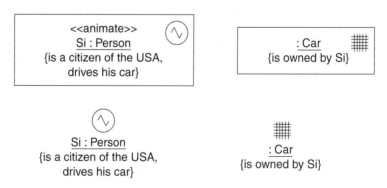

FIGURE 2.12.   Si is animate and his car is inanimate.

2.2.   *Systems and Contexts*

The subject about which we communicate using a language is a system, and the context in which the system resides is its domain or space. Generally, a model is an abstraction of a system used to capture knowledge about the system, an architectural view is an abstraction of a model used to organize knowledge around specific sets of concerns, and a diagram is a graphical presentation of sets of model elements used to depict and communicate knowledge about the system. The relationship between a model, architectural view, and diagram is similar to the relationship between a database that houses data, views that organize subsets of the data into information, and queries that extract subsets of the data and information. This establishes a framework in which a language, such as the UML, allows us to communicate.

2.2.1.   *DOMAINS OR SPACES*

A domain or space is simply an area of interest or world consisting of a collection of concepts and terminology that enable communication about the domain. In systems development, we often use the notion of a business or application domain when discussing a business industry or application using business concepts and terms, analysis domain when analyzing a problem and using analysis concepts, design domain when designing a solution using design concepts, implementation domain when implementing a solution using implementation concepts, and so forth. The world of the problem is called the problem domain, and the world of the solution is called the solution domain. The UML is domain-independent and may be used to communicate regarding various types of domains.

2.2.2.   *SYSTEMS*

A system or physical system is a behavioral unit that consists of an organized collection of connected, collaborating, and interacting elements or units, which may include software, hardware, and people, cooperating to accomplish a purpose and goal or provide some functionality. The elements that constitute a system are called system elements. The UML is system-type independent and may be used to communicate about different types of systems, including hardware systems, software systems, and human systems or organizations.

A system may be recursively decomposed into multiple systems called subordinate systems or subsystems and primitive elements. When fully decomposed, systems consist of primitive elements that are not further decomposable. The functionality of a system is provided as a service to its users via some interface or contract; the system has responsibility for the service and conforms to or offers and supports the interface; and the parts of the system have responsibility for implementing the service and realizing the interface. The functionality of a subsystem is provided as a service to other subsystems via some interface or contract, the subsystem has responsibility for the service and conforms to or offers and provides the interface, and the parts of the subsystem have the responsibility for implementing the service and realizing the interface. Functionality is characterized as behavior, and behavior is characterized as a service. The organization of a system into multiple subsystems and each subsystem into primitive elements results in the system's containment hierarchy where each system contains its subsystems and each subsystem contains its primitive elements. A system is depicted as a package stereotyped with the "topLevel" keyword or a fork symbol icon, and a subsystem is depicted as a package stereotyped with the "subsystem" keyword or a fork symbol icon as shown in Figure 2.13.

For example, a software system may be decomposed into a set of software subsystems, which are recursively decomposed into other software subsystems; and when fully decomposed, a software system consists of instructions that are executed by a computer. A car is likewise a system that may be decomposed into an engine, a body frame, windows, doors, and other physical units. A door may be decomposed into a window, door handle, and other physical units. The door handle may be decomposed into a knob, some screws, and an arm. By having an understanding of a system through multiple layers or levels of decomposition, we can begin to identify the level of detail or level of decomposition at which to best communicate such that the communication is valuable in providing enough detail, but not overly complex in providing too much detail. This is, perhaps, one of the most critical issues in working with systems—establishing agreement among all parties involved concerning the level of detail at which to communicate and work. If I want to communicate that a car may be used for moving between two different points, I would not describe it at the level of a door handle, as I have done above, but perhaps, at the level of a vehicle. However, if I want to communicate how to fix a door handle, I would describe it at a lower level of decomposition, at the level of a door handle.

2.2.3. ARCHITECTURES

The architecture of a system involves the structural and behavioral organization of the system within its context, including the ensemble of elements that collaborate to constitute the system and how these ele-

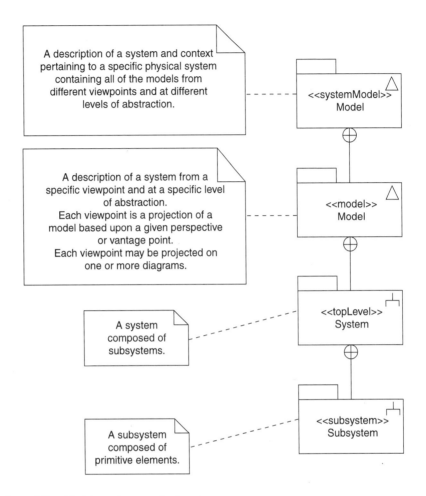

FIGURE 2.13.   Models, systems, and subsystems.

ments interact to provide the overall behavior or functionality of the system, within any other constraints related to the system. The elements that constitute an architecture are called architectural elements. The focus on what ensemble of elements collaborate to constitute a system and their relationships is called the structural or static aspect of the system's architecture. The focus on how these elements interact to provide the functionality of the system is called the behavioral or dynamic aspect of the system's architecture.

As a system may be recursively decomposed into multiple subsystems and primitive elements, and each subsystem may be fully decomposed into primitive elements, the notion of architecture applies to any level of decomposition. A system's architecture includes the subsystems that collaborate to constitute the system and how these subsystems interact to provide the overall functionality of the system. A subsystem's architecture includes the elements that collaborate to constitute the subsystem and how these elements interact to provide the overall functionality of the subsystem, where the elements may be other subsystems or primitive elements. A primitive element's architecture includes the parts that collaborate to constitute the primitive element and how its parts interact to provide the overall functionality of the primitive element.

For example, when describing a car, it is not only important to determine what are the pieces that make up the car, but also how these pieces fit together structurally and work together behaviorally to make a car usable. Figure 2.5 depicts the structural aspect of the car and Figure 2.7 depicts the behavioral aspect of the car. By having an understanding of the architecture of a system, we not only have various levels of decomposition at which to best communicate, but we have two general categories of information to communicate: structure and behavior. This notion of architecture provides a framework for working with and communicating about systems.

2.2.4. MODELS

A model is a description of a system and context from a specific viewpoint or vantage point and at a specific level of abstraction. A model is an abstraction of a system and context for a certain purpose, capturing a set of ideas or concepts about the subject. The concepts are called abstractions, and the technique of identifying these concepts is called abstracting. One of the most critical issues in working with systems is establishing agreement among all parties involved concerning the level of abstraction at which to communicate and work. The system and context are called manifestations of the abstractions, and the technique of exemplifying or instantiating the system and context from the abstraction is called manifesting or instantiation. For example, the idea of a car is an abstraction, and a physical car is the manifestation of the idea. A good abstraction is one that is well defined based on the purpose of the model, and includes essential information required for understanding the subject while excluding any irrelevant or incidental information that may hinder understanding the subject. A good model is one that only contains the necessary concepts for understanding the system.

The elements that constitute a model are called model elements. A model element has structural, or static, features or properties and behavioral, or dynamic, features or properties—essentially, models and model elements have architecture. Models may be viewed via a small set of dimensions or aspects that emphasize particular qualities of a model. The structural model dimension emphasizes the static features of the modeled system, focusing on the static features of a model's model elements, and the behavioral model dimension emphasizes the dynamic features of the modeled system, focusing on the dynamic features of a model's model elements.

As a system may be recursively decomposed into multiple subsystems and primitive elements, and each subsystem may be fully decomposed into primitive elements, a model of a system applies to any level of decomposition. A model of a system is an abstraction of the whole system, a model of a subsystem is an abstraction of the subsystem, and a model of a primitive element is an abstraction of the primitive element. A model from a specific viewpoint and at a specific level of abstraction is depicted as a package stereotyped with the "model" keyword or a triangle icon, and a model pertaining to a specific system containing all of the models from different viewpoints and at different levels of abstraction is depicted as a package stereotyped with the "systemModel" keyword or a triangle icon as shown in Figure 2.13.

Figure 2.14 shows a model of a car, including various subsystems. The Requirements Specification package represents a model capturing the requirements for the car, the Production Schematic package represents a model capturing the information necessary to build and produce the car, and the Design package represents a model capturing the design of the car.

A model is essentially a "blueprint" of a system, a simplification of reality or the real system. A model is valuable for communicating and managing the complexity involved in working with a system by enabling us to focus on the essential rather than incidental concepts that constitute the system, and likewise raise the level of abstraction at which we work with the system such that we can focus on what the system should do in satisfying its objectives rather than how it is implemented and conduct experiments to ensure the resulting system will satisfy its objectives. A model may be used to ensure a system will satisfy its requirements and usability constraints, and verify our understanding of the system before we expend resources to construct it. For example, it may be very costly to simply build a car to determine if it will satisfy its appropriate safety requirements and usability constraints, thus we model it before we build it to determine if it will satisfy its requirements; and once we determine the design we have derived is feasible, we apply resources or assign the work to specific teams for constructing each part of the car using the model as a specification or "blueprint." If we were to avoid modeling the car but directly construct it before verifying our understanding of what we ought to construct or how to best construct it, we may later determine that we overlooked something, and a potentially costly and time consuming change to the actual constructed car becomes necessary, which may have been avoided if we had modeled

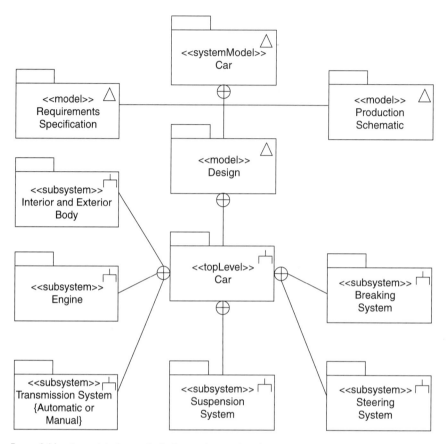

FIGURE 2.14.   A model of a car including various subsystems.

the car prior to building it. Furthermore, it is critical to maintain that it is not necessary to model every thing formally regarding a system, but it is necessary to model what is essential, necessary and sufficient, as formally or informally as required and at a appropriate level of detail or abstraction to allow us to verify our approach and manage the risks of progressing forward with our approach, essentially ensuring the robustness of our approach to address risk sufficiently. The value of a model is not simply when it is used to model a problem or solution, but when it is used to evolve a solution to a problem; and it is the use of a model that makes it valuable. Using a model to document requirements characterized as a problem or a system, including its code, that addresses the requirements characterized as a solution is valuable, but using a model to solve a problem and derive a solution to the problem makes the model potentially significantly more valuable. Modeling focuses on creating systems that are more resilient in addressing change and complexity.

The cost of changing software has significantly decreased given our modern day technologies, potentially to the point of suggesting that we avoid expending time and funds on modeling endeavors and virtually directly implement our systems and leverage the cost and time savings to adapt the implemented systems themselves, as some may argue regarding the use of models. However, in this case, we limit the degree of complex problems we can manageably address by the level of abstraction of our implementation technologies themselves. We should bear in mind that evolving our capabilities to address increasingly more complex problems should not be stifled by the fact that technologies enable us to achieve our objectives faster!

Consider software development languages: rather than manipulate machine language code, we have used assembly language code, and now we use higher-level third- and fourth-generation programming languages and modeling languages. This evolutionary progression has allowed us to raise the level of abstraction at which we work with systems and manage the complexity of the problems we address and systems we develop, fundamentally enabling us to address increasingly more complex problems with increasingly more elaborate solutions. Machine language programs are used to abstract physical hardware components and are executed by computer hardware. Assembly languages are used to abstract the manipulation of machine language programs or models. Lower-level programming languages are used to abstract the manipulation of assembly language programs or models. Higher-level programming languages are used to abstract the manipulation of lower-level programming language programs or models. Higher-level programming language programs are "executed" or interpreted by developers in code walkthroughs and are translated to lower-level programming language programs by traditional compilers and linkers. Lower-level programming language programs are "executed" or interpreted by developers in code walkthroughs and are translated to assembly language programs by traditional compilers and linkers. Assembly language programs are translated to machine language programs by assembler programs. Machine language programs are executed by computer hardware. We now also utilize just-in-time compilers to translate higher-level language programs into "byte code" language programs that may be executed by virtual software machines, similar to the workings of the Java platform. Fundamentally, higher-level language programs are "blueprints" for lower-level language programs, lower-level language programs are "blueprints" for assembly language programs, and assembly language programs are "blueprints" for machine language programs. Similarly, UML models are "executed" by practitioners in constructing and yielding systems, where computer assisted software engineering (CASE) tools that can "execute," animate, and translate models are becoming more readily available. Therefore, if we had allowed our capabilities to address increasingly more complex problems be stifled by the fact that technologies enable us to achieve our objectives faster, we would have potentially stopped our evolutionary progression of programming languages with the development of the first assembler program!

2.2.5. ARCHITECTURAL VIEWS

An architectural view is a projection of a model based on a given perspective or vantage point, emitting those elements that are relevant to the perspective while omitting elements that are not relevant to the perspective. An architectural view is an abstraction of a model defining a specific perspective through which to view a model. A view focuses on addressing a specific set of concerns, and the model elements projected through the view are those associated in addressing those concerns. A view may be associated with one or more specific stakeholders, anyone impacted by, or who has an impact on or has a stake in an effort. The elements that constitute a model view are called view elements. Architectural views partition the model at a layer or level of abstraction.

The UML supports the following architectural views:

- The use-case or user model view focuses on the functional dimension of a system, that is, what functionality the system provides to its users. Use-case modeling is the subject of Chapter 5.
- The structural or static model view focuses on the static dimension of a system, what elements and their relationships constitute a system. Structural modeling is the subject of Chapter 6.
- The behavioral or dynamic model view focuses on the dynamic dimension of a system, how the elements that collaborate to constitute a system interact to provide the functionality of the system. Behavioral modeling is the subject of Chapter 7.
- The component or implementation model view focuses on the implementation or realization dimension of a system, how a system is implemented. Component modeling is the subject of Chapter 8.
- The deployment or environment model view focuses on the context dimension of a system, how an implementation or implemented system resides in its environment. Deployment modeling is the subject of Chapter 9.

Other model views may be defined and used as necessary, provided that an architectural focus is defined by a set of concerns. For example, security issues may define an architectural focus where a security architectural view includes the set of elements from a model that address security issues.

A car may be perceived via these architectural views:

- The use-case model view allows us to view the car as a vehicle that enables us to move between two different points. The Requirements Specification package of Figure 2.14 captures this view of the overall model of the car.
- The structural model view allows us to view the car as a frame with an engine and other parts that work together to be a drivable vehicle. The Design package of Figure 2.14 captures this view of the overall model of the car.
- The behavioral model view allows us to view how the frame, engine, and other parts work together to be a drivable vehicle. The Design package of Figure 2.14 captures this view of the overall model of the car.
- The component model view allows us to view how the frame, engine, and other parts are packaged together to form the car as a whole. The Production Schematic package of Figure 2.14 captures this view of the overall model of the car.
- The deployment model view allows us to view how the car may be driven on different types of terrains. The Production Schematic package of Figure 2.14 may potentially capture this view of the overall model of the car.

2.2.6. DIAGRAMS

A diagram is a graphical presentation of a set of model elements, rendered as a connected graph of vertices or nodes and arcs or paths. The elements that constitute a diagram are called diagram elements. Any number of diagrams may be used to view a model.

The UML supports the following diagrams, organized around architectural views:

- The use-case or user model view
  - A use-case diagram depicts the functionality of a system. Use-case diagrams are function-oriented.
- The structural or static model view
  - A class diagram depicts the static structure of a system using general concepts and relationships, what general elements constitute a system. Class diagrams are structure-oriented. Figure 2.5 is a class diagram.
  - An object diagram depicts the static structure of a system at a

particular time, that is, what specific concepts and relationships constitute a system at a particular time. Object diagrams are structure-oriented. Figure 2.6 is an object diagram.

- The behavioral or dynamic model view
  - A sequence or interaction diagram depicts the dynamic behavior of a system, how the elements that collaborate to constitute a system interact over time to provide the functionality of the system, using general or specific elements. Sequence diagrams have a temporal focus on an interaction, including concepts and messages or stimuli. Sequence diagrams are time-oriented and emphasize the overall flow of an interaction, and are especially useful for complex interactions.
  - A collaboration or interaction diagram depicts the dynamic behavior of a system, how the ensemble of elements that collaborate to constitute a system interact over time and are related in space to provide the functionality of the system, using general or specific elements. Collaboration diagrams have a spatial and temporal focus on a collaboration and interaction, including concepts, relationships, and messages or stimuli. Collaboration diagrams are time- and space-oriented and emphasize the overall pattern of an interaction relative to the involved elements, and are especially useful for visualizing the impact of an interaction on the various elements. Both sequence and collaboration diagrams are called interaction diagrams. Figure 2.7 is a generic collaboration diagram, and Figure 2.8 is a specific collaboration diagram.
  - A state diagram depicts the dynamic behavior of a system, the status conditions and responses and actions of elements that constitute a system due to events. State diagrams are state- and event-oriented.
  - An activity diagram depicts the dynamic behavior of a system, the activities or workflow (flow of work) and responsibilities of elements that constitute a system. Activity diagrams are activity-oriented.
- The component or implementation model view
  - A component diagram depicts the implementation of a system, that is, its implementation-time configuration. Component diagrams are implementation-oriented.
- The deployment or environment model view
  - A deployment diagram depicts how the implementation or implemented system resides in its environment, that is, its run-time configuration. Deployment diagrams are implementation-environment-oriented. Both component and deployment diagrams are called implementation diagrams.

Other diagrams may be defined and used as necessary. Even though diagrams are organized around architectural views, any diagram may be used in any architectural view to communicate some aspects of a system's architecture—its structure and behavior.

A car may be perceived via these diagrams:

- The use-case model view
  - A use case diagram depicts the car as a vehicle that enables us to move between two different points.
- The structural model view
  - A class diagram depicts that a car has a frame with an engine and other parts, as shown in Figure 2.5.
  - An object diagram depicts a specific frame, engine, and parts, as shown in Figure 2.6.
- The behavioral model view
  - A sequence diagram depicts how the frame, engine, and other parts work together over time.
  - A collaboration diagram depicts how the frame, engine, and other parts work together and how they are structurally related, as shown generically in Figure 2.7 and specifically in Figure 2.8.
  - A state diagram depicts the status conditions and responses of the frame, engine, and other parts as they work together.
  - An activity diagram depicts the activities of the frame, engine, and the parts as they work together.
- The component model view
  - A component diagram depicts how the frame, engine, and other parts are packaged together to form the car as a whole.
- The deployment model view
  - A deployment diagram depicts how the car can be driven on different types of terrains.

2.3. Modeling Mechanisms

The system development lifecycle process involves a problem-solving process at a macro-level and the scientific method at a micro-level. Requirements may be characterized as problems, systems that address the requirements may be characterized as solutions, and problem solving involves understanding or conceptualizing the problem or requirements by representing and interpreting the problem, solving the problem by manipulating the representation of the problem to derive or specify a representation of the solution, and implementing or realizing the solution or system that addresses the requirements by mapping the representation of the solution onto the solution world. Within each problem-solving step, the scientific method involves planning or predicting a hypothesis, executing or empirically testing the hypothesis to gain feedback, evaluating the hypothesis against the results, and deriving a conclusion that is used to update the hypotheses. In a problem-solving process, paradigms determine the possible types of representations that may be used, and the UML facilitates specifying, visualizing, understanding, and documenting the problem or requirements; capturing, communicating, and leveraging knowledge in solving the problem; and specifying, visualizing, constructing, and documenting the solution or system that satisfies the requirements. These macro- and micro-level processes are very natural and often occur subtly and sometimes unconsciously in system development.

A system may be viewed as a mathematical relation: given some input data, the input data is processed to derive some output data, and the output data is provided. The system is said to be a "black box" if nothing is known about the internals of the system and how the input data is processed to derive the output data. The system is said to be a "white box" if the internals of the system and how the input data is processed to derive the output data are known. Modeling mechanisms are modeling practices that allow us to produce more precise and communicable models while managing the complexity involved in working with systems. Furthermore, these modeling mechanisms are commonly observed across domains and modeling languages.

2.3.1. PERSPECTIVES

The first modeling mechanism, perspectives, defines a particular point of view through which to model a system, a viewpoint through which to draw or render and read or interpret a diagram. A perspective enables more effective communication using the UML by clearly communicating a viewpoint through which to view a diagram's subject and goal. Perspectives organize architectural model views around the notion of problem solving as shown in Figure 2.15.

The following three perspectives may be used:

- The conceptualization perspective is concerned with the problem and viewing a system conceptually as a "black box." When modeling through this perspective, our objective is to understand what requirements the system must satisfy and what functionality the system provides to its users, primarily involving use-case modeling using use-case diagrams. The conceptualization perspective is often captured in a document referenced as the problem requirements that de-

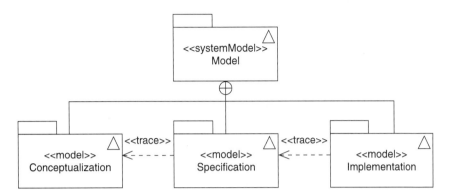

FIGURE 2.15.   Perspectives.

scribes the problem in terms of requirements imposed by the problem on its solution.

■ The specification perspective is concerned with the problem and solution and viewing a system logically as a "white box." When modeling through this perspective, our objective is to understand how
the system will satisfy the requirements, what ensemble of elements
and their relationships collaborate to constitute the system, and how
the elements that constitute the system interact to provide the functionality of the system, primarily involving structural modeling and
behavioral modeling using class, object, sequence, collaboration,
state, and activity diagrams. Figures 2.5–2.8 are all depicted from the
specification perspective. The specification perspective is often captured, as one part, in a document referenced as the solution specification that describes the solution that satisfies the requirements.

■ The implementation or realization perspective is concerned with the
solution and viewing a system physically as a "black box." When modeling through this perspective, our objective is to understand how
the system is packaged or implemented and how the implemented
system resides in its environment, primarily involving component
and deployment modeling using component and deployment diagrams. The implementation perspective is often captured, as the second part, in a document referenced as the solution specification that
describes the solution that satisfies the requirements.

Because the same concept evolves over these perspectives throughout
the software development lifecycle process, a traceability relationship is
used to connect the same element across perspectives, depicted as a
dependency stereotyped with the "trace" keyword as shown in Figure
2.15. This may be used to determine the impact of a change to an ele-

ment across perspectives; that is, as an element changes in one perspective, we can determine which other related elements in the other perspectives are impacted.

For example, a car from the conceptualization perspective is a vehicle that is drivable on land; from the specification perspective is a collection of parts, including an engine, doors, tires, and so forth; and from a implementation perspective is a physical apparatus composed of metal, glass, plastic, and so forth.

2.3.2.   *LEVELS OF ABSTRACTION*

The second modeling mechanism, layers or levels of abstraction, defines a particular level of abstraction at which to draw or render and read or interpret a diagram. A level of abstraction enables more effective communication using the UML by clearly communicating a level of detail at which attention and concentration are focused regarding a diagram's subject. Levels of abstraction organize the decomposition of a system and its model around the notion of problem solving as shown in Figure 2.16.

The following three layers may be used:

- The system level focuses on all of the different perspectives regarding the system as a whole. Figures 2.5–2.8 are all depicted at the system level. A system provides functionality as a service to its users via an interface or contract, and the responsibility for implementing the service and supporting or realizing the contract is distributed across its contents. Users of the system are essentially users of its contents.
- The subsystem level focuses on all of the different perspectives regarding each subsystem that constitutes the system. A subsystem

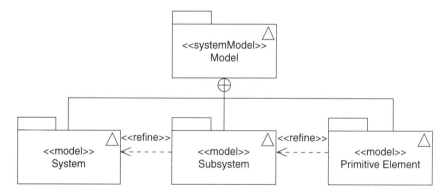

FIGURE 2.16.   Levels of abstraction.

provides functionality as a service to other subsystems via an interface or contract, and the responsibility for implementing the service and supporting or realizing the contract is distributed across its contents. Subsystems are cooperatively responsible for implementing the services and supporting or realizing the contracts provided by their containing system. Users of a subsystem are essentially users of its contents. Furthermore, any number of subsystem levels may be used when modeling a system.

■ The primitive element level focuses on the different perspectives regarding each most fundamental and irreducible element that constitutes the subsystems and system. A primitive element provides functionality as a service to other primitive elements via an interface or contract, and the responsibility for implementing the service and supporting or realizing the contract is distributed across its contents. Primitive elements are cooperatively responsible for implementing the services and supporting or realizing the contracts provided by their containing subsystems and system. Furthermore, primitive elements need not reside in subsystems but may reside directly within a system at the same level as other subsystems.

Because each level of abstraction represents a fuller specification of the next higher level of abstraction, a refinement relationship is used to connect the refining elements to the refined element across levels of abstraction, depicted as a dependency stereotyped with the "refine" keyword as shown in Figure 2.16. Refinement involves scaling elements to be more-or-less granular. The organization of a system in this manner constitutes the system's containment hierarchy. This may be used to determine the impact of a change to an element across levels of abstraction; that is, as an element changes in one level of abstraction, we can determine which other related elements in the other levels of abstraction are impacted.

For example, a car at the system level of abstraction is a vehicle that is drivable on land; at the subsystem level of abstraction, a collection of replaceable parts, including an engine, doors, tires, and so forth; and at the class level of abstraction, a collection of primitive parts, including engine parts, door handles, tire parts, and so forth.

2.3.3. DICHOTOMIES

The third modeling mechanism, dichotomies, defines how the same element may be viewed from two different perspectives or two different levels of abstraction. Dichotomies enable more effective communication using the UML by interconnecting different perspectives and different levels of abstraction; otherwise, the overall system model becomes disconnected and incoherent. Dichotomies are critical for deriving and traversing the roadmap as discussed in Chapter 4.

The following dichotomies may be used:

- The type-instance dichotomy or correspondence allows a general UML sentence involving general constructs, or concepts and relationships, to describe many specific UML sentences involving specific constructs. Type-level diagrams involve general constructs and instance-level diagrams involve specific constructs where the specific constructs are said to instantiate the general constructs. The general constructs are called types. The specific constructs are called instances. Figures 2.5 and 2.7 are type-level diagrams and Figures 2.6 and 2.8 are instance-level diagrams.
- The specification-implementation, or specification-realization or "black-white box," dichotomy specifies that a system may be viewed as a "black box," where it is described from the outside of the box in terms of what it does, and the system may be viewed as a "white box," where it is described from the inside of the box in terms of how it does it. The "black box" description is called the specification or operation and declares what the "box" does. The "white box" description is called the implementation or method and defines how the "box" does what its specification declares. This relationship exists between the conceptualization and specification perspectives, the specification and implementation perspectives, the system level of abstraction and subsystem level of abstraction, and the subsystem level of abstraction and the primitive element level of abstraction. These relationships may be depicted using a dependency stereotyped with the "realize" keyword.
- The static-dynamic, or structural-behavioral, dichotomy specifies that both aspects of an architecture, structure and behavior, are complementary and evolve concurrently and cooperatively as we add more detail across perspectives and levels of abstraction.

2.3.4. EXTENSION MECHANISMS

The final modeling mechanism, extension mechanisms, define a means for customizing and extending the UML, including classifying or marking elements as well as introducing new types of modeling elements and attaching arbitrary information to elements. Extension mechanisms enable the UML to evolve rather than be redefined to satisfy the emerging needs of its users. Extension mechanisms are the subject of Chapter 10.

2.4. *Processes and Methodologies*

Provided with the notion that the system development lifecycle process is a problem-solving process within which the scientific method is applied, a project is a specific problem-solving effort that formalizes the "work hard and hope for the best" approach, a program is a collection or portfolio of projects, a method specifies or suggests how to conduct a project, a process is the execution of a method on a project, and a methodology is a discipline or taxonomy, or well-organized collection, of related methods. Essentially, a methodology is a social contract within a specific culture, an agreement among a community of individuals that provides a context governing their interactions; and a process is the application of a social contract.

A method's descriptive aspect specifies or suggests what knowledge is captured and communicated regarding a problem and solution, and a method's prescriptive aspect specifies or suggests how knowledge is leveraged to solve the problem. A method is known as a process's static aspect since the method describes the process, and a process is known as a method's dynamic aspect since the process involves the execution of the method on a project. Any effort, including a program or project, is not ad hoc, but consists of a semi-ordered collection of steps, has a beginning and end, is planned, has evaluation criteria, requires resources, and aims to produce something demonstrably valuable that will provide feedback in guiding future iterations via the sequence of steps. Feedback makes the overall effort quite empirical.

A methodology specifies who does what activities on what work products, including when, how, why, and where such activities should be done. Workers (who), activities (how), work products (what), and the heuristics concerning them are commonly known as process elements. Methodologies group methods as a family, methods describe processes, and processes execute methods on projects. To provide more flexibility and scalability to address increasingly more diverse problems, where applying a single method may be insufficient and a whole methodology may be impractical, a subset of a whole methodology may be applied where the methodology is called a process framework and the actual subset of all of its methods that are applied on a specific project is called a process instance. A process framework specifies or suggests who does what activities on what work products, including when, how, why, and where such activities should be done for various types of projects. A process instance specifies or suggest who does what activities on what work products, including when, how, why, and where such activities should be done for a specific project. Process frameworks describe process instances as a more flexible and scalable family of related processes, and process instances execute a subset of a process framework on projects.

A collaboration involves an interaction within a context. A collaboration captures who does what activities (how) on what work products. Thus, it establishes the elements of a project. Collaborations involve workers, activities, and work products. A context emphasizes the structural or static aspects of a collaboration, the elements that collaborate, and their conglomeration or spatial relationships. A context captures when and where such activities should be done and work products produced and consumed. Thus, it establishes the context for a project. Contexts involve development cycles and phases, iteration cycles and phases, and iteration phase details. An interaction emphasizes the behavioral or dynamic aspects of a collaboration, the elements that collaborate, and their cooperation or temporal communication. An interaction captures when and why such activities should be done and work products produced and consumed. Thus, it establishes the execution of a project as it is governed by various forces. Interactions involve use cases, iterations, systems and architecture, and risk.

2.4.1. DEVELOPMENT CYCLES AND PHASES

Throughout a process, a management perspective is necessary to manage the effort and a development or engineering perspective is necessary to execute the effort and perform the work. The lifecycle of a system consists of a Conception development cycle in which the system is conceived and the effort initiated, a collection of Evolution development cycles in which the system evolves and the effort is planned, executed, managed and controlled, and a Cessation development cycle where the system is retired and the effort is closed as shown in Figure 2.17. A development cycle is composed of sequential or successive development phases (sometimes known as stages; however, stages often combine development phases) or major milestones at which the project is evaluated against specific objectives and a management decision is made to continue or terminate the effort. The end of a development cycle results in a major system release to external customers or to an internal group, often called a system generation. Development cycles and their development phases embody the macro-level problem-solving process.

The following development phases are common:

1. The inception development phase focuses on delimiting the scope and objectives of the system using a vision or charter, establishing business rationale for the effort, possibly proposing a candidate architecture, and demonstrating the business feasibility of the effort

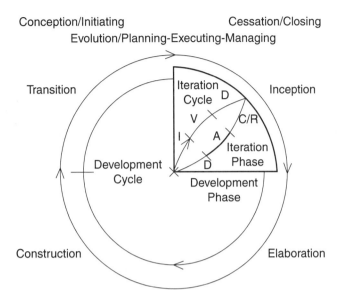

Conception/Initiating   Cessation/Closing
Evolution/Planning-Executing-Managing

Transition   Iteration   Inception
                              Cycle D

                                V ✕ C/R

                              I ✕   A
                                      ✕ Iteration
Development   ✕   D   Phase
Cycle   Development
                   Phase

Construction   Elaboration

FIGURE 2.17.   An iterative, incremental, and parallel lifecycle.

and system—essentially, stabilizing the effort's objectives. This development phase also focuses on identifying risk, any sources of un-
predictability.
2. The elaboration development phase focuses on detailing the require-
    ments, forward planning, establishing a stable architecture that is
    defined, validated, and baselined, and demonstrating the technical
    feasibility of the effort and system to satisfy a stable vision or char-
    ter—essentially, stabilizing the system's architecture. This develop-
    ment phase also focuses on mitigating major risks via feedback from
    prototyping and so forth.
3. The construction development phase focuses on evolving the archi-
    tecture and completing the building of the system.
4. The transition development phase focuses on completing transition-
    ing of the system to the user community.

   The inception and elaboration phases focus on the engineering stage
of a system's lifecycle, where the system is designed. The construction
and transition phases focus on the production stage of a system's lifecycle, where the system is implemented, verified, and deployed. Figure
2.18 shows the focus of each development phase concerning problem
solving. Development phases are not optional but may be minimal. Likewise, development cycles may overlap; however, the more they overlap,
the greater the risk of not communicating something between development cycles.

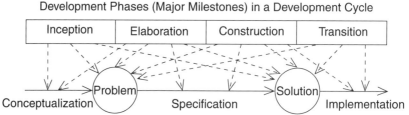

FIGURE 2.18.   Focus of development phases within a development cycle.

2.4.2.   ITERATION CYCLES AND PHASES

A development phase is composed of iteration cycles or minor mile-stones at which the project is evaluated against specific objectives planned at the start of the iteration cycle and a decision is made to continue or alter the technical approach. An iteration cycle, or iteration, is composed of a collaboration among various iteration phases and their content. Each development phase focuses its iteration cycles. The end of an iteration cycle results in a system increment and may result in a minor system release to external customers or to an internal group, often called a system release, which is a stable, demonstrable, and executable system. Within an iteration cycle, there may be any number of system builds where the system is composed to ensure all of its elements integrate, but is not released, which leads to continues integration across the lifecycle. Iteration cycles and their iteration phases embody micro-level applications of the scientific mind.

The following iteration phases are common:

- The management iteration phase focuses on managing the effort, including initiating, planning, executing, controlling, and closing the project.
- The support iteration phase focuses on establishing the infra-structure for the effort, including managing the configuration of work products and change requests (including defects and enhance-ments).
- The process or methodology iteration phase involves defining a pro-cess for the iteration cycles within the effort.
- The context modeling iteration phase focuses on understanding the context of the requirements and system.
- The requirements iteration phase focuses on conceptualizing the re-quirements, establishing what the system should do. This iteration phase generally focuses on the conceptualization perspective.
- The analysis iteration phase focuses on understanding the require-ments enough to specify the system, establishing how an abstract

system that is independent of any real constraints will satisfy the requirements. The result is a description of an application-specific implementation-independent solution that may be executable or verifiable. This iteration phase generally focuses on the specification perspective and understanding the requirements.

- The design iteration phase focuses on understanding the system specification enough to specify the implementation, establishing how a real system that is dependent on the constraints of the context will satisfy the requirements. The result is a description of an implementation-specific solution that may be executable or verifiable. This iteration phase generally focuses on the specification perspective and understanding the system, and also generally focuses on the implementation perspective and understanding the packaging of the system and how the implemented system resides in its environment.
- The implementation iteration phase focuses on building the system. The result is an actual solution. This iteration phase uses the understanding of the packaging of the system from within the implementation perspective to build the system.
- The validation iteration phase focuses on verify the system by validating it against the requirements. This iteration phase validates the implemented system against the conceptualization perspective.
- The deployment iteration phase focuses on making the system available to its users. This iteration phase uses the understanding of how the implemented system resides in its environment from within the implementation perspective.

The management, support, and process or methodology iteration phases are known as supporting iteration phases because they support the other iteration phases. The context modeling, requirements, analysis, design, implementation, validation, and deployment iteration phases are known as core iteration phases because they form the core effort.

Figure 2.19 shows the focus of each iteration phase concerning problem solving. Iteration phases and their contents are optional. Likewise, iteration cycles may only minimally overlap, but are generally successive.

An iteration phase, or workflow, describes a specific discipline or process discipline involving the flow of work between workers or roles, their activities, and work products around a specific area of concern or theme such as requirements, analysis and design, implementation, testing, and so forth. A worker is an individual or team who has responsibility, accountability, authority, and power for performing activities and working with work products while making critical decisions throughout the lifecycle of a system. Roles are not intended to create barriers between team

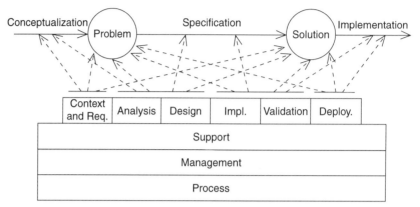

Iteration Phases (Minor Milestones) in an Iteration Cycle

FIGURE 2.19.   Focus of iteration phases within an iteration cycle.

members but are intended to delineate responsibilities of team members. An activity is a unit of work made of multiple tasks or steps that utilize work products as input and produces and maintains work products as output. A task specifies thinking, performing, and reviewing actions or steps to meet the objectives of an activity. A technique provides the means for performing tasks, based on a set of principles and supported tools. A work product or artifact is an element of information, including models and diagrams. These concepts of workers, activities, and work products establish an infrastructure for expressing the heart and soul of a process or methodology.

2.4.3.   ITERATION PHASE DETAILS

Iteration phase details, or workflow details, describe the details of an iteration phase, how a collection of activities are often done together. Iteration phases are performed in parallel, and activities within the same iteration phase may be performed in parallel. Within a use-case-driven process, use cases (or behavior sequences or scenarios for further granularity) are used to drive iteration cycles. Within an architecture-centric or architecture-first process, the effort focuses on architecture throughout the process, and especially the elaboration phase. That is, the use cases selected to drive a given iteration are based on their priority from a user perspective and rank from an architectural perspective, including use cases that require the availability of other use cases in order to be used, the highest business risks they mitigate, highest technical risks they mitigate, how much of the architecture they impact and demonstrate or exercise, and how much of the architecture they stress, especially any delicate points of the architecture. Such use cases are often called architecturally significant use cases. Prioritization must also consider commonly used use cases versus not commonly used use cases. Generally, coarse-grained use cases are useful for managing iteration cycles across phases, and fine-grained use cases are useful for focusing on addressing risk.

The following iteration workers and work products are common, organized around iteration phases:

- The management iteration phase includes a project manager responsible for a project plan, iteration plans and assessments, and risk list. The project manager is also responsible for collaborating and interacting with the various stakeholders to direct the overall effort; that is, anyone impacted by, has an impact on, or has a stake in the project.
- The support iteration phase includes a configuration manager responsible for a configuration management plan and a change request manager responsible for a change request plan.
- The process or methodology iteration phase includes a methodologist or process manager or process coach responsible for a process description or methodology and the development environment in general.
- The context modeling iteration phase includes a business leader responsible for a business model, and business analysts responsible for the details of the business model. A business model describes business functions and how these business functions are realized by the business organization. A business model is often called a context or domain model when it more broadly focuses on the business domain.
- The requirements iteration phase includes a requirements leader responsible for a requirements model, and system requirements analysts responsible for the details of the requirements model. A requirements model describes system functions.
- The analysis iteration phase includes an architect or technical leader responsible for the analysis model, and system analysts responsible for the details of the analysis model. An analysis model describes how the requirements are realized by an abstract system that is independent of any real constraints.
- The design iteration phase includes an architect or technical leader responsible for the design model, and system designers responsible for the details of the design model. A design model describes how a real system that is dependent on the constraints of the context will satisfy the requirements.
- The implementation iteration phase includes an architect or technical leader responsible for an implementation model, and imple-

menters responsible for the details of the implementation model. An implementation model describes the implementation of the system.

- The validation iteration phase includes a test leader responsible for a test model, and testers responsible for the details of the test model. A test model describes what will be verified and how the implemented system will be validated against the requirements.
- The deployment iteration phase includes an architect or technical leader responsible for a deployment model, and deployment personnel responsible of the details of the deployment model. A deployment model describes onto what the system will be deployed.

These workers, their work products, and their activities are not further detailed, but intentionally left very generally defined because the details would be provided in a methodology—which is not the objective of this book. Generally, each worker focuses on some aspect or discipline within the overall effort, for example the business leader and business analysts' focus on the business; and workers capture knowledge about their focus in a model, for example knowledge about the business is captured in the business model which describes the business.

2.4.4. HEURISTICS

Within this overall scheme or process framework, various heuristics are common when executing an effort.

To "kick-start" or engage a project, a contextual iteration cycle, often known as "iteration zero," may be used. The focus of this iteration cycle is to establish a baseline upon which future iteration cycles may be executed. More specifically, this iteration cycle focuses on establishing a general or high-level understanding of the scope and objectives of the system from a business feasibility perspective and the technology that will be used to implement the system from a technical feasibility perspective. The results of this iteration cycle may be a proposal or statement of work and a project kickoff to the future iterations cycles. It also provide an opportunity to learn about the specific context of the effort and the team involved, including the individual's ability to homogenize or gel and become a team, estimate and establish baseline metrics, and so forth.

The distribution of effort within an iteration cycle, including focus and emphasis, across iteration phases varies based on the development phase of the iteration cycle wherein the overall effort results in the parallel evolution and refinement of work products with evolving levels of detail and continuous validation. During the inception development phase, most of the effort is distributed across the context and requirements iteration phases. During the elaboration development phase, most of the effort is distributed across the requirements, analysis, design, and implementation iteration phases. During the construction development phase, most of the effort is distributed across the analysis, design, implementation, and validation iteration phases. During the transition phase, most of the effort is distributed across the validation and deployment iteration phases. The support iteration phase is generally distributed throughout the four development phases, with more emphasis in the construction and transition development phases. The management and process or methodology iteration phases are generally distributed throughout the four development phases, with more emphasis in the beginning of each phase. However, the overall objective is to produce the resulting system; therefore, all of the iteration phases are engaged as soon as possible without introducing risk to the project.

The duration of an iteration cycle is inversely proportional to the level of risk (including change, complexity, and so forth) affecting a project; that is, the more change or complexity a project faces, the shorter the duration of an iteration cycle, and the less change or complexity a project faces, the longer the duration of an iteration cycle such that the changes and complexity impacting and feedback from iteration cycles guides future iteration cycles. Fundamentally, the more risk, the shorter the iteration cycles, and the more feedback received provides guidance for making progress. This feedback is often collected as change requests and various other forms of information derived from the execution of an iteration. Furthermore, iteration cycles may be used better to manage morale. If a team begins to "fester" and become "demoralized" due to the lack of progress, shorter iteration cycles may be used until the team gains confidence and resolve. Likewise, major business risks ought to be addressed during the inception development phase, major technical risks ought to be addressed during the elaboration development phase, and the level of risk should minimize across the construction and transition development phases with minimal and decreasing rework. Given the dynamic nature of iteration cycles, it is possible to move forward or backward across development phases within a development cycle; for example, a project in the construction development phase that encounters such an epochal change that destabilizes the architecture would move backward into the elaboration development phase in order to restabilize the architecture. This notion of "moving backward" involves changing the focus of iteration cycles and the current development phase of a project.

The use cases (or behavior sequences or scenarios for further granularity) that are used to drive an iteration cycle need not evolve through every core iteration phase in one iteration cycle or through every core iteration phase linearly per se, but may only go through a subset of all of the iteration phases due to cost, time, resources, and other limiting project factors, and in succeeding iteration cycles, are promoted and continue their evolution through the remaining iteration phases as necessary and appropriate.

When multiple iteration cycles are used wherein use cases (or behavior sequences or scenarios) evolve through every core iteration phase, the effort gains a deep understanding of the solution for a narrow area of the problem, resulting in a system that only addresses a subset of the requirements. This is often known as a sequential approach. It is often too solution-oriented and micro-focused toward technology. Iteration phases are discretely distributed within iteration cycles and attempt to force a few use cases through all iteration phases in an iteration cycle. The technical team often perceives everything as a technical risk that must be addressed. Such an approach generally delays confronting and resolving use-case-related risks since everything is perceived as an architecture-related risk; causes solutions to be difficult to integrate and validate, and delays sufficient exercising the overall architecture to gain architectural coverage.

When multiple iteration cycles are used wherein the first group of iteration cycles focus on the requirements iteration phase until the requirements model is almost 100% complete, the next group of iteration cycles focus on the analysis iteration phase until the analysis model is almost 100% complete, and so on, the effort gains a shallow understanding of the solution for a wide area of the problem, resulting in a complete system only at the end of the development cycle. This is often known as a linear approach. It is often too problem-oriented and macro-focused toward management. Iteration phases are discretely disturbed across iteration cycles and attempt to force all uses through a few iteration phases in an iteration cycle. The management team often perceives everything as a business risk that must be addressed. Such an approach generally delays confronting and resolving architecture-related risks since everything is perceived as a use-case-related risk, delays demonstrable validation since a complete system only results at the end of the development cycle, and precludes opportunistic deployment throughout the development cycle.

An iterative approach involves using a mixture of sequential and linear approaches wherein sequential approaches focus on addressing risk and gaining depth into the solution, while linear approaches focus on progressively achieving the resulting system and gaining breadth across the problem, and together these approaches leverage feedback from the iteration cycles and allow for the introduction of changes at the end of an iteration cycle and before the next iteration cycle. Indifferent to any specific pattern of iterations, the overall objective is to produce a demonstrable or executable system as soon as possible; therefore, the implementation iteration phase and the production of the actual resulting system is started as early as possible without jeopardizing the effort. During the inception development phase, linear approaches are used to focus on scope while sequential approaches are used to focus on proving the architectural approach (often called an architectural proof-of concept). During the elaboration development phase, linear approaches are used to focus on gaining architectural coverage while sequential approaches are used to focus on addressing architectural risks. During the construction development phase, sequential approaches are used to promote deployment opportunities. During the transition development phase, sequential and linear approaches are used to reach completion.

An iteration cycle is time-boxed; that is, the time planned for the iteration cycle is fixed and not changed, but the scope is managed where the use cases (or behavior sequences or scenarios) driving the iteration cycle may be re-planned for future iteration cycles should there be insufficient time, resources, or other limiting factors. The use of time-boxes and time boxing allows stakeholders to have better visibility concerning the progress of the overall effort rather than simply achieving the planned objectives or ends of an iteration cycle without regard to the means for achieving those objectives. Furthermore, a time-box is not simply dictated to the team, but is rather negotiated (that is, a negotiated time-box rather than a dictated time-box) among the various stakeholders before the iteration cycle begins and is generally not altered once the iteration cycle begins. If there are critical or potentially catastrophic changes, "killing" (or "castrating") the current iteration cycle may be more feasible than expending resources to complete the current iteration cycle, which may result in nothing other than delaying addressing the change. If there are critical use cases (or behavior sequences or scenarios) that would result in a potentially catastrophic result if they were not implemented in the current iteration cycle, "extending" (or "mutating") the current iteration cycle may be more feasible than re-planning the use cases (or behavior sequences or scenarios) in future iteration. Modifying the scope of the current iteration cycle will "pollute" (or "adulterate") it and will make the ramifications of the iteration cycle and genuine status of the effort less visible to stakeholders. However, "killing," "extending," and "polluting" iteration cycles should not be the norm as it impacts metrics collection for iteration cycles and works against most of the value of an iterative approach. When using metrics, focus on trends between iteration cycles as this will provide insight into the overall pattern of the effort. Within an iterative approach, metrics and estimates are iteratively derived, and trends across iterations form the basis for metrics and estimation for the overall effort. Time-boxing may also be applied to development cycles and phases as well as iteration cycles and phases and their content.

A common question concerning any model (or its model elements) is its quality. As quality is very difficult to measure, a common mistake is to only use two extremes, worst and best, rather than pragmatically use worse and better. The quality of a model may be considered via two directions, backwards and forwards. First, looking backward from the model toward the iteration phase responsible for the model does the model or model element achieve agreement and consensus given the focus of its iteration phase? Addressing this question hinges on collaborating with the involved stakeholders. Second, looking forward from the model toward the other iteration phases that will use the model, does the model or model element allow us to make progress throughout the other iteration phases? Addressing this question hinges on leveraging the model or model element. For example, how can we judge the quality of a use case from a requirements model? First, does the use case allow us to achieve agreement and consensus concerning requirements? And second, can we sufficiently leverage the use case throughout the other iteration phases? If so, and we are able to produce the resulting system, the use case is of sufficient quality. Another common question concerning any model (or its model elements) is its completeness. As completeness is very difficult to measure, rather than quantify completeness itself, we can qualify it via some criterion—that is, define what can be done next with it at the level of completeness of the model or model element.

The principal set of dynamics within this scheme occurs between the project manager, the methodologist or process manager or process coach, and the architect or technical leader. The dynamics involving the other workers are not particularly secondary to these dynamics, but collate around these principal set of dynamics. While all workers including these three are responsible for answering back to the business stakeholders defining the context of the overall project, the project manager is specifically responsible for directing the execution of the project, the architect is specifically responsible for the target system and perhaps conducting experiments to ensure the technical feasibility of the system as it evolves throughout the project, and the process manager is specifically responsible for uniting the execution of the effort with the target system. This unification involves a project where the architect defines the pieces that constitute the target system, the process manager defines and suggests the workers, activities, and work products required for deriving the target system, and the project manager applies resources for executing the activities against work products to derive the target system. This unification involves a healthy tension between the project manager, architect, process manager, and the rest of the team to enable progress via the most feasible route by prioritizing, dialoguing, negotiating, agreeing, and attaining consensus to achieve the overall purpose and objectives of the effort. For example, given a very simple project directive "Si eat dinner," the architect defines dinner, the process manager defines that a person is required who must carry out the eating activity on the dinner work product, and the project manager applies Si as the resource who will play the role of the person. Grammatically, the architect defines the object within the directive statement, the process manager defines the subject and verb within the directive statement, and the project manager applies resources to execute the subject-verb-object combined directive statement. Most traditional projects combine the project manager and process manager roles, which essentially results in distorting this balance, causing a conflict of interest, and potentially risking project failure. For example, if there isn't ample time or resources for executing a project, the process is compromised and may increase the possibility of failure if key activities and work products are not leveraged. The different roles must constantly leverage each other's knowledge: the architect knows the target system best and advises what pieces constitute the target system, the process manager knows the process best and advises what process elements (workers, activities, work products, and so forth) are feasible for deriving the target system, and the project manager knows the available resources best and advises what resources are feasible for deriving the target system. The success of a project is fundamentally based on the effective and successful interaction, counterbalancing, and reinforcement of these dynamics that are separated, distributed, and balanced across workers representing sets of responsibilities and accountabilities with authority and power, their work products capturing knowledge, and their activities capturing the application of knowledge to progressively attain the project goals and objectives.

When empowered, the localization of the forces in between the project manager, architect, and process manager and the rest of the team significantly heightens the potential for project success because it establishes a context for achieving balance. The project manager must be a leader and simply a project administrator or rigid dictator. The architect must also be a leader and not simply a theoretician or technologist who is overly pedantic or pragmatic. The process manager must be a facilitator or enabler and not a process enforcer. The team must be able to stretch to address challenges and seize opportunities without breaking. Each iteration phase has a worker who leads the overall effort and who is responsible for the mode ("big picture") associated with the iteration phase, and each iteration phase has other workers who are responsible for the details ("small picture") within the model. Generally, an effort ought to strategize, execute, assess, and be agile (reactively adapt and proactively evolve) across the lifecycle. To succeed, an effort ought to localize forces that facilitate success in the context of forces that impede success; and then focus, balance, and iterate to bridge the chasm between culture and vision in order to succeed.

Within this overall scheme or process framework, a paradigm is required to define a set of foundational terms and concepts, and any specific methodology would define various heuristics, empirical or experience-based guidelines or rules of thumb that have proved valuable on previous projects utilizing the methodology. Workers, activities, work products, and the heuristics concerning them are commonly known as process elements. The UML rests heavily on the object-oriented paradigm for conceptualizing requirements and specifying systems, and the component-based paradigm for specifying and realizing systems. The principles and concepts of these paradigms are discussed in Chapter 3. Various heuristics are discussed throughout Chapters 5–9.

2.5. *The Value of Processes and Methodologies*

As the UML does not prescribe a particular process, it does not specify any specific process elements. A heavyweight process or methodology would define many process elements within this overall scheme, and a lightweight process or methodology would define very few process elements within this overall scheme. A methodology or process specifically addresses or suggests who does what activities on what work products, including when, how, why, and where such activities should be done.

2.5.1. *The Question*

The question of how lightweight or heavyweight a process ought to be can best be answered if we address an even more fundamental question: What is the value of a process or methodology, independent of how heavyweight or lightweight it is, and why would one process or methodology be more suitable than another?

The various answers to this question are as diverse as there are different types of communities of practitioners, particularly due to the fact that each community has its own unique culture and vision involving people and teams, processes, tools, and technologies founded on a set of values and principles establishing techniques and practices as well as concepts and a language.

Does a process or methodology unify teams with a common approach? Does it optimize workers, their activities, and their work products within the team? Does it simplify the overall approach to providing more functionality, in less time, and with a lower cost while managing risk, complexity, and change? Does it enable systems development to be less ad hoc, more repeatable and predictable, better-defined, well-managed, optimized, stable and flexible? Does it help address our fears, perhaps viewed negatively, or does it enable us, perhaps viewed more positively, to naturally evolve and improve? What is process really about? Is it about speed, size, continuous adaptability, discrete evolution, responding to the environment, fitness, feedback, or some other metric or characteristic within a specific context?

2.5.2. FINE CUISINE AND SYSTEMS DEVELOPMENT

Consider an analogy between fine cuisine and systems development.

Fine Cuisine

A method is comparable to a recipe, a process is comparable to cooking using a recipe, and a methodology is comparable to a book of related recipes. A recipe advises us on how to combine different ingredients in different proportions to produce a resulting dish for a specific audience with particular tastes. As a team of chefs follows a recipe, a team of practitioners executes a method. As chefs require utensils to follow the recipe, team members require tools to execute the method. As chefs require ingredients to follow the recipe, team members require a domain in which to execute the method using input information from all parties involved regarding the problem and solution. As chefs routinely tailor the recipe to add their unique perspectives based on the tastes of their audience, team members must tailor and adapt the method to address the particular needs and requirements of the domain, problem, solution, various other constraints, and culture and vision of the effort. Clearly, systems development has many similarities to fine cuisine. Therefore, the question regarding the value of a process or methodology may be rephrased: What is the value of a recipe or book of recipes, independent of how involved a recipe is, and why would one recipe or book of recipes be more suitable than another?

Various responses to this question may be summarized:

- The value of a recipe lies heavily in how various ingredients are combined, interact, accentuate or not accentuate, and generally affect each other as well as the various characteristics of the resulting dish, including flavor, aroma, texture, and so forth. This can be described as an amalgamation of ingredients into equilibrium.
- We can use the recipe to determine how the resulting dish may differ if we alter the ingredients. A recipe might include hints and variations of how additional ingredients, substitute ingredients, or ingredients in different proportions may be used to alter the various characteristics of the resulting dish.

- We can use the recipe to determine how much of each ingredient we ought to use based on the serving size, audience size, the amount of available ingredients, and so forth.
- The suitability of a recipe is fundamentally based on whether we can execute the recipe, the recipe accommodates the available ingredients, the resulting dish satisfies the tastes of the audience, and various other factors specific to our situation.

Because there are many different recipes, it would be most difficult to compile all recipes into a single book of recipes. Likewise, because there are many different ingredients, it would be most difficult to capture how various ingredients may be amalgamated. However, if there were a finite number of ingredients with a finite number of characteristics, rather than attempt to compile all recipes into a single book of recipes, we could capture a general recipe and use our understanding of the ingredients, including their numerous individual characteristics and amalgamation properties, to tailor the recipe to satisfy the tastes of any audience while considering any other factors specific to our situation.

Systems Development

Given this analogy, a similar approach may be applied to processes and methodologies. There are no "silver bullets" regarding systems development; rather, there are known best engineering practices, which have been unified into the UML as modeling techniques, that are commonly observed by effective and successful projects and organizations. Processes can only provide advice and recommendations, however they don't eradicate "thinking" activities throughout the lifecycle. Tools can only assist in the automation of a process, however they don't eradicate "doing" activities throughout the lifecycle. To succeed as a team, we need a common language that allows us to communicate and collaborate, and a common approach for achieving our objectives. A language establishes the boundaries of thought and behavior; it defines concepts similar to defining all possible ingredients that may be used by any recipe. A process establishes behavior within that boundary; it applies concepts similar to a recipe applying ingredients. Tools establish the automation of behavior within that boundary; they automate the application of concepts similar to cooking utensils used in the execution of a recipe.

The various responses to the recipe analogy may be reexamined and rephrased to address the original question:

- The value of a method lies heavily in its checks and balances between process elements across the lifecycle, where process elements interact, counterbalance, and reinforce one another due to their interdependencies such that quality results may be achieved. Checks involve looking back to validate a step or work product throughout the overall process and test assumptions in the face of change and complexity; and balances involve looking forward to adjust our approach as necessary given the results of a check. Similar to how various ingredients are amalgamated into equilibrium, checks and balances intertwine to enable us to amalgamate processes elements into equilibrium in order to manage risk and make progress toward our objectives. This can be described as an amalgamation of process elements into equilibrium where effort is separated, distributed, and balanced across workers involving checks and balances between responsibilities and accountabilities with authority and power, work products involving checks and balances between knowledge, and activities involving checks and balances between the applications of knowledge. As knowledge is distributed across the lifecycle with explicit intertwining points of checks and balances, systems development is quite closely related to the discipline of "knowledge management" in that the primary asset is knowledge. The checks and balances of a process or methodology are its heart and soul, expressed via workers, activities, and work products, and they define the robustness and rigor of the process or methodology. At the core of this equilibrium are the principal set of dynamics between the project manager, process manager, and architect. Furthermore, checks and balances combined with the evolution of work products with evolving levels of detail and continuous validation with feedback are critical for confronting risk rather than deferring risk. Different views, diagrams, and iteration cycles provide checks and balances between different stakeholders, aspects of a system, and aspects of an effort in order to align the various forces impacting an effort's vision such that decisions may be made while reconciling against risk and achieving quality results.

- We can use the method to determine how change traces between process elements. Traceability involves determining the ramification of a change to a given process element onto other process elements; that is, tracing an element to other related elements. Similar to how a recipe may be used to determine how the resulting dish may differ if we alter the ingredients using hints and variations, traceability between process elements enables us to manage change and the resulting complexity due to change.

- We can use the method to determine how to scale process elements. Scalability involves appropriately sizing process elements based on the size and complexity of a problem, solution, and team. Similar to how a recipe may be used to determine how much of each ingredient we ought to use based on the servicing size, audience size, the amount of available ingredients, and so forth, scalability enables us to scale a method to be as lightweight or heavyweight as necessary to enable us to succeed.

■ The suitability of a method is fundamentally based on whether we can execute the method, the method accommodates our various situational constraints, and we are enabled as a community of practitioners with our own unique culture, incentives, and vision to reasonably attain our vision.

Because there are many different methods, it would be most difficult to compile all methods into a single methodology. However, because a language establishes the boundaries of thought and behavior in defining concepts similar to defining all possible ingredients that may be used by any recipe, and because a process establishes behavior within that boundary in applying concepts similar to a recipe applying ingredients, given that known best engineering practices have been unified into the UML as modeling techniques, and given that there are a finite number of concepts defined by the core UML, rather than attempt to compile all methods that may apply the UML into a single methodology, we can apply the various modeling mechanisms to define a general infrastructure for applying the UML concepts, and use this infrastructure as necessary to satisfy our objectives and vision. This infrastructure combined with the UML establishes the UML roadmap.

2.5.3.   *THE ROADMAP*

The roadmap is a practical tool-, process-, and technology-independent approach to the effective and successful application of the UML. The roadmap is specifically derived from the UML and does not prescribe any particular process or process elements, but focuses on emphasizing what ought to be addressed when applying the UML, including the decision points and their relationships, emphasizing the following at each decision point and across each relationship:

■ Checks and balances by indicating or suggesting what to model, why, and how to model it using the UML. This can be described as an amalgamation of UML elements into equilibrium, or the holistic and cohesive integration of UML elements.

■ Traceability between UML constructs, holistically and cohesively across perspectives.

■ Scalability between UML constructs, holistically and cohesively across levels of abstraction.

■ Suitability to be as lightweight or heavyweight as necessary to enable success.

Having a general description of heavyweight, lightweight, and a road-map approach to process and methodology, it is worthwhile to compare, at least minimally if not exhaustively since an extensive comparison would require explicit methodologies and is beyond the scope of this discussion, these different approaches and their emphasis on the different types of process elements. All of these approaches may be applied as use-case-driven, architecture-centric, iterative and incremental, and risk-confronting processes that are object oriented and component based while focusing on providing more functionality, in less time, and with a lower cost while managing risk, complexity, and change. However, each approach has a different focus and emphasis.

All of these approaches have values or goals, principles embodying values or rules for attaining their goals and choosing between alternatives, techniques or means for applying rules, and practices or guidelines using the various techniques, making them habits. For example, if we value managing change and complexity, we need principally to be able to introduce change non-chaotically and adapt due to complexity, we need to apply techniques involving the stepwise introduction of change and adapting a system structurally and behaviorally due to complexity throughout the system development lifecycle process; and we need to leverage the practices of iterative and incremental development and an architecture-centric approach where effort may be performed in parallel.

Heavyweight Approaches

A heavyweight approach involves a discipline with a fairly significant number of rules and practices reified in numerous process elements, and is therefore process-oriented.

- A heavyweight approach may specify numerous process elements, including significant detail describing each worker, how to conduct each activity, and what constitutes each work product; thus, potentially providing significant detail in terms of process elements.
- A heavyweight approach furthermore leverages the various work products to facilitate communication, and is often perceived as being quite documentation-centric, giving prominence to the idiom "the design is the code," where the objective is to execute or demonstrate the design that will eventually translate into the physical system. Notice that the focus is not simply documentation, but modeling and communication.
- Thus, such an approach puts a project's burden of success quite heavily on the work products of an effort and focuses on predictably planning for change and prescriptively controlling change and complexity via the numerous defined process elements.

Fundamentally, the checks and balances within a heavyweight approach are distributed across process elements and may be unintentionally lost as different process elements are compromised, removed, or curtailed in order to satisfy the time, cost, resource constraints, culture, and vision of an effort. Essentially, due to the significant detail describing each worker, how to conduct each activity, and what constitutes each work product, the checks and balances between process elements become very obscured and hidden within the process. Furthermore, as decisions concerning process implementation are being made, such approaches don't readily indicate which checks and balances are being impacted such that their ramifications may be explored and risks addressed. Likewise, traceability and scalability become dependent on how well the process elements are defined, interrelate, and scale.

Lightweight Approaches

A lightweight approach involves a discipline with very few rules and practices not reified at all or only implicitly reified in any process elements, but heavily dependent on and emphasizes practitioners appropriately leveraging the practices, and is therefore people-oriented.

- A lightweight approach may specify practices or guidelines, while only implicitly, if at all, identify and describe each worker, the details of how to conduct each activity, and the details of what constitutes each work product, thus, potentially requiring significant interpretation in terms of process elements.
- A lightweight approach furthermore leverages face-to-face communication and the system implementation or code as the primary work product capturing the communication, where very little if any documentation beyond the code exists, giving prominence to the idiom "the code is the design," where the primary objective is to arrive at the system implementation and use the system implementation as the primary means of communication.
- Thus, such an approach puts a project's burden of success quite heavily on the people executing the effort and focuses on adaptively reacting to change and complexity by defining very few practices underlying any implicit process elements while emphasizing that people will appropriately leverage the practices.

Fundamentally, the checks and balances within a lightweight approach are embodied in the practices themselves and may be unintentionally lost because practices require interpretation in terms of process elements when being applied in the context of an effort. Essentially, worker responsibilities, accountabilities, authority, and power may be informally separated and distributed to every individual on the team, thus diluting the checks and balances between process elements; and the implicit, if any, descriptions of the details of how to conduct each activity, and the details of what constitutes each work product further dilute the checks and balances between process elements. Furthermore, as practices are being interpreted and applied in the context of an effort, such approaches don't readily indicate which checks and balances are being impacted such that their ramifications may be explored and risks addressed. Likewise, traceability and scalability become virtually completely informal and dependent on how the practitioners interpret the practices and execute the effort.

2.5.4. *THE ANSWER*

Various tactics attempting to reconcile or debate heavyweight approaches and lightweight approaches miss the opportunity to address the fundamental question regarding the value of a process or methodology, and often result in a cultural war for the heart and soul of process.

The roadmap establishes a continuum in which the best approach, independent of its weight, can be derived and applied. The derived approach would include what is necessary, sufficient, and consistent for succeeding in meeting our objectives and vision. Something is necessary if it is required; sufficient if it, by itself, is enough to satisfy a given purpose; and consistent if it does not have contradictory suppositions or conflicting imperative expressions that have contradictory consequences.

The roadmap approach focuses explicitly on checks and balances, traceability, scalability, and suitability and may be as process-oriented or people-oriented as necessary to be effective and successful.

- This approach avoids over engineering process elements similar to heavyweight processes, as heavyweight approaches potentially specify too much detail while portraying overengineered processes as a panacea and underengineered processes as backlashes to process in general, and potentially causing confusion when process elements must be scaled back.
- This approach avoids under engineering process elements similar to lightweight processes, as lightweight approaches potentially insufficiently specify enough detail while portraying underengineered processes as a panacea and overengineered processes as reactions to fear, and potentially leaving much to interpretation in applying a collection of practices.

Process and methodology cannot be reduced to a question of people-orientation or process-orientation but must be a well-balanced mix of all aspects. People leverage a process to focus on predictably planning for change and prescriptively controlling change and complexity while adaptively reacting to change and complexity so as to evolve. Furthermore, as the roadmap is scaled to be more heavyweight or lightweight in the context of an effort, we can readily identify which checks and balances are being impacted such that their ramifications may be explored and risks addressed.

The roadmap leverages the UML to facilitate communication, and thus puts a project's burden of success quite heavily on the use of the language in the context of the various modeling mechanisms, while focusing on being accommodating of change via the language's support for traceability and accommodating of complexity via the language's support for scalability. Because the roadmap puts a project's burden of success quite heavily on checks and balances within the context of the various modeling mechanisms, any modeling language other than the UML may likewise be used so long as there are corresponding concepts. Furthermore, a modeling language, not a computer programming language, is used such that the language is broadly applicable across the system lifecycle rather than only the later part of the lifecycle and such that we can apply our most valuable mental capability of abstraction to manage complexity and change.

After recognizing the value of the roadmap, we are empowered to leverage the roadmap in adopting a process, evolving an adopted process, and generally improving an approach to meeting our objectives and vision effectively and successfully. The roadmap is described in Chapter 4 and elaborated throughout Chapters 5–9

CHAPTER 3

Object Orientation

This chapter introduces object orientation, including the principles of object orientation, the foundational structural and behavioral concepts that enable us to model systems using the object-oriented paradigm, and how to communicate these concepts using the UML. Chapters 5–9 elaborate with more detail on these and other concepts. Our goal in this chapter is to gain a detailed tutorial overview of the UML notation.

3.1. *Principles of Object Orientation*

The object-oriented paradigm focuses on constructing reusable units and encompasses conceptualization and specification concepts, while the component-based paradigm focuses on the assembly of reusable units and encompasses specification and realization concepts, both of which are based on the principles of abstraction, encapsulation, generalization, and polymorphism. These principles enable a system to be more resilient in addressing change and complexity, which leads to system stability. Systems that are utterly simple or more algorithmic may not benefit as much from these paradigms as complex and more volatile systems.

3.1.1. ABSTRACTION

An abstraction is a concept or idea, and the technique of identifying abstractions is called abstracting. A manifestation of an abstraction is an example of the abstraction, and the technique of exemplifying or instantiating abstractions is called manifesting or instantiation. An abstraction may also be a concept of a relationship that relates other concepts. For example, the idea of a car is an abstraction and a physical car is the manifestation of the idea; and the idea of ownership of a car is an abstraction and ownership of a physical car is the manifestation of the relationship.

An abstraction is derived from a problem or solution domain and used in problem solving. A good abstraction is well defined by a boundary where it includes essential information required for understanding the concept while excluding any irrelevant or incidental information that may hinder understanding the concept. Well-defined abstractions enable us better to manage complexity by being able to focus on what is essential rather than being distracted by what is incidental. By capturing an agreed upon set of abstractions, we can manage the complexity caused by the exuberant amount of information involved in systems development. Otherwise, trying to know *every thing* about *everything* easily and quickly overwhelms our ability to manage change and complexity.

For example, in order to understand what it means to be a person within the context of a bank, we need to understand that a person has an identification number (for example, a social security number) and a collection of accounts among other pertinent information. But it is not essential for us to maintain the number of pets a person owns in the context of the bank. However, in order to understand what it means to be a person within the context of a pet store, we need to understand that a person owns pets, whose names, types, and ages may be pertinent. The relevance of information differs not only between domains, but also between different views within the same domain because each stakeholder has unique goals and needs, and the distinction of what is relevant and essential versus what is irrelevant and incidental differs based on these different goals and needs.

An abstraction has structural, or static, features or properties and behavioral, or dynamic, features or properties—essentially, abstractions have architecture. For example, a car may have a color, a structural characteristic, and may be able to accelerate or decelerate, both behavioral characteristics. This applies the static-dynamic dichotomy as discussed in Chapter 2.

An abstraction may be general or specific. A general abstraction represents a general concept. For example, person is a general abstraction and ownership is a general relationship between a person and some thing. A specific abstraction represents a specific concept. For example, Si, who is a person, owns some car, that is, some thing. This applies the type-instance dichotomy as discussed in Chapter 2, where Si is an instance of a person, the car is an instance of a thing, and the relationship between Si and the car is an instance of the ownership relationship. By classifying concepts by their similarities and separating concepts by the differences, general abstractions may be identified by virtue of this classification scheme.

Classification is very dependent on context, perspective, and level of abstraction. For example, there are numerous ways to perceive a car. A mechanical engineer in a factory may perceive a car as a collection of parts to be assembled. A salesperson in an automobile dealership may perceive a car as a product to be sold. A potential buyer in an automobile dealership may perceive a car as a "toy"—such as a sports car used for enjoyment—or as a "utility"—such as a family car used for transportation. Notice that even within the same context, a car may be perceived differentially given the buyer's needs. A mechanical engineer in an automobile dealership may perceive a car as a collection of parts to be repaired. Notice that even the same individual may perceive a car differently depending on the context. Quite often, people are more appeased with simpler rather than more complex problems because they presume such problems are easier to solve. However, there is not always a correlation between the simplicity or complexity of a problem and its solvability. Other practitioners are quite often attracted to more complex problems because they feel more comfortable with the context of the problem and are more adept at managing the level of abstraction to derive classifications that best enable them to solve the problem.

3.1.2. ENCAPSULATION

Encapsulation involves packaging an abstraction based on the principles of localization and information hiding. Localization involves grouping related parts together to maintain their unity in order to increase cohesion and decrease coupling.

Cohesion is a measure of relatedness, how parts of a whole are logically related to each other. The higher the cohesion of a collection of parts, where interdependencies between parts within a whole are maximized, the more likely that changes will be localized to those parts within the whole. For example, two rooms within the same house are highly cohesive since they are part of the same house; and if one room changes, the room most likely impacted is a room in the same house. Localization is maximized when cohesion is high, when related parts are packaged together.

Coupling is a measure of dependence, the strength of the connections or dependencies between wholes, where each whole is a collection of parts. The looser the coupling among wholes, where intradependencies between wholes is minimized, the more likely that changes will be localized to each whole collection of parts and not ripple to effect other wholes. For example, two rooms within two different houses are loosely coupled since they are parts of different houses; and if a room in one house changes, the other room in the second house is most likely not to be impacted. Localization is maximized when coupling is loose, when non-related parts are packaged separately from one another.

Information and implementation hiding involve defining a specification, which is exposed or visible from the external view of an abstraction, and an implementation, which is hidden or visible from the internal view of the abstraction but not visible from the outside of the abstraction, such that the abstraction has a well-defined boundary. This applies the specification-implementation dichotomy as discussed in Chapter 2, where the specification describes what services and information may be requested by users of the abstraction and the implementation or realization describes how the services and information that the abstraction offers are implemented or realized. A service is a characterization of the behavior of an element. An encapsulated abstraction enables us better to manage change by being able to modify the implementation without necessarily impacting the specification and requiring users of the abstraction to change, thus localizing changes to the internal view of the abstraction and reducing the external user's dependency on the implementation, provided that the user is using the abstraction via its specification.

For example, when a person, whether real or as an abstraction, is requested to do something such as opening a door, the request or specification may be verbal while the means or implementation of how the person opens the door is hidden from view. We may be able to see the person open the door with the person's right or left hand, however, the actual sequence of muscle movements and the internal workings of the physical body remain hidden and only visible through outward manifestations. Therefore, altering or changing the internal workings of the body would not impact whoever made the request.

Modularity, as it relates to encapsulation, involves the purposeful partitioning of an abstraction into multiple smaller and simpler abstractions. Modularity enables us better to manage change and complexity by being able to break down and decompose or build up and compose an abstraction as necessary to an appropriate level of granularity where its complexity and likelihood of being changed are minimized but its usability is maximized. For example, it is more feasible to separate the abstraction of a person from the abstraction of the person's bank account such that either abstraction may be used independently. If these two concepts are combined, the conglomerate abstraction, person–bank-account, would be more complex because it combines two concepts into one and more apt to change because it may be impacted by changes to either concept. If these two concepts are separated, the bank account abstraction may be associated with a person, organization, and so forth, and if either concept changes, the other concept need not necessarily be impacted. Modularity enables us better to manage complexity and change at different levels of abstraction or granularity. For example, a system is modularized into a collection of subsystems such that changes to one subsystem need not necessarily impact other subsystems.

3.1.3. GENERALIZATION

Generalization involves the relating of a collection of abstractions taxonomically based on similarities and differences where more specific or specialized abstractions may be defined as variations of more general or generalized abstractions. Generalization also allows more specific or specialized abstractions to be substituted for their more general or generalized abstractions. The more general abstraction is often called the generalization of the more specific abstraction, and the more specific abstraction is often called the specialization of the more general abstraction. Generalization enables us better to manage change and complexity by being able to reuse the specification and implementation of existing abstractions to define new abstractions. Specialized abstractions receive or inherit the structural and behavioral characteristics, including specifications and implementations, of their related generalized abstractions. The more specific abstractions may add their own more specialized structural and behavioral characteristics, and may override implementations while maintaining the specifications of the behavior provided by the more general abstractions they specialize. The more specific abstractions are called the children or descendants (for non-immediate children) of the more general abstractions, and the more general abstractions are called the parents or ancestors (for non-immediate parents) of the more specific abstractions.

For example, given the more general or generalized abstraction of vehicle, we can establish two more specific or specialized abstractions of land-vehicle and water-vehicle based on the mediums through which the vehicle will operate. The vehicle abstraction may provide behaviors for activating or and deactivating any vehicle, and the land-vehicle and water-vehicle abstractions would receive and share the specification and implementation of these services. The vehicle abstraction may also provide a specification for the behavior of veering-left and veering-right, possibly with default implementations, and the land-vehicle and water-vehicle abstractions would use the same specifications for the behaviors but provide their own specific implementations for veering in water or on land. Because the land-vehicle and water-vehicle abstractions share the behaviors for activating and deactivating a vehicle, should these shared behaviors be modified, the modification would impact both specialized abstractions as they share the specifications and implementations of the vehicle abstraction. Furthermore, when discussing a generic vehicle, so long as we don't refer to anything specific to a land-vehicle or water-vehicle, we can substitute either type of vehicle in place of the more general or generalized vehicle abstraction.

3.1.4. Polymorphism

Polymorphism involves the relating of a collection of abstractions that share a specification but provide their own unique or specific implementations. An abstraction providing the implementation is said to realize or implement the abstraction providing the specification. This involves the ability to make the same request of two or more different abstractions where each abstraction has its own unique or specific implementation for handling the request. Polymorphism allows an abstraction to be substituted for other abstractions realizing the same specification when the user of the abstraction relies on that specification. Polymorphism enables us better to manage change and complexity by being able to reuse specifications without unique or specific implementations of existing abstractions to define new variations with their own implementation. An implementing abstraction receives the specifications of the structural and behavioral characteristics of a specifying abstraction. The implementing abstraction may have other structural and behavioral characteristics, but must provide implementations while maintaining the specifications of the realized specifying abstractions.

For example, a person or a dog may be requested to walk to a door; the same request or specification will evoke the person and dog to apply two different means or implementations to respond to the request. The person and dog will utilize the same operation or specification of walking but their own methods or implementation for walking to the door even though they received the same request.

3.2. Structural (Static) Concepts

The foundational structural concepts include classes and objects, which form the basis for various other structural concepts. The foundational structural relationships include associations and links, which form the basis for various other relationships.

3.2.1. Class and Object Diagrams

Class diagrams, from the structural or static model view, depict the static structure of a system using classes and associations. Object diagrams, from the structural or static model view, depict the static structure of a system at a particular time using objects and links. Structural modeling is the subject of Chapter 6.

Classes

A class is a general abstraction representing a concept. A classifier abstractly defines structural features and behavioral features as discussed in Chapter 6; that is, it is a generalized concept representing various more concrete concepts, including classes, interfaces, nodes, components and subsystems. A class concretely defines structural features and behavioral features. The most crucial aspect of a class is its semantics, the meaning of the abstraction.

Structural features, including attributes and relationships called associations, define what elements constitute an abstraction. An attribute is an element of information or data with visibility, name, multiplicity, type, and an initial value. Visibility is applied to elements relative to their containers. The visibility symbol "+" means public and the element is accessible from outside of its container, "-" means private and the element is inaccessible from outside of its container, "#" means protected and the element is inaccessible from outside of its container but is accessible from descendant elements, and "~" means package visibility and other elements in the same container package may access the element. UML provides data types for Boolean true and false values, integers, real numbers, and strings. A relationship is a connection between classes.

Behavioral features, including operations and methods, define how the constituents of the abstraction interact to provide the behavior of the abstraction. An operation is a specification of a service or processing with visibility, name, parameter list, and return type list. A method is an implementation of a service or processing. This applies the specification-implementation dichotomy as discussed in Chapter 2, where the operation is a specification describing what service may be requested by users of the class, and the method is an implementation or realization describing how the service that the class offers is implemented or realized.

A class is depicted as a solid-outline rectangle with three standard compartments separated by horizontal lines. The top compartment is required and contains the class name string; the middle list compartment is optional and contains a list of attributes; and the bottom list compartment is optional and contains a list of operations. A list compartment holds a list of text strings and may have a name depicted centered at the top of the compartment. For the attributes compartment, the string "attributes" may be used. For the operations compartment, the string "operations" may be used. Other compartments may be used as necessary; each compartment need only show what is relevant to the diagram, and optional compartments may be suppressed. An attribute is shown as a text string in the middle compartment of the class rectangle. An operation is shown as a text string in the bottom compartment of the class rectangle.

Figure 3.1 shows various ways to depict classes. Not all details of a modeling element need to be depicted on a diagram, but only those that are relevant to the purpose of the diagram. Notice how attributes are depicted, where a Person class has a private Name attribute of type String with an initial value of "No Name"; and also notice how operations are specified, where a Person class has a public verifyPassword operation that requires a parameter that it names thePassword of type String and returns a Boolean type value.

Objects

An object is a specific abstraction representing a specific concept. An instance abstractly defines specific classifiers as discussed in Chapter 6; that is, it is a generalized concept representing various more concrete concepts, including objects, node instances, component instances, and subsystem instances. An object is an instance of a class, and a class is instantiated as an object. A class defines the structural and behavioral characteristics of its objects; furthermore, the stereotypes and properties of a class apply to the objects of the class.

An object concretely defines values for its structural features, attribute values and specific relationships called links, and shares the behavioral features of its class. The state of an object is the condition or situation

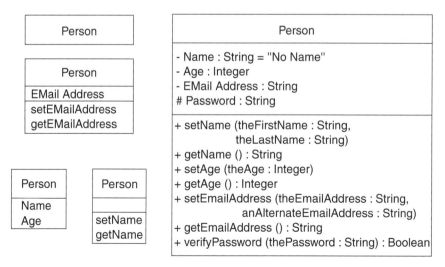

FIGURE 3.1. Classes.

of the object during its life during which it satisfies some condition. The state of an object is defined by the values of the object's structural features, what an object knows. The most crucial aspect of an object is that it has its own identity. No two objects are the same, even if they have the same values for their structural features. The behavior of an object is defined by the behavior of its class, what an object can do.

An object is depicted as a solid-outline rectangle with two standard compartments separated by horizontal lines. The top compartment is required and contains the object name followed by a colon followed by the object's class name (or a comma-separated list of class names) fully underlined, both names are optional and the colon is only present if the class name is specified; the second compartment is optional and contains a list of attributes, each with an equal symbol and it value. Other compartments may be used, and each compartment need only show what is relevant to the diagram. To show the presence of an object in a particular state of a class, follow the name of the object with the state name (or a comma-separated list of names of states) enclosed within square brackets.

An active object is an object that owns a thread of control and may initiate control activity. A passive object is one that holds data but does not initiate control, though it may communicate with other objects in the course of processing a request that it has received. An active element is shown as a rectangle with a heavy border. Alternatively, the property keyword "active" may also be used to indicate an active object. A multiobject is a collection of objects. A multiobject is depicted as two rectangles in which the top rectangle is shifted slightly vertically and horizontally to suggest a stack of rectangles. Multiobjects are also used on class diagrams as multiobject classes using the class notation.

Figure 3.2 shows various ways to depict objects. Again, not all details of a modeling element need to be depicted on a diagram, but only those that are relevant to the purpose of the diagram. Notice how attributes have values, where an anonymous object of the Person class has a Name attribute value of "Sinan Si Alhir"; and also notice how operations are not specified. Also notice how the multiobject collection of files is depicted and how active objects are depicted.

Types

A type is a class defining a set of objects to which a collection of operations and structural features (attributes and relationships) apply; it focuses on a role or a part a class or objects of a class may play in a particular situation without defining the physical implementation of objects of the class. A role is a named specific behavior of a class participating in a particular context. The structural features of a type are solely for the purpose of specifying the behavior of the type's operations and do not represent any actual implementation. A type cannot be instantiated. An object may have or conform to any number of types since a type is a role that an object may adopt or abandon.

A type is depicted as a class stereotyped with the "type" keyword. The attribute compartment contains a list of the attributes specified by the type. The operations compartment contains a list of the operations spec-

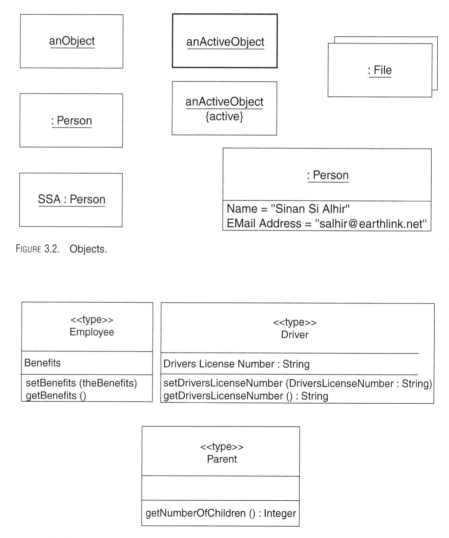

Figure 3.2.   Objects.

Figure 3.3.   Types.

ified by the type. Figure 3.3 shows three different types or roles that objects may play, including employee, driver, and parent.

Implementation Classes

An implementation class is a class defining an implementation for behavioral features (operations and methods) and structural features (attributes and relationships). An object may have only one implementation class since an implementation class specifies the physical implementation of the object.

An implementation class is depicted as a class stereotyped with the "implementationClass" keyword. The attribute compartment contains a list of the attributes implemented by the implementation class. The operations compartment contains a list of the operations implemented by the implementation class. Figure 3.4 shows a physical implementation of an employee.

Interfaces

An interface is a class defining a service or contract as a collection of externally visible operations without any structural features. An interface does not specify any internal structure (attributes and relationships) or implementation (methods) and only specifies operations. An interface may be the target of a relationship that other elements can navigate or traverse to reach the interface, but it may not have relationships it can navigate or traverse to reach other elements. An interface cannot be instantiated. Any abstraction that conforms to or realizes an interface

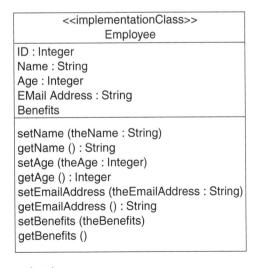

FIGURE 3.4. Implementation classes.

must faithfully carry out or support and implement the operations of the interface; that is, the elements that constitute the abstraction must implement the operations. Any abstraction that conforms to an interface may be substituted for other abstractions that conform to or realize the same interface.

An interface is depicted as a class stereotyped with the "interface" keyword. The attribute compartment may be omitted because it is always empty. The operations compartment contains a list of the operations specified by the interface. An interface may also be depicted as a small circle with the name of the interface placed near the symbol. The operations specified by the interface are not shown using the circle notation. The circle may be attached by a solid line to an element that supports the interface or provides an implementation for the operations the interface specifies. In a realization relationship, abstractions share specifications without any implementations where a more specialized abstraction must provide an implementation.

Figure 3.5 shows five different interfaces or contracts that objects may implement or support and use when implemented by other objects, including IDrive, ITransaction, IEmployee, IDatabase, and IConnection. The operations are depicted for each interface other than the IEmployee because it is depicted using the circle notation.

Associations

An association is a general abstraction representing a relationship between classes. A binary association involves two classes, and an *n*-ary association involves three or more classes. An association may have a related class called an association class defining structural features and behavioral features of the association itself.

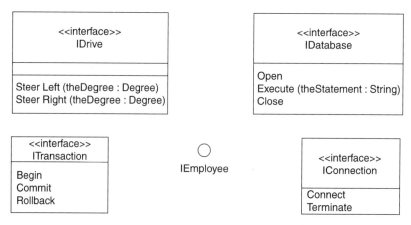

FIGURE 3.5.   Interfaces.

Binary Associations

A binary association, a relationship between two classes, is depicted as an arc or a solid path made of a connected series of line segments connecting two classes. A binary association may be labeled with a name. The name is usually read from left to right and top to bottom. The name may have a small black solid triangle next to it, called a name-direction arrow, where the point of the triangle indicates the direction in which to read the name; but the arrow is purely descriptive and has no semantics associated with it. Figure 3.6 shows that a person may own cars and lives in a home.

N-ary Associations

An *n*-ary association, a relationship between three or more classes, is depicted as a large diamond with an arc or a solid path made of a connected series of line segments from the diamond to each participating class. An *n*-ary association may be labeled with a name near the diamond. The name is usually read from left to right and top to bottom. The name may have a small black solid triangle next to it, called a name-direction arrow, where the point of the triangle indicates the direction in which to read the name; but the arrow is purely descriptive and has no semantics associated with it. Aggregation and composition may not be used with *n*-ary associations. Figure 3.7 shows that a purchase involves a person, a dealer, and a car.

Association Classes

An association class, a class representing an association, is depicted as a class rectangle attached by a dashed line to its association path in a binary association, or to its association diamond in an *n*-ary association.

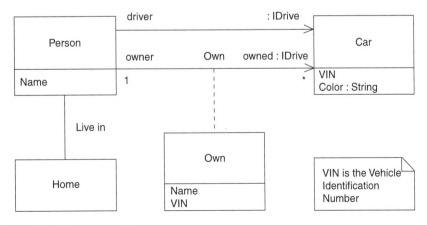

FIGURE 3.6. Binary associations.

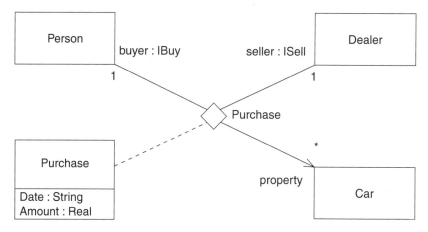

FIGURE 3.7. *N*-ary associations.

The name in the class symbol and the name attached to the association are redundant and should be the same, and only one name need appear, but association names are optional.

Figure 3.6 shows the Own association class and its attributes, including the Name attribute of a person and the VIN or vehicle identification number of a car. Figure 3.7 shows the Purchase association class and its attributes, including the Date attribute and the Amount attribute of the purchase.

Association Ends

An association end is an endpoint of an association, which connects the association to a class.

Given a class involved in an association, a rolename may be used to indicate how the class participates in the association, the "face" it projects in the relationship. A role is a named specific behavior of a classifier participating in a particular context. A rolename may be placed near the end of the association attached to the class. A visibility symbol may be attached in front of a rolename to specify the visibility of the association traversing in the direction toward the rolename.

Figure 3.6 shows that within the Own association, a person plays the role of owner while a car plays the role of something that is owned. Figure 3.7 shows that within the Purchase association, a person plays the role of buyer, a dealer plays the role of seller, and a car plays the role of property.

Given a class involved in an association, an interface specifier (or a comma-separated list of interface specifiers) may be used to indicate the behavior expected of the class by other classes that participate in the association; that is, a class's responsibilities. In the context of an association, a class may present only one or more of its interfaces as relevant. The specifier indicates what role a class presents to its associated classes in that context, where only the specified properties are relevant and visible. An interface specifier may be placed following a rolename and a colon. If no interface specifier is indicated, full access to the class is permitted. An interface specifier may use interface and type names.

Figure 3.6 shows that the Car class indicates that the Person class expects it to be drivable using the IDrive interface. Figure 3.7 shows that within the Purchase association, the Person class indicates that the other classes expect it to play the role of buyer using the IBuy interface, the Dealer class indicates that the other classes expect it to play the role of seller using the ISell interface, and the buyer and seller don't have any expectations of the car providing any interface but via the relationship, they obtain full access to the car.

Given a class involved in an association, navigation may be used to indicate that the class is identifiable and referenceable from associated classes. Furthermore, an interface may be the target of a one-way association, but it may not have an association that it can navigate. Navigation is depicted as an arrow attached to the end of an association path to indicate that navigation is supported toward the class attached to the arrow, otherwise the association is assumed to be bi-directional and navigable in all directions.

Figure 3.6 shows that within the Own association, if we know of a person, we can determine what car or cars are owned by the person, but if we know of a car, we cannot determine who owns the car. Also, if we know of a person, we can determine what home they live in, and if we know of a home, we can determine who lives there. Figure 3.7 shows that within the Purchase association, if we know of a person, we can determine the dealer and car. If we know of a dealer, we can determine the persona and car. However, if we know of a car, we cannot determine either the person or dealer involved in the purchase.

Given a class involved in an association, multiplicity may be used to indicate how many instances of the class may participate in the relationship when the associated classes are fixed. Multiplicity is depicted as a comma-separated sequence of integer intervals, including literal integer values, closed ranges depicted as "lower-bound .. upper-bound," and a single asterisk to denote an unlimited range. There is no default multiplicity for association ends, it is simply undefined.

Figure 3.6 shows that within the Own association, a person may own zero or more cars and a car may only be owned by one person. The diagram does not specify how many people may live in the same home or how many homes a single person may live in. Figure 3.7 shows that within the Purchase association, only one person and one dealer may be involved in the purchase of zero or more cars.

Links

A link is a specific abstraction representing a specific relationship between objects. A link is an instance of an association. If its association has a related association class, the link has a corresponding link object, which defines values for its structural features and shares the behavioral features of the association class.

Binary Link

A binary link, a specific relationship between two objects, is depicted as an arc or a solid path made of a connected series of line segments connecting two objects. A link may have its association name depicted near the path fully underlined, but links do not have instance names as they take their identity from the instances that they relate.

Figure 3.8 shows that Nora, who is a person, owns a red car with a VIN of 1, a white car with a VIN of 2, and a blue car with a VIN of 3. The diagram also shows that Phillip, who is a person, owns a black car with a VIN of 4, and that both Nora and Phillip live in the same home.

N-ary Link

An *n*-ary link, a relationship between three or more objects, is depicted as a large diamond with an arc or a solid path made of a connected series of line segments from the diamond to each participating object. A link may have its association name depicted near the path fully underlined, but links do not have instance names as they take their identity from the instances that they relate. Aggregation and composition may not be used with *n*-ary links.

Figure 3.9 shows that a person with the name of "Phillip" purchased a red car from a dealer with the name of "Dealer 1" in January 1999 and a white car from the same dealer in January 2000; furthermore, the same person also purchased a blue car from a dealer with the name of "Dealer 2" in January 2001.

Link Objects

A link object, an object representing a link, is depicted as an object rectangle attached by a dashed line to its link path in a binary link, or to its link diamond in an n-ary link. The name in the object symbol and the name attached to the link are redundant and should be the same, and only one name need appear but link names are optional. Figure 3.8 and Figure 3.9 show various link objects for the relationships.

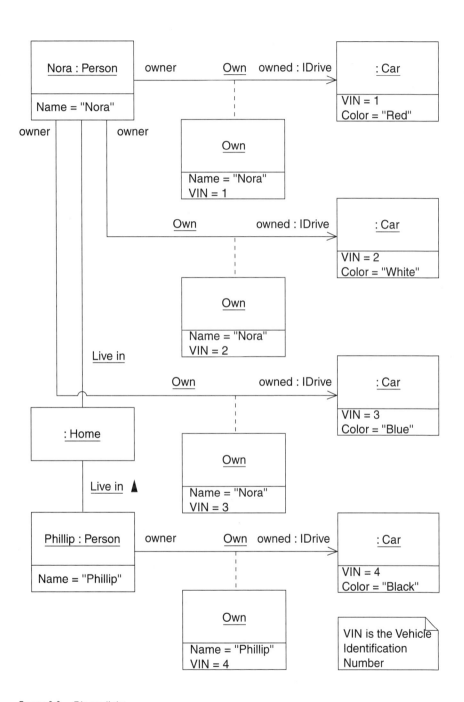

FIGURE 3.8. Binary links.

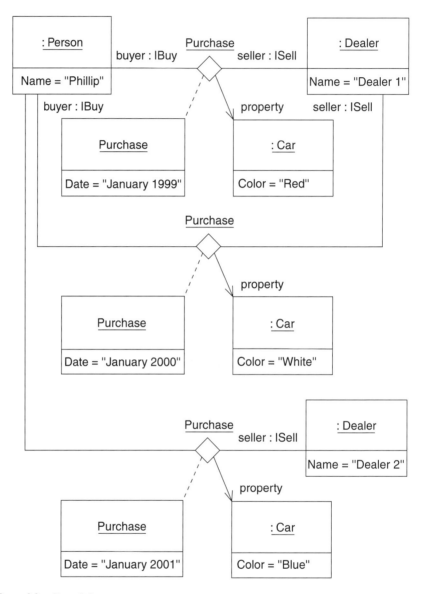

FIGURE 3.9.   *N*-ary links.

Link Ends

A link end, similar to an association end, is an endpoint of a link, which connects the link to an object. Visibility, rolenames, interface specifiers, and navigation may be shown for links.

Aggregation Associations

An aggregation association is an association representing a whole-part relationship between an aggregate, the whole, and its parts. Likewise, a part cannot own its whole; that is, there cannot be any cycles among whole and part objects. An aggregation association is often called a "has-a"(for objects) or "has-a-kind-of" (for classes) relationship because the whole has its parts.

An aggregation association is depicted using a hollow diamond attached to the end of the path connected to the class that is the aggregate. Aggregation is depicted for binary associations and links, and is not used with *n*-ary associations and links.

Figure 3.10 shows that a team has 3 to 5 employees who play the role of members, and a member may belong to zero or up to two teams.

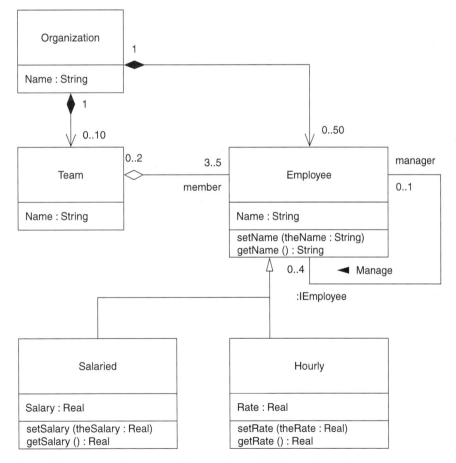

FIGURE 3.10.   Aggregations, compositions, and generalizations between classes.

Notice that an employee playing the role of a manager manages employees using the IEmployee interface, where a manger may manage zero to four employees and an employee may have no more than one manager but need not have a manager. The Manage association between the employee class and itself is called a self-referential or reflexive association since it involves two objects of the same class. Figure 3.11 shows that Phillip, Jill, Andy, Nora, and Si are members of the Product Development team, and Phillip, Jack, and Jill are members of the Sales and Marketing team. Notice that Nora manages Andy and Si, and Jill manages Jack.

Composition Associations

A composition association, also called composite aggregation, is an aggregation association where the part may belong to at most one whole, called strong ownership, and the whole is responsible for destroying its parts when the whole is destroyed, called coincident lifetime. The whole is responsible for the life of the part. A composition association is often called a "contains-a" (for objects) or "contains-a-kind-of" (for classes) relationship because the whole contains its parts.

A composition association is depicted using a filled diamond attached to the end of the path connected to the class that is the composite. Composition is depicted for binary associations and links, and is not used with *n*-ary associations and links.

Figure 3.10 shows that an organization may have zero to ten teams, an organization may have zero to fifty employees, a team may only belong to one organization, and an employee may belong to only one organization. Also, if an organization is destroyed or should go bankrupt, its teams and employees are destroyed. Figure 3.11 shows that the Product Development team and Sales and Marketing team belong to the same organization.

Alternately, composition may be depicted by graphically nesting elements. A nested element's multiplicity may be depicted in its upper right corner and its rolename may be indicated in front it its class name followed by a colon. Attributes are, in effect, composition relationships between a class and the classes of its attributes. Figure 3.12 is equivalent to Figure 3.10 but uses the graphical nesting of elements to depict composition. This notation may be used for classes and objects.

Generalizations

A generalization relationship represents generalization between a more general element and a more specific element, where the more specific element receives the structural features (attributes and relationships) and behavioral (operations and methods) features from the more general element and instances of the more specific element may be substi-

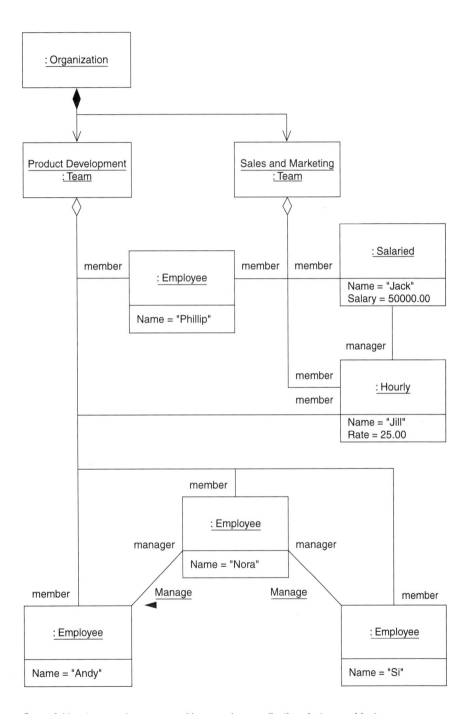

FIGURE 3.11. Aggregations, compositions, and generalizations between objects.

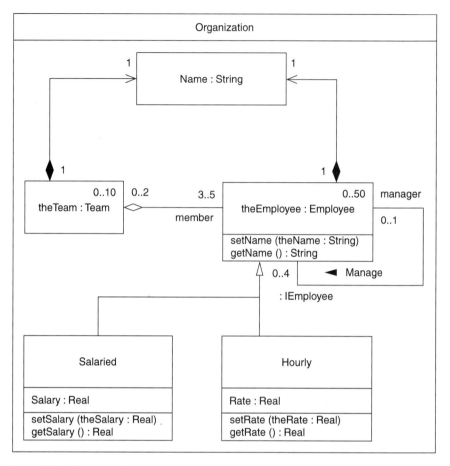

FIGURE 3.12.   Alternative form of composition.

tuted in the place of instances of the more general element. The more
specific element may add its own more specialized structural and behavioral characteristics, and may override implementations or methods
while maintaining the specifications or operations of the behavior provided by the more general element it specializes. The more general element and the more specific element must be consistent with one another; that is, they must be of the same type of modeling element (types,
interfaces, implementation classes). The more general element is called
a supertype, superclass, or generalization and the more specific element
is called a subtype, subclass, or specialization. Inheritance is the sharing
mechanisms through which more specific elements acquire the characteristics of more general elements. Single inheritance involves only a
single more general element, and multiple inheritance involves at least

two or more general elements. A generalization relationship is often called a "is-a-kind-of" relationship because the more specific element is a specialized type of the more general element.

A generalization relationship is depicted as a solid-line path from the more specific element to the more general element, with a large hollow triangle at the end of the path connected to the more general element. In a generalization relationship, abstractions share specifications and implementations where a more specialized abstraction may override the default or provided implementation with a more specialized implementation.

Figure 3.10 shows that the organization has two types of employees, salaried and hourly. Salaried employees not only have a name similar to other employees, but they also receive a salary. Hourly employees not only have a name similar to other employees, but they have an hourly rate. Salaried and hourly employees may also participate in the management of other employees via the Manage association and participate as team members. Furthermore, we may substitute salaried and hourly employees for general employee.

Figure 3.11 shows that Phillip, Nora, Andy, and Si are general employees, but Jack and Jill are more specific employees. Notice how Jack, who is a salaried employee, has a name similar to other employees, but also has a salary; and notice how Jill, who is an hourly employee, has a name similar to other employees, but also has an hourly rate. Furthermore, we have substituted Jack and Jill as members of the Sales and Marketing team because they are employees. Also notice that Jill is Jack's manager because they are employees.

Dependencies

A dependency is an abstraction representing a relationship between elements indicating that one element, the source or client, uses or depends on another element, the target or supplier; and a change to the target element may require a change to the source element.

A dependency is depicted as a dashed arrow from the dependent client element to the independent supplier element, and it may also be named. A dependency may be stereotyped with the "use" keyword to indicate that one element requires the presence of another element for its correct functioning. A dependency may be stereotyped with another keyword to indicate the exact nature of the dependency, but this is often evident from the context in which the dependency is used. Note that a dependency may be traversed in either direction, and the direction of the arrow does not limit traversal but only indicates the dependent and independent elements.

A dependency may exist for a set of elements, depicted as one or more arrows with their tails on the clients connected to the tails of one or more arrows with their heads on the suppliers, where a small dot can be placed on the junction and a note on the dependency should be attached at the junction point describing the dependency. A dependency may be stereotyped with the "instanceOf" keyword to specify that the source is an object or link and the target is its class or association respectively.

Figure 3.13 shows Nora is a person who owns a blue car with a VIN of 3; and that a person, and more specifically Nora, uses the IDrive interface. Figure 3.14 shows that Phillip is a person who purchased a red car from a dealer with the name of "Dealer 1" in January 1999; and that a person, and more specifically Phillip, uses the ISell interface to communicate with the dealer; and that a dealer, and more specifically "Dealer 1," uses the IBuy interface to communicate with Phillip in the purchasing of the car. Figure 3.15 shows that Nora and Si are both employees;

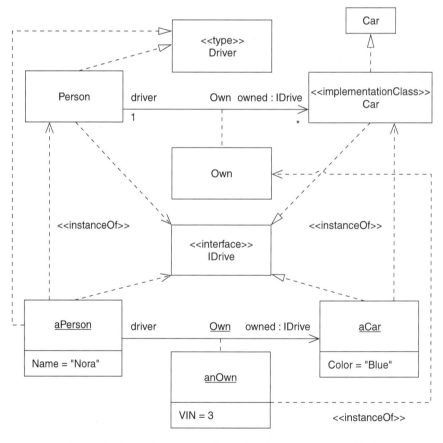

FIGURE 3.13.   Dependencies and realization relationships between classes, objects, binary associations, and binary links.

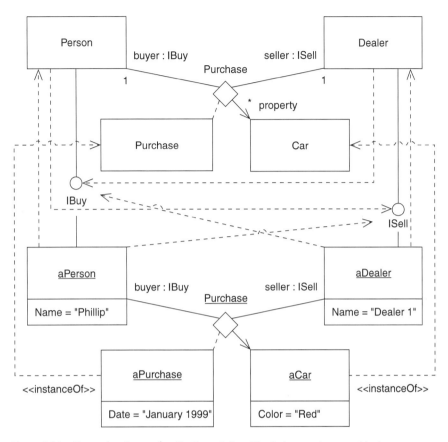

FIGURE 3.14.   Dependencies and realization relationships between classes, objects, *n*-ary
associations, and *n*-ary links.

and that an employee, more specially Nora, uses the IEmployee interface
to manage Si.

Notice that a class or object depends on the interfaces identified by
the interface specifiers of the classes or objects to which it is associated
or linked. For example, in Figure 3.13, the Person class depends on the
IDrive interface that is identified by the interface specifier of the Car
class in the association with the Person class.

Realizations

A realization relationship represents a relationship between an element
providing a specification and an element providing an implementation
for the specification. The realizing elements is said to realize or implement the specifying element. Any element may be used as a specification

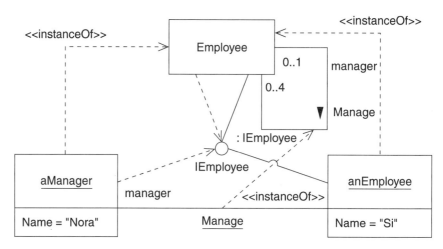

FIGURE 3.15.   Dependencies and realization relationships between classes and objects
without associations or links.

or realization element because a realization relationship indicates conformance of behavior, where the client supports at least all of the operations defined in the supplier without necessity to support any structural
features of the supplier (attributes and associations).

A realization relationship is depicted using a dependency stereotyped
with the "realize" keyword drawn from the implementing source element
to the specifying target element or a dashed line with a solid triangle arrowhead attached to the specifying target element. When the specifying
element is an interface that is depicted as a small circle with the name of
the interface placed near the symbol, the realization relationship is depicted as a solid line from the implementing element to the interface.

Figure 3.13 shows that a car, and more specifically Nora's blue car,
realizes the IDrive interface. Figure 3.14 shows that a person, and more
specifically Phillip, realizes the IBuy interface and that a dealer, and
more specifically "Dealer 1," realizes the ISell interface in order for the
purchasing of the car. Figure 3.15 shows that an employee, and more
specially Si, realizes the IEmployee interface such that Si maybe managed by Nora.

Notice in Figures 3.13–3.15 that interfaces and types do not have instances and are not instantiated because they require a class or object
to realize them. Also notice that a class or object realizes the interfaces
identified by the interface specifiers of the class or object. For example,
in Figure 3.13, the Car class realizes the IDrive interface that is identified
by the interface specifier of the Car class in the association with the
Person class.

3.2.2. Use-Case Diagrams

Use-case diagrams, from the use-case or user model view, depict the functionality of a system using actors, use cases, and their relationships. Use-case modeling is the subject of Chapter 5.

Actors

An actor is a class representing a set of roles outside of an entity that users of the entity can play when interacting with the entity. An entity may be a system, subsystem, or class. An actor may have binary associations with use cases, subsystems, and classes, and may offer interfaces that describe how other elements may communicate with the actor. An actor is depicted as a class stereotyped with the "actor" keyword or a "stick figure" icon.

Figure 3.16 shows four different actors: including a person, manager, buyer, and dealer. Figure 3.17 shows that Nora is a person playing the role of a driver. Figure 3.18 shows that Phillip is a buyer and shows a dealer actor with the name of "Dealer 1." Figure 3.19 shows that Nora is a manager.

Use Cases

A use case is a class representing a specification of general functionality, which is observable and testable, provided by an entity to its users as a complete sequence of actions that the entity performs in an interaction or dialog, including its variant interactions or complete sequences of actions, with actors in order to provide results and value to at least one

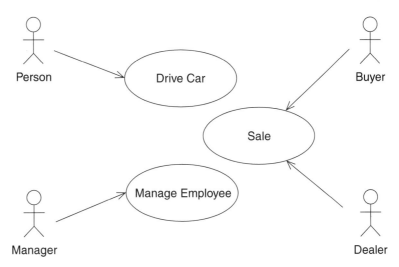

FIGURE 3.16. Actors and use cases.

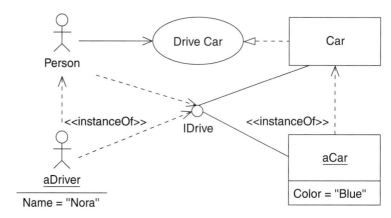

Figure 3.17.   A person who drives a car.

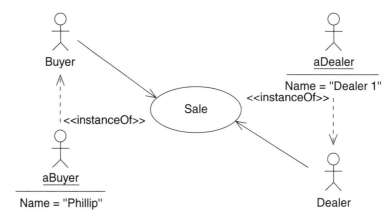

Figure 3.18.   A buyer and dealer involved in a sale.

of its actors or users. A behavior sequence is generally an individual sequence of actions and interactions from the basic or normal and variant or alternative sequences of actions and interactions.

A use-case instance is called a scenario and represents a specific use of the general functionality provided by an entity as a specific sequence of actions that the entity performs in an interaction or dialog with specific actors. A use case may have attributes, operations, binary associations, and may offer interfaces that define a subset of the entire interaction defined in the use case, where different interface offered by the use case need not be disjoint. A use case is depicted as an ellipse containing the name of the use case. Use cases may be enclosed by a rectangle that represents the boundary of the containing entity.

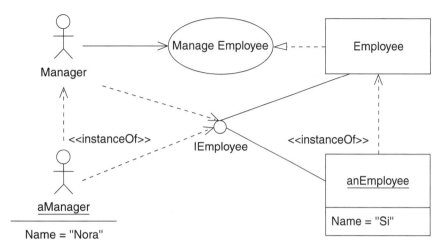

FIGURE 3.19.   A manager who manages employees.

Figure 3.16 shows three different use cases, including driving a car, managing employees, and a sale. Various relationships may be used between use cases to indicate common, optional, and variations of existing functionality as discussed in Chapter 5.

Relationships

An association between an actor and a use case indicates that the actor communicates and participates in the use case and collaborates and interacts with other involved actors and the entity to which the use case pertains; that is, instances of the actor, instances of other involved actors, and instances of the entity to which the use case pertains communicate with each other. An actor plays a separate role with regard to each use case within which it participates.

A navigation arrow indicates who initiates the interaction. A navigation arrow pointing toward a use case indicates that the associated actor initiates the interaction. A navigation arrow pointing toward an actor indicates that the entity to which the use case pertains initiates the interaction.

When an actor participates in a use case, the actor interacts with the entity via an interface that the entity provides. The actor depends on the interface and the entity realizes the interface. The functionality or use case of an entity is provided as a service to its users or actors via some interface, the entity has responsibility for the service and conforms to or offers and supports the interface, and the parts within the entity have responsibility for implementing the service and realizing the interface.

Figure 3.17 shows that a person driver uses the IDrive interface to drive a car, and a car realizes or implements the use case and interface. Figure 3.18 does not identify any interfaces for the actors or any elements that realize the use case. Figure 3.19 shows that a manager uses the IEmployee interface to manage employees, and an employee realizes or implements the use case and interface. Figure 3.6 shows that a person may play the role of a driver, Figure 3.13 shows that a person uses the IDrive interface when playing the role of a driver, and Figure 3.17 shows the Person actor using the IDrive interface to drive a car. Notice that interfaces are based on the roles actors play in relation to the use cases. Also notice that the Manager, Buyer, and Dealer actors are more specific sets of roles than the Person actor; however, the Person actor may have been used for all of the actors in these figures, and the specific role of the Person actor would have been captured via the interfaces.

3.2.3.   COMPONENT DIAGRAMS

Component diagrams, from the component or implementation model view, depict the implementation of a system using components and their relationships. Component modeling is the subject of Chapter 8.

A component is a class representing a modular, deployable, and replaceable physical implementation that has identity during execution time. A component is depicted as a rectangle with two small rectangles protruding from its side. A component realizes interfaces and implementation classes, objects, associations, and links; that is, the elements reside on the component. A single element may reside in multiple components; that is, each component requires it to be resident. Active elements constitute the active parts of a component. A component does not have its own features, but is a container for its elements. A component may have dependency relationships on these elements, including other components, or may have composition relationships with these elements. A dependency may be stereotyped with the "reside" keyword to specify that the target element resides on the source component.

Figure 3.20, related to Figure 3.16, shows three different components, including a car, employee, and sales system. Notice how the components realize interfaces that actors use to interact with the components. Also notice that the sales system uses its source code and uses a security library via the ISecurity interface. The entities with which actors interact may be represented as components. A component realizes and conforms to interfaces and operations, which represent the services implemented by the elements residing inside the component. The parts of an entity realize the use cases that pertain to the entity and the component realizes the interfaces through which actors interact with the entity. Figures 3.21–3.23, respectively, show how Figures 3.17–3.19 are represented using components.

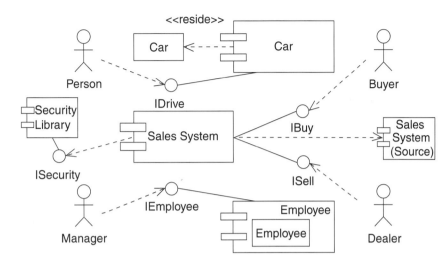

FIGURE 3.20.   Components.

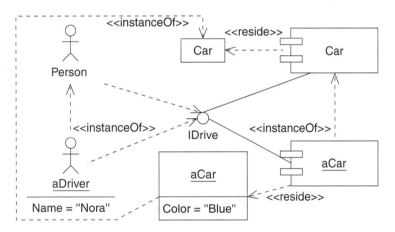

FIGURE 3.21.   A car component.

3.2.4.   DEPLOYMENT DIAGRAMS

Deployment diagrams, from the deployment or environment model view, depict how an implementation or implemented system resides in its environment using nodes and their relationships. Deployment modeling is the subject of Chapter 9.

A node is a class representing a resource in the execution environment on which components reside. A node is depicted as a three-dimensional cube figure. A node may contain components; that is, the components live or execute on the node. A node may be connected to other nodes

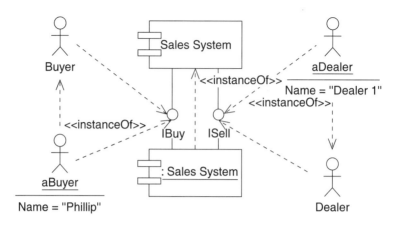

FIGURE 3.22.   A sales system component.

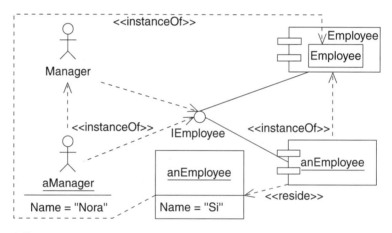

FIGURE 3.23.   An employee component.

using communication associations that provide a communication path between the nodes through which the components on the nodes may communicate with one anther. A dependency may be stereotyped with the "deploy" keyword to specify that the target node may contain or support the source component and that the source component may be deployed on the target node.

Figure 3.24, related to Figures 3.16 and 3.20, shows three different nodes: a terrain, desktop computer, and reality. The environments of entities with which actors interact may be represented as nodes. A node is a resource necessary for a component to execute, and an entity uses a node as a resource upon which to execute. Figures 3.25–3.27, respectively, show how Figures 3.17 with 3.21, 3.18 with 3.22, and 3.19 with 3.23 are represented using nodes.

3.3.   Behavioral (Dynamic) Concepts

The foundational behavioral concepts include collaborations and inter-actions, which form the basis for various other behavioral concepts.

A collaboration of objects interact to accomplish a purpose by ex-changing stimuli via links in order to convey information with the ex-

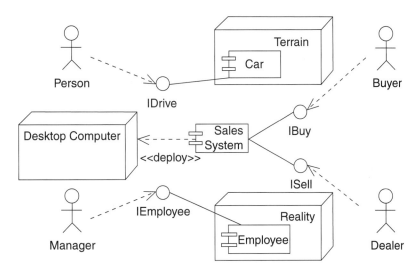

FIGURE 3.24.   Nodes.

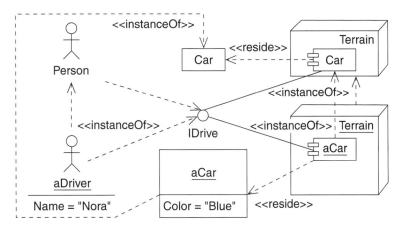

FIGURE 3.25.   A terrain node.

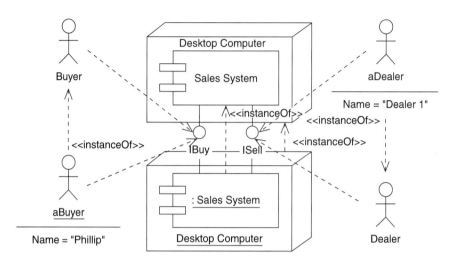

FIGURE 3.26.   A desktop computer node.

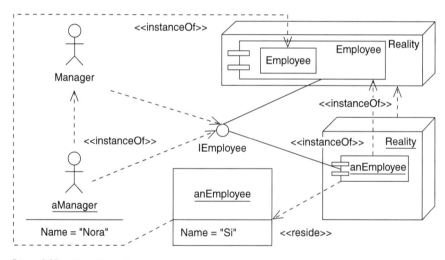

FIGURE 3.27.   A reality node.

pectation that action will ensue, and a collaboration of classes interact to accomplish a purpose by exchanging messages via associations in order to convey information with the expectation that action will ensue. A collaboration involves participating elements collaborating or cooperatively working together. An interaction involves communicating elements interacting or reciprocally acting on one another. A collaboration focuses on elements and their relationships, while an interaction focuses on elements and their communication. A message specifies a stimulus, indicating the sender, receiver, and what is communicated. A stimulus is a communication conforming to a message. A stimulus is an instance of a message, similar to an object being an instance of a class. A stimulus is communicated via a link, while a message is communicated via an association. An event is an occurrence, for example receiving a message or stimulus. An action is an executable or interpretable statement (or part of a set of statements or computation called a procedure), for example, responding to a message or stimulus. Generally, wherever an action may be used, a procedure or collection of actions may be used.

3.3.1.   SEQUENCE AND COLLABORATION DIAGRAMS

Sequence and collaboration diagrams, both known as interaction diagrams, capture patterns of collaboration and interaction among participating elements. Sequence diagrams, from the behavioral or dynamic model view, depict the dynamic behavior of a system via a temporal focus on an interaction using class roles and messages or using objects and stimuli. Collaboration diagrams, from the behavioral or dynamic model view, depict the dynamic behavior of a system via a spatial and temporal focus on a collaboration and interaction using class roles, association roles, and messages or using objects, links, and stimuli. Behavioral modeling is the subject of Chapter 7.

Interactions and Collaborations

An interaction is an abstraction representing a pattern of communication meaningful for a purpose—the behavioral or dynamic aspect of interacting or communicating elements. A pattern of communication is a set of partially ordered messages, each specifying one communication. Fundamentally, an interaction defines elements and their communication. An interaction is defined in the context of a collaboration.

A context is an abstraction representing participating elements and their relationships meaningful for a purpose—the structural or static aspect of collaborating or participating elements. Fundamentally, a context defines an ensemble of elements and their relationships.

A collaboration is an abstraction representing an interaction within a context. A collaboration owns zero or more interactions. A collaboration shows the full context of an interaction because it combines the dynamic features of the interaction with the static features of its context. Fundamentally, a collaboration defines an ensemble of elements, their relationships, and their communication.

Roles, Classes, Associations, Objects, and Links

A role is a specific placeholder or part played by a participant in a collaboration and interaction; it specifies a usage of an element. A class defines the features and properties of its objects, and an association defines the features and properties of its links. A class role defines a specific usage of a class or object, and an association role defines a specific usage of an association or link. An object conforms to its class, and a link conforms to its association. An object must conform to a class role in order for it to participate in the place of that class role within a collaboration or interaction, and a link must conform to an association role in order for it to participate in the place of that association role within a collaboration or interaction. An object or link conforms to its role if it supports the structural and behavioral features required of its role within a collaboration or interaction. A collaboration or interaction executes when objects and links are bound to the roles defined by the collaboration or interaction, and the pattern of communication is executed. Fundamentally, a class role is a specific use of a class or its specializations and an association role is a specific use of an association or its specializations within a collaboration and interaction, an object is an instance of a class and a link is an instance of an association, and an object must conform to a class role and a link must conform to an association role within a collaboration and interaction in order for the pattern of communication to execute. The ensemble of objects and links that collaborate form a collaboration instance set, and the stimuli they exchange form an interaction instance set.

A class role is depicted using the notation for a class, including adornments, but the name string is depicted as a forward slash followed by the class rolename followed by a colon followed by the class name (or a comma-separated list of class names) to which participants must conform. An association role is depicted using the notation for an association, including adornments (with association end adornments), but the name follows the same syntax as for a class rolename.

When multiobjects are used, a message to the multiobject symbol indicates a message or stimulus to the set of objects, and a message to a simple object symbol indicates a message or stimulus to an individual object that is part of the set. Typically a selection stimulus to a multiobject returns a reference to an individual object, to which the original sender then sends a stimulus. The object from the set is shown as a normal object symbol, but it may be attached to the multiobject symbol using a composition link to indicate that it is part of the set.

The use of a collaboration is depicted as a dashed ellipse. A collaboration may be labeled with a name in the collaboration symbol. A collaboration may be left anonymous if it is attached to an element via a realization relationship, as a collaboration may realize an operation, use case or behavior sequence, or a class to define its static structure. A dashed line is drawn from the collaboration symbol to each of the symbols denoting elements that participate in the collaboration. Each dashed line may be labeled with the role of the participant, alternatively each participant may be labeled to indicate the role it plays. A role corresponds to an element within the context of the collaboration, where the role is a parameter that is bound to the specific element to which the role is attached on each occurrence or use of the collaboration. A collaboration instance set is depicted as a dashed ellipse with the name of the collaboration underlined.

Figure 3.28 shows a collaboration among classes and associations for transferring a file, and Figure 3.29 shows the same collaboration among objects and links for transferring a file using a collaboration instance set.

A class or association conforming to or playing the role defined by a class role or association role is depicted using the notation for a class or association, including adornments (with association end adornments for association roles), but the name is depicted as a forward slash followed by the class or association rolename followed by a colon followed by the class or association name, all names are optional and the forward slash is present if the class or association rolename is specified and the colon is present if the class or association name is specified.

Figure 3.28 shows that a person plays the class role of sender, a dealer plays the class role of receiver, a file plays the class role of content, and an Own association plays the association role of ownership.

An object or link conforming to or playing the role defined by a class

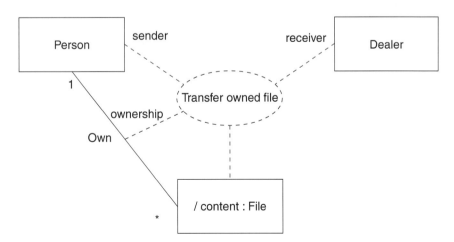

FIGURE 3.28.   A collaboration among classes and associations for transferring files.

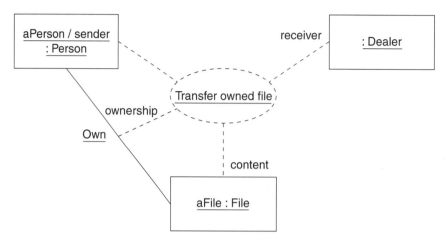

FIGURE 3.29.   A collaboration among objects and links for transferring files.

role or association role is depicted using the notation for an object or link, including adornments (with link end adornments for links), where the name is depicted as the object or link name followed by a forward slash followed by the class or association rolename followed by a colon followed by the class or association name (or a comma-separated list of class or association names) fully underlined, all names are optional and the forward slash is present if the class or association rolename is specified and the colon is present if the class or association name (or a comma-separated list of class or association names) is specified.

Figure 3.29 shows that the aPerson object plays the class role of sender, an anonymous dealer object plays the class role of receiver, the aFile object plays the class role of content, and an Own link plays the association role of ownership.

Because a collaboration may realize an operation, use case or behavior sequence, or a class to define its static structure, collaborations are the vehicle for integrating the structural or static aspect and behavioral or dynamic aspect of an entity as well as bridging the gap from the specification of the entity versus the implementation of the entity using the specification-implementation dichotomy as discussed in Chapter 2. An entity may be a system, subsystem, or class. That is, a use case allows us to view an entity as a "black box" via the specification perspective—focusing on what requirements the entity must satisfy and what functionality the entity provides to its users—and a collaboration allows us to view an entity as a "white box" via the implementation perspective—focusing on how the entity will satisfy the requirements, what ensemble of elements and their relationships collaborate to constitute the entity, and how the elements that constitute the system interact to provide the functionality of the entity.

Sequence Diagrams

A sequence diagram is used to depict one or more interactions within a single collaboration. An interaction has a generic and instance form. A generic-form interaction describes two or more possible sequences of interaction. An instance-form interaction, also called an individual behavior sequence or specific scenario, describes one actual sequence of interaction consistent with its generic-form interaction. A generic-form and instance-form sequence diagram depicts an interaction among class roles or objects that conform to the class roles, messages or stimuli that conform to the messages, and additional classes or objects as necessary. A generic-form sequence diagram describes two or more possible sequences of interaction, but an instance-form sequence diagram describes one actual sequence of interaction.

A sequence diagram has two dimensions. The vertical dimension represents time where time proceeds down the page. The horizontal dimension represents the different class roles or objects that participate in an interaction. There is no significance to the horizontal ordering of the elements. A lifeline is a graphical construct representing the existence of an element over time. A lifeline is depicted as a vertical dashed line from a class role or object. A lifeline may split into two or more concurrent lifelines to show conditionality, where each separate track represents a conditional branch in the interaction, and the lifelines may subsequently merge together again.

An activation, also known as a focus of control, is a graphical construct representing the period during which an element is performing an action or procedure, capturing the duration of the performance of the action in time and the control relationship between the activation and its callers. An activation is depicted as a tall thin rectangle on a lifeline whose top is aligned with its initiation time and whose bottom is aligned with its completion time. The action or procedure being performed may be labeled in text next to the activation symbol or in the left margin.

A message is a specification of a stimulus; it specifies the roles that the sender and receiver must conform to and the content of the communication. A stimulus is a communication between instances conforming to roles that conveys information with the expectation that action will ensue. A message or stimulus is depicted as a horizontal solid arrow from the lifeline or activation of the sender to the lifeline or activation of the receiver. The arrow is labeled with an optional guard condition enclosed in square brackets, indicating when the message or stimulus is sent, followed by an optional sequence number indicating the order within the overall interaction in which the message or stimulus is sent followed by a colon followed by the message or stimulus being communicated, including the return values, message name, argument list, and other control information. Because an incoming arrow indicates an action or procedure, the action or procedure may be omitted on the activation of the receiving element itself.

Similar to a self-referential association or link, a role may communicate with itself where a message or stimulus is sent from the role to itself, called a self-referential or reflexive message or stimulus. A self-referential message or stimulus is depicted as a horizontal solid arrow from the lifeline or activation of a role that loops back to the same lifeline or activation of the role, the arrow starts and finishes on the same role lifeline or activation where the sending point is above the receiving point.

The message arrowhead indicates the type of communication. A filled solid arrowhead indicates an operation call or other nested flow of control where the entire nested sequence is completed before the outer level sequence resumes. A stick arrowhead indicates an asynchronous message or stimulus, called a signal, without nesting of control where the sender dispatches the communication and immediately continues with its next step. A dashed arrow with stick arrowhead indicates a return from a message. The message label may also indicate other control information, including call nesting, iteration or looping, branching, concurrency, and synchronization as discussed in Chapter 7.

Figure 3.30, related to Figure 3.28, shows a generic-form interaction of how a file is transferred from a sender to a receiver using class roles:

1. A connection is opened between the sender and receiver via a connection class role.
2. A transaction is started or began via a transaction class role.
3. A file sends itself via the transaction class role.
4. The sender decides to rollback the transfer or commit the transfer via the transaction class role.
5. If the sender decides to commit the transfer, the transaction class role sends the data and the receiver receives the data; otherwise, the transaction is rolled back or canceled.
6. The connection is closed between the sender and receiver via the connection class role.

Figure 3.31, related to Figure 3.29, shows a generic-form interaction of how a file is transferred from a sender to a receiver using objects conforming to class roles. Figure 3.31 is an instance of Figure 3.30. Figure 3.32, related to Figure 3.28, shows an instance-form interaction or individual behavior sequence or specific scenario of how a file is transferred and committed to, in steps 4 and 5 above, from a sender to a receiver using class roles. Figure 3.32 is an instance of Figure 3.30. Figure 3.33, related to Figure 3.29, shows an instance-form interaction or

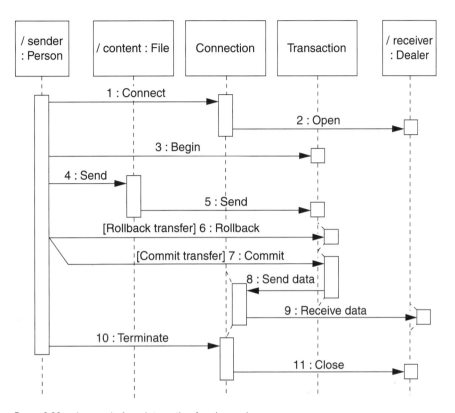

FIGURE 3.30.   A generic-form interaction for class roles.

individual behavior sequence or specific scenario of how a file is transferred and committed to, in step 4 and 5 above, from a sender to a receiver using objects conforming to class roles. Figure 3.33 is an instance
of Figure 3.31.

Collaboration Diagrams

A collaboration diagram is used to depict a collaboration with zero or
more interactions. A collaboration has a specification and instance level.
A specification-level collaboration describes class roles, association
roles, and their messages. An instance-level collaboration describes
objects, links, and their stimuli conforming to the class roles, association roles, and messages of its specification-level collaboration. A
specification-level collaboration diagram depicts a collaboration among
class roles, association roles, messages, and additional classes and associations as necessary. An instance-level collaboration diagram depicts
a collaboration among object that conform to class roles, links that con-

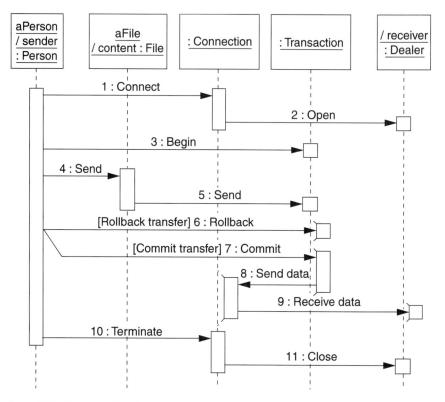

FIGURE 3.31. A generic-form interaction for objects.

form to association roles, stimuli that conform to messages, and additional objects and links as necessary.

On collaboration diagrams, a message or stimulus is depicted as an arrow labeled using the same syntax as messages and stimuli on sequence diagrams, but with required sequence numbers, placed near an association role or link. The relationship is used for transportation of the communication and the arrow points along the line in the direction of the receiving class role or object. A self-referential message or stimulus is depicted as a message on a self-referential association or link. Sequence numbers start at 1 and increment by 1. Nesting and conditionality are shown by means of the dot notation where communication 1 is followed by 2 at the same level of nesting and 1.1 is followed by 1.2 at the next level of nesting, and so forth. Nesting is also used to show conditionality, similar to the splitting of a lifeline on a sequence diagram, where communication 1.1.1 only occurs if the condition on communication 1.1 is satisfied, and communication 1.1 only occurs if the condition on communication 1 is satisfied.

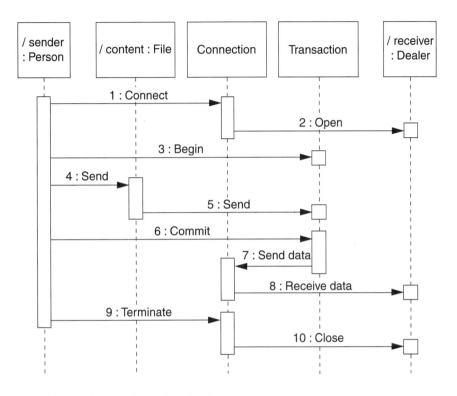

FIGURE 3.32. An instance-form interaction for class roles.

Figure 3.34, related to Figures 3.28 and 3.30, shows a specification-level collaboration for a generic-form interaction of how a file is transferred from a sender to a receiver using class roles and association roles. Figure 3.35, related to Figures 3.29 and 3.31, shows an instance-level collaboration for a generic-form interaction of how a file is transferred from a sender to a receiver using objects conforming to class roles and links conforming to association roles. Figure 3.35 is an instance of Figure 3.34. Figure 3.36, related to Figures 3.28 and 3.32, shows a specification-level collaboration for an instance-form interaction or individual behavior sequence or specific scenario of how a file is transferred and committed to from a sender to a receiver using class roles and association roles. Figure 3.36 is an instance of Figure 3.34. Figure 3.37, related to Figures 3.29 and 3.33, shows an instance-level collaboration for an instance-form interaction or individual behavior sequence or specific scenario of how a file is transferred and committed to from a sender to a receiver using objects conforming to class roles and links conforming to association roles. Figure 3.37 is an instance of Figure 3.35.

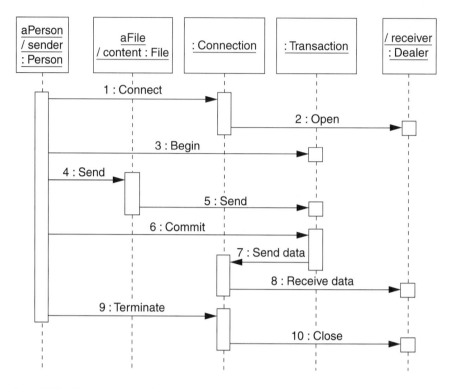

FIGURE 3.33.   An instance-form interaction for objects.

3.3.2.   STATE DIAGRAMS

State diagrams, from the behavioral or dynamic model view, depict the dynamic behavior of a system using states and transitions. Behavioral modeling is the subject of Chapter 7. State diagrams are also known as statechart diagrams.

States

Each object has a lifecycle in which it is created, passes through or transitions between various states, and is destroyed. The state of an object is the condition or situation of the object during its life during which it satisfies some condition. The state of an object is defined by the values of the object's structural features. A transition between states indicates how an object changes state due to an event. An event is an occurrence, for example receiving a message or stimulus. An action is an executable or interpretable statement (or part of a set of statements or computation called a procedure), for example responding to a message or stimulus.

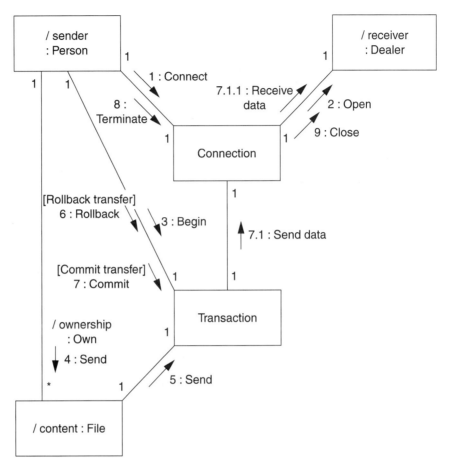

Figure 3.34.   A specification-level collaboration for a generic-form interaction.

Generally, wherever an action may be used, a procedure or collection of actions may be used.

A state is depicted as a rectangle with rounded corners containing the name of the state. Figure 3.38 shows the lifecycle of Transaction class objects, where the Idle state represents when no transaction has started and the inTransaction state represents when a transaction has started. States may be nested, and objects may have current substates, where an object may be in multiple substates simultaneously, as discussed in Chapter 8.

Transitions

An event is depicted with an event name and an optional comma-separated list of parameters enclosed in parentheses. Figure 3.38 shows

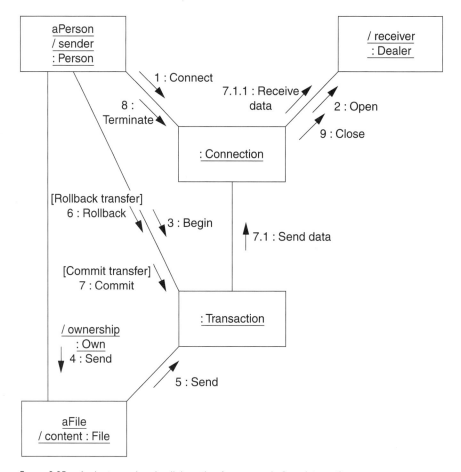

FIGURE 3.35.   An instance-level collaboration for a generic-form interaction.

the various events associated with incoming messages to Transaction class objects.

A transition is depicted as a solid line originating from a source state and terminating to a target state labeled with an event followed by an optional guard condition enclosed in square brackets, indicating when the transition is enabled, followed by a forward slash followed by an optional action or procedure. The forward slash is only present if an action is specified. This indicates that an object in the first state will enter the second state and perform the specific action, which should take a negligible amount of time such that an object always has a current state, when the specified event occurs provided that the specified guard condition is satisfied. The transition is said to fire on such a change of

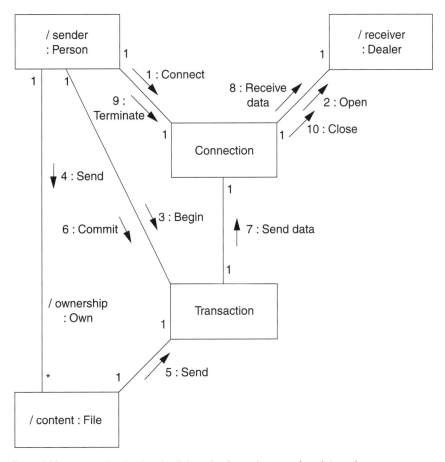

FIGURE 3.36.   A specification-level collaboration for an instance-form interaction.

state. Figure 3.38 shows the various transitions using events and actions between the states of Transaction class objects.

A newly created object enters its initial state, also called a pseudostate as an object never is in that state and only transitions from the state. An initial state is depicted as a small solid filled circle, and the default transition originating from the initial state may be labeled with the event that creates the object and may have an action; otherwise, it must be unlabeled. Figure 3.8 shows that the initial state of a transaction is the Idle state reached via the Create transition.

An object that transitions to its final state, also called a pseudostate, is terminated or destroyed. A final state is depicted as a circle surrounding a small solid filled circle (a bull's eye), and the transition to the final state may be labeled with the event that destroys the object, but is usually

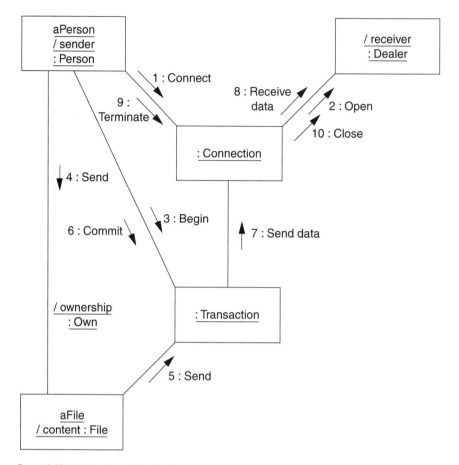

Figure 3.37.   An instance-level collaboration for an instance-form interaction.

displayed as an unlabeled transition. Figure 3.8 shows that the final state of a transaction is triggered on the Idle state via the Destroy transition.

3.3.3.   Activity Diagrams

Activity diagrams, from the behavioral or dynamic model view, are variations of state diagrams that depict the dynamic behavior of a system using action states and flows. Behavioral modeling is the subject of Chapter 7. Activity diagrams are also known as activity graphs.

Action States

An action state is a state with an action and at least one outgoing transition that is triggered upon completion of the action. An action state is depicted as a shape with straight top and bottom and with convex arcs

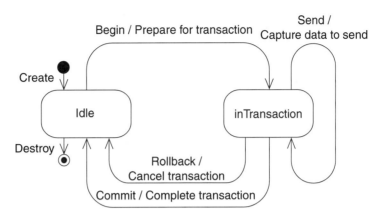

FIGURE 3.38.   Lifecycle of Transaction class objects.

on the two sides containing the action of the state. An action state may take a non-negligible amount of time and thus may be interrupted. Figure 3.39 shows the various action states for transferring files. The action states are associated with incoming messages to the various elements. A transition leaving an action state does not include an event, as it is trigged by the completion of the action, but may include a guard condition and action. Action states may be nested to form activities that take a non-negligible amount of time as discussed in Chapter 7.

A swimlane is a region of responsibility for action states. Swimlanes are depicted as visual regions separated from neighboring swimlanes by vertical solid lines on both sides. Each action is assigned to one swimlane and transitions may cross swimlanes. A swimlane may be labeled at the top with who or what class has responsibility for the actions within the swimlane. Figure 3.39 shows five swimlanes, including person, file, connection, transaction, and dealer.

Flows

An object flow determines the objects input to and output from action states. An object flow is depicted as a dashed arrow drawn from an action state to an output object or drawn from an input object to an action state. The same object may be used with multiple action states. A transition or control flow may be omitted when an object flow specifies a redundant ordering; that is, when an action state produces an output that is input to a subsequent action state, the object flow implies a control or transition flow. One object may have transitions to and from all of the relevant action states that pertain to the object. However, for greater clarity, the object may be depicted multiple times where each

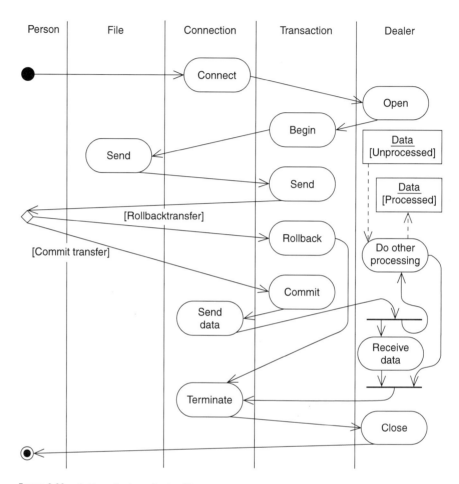

Figure 3.39.   Actions for transferring files.

occurrence of the object represents a different point during the object's life, and the state of the object at each point may be placed in brackets following the name of the object. Figure 3.39 shows a data object twice in the dealer swimlane: one occurrence specifies that it is unprocessed and is input to the "Do other processing" action state, and the second occurrence specifies that it is processed and is output from the "Do other processing" action state.

A decision involves different possible transitions that depend on various conditions. A decision may be depicted by labeling multiple output transitions of an action with different guard conditions. A decision may be depicted using the traditional diamond shape, with one incoming transition and with two or more outgoing transitions, each labeled with a distinct guard condition with no event trigger. All possible outcomes should be considered; otherwise, the keyword "else" may be applied as a guard condition to at most one outgoing transition which is triggered if all the other guard conditions on the other transitions are false. A merging of decision branches back together may be depicted using the traditional diamond shape, in which case it is called a merge, with two or more incoming transitions and one outgoing transition. The outgoing transition from a merge may not have a trigger or guard condition. A set of decisions may be chained together, where only the first incoming transition may contain an event trigger, while all other transitions may have guard conditions. Figure 3.39 shows a decision in the person swimlane determining to rollback or commit the file transfer.

A concurrent transition is a transition that represents the synchronization or splitting of control. A concurrent transition is depicted as a short heavy bar. If the bar has one or more incoming transitions from action states to the bar, it represents a synchronization of control and the outgoing transition fires after the incoming transitions have fired. If the bar has one or more outgoing transitions from the bar to action states, it represents a splitting of control and the outgoing transitions fire concurrently after the incoming transition has fired. A transition string may appear near the short heavy bar and each transition does not have its own transition string. Figure 3.39 shows that a dealer will split control to receive data and do other processing concurrently and then synchronize and continue in the interaction.

3.4. Object-Oriented Systems

An object-oriented system is a society of elements organized together for some purpose, where the types of elements are defined by the object-oriented and component-based paradigms. As a system may be recursively decomposed into multiple subsystems and each subsystem may be fully decomposed into primitive elements within a containment hierarchy, a society of elements may be decomposed into multiple subordinate societies or sub-societies; and each sub-society may be fully decomposed into primitive society elements, including classes, objects, associations, and links whose structural, or static, features or properties and behavioral, or dynamic, features or properties may be captured and communicated using static or structural concepts and dynamic or behavioral concepts via UML diagrams. Because the most basic constructs in the object-oriented paradigm are objects, the notion of a society of elements is often known as a society of objects.

Generally, objects live within a society, encapsulate knowledge in attributes (what an object knows) and skills (what an object can do) in operations, may be classified based on common operations and interfaces (using realization relationships) or methods and implementations (using generalization relationships), inherit characteristics from their ancestors, communicate via stimuli, fulfill requests made by other objects when receiving stimuli, perform operations via methods in response to requests, may respond differently to the same request based on their classification, need not disclose exactly how they respond to requests, may not express exactly how they want other objects to respond to requests, and may determine the appropriate response to a request when the request is received given their classification.

The system development lifecycle process involves the development of a society of elements, and the roadmap of Chapter 4 focuses on the checks and balances among, traceability between, and scalability of elements within a society.

3.4.1. PACKAGES

A package is a general means for grouping and organizing elements. A package owns its contents and defines a namespace, a part of a model in which a name may be uniquely defined and used. A package is used to organize a society of elements, similar to organizing a society into sub-societies or groups. A package is depicted as a large rectangle with a small rectangle or "tab" attached to the left side of the top of the large rectangle. Packages may be nested and elements within a package see or have visibility all the way out through nested packages to the outermost package.

A package may have a dependency on other packages to indicate that its contents use the contents of those packages. This dependency may be stereotyped with the "use" keyword, but the meaning of the dependency is often evident form the context in which the dependency is used. However, a dependency may be stereotyped with other keywords to indicate the exact nature of the dependency, including the "import" or "access" keywords.

A package with an import dependency, depicted as a dependency stereotyped with the "import" keyword, on another package indicates that the elements having public visibility within the independent supplier package and other packages it imports may be directly accessed from within the dependent client package since they are imported into the namespace of the dependent client package. An imported element may be assigned an alias to avoid name conflicts with other names in the namespace and by default becomes private to the importing package, but may be assigned another visibility. Figure 3.40 shows that the Sentence package imports the Relationships package and aliases the Occupy class with "Live in.". Notice that "Live in" is then used in the Sentence package.

A package with an access dependency, depicted as a dependency stereotyped with the "access" keyword, on another package indicates that the elements having public visibility within the independent supplier package only and not any other packages it access are visible and may be accessed from within the dependent client package using the pathnames of the elements. A pathname is a series of names linked together and separated by a double colon (::) delimiter where the chaining together of package names and the element name starting from the root of the system or from some other point selects the element. By default, an element shown within a package is assumed to be defined within that

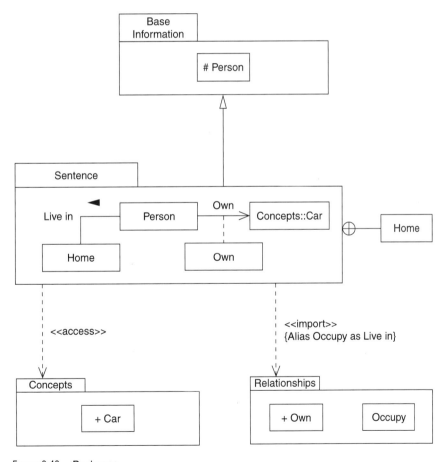

FIGURE 3.40. Packages.

package, and a reference to an element defined in another package is shown using a pathname to the element. Figure 3.40 shows that the Sentence package accesses the Concepts package. Notice that a pathname is utilized to use the Car class in the Sentence package.

A package with a generalization relationship to another package indicates that the elements having public and protected visibility that are owned or imported within the more general package are available to the more specific package. Figure 3.40 shows that the Sentence package inherits the Person class from the Base Information package and use it.

A package may have branching lines to contained elements that are depicted outside of the package with a plus sign (+) within a circle drawn at the end attached to the container, called tree notation using an "anchor" icon. Figure 3.40 shows that the Sentence package contains the Home class using the tree notation.

3.4.2. Templates

A template or parameterized element is a descriptor of an element with one or more unbound parameters defining a family of elements; each actual element is specified by binding the parameters to actual values. A template is used to generalize the structure and behavior of a society of elements. A template element is not directly usable because it has unbound parameters, and it must be bound to actual values before it is used via a binding dependency, depicted as a dependency stereotyped with the "bind" keyword with a comma-separated list of actual parameters enclosed in parentheses, from the non-parameterized class to the template class. A template class is depicted with a small dashed rectangle that is superimposed on the upper right-hand corner of the rectangle for the class (or to the symbol for another modeling element) containing a comma-separated formal parameter list or one formal parameter per line including the parameter's name, implementation type, and optional initial value following an equal sign. If the type of a parameter is omitted, it is assumed to be a class. The contents of the template class appear as normal in the class rectangle; however, they may use the formal parameters. Parameterization may be applied to classes, associations, collaborations, packages, and other modeling elements.

Figure 3.41 shows a parameterized container from which two container classes are created, each having one container object instance, and one container object directly created from the parameterized Container class. The People class uses the "bind" dependency and has one "Group of People" object that may have up to five people in the container. The "Container of People" object is an instance of a class using an alternative notation combining the "bind" dependency directly within the class definition and may have up to 10 people in the container. The Team

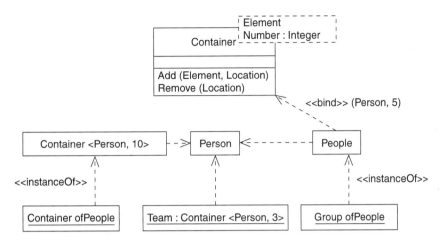

FIGURE 3.41.   Template or parameterized elements.

object directly instantiates the container without an intermediate class and may have up to three people in the container.

3.4.3.   PATTERNS AND FRAMEWORKS

A pattern is a generalized solution to a problem in a given context, where each pattern has a description of the problem, solution, context in which it applies, and heuristics, including use, advantages, disadvantages, and trade-offs. A pattern is used to generalize the use and application of a society of elements. A solution is described using a static structure, identifying the participating elements and their relationships, and a dynamic behavior, identifying how the elements collaborate and interact. Patterns that apply to specific programming languages are called idioms. Patterns that are applied during analysis are called analysis patterns. Patterns that are applied during design are called design patterns. Patterns that apply to the structural organization of a system are called structural or architectural patterns and are concerned with larger structures composed of smaller structures. Patterns that apply to the behavior of a system are called behavioral patterns and are concerned with assigning responsibilities among a collection of objects. Patterns that apply to the instantiation of objects are called creational patterns and are concerned with decoupling the type of an object from the process of constructing objects of that type. A pattern is depicted as a template or parameterized collaboration, where the formal parameters are the roles used in the collaboration.

Figure 3.42 shows various patterns. Common Error Handler is a collaboration. The Factory Method creational pattern defines a means for a creator to be invoked in order to instantiate objects of a product where the creator differs instantiation to subclasses for deciding which product class to instantiate. The Facade structural pattern defines a means for a single interface to be used to gain access to a collection of interfaces where clients communicate requests to the facade and the facade delegates the requests to the appropriate server via its interface. A facade may also be depicted as a package stereotyped with the "facade" keyword to indicate that the package only contains references to model elements owned by other package and is used to provide a public view of the model elements. The Proxy structural pattern defines a means for a surrogate or placeholder to manage access to another object where clients communicate requests to the proxy and the proxy forwards the requests to the server. The Observer behavioral pattern defines a means to capture a one-to-many dependency among objects such that when one subject object changes state, all of its dependent observers are notified and can update themselves appropriately. The "Transfer owned file" pattern represents the collaboration of Figure 3.28. The "Transfer content" pattern is a more general and abstract pattern for communicating content, and may be used to instantiate the "Transfer owned file" pattern, as shown in the Figure 3.42.

Figure 3.43 shows the use of the Facade structural pattern in the context of an Object Request Broker class, Supplier classes, and Consumer class. The Consumer class, playing the role of a client, sends a request to the Object Request Broker class, playing the role of a facade, who in turn forwards the request to the appropriate Supplier object that it man-

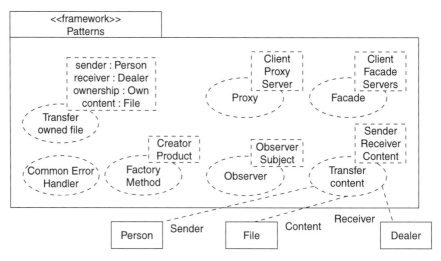

FIGURE 3.42. Patterns and frameworks.

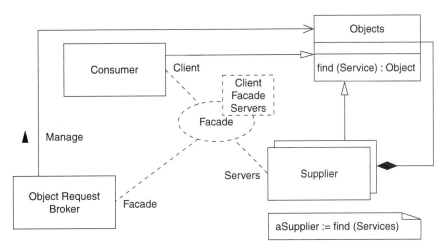

FIGURE 3.43. Applying the Facade structural pattern.

ages after finding the specific Supplier object using a selection operation to identify who handles the request.

A mechanism is a specific pattern that may use any number of other patterns and that applies to a society of elements whose cooperation provides some capability. A mechanism is an instance of one or more patterns. A collaboration is used to model a specific society of elements and a mechanism is used to model the essential aspects of the mechanism in a domain-independent manner such that the mechanism may be bound and used within a specific context. Figure 3.42 shows various patterns that may be used as mechanisms. Other capabilities that may be defined as mechanisms include means for error detection, handling, and recording, security management, interfacing with legacy systems, information exchange, transaction management, resource management, communication and distribution, persistence, and other capabilities.

A framework is a collection of patterns defined as template collaborations with their supporting elements. A framework is depicted as a package stereotyped with the "framework" keyword. Frameworks are societies of elements that are focused on specific domains and provide appropriate plug-points or roles for adaptability within other societies of elements. Essentially, a framework is a skeletal solution in which specific elements must be plugged-in in order to establish an actual solution. Figure 3.42 organizes various patterns into a framework.

3.4.4. SYSTEMS

A system is a society of elements where the system may be recursively decomposed into multiple subsystems and each subsystem may be fully decomposed into primitive elements within a containment hierarchy. The functionality of a system is provided as a service to its users via some interface, the system has responsibility for the service and conforms to or offers and provides the interface, and the parts of the system have responsibility for implementing the service and realizing the interface. A system is depicted as a package stereotyped with the "topLevel" keyword or a fork symbol icon.

A subsystem is a sub-society of elements representing a behavioral unit that may have associations and offers interfaces. It may have operations, may specialize other subsystems similar to using generalization relationships between packages, and may have its contents partitioned into specification elements and realization elements. Specification elements include use cases. Realization elements are those elements of the subsystem that realize the use cases or behavior sequences and operations. The subsystem may be instantiable once it is implemented as a component; however, if the subsystem is non-instantiable, it serves as a specification unit for the behavior of its contained elements. The functionality of a subsystem is provided as a service to other subsystems via some interface, the subsystem has responsibility for the service and conforms to or offers and provides the interface, and the parts of the subsystem have the responsibility for implementing the service and realizing the interface. Each element within a subsystem has its own visibility. The notion of a society or sub-society of elements is founded on the concepts of responsibilities, requirements, features, behaviors, services, use cases, interfaces, operations, methods, invariants, preconditions, and postconditions.

Responsibilities, Requirements, and Services

A responsibility defines a purpose, obligation, or required capability of an element given the context of the element and its users and their needs, goals, and objectives. Responsibilities focus on the context of an element and the users of the element. For example, a project manager has the responsibility or need to manage projects. A responsibility may be modeled as a note or comment stereotyped with the "responsibility" keyword and attached to an element indicating the contract or obligation of the element in its relationship to other elements. Furthermore, one can take various approaches in dealing with such a society, including use-case-driven, data-driven, function-driven, responsibility-driven, and various other types of approaches to further the exploration and understanding of a society of elements.

A requirement is a desired feature or property of an element. A requirement may be modeled as a note or comment stereotyped with the "requirement" keyword and attached to an element indicating the desired feature, property, or behavior of the element as part of a system. A feature or property is a characteristic of an element. A behavior is an externally visible effect of an element as it interacts with its users. A service is a characterization of the behavior of an element. A project management system provides project management functionality or services to allow a project manager to manage projects, including services to manage tasks and resources. A use case is a specification of a service as a sequence of communications or dialog between an element and actors and a sequence of actions performed by the element. An interface is a specification of a service as a collection of externally visible operations. An operation is a specification of a service. The project management system provides various operations to manage tasks and resources. These operations are combined to form use cases or cases of how a project manager wants to use the system to fulfill their responsibilities. The system provides interfaces for the project manger to use. A method is an implementation of a service or processing, it defines how a service is implemented.

As a service is a characterization of the behavior of an element; the distinction between an operation, interface, and use case is one of granularity of a service or behavior. An operation is processing offered as a service by a class or subsystem, an interface is a collection of operations offered as a service by a class or subsystem, and a use case is a sequence of actions or dialog offered as a service by a class, subsystem, or system. An operation is a fragment of an interface or use case, while a use case is a complete and well-defined sequence of one or more actions or operations, and an interface is simply a collection of one or more actions or operations. An operation is equivalent to an interface with only one operation or a use case with only one operation in its sequence of actions or operations. As a specification declares what something is or what it does, a use case declares an interaction and actions, an interface declares collections of operations, and an operation declares processing. As an implementation defines how something is or how it does what its specification declare, collaborations define the realization of services, and components implement the services. A responsibility is implemented by any number of operations and any number of attributes, and an operation is implemented by a method.

Invariants, Preconditions, and Postconditions

A constraint is a semantic condition. An invariant is a constraint or rule for an element that must hold true over time and defines an internal consistency condition, a condition that must be internally satisfied. For example, in the project management system, a task may not be assigned to multiple resources simultaneously. An invariant is modeled as a constraint or note stereotyped with the "invariant" keyword and attached to a class or association indicating the conditions of the constraint that must hold over time for the element and its instances.

A precondition is a constraint or rule for an operation that must hold true for the invocation of an operation and defines a correctness condition that is the responsibility of the client or invoker of the operation. For example, in the project management system, a project must exist before it is managed. A precondition is modeled as a constraint or note stereotyped with the "precondition" keyword and attached to an operation indicating the conditions of the constraint that must hold for the invocation of the operation.

A postcondition is a constraint for an operation that must hold true after the completion of an operation and defines a correctness condition that is the responsibility of the supplier or provider of the operation. For example, in the project management system, once a project is created, it may be managed. A postcondition is modeled as a constraint or note stereotyped with the "postcondition" keyword and attached to an operation indicating the conditions of the constraint that must hold after the invocation of the operation.

Specification and Realization Elements

A subsystem is depicted as a package stereotyped with the "subsystem" keyword or a fork symbol icon. The large rectangle may have three compartments, one for operations, one for specification elements, and one for realization elements, delineated by dividing the rectangle with a vertical line, and then dividing the area to the left of this line into two compartments with a horizontal line. Operations are depicted in the upper left compartment, which is not labeled; specification elements are depicted in the bottom left compartment, which is labeled "Specification Elements"; and realization elements are depicted in the right compartment, which is labeled "Realization Elements". This general notation may be customized as necessary: compartments may be collapsed or suppressed if they are not relevant in a particular diagram; all contained elements may be depicted together in one non-labeled compartment; the contexts of a subsystem may be depicted using the tree notation using an "anchor" and labeling branches appropriately, or compartments may be rearranged.

Any element may be used as a specification or realization element because a realization relationship indicates conformance of behavior, where the client supports at least all of the operations defined in the supplier without necessity to support any structural features of the supplier (attributes and associations). When a realization element realizes a specification element, the realization element conforms to the role specified by the specification element. Subsystems within the realization

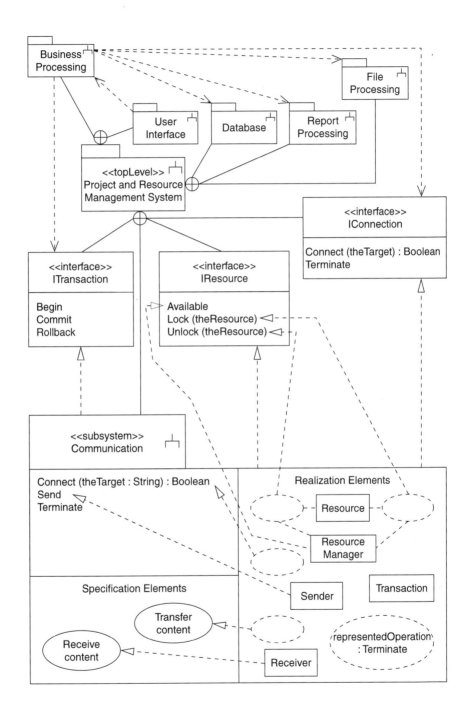

FIGURE 3.44.   A Project Management System.

compartment represent subordinate subsystems relative to the encompassing subsystem. Realization relationships are depicted between specification elements and realization elements within the package. A subsystem package or its elements may have realization relationships to specification elements that are external to the subsystem, including interfaces and operations. A subsystem may realize several interfaces and an interface may be realized by several subsystems. Each operation of every interface offered by a subsystem must be offered by the subsystem itself or at least one contained specification element must have a matching operation. Generally, system use cases, interfaces, and operations are realized by subsystems, classes, and collaborations; subsystem use cases, interfaces, and operations are realized by subsystems, classes, and collaborations; and class use cases, interfaces, and operations are realized by class operations. A collaboration may be labeled with the string "representedOperation" followed by a colon followed by the operation the collaboration realizes.

Figure 3.44 shows a Project Management System consisting of various subsystems: User Interface, Business Processing, Database, File Processing, and Report Processing. All of these subsystems, the interfaces they realize, and their relationships are contained in the system. Even though these are depicted using the tree notion, they may have been rendered inside the system level package which is stereotyped with the "topLevel" keyword. The Connect and Terminate operations of the IConnection interface are depicted in the operation compartment of the Communication subsystem and realized by collaborations in the realization compartment. The Send operation is specified in the operation compartment and is realized by the Sender class in the realization compartment. The use cases specified in the specification compartment are realized by a collaboration and a class in the realization compartment. The diagram does not indicate if the Begin, Commit, and Rollback operations of the ITransaction interface are operations of specification elements used in use cases or use case interactions, or are operations of the subsystem itself; in either case, they may be potentially realized by the Transaction class (or any other class or collaboration) in the realization compartment of the subsystem. The IResource interface is realized by the Communication subsystem, Lock and Unlock operations are realized by collaborations involving the Resource class and the Resource Manager class, while the Available operation is realized by the Resource Manager class.

CHAPTER 4

The Roadmap

This chapter provides an essential and practical tool-, process-, and technology-independent approach, as a roadmap, for effectively and successfully applying the UML. The roadmap demonstrates how the elements of the UML are holistically and cohesively integrated, how the UML supports traceability throughout the system development lifecycle process, and how the UML scales. Our goal, in this chapter, is to gain an overview of the roadmap by conglomerating the contents of Chapters 2 and 3. Use this overview chapter as a launching point into the detailed Chapters 5–9.

The roadmap is derived by exploring the UML sentence, establishing a roadmap space, defining a general roadmap, elaborating a detailed roadmap, and specifying a notational roadmap.

The UML sentence conglomerates the key concepts of the UML as discussed in Chapter 2. The roadmap space provides a context for the roadmap, including the decision points (or critical points within an effort at which decisions must be made) and their relationships using the modeling mechanisms as discussed in Chapter 2. The general roadmap relates the process disciplines of context modeling, requirements, analysis, design, implementation, validation, and deployment as discussed in Chapter 2 to the roadmap space.

The detailed roadmap provides general guidance, including what to model and why, for each point across the roadmap space. The notational roadmap provides notational guidance, including how to model various aspects of a system, as a society of elements, for each point across the roadmap space using the foundational structural and behavioral concepts of the object-oriented paradigm and component-based paradigm via the UML as discussed in Chapter 3.

The roadmap emphasizes checks and balances by indicating or suggesting what to model, why, and how to model it using the UML, traceability and scalability between UML constructs, and how they are holistically and cohesively integrated. Chapters 5–11 provide various essential rules, principles, and style guidelines for effectively applying the UML within the context of the roadmap, providing pragmatic descriptive and perspective information collated around the UML concepts.

4.1. The Unified Modeling Language (UML) Sentence

To derive the roadmap, the UML sentence, which is the foundation for the roadmap, must be explored. The UML sentence conglomerates the key concepts of the UML as discussed in Chapter 2.

4.1.1. COLLABORATING AND INTERACTING SYSTEMS

Consider two collaborating and interacting systems. One system conforms to being a client who requests services from the other system. The other system conforms to being a supplier who provides services that may be requested by other systems. Figure 4.1 shows two systems where one conforms to being a client and one conforms to being a supplier.

In order for these systems to collaborate and interact, they exchange messages via an association. Within this collaboration and interaction via the relationship, the system that conforms to being a client plays the role of a sender that passes a message to the other system and expects the appropriate behavior, and the system that conforms to being a supplier plays the role of a receiver that receives the message from the other system and is required to provide the behavior specified by the interface enabling the association, as shown in Figure 4.2.

4.1.2. SERVICES

The functionality of a system is provided as a service to its users via some interface where the service is a characterization of the behavior of the

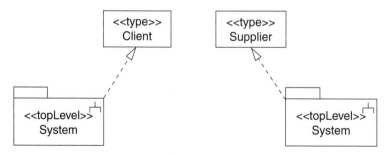

FIGURE 4.1. Two collaborating and interacting systems.

system. The system has responsibility for the service and conforms to or offers and provides the interface, and the parts of the system have the responsibility for implementing the service and realizing the interface.

From the client's view of this service, the client participates in the use case that specifies the functionality of the service provided by the supplier, as shown in Figure 4.3. From the supplier's view of this service, the supplier provides an interfaces that specifies the service realized by the supplier and required by the client where the client depends on and uses the interface, as shown in Figure 4.4.

Even though the client and supplier interact or communicate with one another as they participate in a use case, they need not both offer interfaces. The client communicates with the supplier via an interface, and the supplier communicates with the client via an explicit interface or another means internal to the supplier. For example, a human user communicates with an information system via a graphical form and keyboard, and the information system communicates with the human user via a graphical form that is internal to the system; thus, the human user need not offer an explicit interface, but must interpret the contents of the graphical form. Likewise, two information systems may communicate via explicit interfaces; thus, they both may offer explicit interfaces, often called a protocol.

FIGURE 4.2.   A relationship between two collaborating and interacting systems.

FIGURE 4.3.   The client's view of a service.

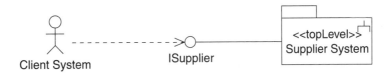

FIGURE 4.4.   The supplier's view of a service.

Figure 4.5 combines Figures 4.3 and 4.4 and shows the relevant operations on the interface and use case. This diagram uses the canonical form for expressing interfaces and use cases in order to depict the relevant operations, but uses the elided form for expressing the supplier system. The interface is shown as a class stereotyped with the "interface" keyword, and the use case is shown as a class stereotyped with the "use case" keyword.

4.1.3. SERVICE REALIZATIONS

When an element realizes a service specified as a use case or behavior sequence, interface, or operation, the element has responsibility for offering and supporting the service and the parts that constitute the element have responsibility for implementing the service. Figure 4.6 shows a collaboration involving a supplier that realizes the use case. This applies the specification-implementation dichotomy as discussed in Chapter 2. The system may be viewed as a "black box" and is described from the outside of the box in terms of what it does using use cases, interfaces, and operations. The system may be viewed as a "white box" and is described from the inside of the box in terms of how it does what it does using collaborations and interactions. Notice that the supplier system realizes the interface because both, the system and interface, are static constructs where the interface specifies a contract or service and the system realizes or conforms to the interface. Also notice that the collaboration realizes the use case because both the use case and collabo-

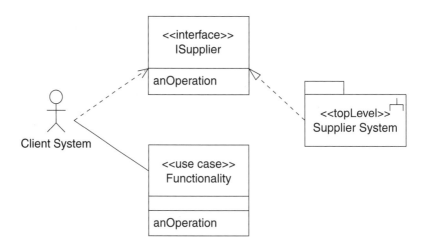

FIGURE 4.5.   Combining the client's view and supplier's view of a service using the canonical form of interfaces and use cases and the elided form of systems.

ration are dynamic constructs where the use case provides the specification of the behavior and a collaboration provides the realization of the behavior. Traversing the diagram from the client system actor to the supplier system via the interface, as shown on the top portion of the figure, demonstrates how the elements are structurally connected. Traversing the diagram from the client system actor to the supplier system via the use case, as shown on the bottom portion of the figure, demonstrates how the elements are behaviorally connected. This applies the static-dynamic dichotomy as discussed in Chapter 2 where the structure and behavior of system are complementary and evolve concurrently and cooperatively.

Figure 4.7 is equivalent to Figure 4.6 but uses the canonical form for expressing the system in order to depict the relevant operations within the system and uses the elided form for expressing interfaces and use cases. Note that each operation of every interface offered by a system must be offered by the system itself or at least one contained specification element must have a matching operation. For Figure 4.7, if there were other operations specified by the interface or directly offered by the system that did not match an operation used by the use case, they would have to be identified in the operation compartment and have a corresponding realizing element, an element contained in the realization elements compartment of the supplier system.

Figure 4.8 shows a component within which the system resides and a node that supports the component or on which the component is deployed.

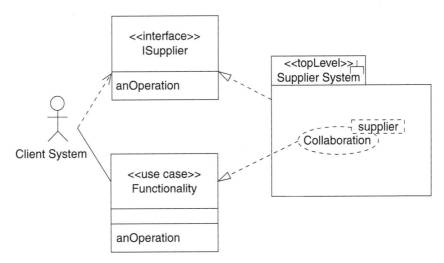

FIGURE 4.6.   The supplier's realization of a use case, interface, and operation.

4.1.4.   *The Unified Modeling Language (UML) Sentence*

Figure 4.9 shows the UML sentence, generalized from Figure 4.8, which conglomerates the key concepts of the UML such that the UML may be applied in the context of the roadmap space. The container may be a system, subsystem, or class; it is depicted as a package for generality. The UML sentence unites the various model views via their elements, including actors and use cases from the user model view, the system from the structural model view, collaborations from the behavioral model view, components from the implementation model view, and nodes from the deployment model view.

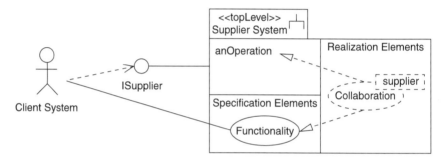

FIGURE 4.7.   Combining the client's view and supplier's view of a service with the supplier's realization of the use case, interface, and operation using the elided form of interfaces and uses cases and the canonical form of systems.

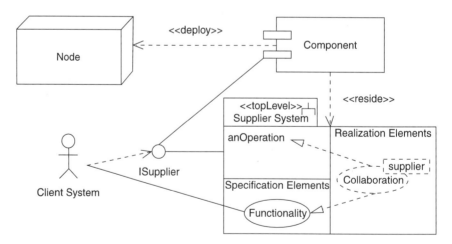

FIGURE 4.8.   A system implementing a service and a node supporting the system.

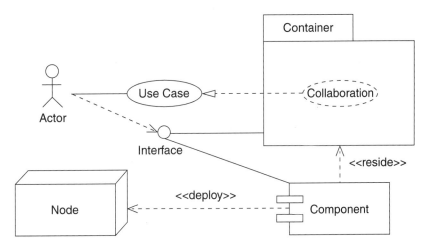

FIGURE 4.9.   The UML sentence.

We can use the UML sentence to determine how change traces between model elements across perspectives. Traceability involves determining the ramification of a change to a given model element onto other model elements, that is, tracing an element to other related elements. Traceability between model elements enables us to manage change and the resulting complexity due to change. For example, if an actor changes, we can determine what use cases they participate in and interfaces they use, what system they use, what elements collaborate in providing the use case, the component within which the system resides, and the node that supports the component or on which the component is deployed. As another example, if a node changes, we can determine which components it supports, what systems reside on the components, what use cases the systems realize and interfaces they offer, and what actors participate in the use cases and use the interfaces. Thus, the UML sentence may be traversed in either direction across perspectives, forward from actors or backward from nodes.

Furthermore, to this sentence, the type-instance dichotomy as discussed in Chapter 2 may be applied, where general UML sentences may be derived using general constructs and specific UML sentences may be derived using specific constructs. General constructs include classifiers, classes, associations, operations, attributes, messages, and roles; and relative to these general constructs, specific constructs include instances, objects, links, methods, attribute values, stimuli, and elements playing roles.

4.2.   *The Roadmap Space*

The roadmap space provides a context for the roadmap, including the decision points (or critical points within an effort at which decisions must be made) and their relationships using the modeling mechanisms as discussed in Chapter 2.

4.2.1.   PERSPECTIVES AND LEVELS OF ABSTRACTION

Consider a system. The system may be viewed from various perspectives and various levels of abstraction as discussed in Chapter 2.

Perspectives define particular points of view, including the conceptualization, specification, and implementation perspectives. Because a model element evolves across these perspectives, a traceability relationship is used to connect the same element across perspectives such that we can determine the impact of a change to an element across perspectives; that is, as an element changes in one perspective, we can determine which other related elements in the other perspectives are impacted.

Levels of abstraction define particular levels of decomposition, including the system, subsystem, and primitive elements or class and object levels within a containment hierarchy. Because each level of abstraction represents a fuller specification of the next higher level of abstraction, a refinement relationship is used to connect the refining elements to the refined element across levels of abstraction such that this scaling of elements may be used to determine the impact of a change to an element across levels of abstraction; that is, as an element changes in one level of abstraction, we can determine which other related elements in the other levels of abstraction are impacted.

4.2.2.   CARTESIAN PRODUCT

Because each perspective may be applied to each level of abstraction and because each level of abstraction may be applied to each perspective, the Cartesian product may be used to determine all possible combinations of perspectives and levels of abstraction. The Cartesian product involves two sets of information where each element from the first set is applied against each element in the second set until all possible combinations are determined.

Figure 4.10 shows the Cartesian product of perspectives and levels of abstraction where each perspective is applied to every level of abstraction and each level of abstraction is applied to every perspective. This results in nine models, including the system conceptualization model,

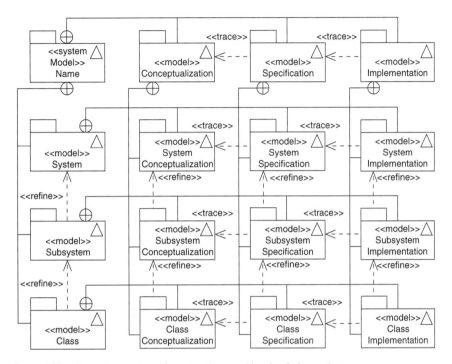

FIGURE 4.10.   Cartesian product of perspectives and levels of abstraction.

system specification system implementation, subsystem conceptualization, subsystem specification, subsystem implementation, class conceptualization, class specification, and class implementation models, where each model is a description of the system from a specific perspective and at a specific level of abstraction. Each model in Figure 4.10 represents a decision point (or critical points within an effort at which decisions must be made, and each relationship between models represents a path or relationship between decision points.

Because each level of abstraction is concerned with a specific level of decomposition as discussed in Chapter 2, Figure 4.10 is refined into Figure 4.11, where the models resulting from the Cartesian product are replaced by packages stereotyped for the appropriate level of abstraction. System packages are stereotyped with the "topLevel" keyword, subsystem packages are stereotyped with the "subsystem" keyword, and packages containing primitive elements are not stereotyped. Because each model consists of a system that may be recursively decomposed into multiple subsystems and each subsystem may be fully decomposed into primitive elements as discussed in Chapter 2, Figure 4.11 is refined into Figure 4.12, where the tree notation using an "anchor" icon is

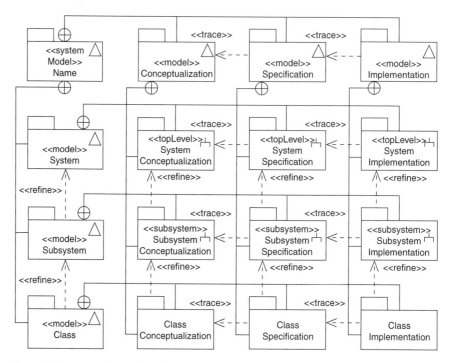

FIGURE 4.11.   Cartesian product of perspectives and levels of abstraction only with content specific to each level of abstraction.

used to relate the different levels of abstraction. The organization of a system in this manner constitutes the system's containment hierarchy.

4.2.3.   THE ROADMAP SPACE

Figure 4.13 shows the roadmap space, extracted from Figure 4.12, which includes the decision points and their relationships such that the roadmap space provides a general infrastructure and context for applying the UML sentence. The roadmap space enumerates all possible perspectives and levels of abstraction. Undoubtedly, to maintain consistency within any project, there should exist standards and guidelines for the various elements depicted in Figures 4.10–4.13.

The UML sentence unites the various model views. Because each perspective may be applied to each level of abstraction, the roadmap space is derived by using the Cartesian product between perspective and levels of abstraction to determine all possible decision points and relationships. Because each perspective primarily involves a subset of all of the model views, portions of the UML sentence apply to any perspective. Figure 4.14 shows the portion of the UML sentence relevant to the con-

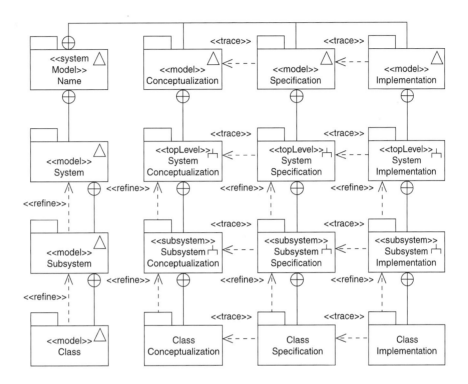

FIGURE 4.12. Cartesian product of perspectives and levels of abstraction only with content specific to each level of abstraction using the tree notation.

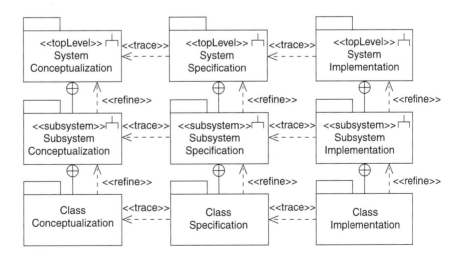

FIGURE 4.13. The roadmap space.

ceptualization perspective, including the actor, use case, interface, and container. Figure 4.15 shows the portion of the UML sentence relevant to the specification perspective, including the use case, interface, and container. Figure 4.16 shows the portion of the UML sentence relevant to the implementation perspective, including the interface, container, component, and node.

We can use the roadmap to determine how change traces perspectives and levels of abstraction. Moreover, we can use the roadmap to determine how to scale model elements across levels of abstraction. Scalability involves appropriately sizing model elements in accordance with their level of decomposition or levels of abstraction, that is, refining an element to other related elements. Scalability between model elements enables us to manage change and the resulting complexity due to change. For example, if an actor changes at a given level of abstraction, we can determine what use cases they participate in and interfaces they use, what system they use, what elements collaborate in providing the use case, and move to the next lower level of abstraction regarding the collaborating elements. As another example, if a node changes, we can determine which components it supports, what elements reside on the

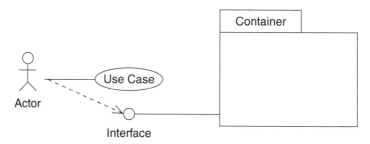

FIGURE 4.14. Portions of the UML sentence relevant to the conceptualization perspective.

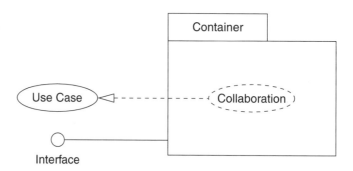

FIGURE 4.15. Portions of the UML sentence relevant to the specification perspective.

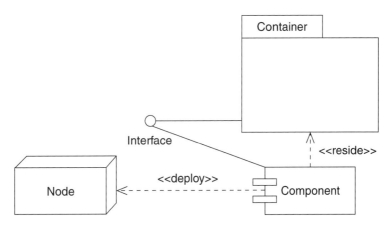

FIGURE 4.16.   Portions of the UML sentence relevant to the implementation perspective.

components, and what collaborations the elements participate in within the next higher level of abstraction. Thus, the UML sentence may be traversed in either direction across levels of abstraction, forward from actors to lower levels of abstraction or backward from nodes to higher levels of abstraction.

From the application of the UML sentence within the roadmap space, we can derive general guidance focusing on what to model, why, and how to model it using the UML for each point across the roadmap space.

4.3.   The General Roadmap

The general roadmap relates iteration phases or the process disciplines of context modeling, requirements, analysis, design, implementation, validation, and deployment as discussed in Chapter 2 to the roadmap space.

4.3.1.   PERSPECTIVES AND LEVELS OF ABSTRACTION

While viewing a system from the conceptualization perspective, our objective is to understand what requirements the system, its subsystems, and its classes must satisfy and what functionality they provide to their users; this primarily involves use-case modeling using use-case diagrams. Therefore, at the system level of abstraction, the conceptualization perspective focuses on system functionality and requirements captured in a system conceptualization model; at the subsystem level of abstraction, the conceptualization perspective focuses on subsystem functionality and requirements captured in a subsystem conceptualization model; and at the class level of abstraction, the conceptualization perspective focuses on class functionality and requirements captured in a class conceptualization model.

While viewing a system from the specification perspective, our objective is to understand how the system, its subsystems, and its classes will satisfy their requirements, what elements and their relationships collaborate to constitute the system, its subsystems, and its classes, and how these elements interact to provide functionality to their users; this primarily involves structural modeling and behavioral modeling using class, object, sequence, collaboration, state, and activity diagrams. Therefore, at the system level of abstraction, the specification perspective focuses on what elements structurally constitute a system and how these elements behaviorally provide the functionality of the system captured in a system specification model, and more specifically, what subsystems constitute the system and how these subsystems collaborate and interact to realize the behavior of the system; at the subsystem level of abstraction, the specification perspective focuses on what elements structurally constitute a subsystem and how these elements behaviorally provide the functionality of the subsystem captured in a subsystem specification model, and more specifically, what classes constitute the subsystem and how these classes collaborate and interact to realize the behavior of the subsystem; and at the class level of abstraction, the specification perspective focuses on what elements structurally and behaviorally constitute a class captured in a class specification model, and more specifically, what attributes constitute the class and how operations realize the behavior of the class. Furthermore, any number of subsystem levels may be used, and classes may be used at the subsystem level of abstraction.

While viewing a system from the implementation perspective, our objective is to understand how the system, its subsystems, and its classes are packaged or implemented and how they reside in their environment; this primarily involves component and deployment modeling using component and deployment diagrams. Therefore, at the system level of abstraction, the implementation perspective focuses on the implementation of a system and its environment captured in a system implementation model; at the subsystem level of abstraction, the implementation perspective focuses on the implementation of a subsystem and its environment captured in a subsystem implementation model; and at the class level of abstraction, the implementation perspective focuses on the implementation of a class and its environment captured in a class implementation model.

Because each level of abstraction is concerned with a specific level of decomposition and because each model consists of a system that may be recursively decomposed into multiple subsystems and each subsystem may be fully decomposed into primitive elements, all of the models for a given perspective are collated into one model for the perspective and each of its subordinate models only focuses on the content for the appropriate level of decomposition as depicted in Figure 4.13.

4.3.2. Process Disciplines

The context modeling process discipline focuses on understanding the context of requirements and a system, subsystem, or class. The context of an element at a specific level of abstraction is the next higher level of abstraction; that is, the context of a class is a subsystem, the context of a subsystem is a system, and the context of an information system is a business system. An information system is a technical solution and a business system is a business organization that the information system automates. Essentially, all of the process disciplines that apply to an information system may likewise be applied to a business system where the business organization is the system, smaller business organization elements or departments are subsystems, and the smallest business organization elements or people and their work products are classes. The context process discipline results in a business model that describes business functions and how these business functions are realized by the business organization. A business model is often called a context or domain model when it more broadly focuses on the business domain.

The requirements process discipline focuses on conceptualizing the requirements, establishing what a system, subsystem, or class should do by addressing the question of "why" it should do it. This generally focuses on the conceptualization perspective. The requirements process discipline results in a requirements model that describes system functions.

The analysis process discipline focuses on understanding the requirements enough to specify a system, subsystem, or class, establishing how an abstract system, subsystem, or class that is independent of any real constraints will satisfy the requirements by addressing the question of "what" it should do. This generally focuses on the specification perspective and understanding the requirements. The analysis process discipline results in an analysis model that describes how the requirements are realized by an abstract system that is independent of any real constraints.

The design process discipline focuses on understanding the system, subsystem, or class specification enough to specify the implementation, establishing how a real system, subsystem, or class that is dependent on the constraints of the context will satisfy the requirements by addressing the question of "how" it will do "what" it should do. This generally focuses on the specification perspective and understanding the system, subsystem, or class, and also generally focuses on the implementation perspective and understanding the packaging of the system, subsystem, or class and how it resides in its environment. The design process discipline results in a design model that describes how a real system that is dependent on the constraints of the context will satisfy the requirements.

The implementation process discipline focuses on building the system, subsystem, or class. This involves understanding the packaging of the system, subsystem, or class from within the implementation perspective to construct it. The implementation process discipline leverages the implementation model, established during design, which describes the implementation of the system.

The validation process discipline focuses on verify the system, subsystem, or class by validating it against its requirements. This involves validating the implemented system, subsystem, or class against its conceptualization perspective. The validation process discipline results in a test model that describes what will be verified and how the implemented system will be validated against the requirements.

The deployment process discipline focuses on making the system, subsystem, or class available to its users. This involves understanding how the implemented system, subsystem, or class resides in its environment from within the implementation perspective to install it within its environment. The deployment process discipline leverages the deployment model, established during design, which describes onto what the system will be deployed.

Conceptualization perspective information is often captured in a document referenced as the problem requirements that describes the problem in terms of requirements imposed by the problem on its solution. Specification and implementation perspective information is often captured in a document referenced as the solution specification that describes the solution in terms of how the solution satisfies the requirements.

4.3.3. THE GENERAL ROADMAP

Figure 4.17, an activity diagram, shows the general roadmap which relates the process disciplines of context modeling, requirements, analysis, design, implementation, validation, and deployment to the roadmap space. The process disciplines are shown as action states with object flows to and from roadmap space decision points. Notice that the specification and implementation perspectives at a given level of abstraction provide the context for the next lower level of abstraction, and that the

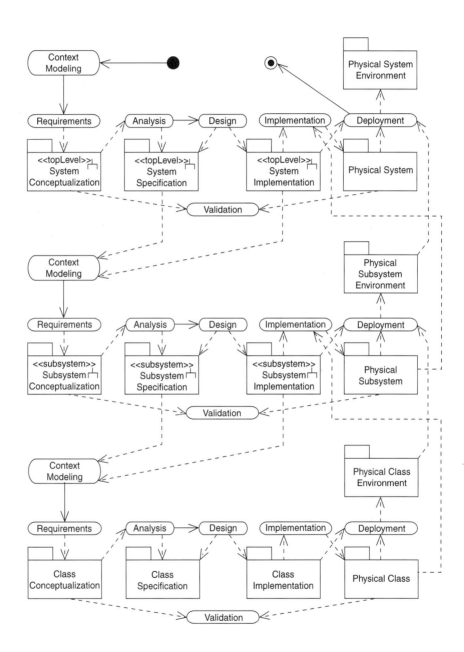

FIGURE 4.17.   The general roadmap.

physical implementation and its environment at a given level of abstraction are incorporated into the physical implementation and environment of the next higher level of abstraction. Undoubtedly, to maintain consistency within any project, there should exist standards and guidelines for the various elements depicted in Figure 4.17.

These process disciplines, and their relationships to the roadmap space, may leverage the UML via a use-case-driven, architecture-centric, iterative and incremental, and risk-confronting process that is object-oriented and component-based where they are performed or some aspects thereof may be performed in parallel.

4.4.   Detailed and Notational Roadmap

The detailed roadmap provides general guidance, including what to model and why for each point across the roadmap space. The notational roadmap provides notational guidance, including how to model various aspects of a system, as a society of elements, for each point across the roadmap space using the foundational structural and behavioral concepts of the object-oriented paradigm and component-based paradigm via the UML as discussed in Chapter 3.

The detailed roadmap strives to balance the power of applying abstraction to manage complexity with the objective of deriving a description of a system that may be implemented and made real for its users. To achieve this balance, conceptual, candidate, and actual elements are used with conceptual, logical, and physical mechanisms.

4.4.1.   CONCEPTUAL ELEMENTS

A system may be viewed as a mathematical relation: given some input data, the input data is processed to derive some output data, and the output data is provided. This scheme is objectified or described using object-oriented concepts by applying the conceptual elements of boundary, control, and entity concepts or classes and objects.

Boundary Concepts

A boundary concept is an abstraction representing a means for input or output through which actors interact with a system. A boundary concept represents a user interface for users of the system or a system or device protocol for other systems that interact with the system under discussion. A boundary concept has responsibility for coordinating the interaction between a system and its actors.

A boundary concept is depicted as a class stereotyped with the "boundary" keyword or an icon consisting of a circle with a vertical line connected to it via a horizontal line on its left side. Figure 4.18 shows two boundary concepts, including a Customer Form boundary concept and Bank System boundary concept.

Control Concepts

A control concept is an abstraction representing processing by which input is processed into output. A control concept represents an interaction, transaction, or process involving a collection of elements where the control concept itself does not do the processing but coordinates and manages the processing by delegating responsibility for the processing to other elements. A control concept has responsibility for coordinating the processing provided by the system via the elements that constitute the system.

A control concept is depicted as a class stereotyped with the "control" keyword or an icon consisting of a circle with a small arrow pointing counterclockwise attached at the top of the circle. Figure 4.18 shows a Financial Transaction Manager control concept.

Entity Concepts

An entity concept is an abstraction representing passive data and information that is input, processed, and output by a system. Entity concepts may be derived from the context process discipline and its resulting business, context, or domain model. An entity concept has responsibility for storing and managing data and information.

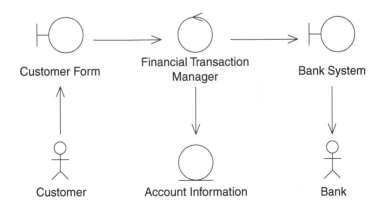

FIGURE 4.18. Boundary, control, and entity concepts.

An entity concept is depicted as a class stereotyped with the "entity" keyword or an icon consisting of a circle with a small horizontal line attached at the bottom of the circle. Figure 4.18 shows an Account Information entity concept.

Boundary, Control, and Entity Concepts

An actor may have a navigable relationship to a boundary class in order for the actor to communicate with a system. A boundary class may have a navigable relationship to an actor in order for a system to communicate with an actor. An entity class may only have a navigable relationship to an entity class because an entity is passive and does not initiate an interaction on its own. A boundary class may have a navigable relationship to a boundary, control, or entity class. A control class may have a navigable relationship to a boundary, control, or entity class.

Levels of Abstraction

Conceptual elements may be applied at all levels of abstraction.
At the system level of abstraction:

- Boundary classes represent and often evolve into system interfaces or operations of system interfaces.
- Control classes represent and often evolve into active system parts, including subsystems and classes, which may initiate control activity.
- Entity classes represent and often evolve into passive system parts, including packages and classes, which do not initiate control activity on their own behalf, but may communicate with other elements in the course of processing a request that was received.

At the subsystem level of abstraction:

- Boundary classes represent and often evolve into subsystem interfaces or operations of subsystem interfaces.
- Control classes represent and often evolve into active subsystem parts, including enclosed subsystems and classes.
- Entity classes represent and often evolve into passive subsystem parts, including packages and classes.

At the class level of abstraction,

- Boundary classes represent and often evolve into class operation specifications.
- Control classes represent and often evolve into class operation implementations or methods.
- Entity classes represent and often evolve into class attributes.

Furthermore, as conceptual elements are classes, the use of these stereotypes may be dropped as the use of these elements progresses to the next level of abstraction. These concepts are introduced, combined, and split as necessary when traversing the roadmap.

Abstract or Conceptual Programming Language

This scheme of objectification results in a pseudo–"abstract programming language" or "conceptual programming language" that uses conceptual elements to express conceptual solutions.

The use of conceptual elements establishes a conceptual solution, an abstract or ideal solution disconnected from any implementation and void of real constraints. The conceptual solution enables us to manage complexity by steadily evolving it into an actual system via the evaluation of candidate solutions that integrate the elements of the conceptual solution. A candidate solution is a proposed or possible solution whose elements are known as candidate elements, and an actual solution is a proposed solution that has been justified via the conceptual solution with consideration of real constraints and whose elements are known as actual elements, both of which are composed of subsystems, packages, and classes.

The conceptual solution establishes fit or fitness criteria for assessing a candidate solution before accepting it as the actual solution; and the conceptual solution also provides detail for evolving the candidate solution into the actual solution before it is physically implemented. A fit criterion is a rule or standard by which something may be judged for suitability or accordance with something else; it quantifies and qualifies constraints such that we can ensure that an actual system satisfies or fits the conceptual system, and in turn when implemented, the implemented system will satisfy the requirements. A fit criterion is not a test, but input to define tests for any type of requirement. A use case may be considered a cluster of functional requirements where the fit criterion for a use case includes all of the fit criteria for all of the functional requirements within that use case.

For example, if a requirement indicates a system should be "usable," the fit criterion would describe how we would measure usability, and tests would be developed to measure the fit of a system in satisfying the usability scale or metric. Fundamentally, something may be measured only after a measurement scale or metric is defined.

The validation process discipline involves validating an implementation against its conceptualization using tests; however, this validation occurs after a physical system is implemented. A validation of a system specification would be valuable in minimizing the cost of potentially building the wrong system; thus, a conceptual solution establishes fit criterion for evaluating candidate solutions, and the candidate solution that best fits becomes the actual solution that is then implemented.

Thus, a system evolves from a candidate solution to an actual solution by satisfying the fit criterion of a conceptual solution and by incorporating the conceptual solution to evolve the detail of the candidate solution.

4.4.2. *Mechanisms*

As a system evolves through the development lifecycle process, earlier in the effort, focus is primarily on the requirements or problem being addressed, and later in the effort, focus is primarily on the system or solution that addresses the requirements. Throughout this evolution, focus must steadily transition from the problem or requirements to the solution or system; otherwise, we can easily begin to focus on implementation issues much too early rather than focus on the problem, or we can easily remain focused on requirements for much too long rather than begin to focus on the solution. This transition of focus is facilitated by applying mechanisms.

A constraint is a semantic condition that may be used to capture requirements, desired features, or properties of an element. A functional requirement is a use case that describes the functionality of an element. A non-functional requirement is a condition or characteristic that pertains to a specific use case of an element, all of the use cases of an element, a subset of all of the use cases of an element, or to an element in general. Non-functional requirements include usability, reliability, performance, and other such characteristics, including business rules. Constraints include environmental, technological, political, economic, system, feasibility, and other such characteristics. There are various options regarding satisfying a requirement; however, a constraint does not allow for any options, and must be satisfied. Non-functional requirements and characteristics may be captured using property strings attached to modeling elements. Each modeling element has properties used to capture the constraints and characteristics of the element. Functional requirements, non-functional requirements, and constraints are integrated via the evolution of the solution and via mechanisms as focus steadily transitions from the problem or requirements to the solution or system.

A pattern is a generalized solution to a problem in a given context. A mechanism is a specific pattern that is applied to a society of elements whose cooperation provides some capability, the solution to the problem. For example, mechanisms include means for error detection and handling, security management, interfacing with legacy systems, information exchange, transaction management, resource management, communication and distribution, persistence, and other capabilities. Mechanisms may be used to utilize standards more effectively.

Conceptual Mechanisms

A conceptual mechanism captures the key characteristics of an implementation-independent solution. A conceptual mechanism identifies a need for a capability. For example, a conceptual mechanism for persistence allows an object to exist beyond the program or process execution that created it.

Figure 4.19 shows an Account Information entity class with two conceptual mechanisms, including Persistence and Distribution.

Logical Mechanisms

A logical mechanism is a refinement of a conceptual mechanism and captures the key characteristics of a solution, assuming some implementation environment detail, but not assuming a specific implementation. A logic mechanism identifies various options for satisfying the capabilities required of a conceptual mechanism.

For example, a logical mechanism for persistence may be a relational database management system (RDBMS) or an object-oriented database management system (OODBMS), but perhaps a flat-file solution is not viable since it may be inefficient and an in-memory storage solution is not viable since it may require too much costly memory. The specific implementation environment constraints would dictate the viability of logical mechanisms. Figure 4.19 shows that the Account Information entity class's logical mechanism for persistence includes an RDBMS or OODBMS, and the class may be distributed on a client or server.

Physical Mechanisms

A physical mechanism is a refinement of a logical mechanism and specifies a specific solution implementation. A physical mechanism specifies an exact solution. Prototyping logical mechanisms, the various options, provides the basis and justification for selecting physical mechanism that fulfill the needs of conceptual mechanisms.

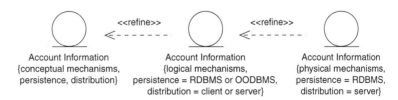

FIGURE 4.19. Conceptual, logical, and physical mechanisms.

A physical mechanism for persistence may be a specific implementation of an RDBMS or OODBMS from a specific vendor. Many practitioners criticize object orientation on the basis that performance is compromised when applying object-oriented approaches; however, feedback from prototyping efforts must be leveraged in order to fine tune and adjust the specification of object-oriented systems before they are actually constructed. It is not object orientation that leads to a degradation of performance, but practitioners' not leveraging prototyping to fine tune their specifications. Figure 4.19 shows that the Account Information entity class's physical mechanism for persistence is a RDBMS, and the class will be distributed on the server.

Conceptual, Logical, and Physical Mechanisms

Mechanisms enable us to manage complexity and enforce consistency within a system while ensuring that premature technology decisions are not made, but such technology decisions are not completely overlooked either. Logical mechanisms bridge movement between conceptual mechanisms and physical mechanisms. They allow us to avoid obscuring a solution with implementation detail, and they allow us to establish the potential for substituting one specific actual mechanism or implementation for another without adversely impacting the solution. Thus, as a system evolves from a candidate solution to an actual solution by satisfying the fit criterion of a conceptual solution, the system uses physical mechanisms that have evolved from logical options to satisfy the needs of conceptual capabilities.

4.4.3. THE ROADMAP

As the detailed roadmap provides general guidance, including what to model and why for each point across the roadmap space, focus is on a specific construct, including a system, subsystem, or class, at a given level of abstraction. As the notational roadmap provides notational guidance, including how to model various aspects of a system, as a society of elements, for each point across the roadmap space using the foundational structural and behavioral concepts of the object-oriented paradigm and component-based paradigm via the UML as discussed in Chapter 3, focus is on communication regarding a specific construct, including a system, subsystem, or class, at a given level of abstraction.

The detailed and notational roadmap may be elaborated and understood in general via the three perspectives, and then followed by a Project Management System example. Within the roadmap, specification elements include use cases, interfaces, and operations; realization elements include subsystems, classes, and collaborations; construct elements include any elements that may constitute the construct or system, including subsystems, packages, and classes which evolve from proposed candidate elements to accepted actual elements; implementation elements are components; and environment elements are nodes. Properties capture constraints and characteristics of elements.

Checks and balances involve indicating or suggesting what to model, why, and how to model it using the UML, and how this amalgamation of UML elements are validated and verified into equilibrium where the UML elements are holistically and cohesively integrated into a model. Traceability involves propagating information through a model by tracing an element to other related elements such that the ramification of a change to a given model element onto other model elements across perspectives may be determined, that is, tracing an element to other related elements. Scalability involves appropriately sizing model elements in accordance with their level of decomposition or levels of abstraction by refining an element to other related elements such that the ramification of a change to a given model element onto other model elements across levels of abstraction may be determined, that is, refining an element to other related elements.

In practice, the roadmap is applied via iterations where each successive iteration evolves, elaborates, and refines the work of previous iterations with more detail. Steps need not be sequential, but may be executed in parallel, were multiple efforts regarding the same system are carried out concurrently. Fundamentally, every constituent of the roadmap is optional and should only be applied if it adds value to the body of knowledge concerning the construct and facilitates achieving the overall objectives of the effort within the specific context of the effort. Those constituents of the roadmap that are applied constitute a roadmap instance. Likewise, refactoring techniques may be applied, where a system is modified in such a way that its external behavior is not altered, but its internal structure is improved.

Conceptualization

For construct (system, subsystem, or class) conceptualization, our objective is to understand what requirements the construct must satisfy and what functionality it provides to its users. This is accomplished with use-case modeling using use-case diagrams.

Chapter 5 provides various essential rules, principles, and style guidelines concerning construct conceptualization for the steps below. Reference the relevant portions of Chapter 5 for more detail.

1. Identify construct actors.
    - Identify actors.
    - For each actor, model the user view to establish a placeholder for information about the actor.

2. Describe construct actors.
   - For each actor, capture the actor's properties.
3. Identify the construct.
   - Identify the construct.
   - For the construct, model the structural view to establish a place-holder for information about the construct.
4. Describe the construct.
   - For the construct, capture the construct's properties.
5. Identify construct specification elements.
   - For each actor and the construct, identify specification elements.
   - For each actor, update the user view with specification elements in order to establish placeholders for information about the spec-ification elements.
   - For the construct, update the structural view with specification elements in order to establish placeholders for information about the specification elements.
6. Describe construct specification elements, effectively capturing the requirements of the construct by addressing the question of why it should have the requirements. See the Requirements section of Chapter 5 for more information.
   - For each specification element, capture the specification ele-ment's properties based on its actor's properties and the con-struct's properties to ensure traceability between its actors and the construct and the specification element.
   - For each specification element, model the structural and behav-ioral views in order to describe the specification element.
   - For each specification element, reconcile the structural and be-havioral views in order to ensure that the description of the spec-ification element is consistent.
7. Unify construct conceptualization, effectively synchronizing and concluding construct conceptualization.
   - Reconcile all of the elements used in construct conceptualization to ensure homogeneity and consistency.
   - Reconcile the construct conceptualization at the current level of abstraction with the construct conceptualization at the next higher level of abstraction to ensure that the conceptualization perspective is consistent.

Figure 4.20 shows how the portion of the UML sentence relevant to the conceptualization perspective as depicted in Figure 4.14 scales across levels of abstraction via refinement relationships. Subordinate elements refine super-ordinate elements and subordinate elements structurally constitute and cooperate to perform (collaborate and inter-act) the behavior of super-ordinate elements. A system is refined into

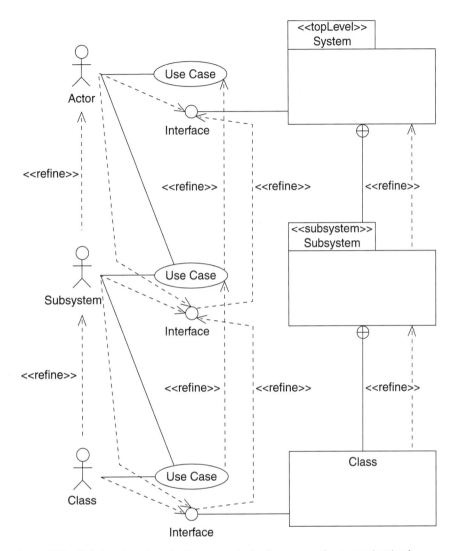

FIGURE 4.20.   Notational roadmap for the conceptualization perspective across levels of
abstraction.

subsystems that constitute the system. A subsystem is refined into
classes that constitute the subsystem. A super-ordinate use case is refined into subordinate use cases that cooperate to perform the super-
ordinate use case. A super-ordinate interface is refined into subordinate
interfaces that constitute the super-ordinate interface. The organization
of a system in this manner constitutes the system's containment hierarchy for the conceptualization perspective.

Specification

For construct (system, subsystem, or class) specification, our objective is to understand how the construct will satisfy its requirements, what elements and their relationships collaborate to constitute the construct, and how these elements interact to provide functionality to its users. This is accomplished with structural and behavioral modeling using class, object, sequence, collaboration, state, and activity diagrams.

Chapters 6 and 7 provide various essential rules, principles, and style guidelines concerning construct specification for the steps below. Reference the relevant portions of Chapters 6 and 7 for more detail.

1. Identify construct elements.
   - For the construct, identify candidate elements.
   - For the construct, model the structural view to establish placeholders for information about the construct elements.
   - Identify conceptual mechanisms.
2. Describe construct elements.
   - For each candidate element, capture the candidate element's properties based on the construct's properties to ensure traceability between the construct and the candidate element.
   - Describe conceptual mechanisms.
3. Identify construct realization elements.
   - For each specification element, identify realization elements.
   - For the construct, model the structural view to establish placeholders for information about the realizations of the specification element.
4. Describe construct realization elements, effectively analyzing and understanding construct specification elements, what the construct specification elements involve, by addressing the question of what the construct should do. See the Analysis section of Chapter 6 for more information.
   - For each realization element, capture the realization element's properties based on its specification element's properties to ensure traceability between the specification element and the realization element.
   - For each realization element, identify conceptual elements.
   - For each realization element, model the structural and behavioral views in order to describe the realization element.
   - For each realization element, reconcile the structural and behavioral views in order to ensure that the description of the realization element is consistent.
   - For each conceptual element, capture the conceptual element's

properties based on its realization element's properties to ensure traceability between the realization element and the conceptual element.

■ For each conceptual element, consider the conceptual element's use of conceptual mechanisms.

5. Distribute construct realization elements to construct elements, effectively designing and understanding construct realization elements, how the construct provides its services, by addressing the question of how the construct will do what it should do. See the Design section of Chapter 6 for more information.

   ■ Map conceptual elements to candidate elements in order to refine the candidate elements and identify actual elements.
   ■ For the construct, update the structural view with actual elements.
   ■ For each actual element, capture the actual element's properties based on its candidate element's properties and its conceptual element's properties to ensure traceability between the candidate element and the conceptual element and the actual element.
   ■ Identify logical mechanisms.
   ■ Map conceptual mechanisms to logical mechanisms.
   ■ Describe logical mechanisms.

6. Describe construct realization elements using construct elements, effectively validating the design against the analysis of the construct. See the Validation section of Chapter 6 for more information.

   ■ For each realization element, update the structural and behavioral views based on the actual elements to which the conceptual elements were mapped.
   ■ For each actual element, validate that the actual element supports the structure and behavior of its conceptual element.
   ■ For each actual element, validate that the actual element's properties are consistent with its conceptual element's properties.
   ■ Identify physical mechanisms.
   ■ Map logical mechanisms to physical mechanisms.
   ■ Describe physical mechanisms.
   ■ For each actual element, incorporate the actual element's use of physical mechanisms.

7. Unify construct specification, effectively synchronizing and concluding construct specification.

   ■ Reconcile all of the elements used in construct specification to ensure homogeneity and consistency.
   ■ Reconcile the construct specification at the current level of abstraction with the construct specification at the next higher level of abstraction to ensure that the specification perspective is consistent.

Figure 4.21 shows how the portion of the UML sentence relevant to the specification perspective as depicted in Figure 4.15 scales across levels of abstraction via refinement relationships. Subordinate elements refine super-ordinate elements and subordinate elements structurally constitute and cooperate to perform (collaborate and interact) the behavior of super-ordinate elements. A system is refined into subsystems that constitute the system. A subsystem is refined into classes that constitute the subsystem. A super-ordinate use case is refined into subordinate use cases that cooperate to perform the super-ordinate use case. A super-ordinate interface is refined into subordinate interfaces that constitute the super-ordinate interface. A super-ordinate collaboration is refined into subordinate collaborations that cooperate to perform the super-ordinate collaboration. The organization of a system in this manner constitutes the system's containment hierarchy for the specification perspective.

Implementation

For construct (system, subsystem, or class) implementation, our objective is to understand how the construct is packaged or implemented and how it resides in its environment. This is accomplished with component and deployment modeling using component and deployment diagrams.

Chapters 8 and 9 provide various essential rules, principles, and style guidelines concerning construct implementation for the steps below. Reference the relevant portions of Chapters 8 and 9 for more detail.

1. Identify the construct implementation element.
   - For the construct, identify the implementation element.
   - For the construct, model the implementation view to establish a placeholder for information about the implementation of the construct.
2. Describe the construct implementation element, effectively capturing the implementation of the construct. See the Implementation section of Chapter 8 for more information.
   - For the implementation element, capture the implementation element's properties based on the construct's properties to ensure traceability between the construct and the implementation element.
   - For each specification element of the implementation element, validate that the specification element's properties are consistent with the construct's specification element's properties.
3. Identify the construct environment element.
   - For the construct, identify the environment element.
   - For the construct, model the environment view to establish a

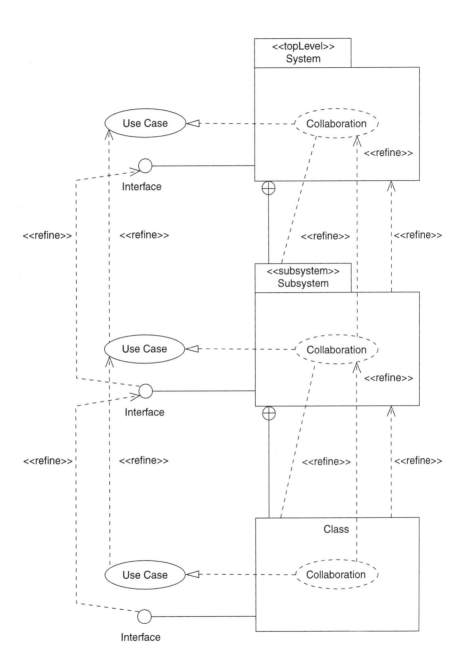

FIGURE 4.21.   Notational roadmap for the specification perspective across levels of abstraction.

placeholder for information about the environment of the construct.

4. Describe the construct environment element, effectively capturing the environment of the construct. See the Deployment section of Chapter 9 for more information.

   ■ For the environment element, capture the environment element's properties based on the construct's properties to ensure traceability between the construct and the environment element.

   ■ For the environment element, validate that the environment element's properties are consistent with the implementation element's properties.

5. Unify construct implementation, effectively synchronizing and concluding construct implementation.

   ■ Reconcile all of the elements used in construct implementation to ensure homogeneity and consistency.

   ■ Reconcile the construct implementation at the current level of abstraction with the construct implementation at the next higher level of abstraction to ensure that the implementation perspective is consistent.

Figure 4.22 shows how the portion of the UML sentence relevant to the implementation perspective as depicted in Figure 4.16 scales across levels of abstraction via refinement relationships. Subordinate elements refine super-ordinate elements and subordinate elements structurally constitute and cooperate to perform (collaborate and interact) the behavior of super-ordinate elements. A system is refined into subsystems that constitute the system. A subsystem is refined into classes that constitute the subsystem. A super-ordinate interface is refined into subordinate interfaces that constitute the super-ordinate interface. A super-ordinate component is refined into subordinate components that constitute the super-ordinate component. A super-ordinate node is refined into subordinate nodes that constitute the super-ordinate node. The organization of a system in this manner constitutes the system's containment hierarchy for the implementation perspective.

4.4.4.   A ROADMAP EXAMPLE

Consider a Project Management System that has a user who wishes to print a report. In order to demonstrate the overall flow through the roadmap, element constraints and the use of mechanisms is not discussed in this example.

Project Management System

For system conceptualization, we apply the following steps:

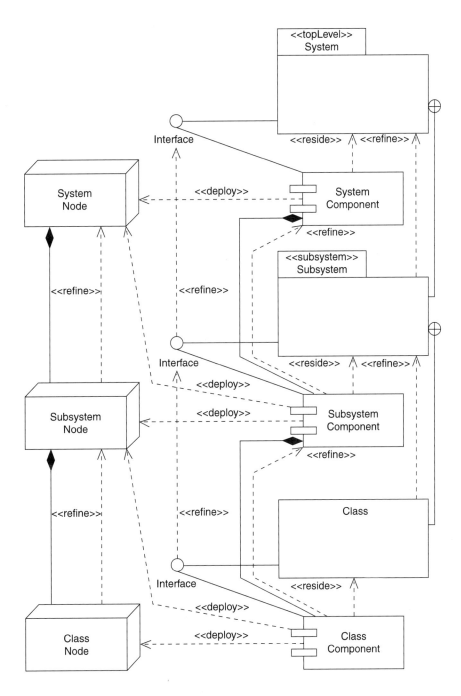

FIGURE 4.22.   Notational roadmap for the implementation perspective across levels of abstraction.

1. Identify system actors.
    - Identify actors. There are two actors involved, including User and Printer. The User actor is responsible for managing projects. The Printer actor is responsible for generating printed documents of information.
    - Model the user view. Figure 4.23 shows the two system actors.
2. Identify the system.
    - Identify the system. The system under discussion is the Project Management System, which is responsible for automating the management of projects.
    - Model the structural view. Figure 4.24 shows the Project Management System.
3. Identify system specification elements.
    - Identify specification elements. We are only interested in the Print Report service, which involves printing a report.
    - Update the user view with specification elements. Figure 4.23 shows a Print Report use case that the User actor initiates and in which the Printer actor participates.
    - Update the structural view with specification elements. Figure 4.24 shows the IUser interface through which the User actor communicates with the Project Management System and the IPrinter interface through which the Project Management System communicates with the Printer actor.
4. Describe system specification elements, effectively capturing the requirements of the system.
    - Model the structural and behavioral views. Figure 4.25 shows the behavioral view of the Print Report use case. Figure 4.26 shows the corresponding structural view of the Print Report use case.

FIGURE 4.23.   System conceptualization—User view.

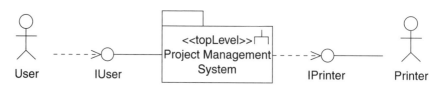

FIGURE 4.24.   System conceptualization—Structural view.

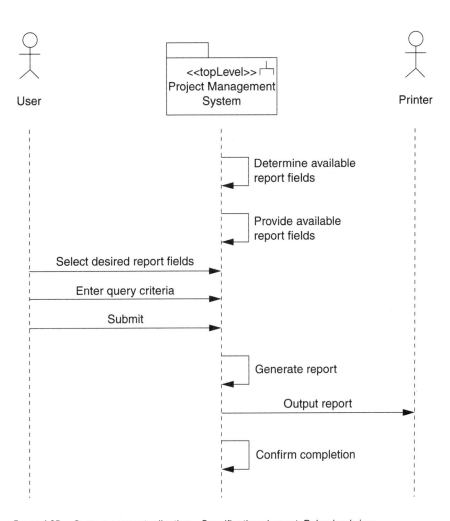

FIGURE 4.25.   System conceptualization—Specification element: Behavioral view.

5. Unify system conceptualization, effectively synchronizing and con-
    cluding system conceptualization. At this point, we understand what
    requirements the system must satisfy and what functionality it pro-
    vides to its users.

    For system specification, we apply the following steps:

1. Identify system elements.
    ■ Identify candidate elements. We identify three packages, includ-
       ing User Interface, Report Processing, and Data Management.
       The User Interface package is used for providing an interface to

the User actor. The Report Processing is used for executing the processing associated with the Project Management System. The Data Management package is used for managing data.
- Model the structural view. Figure 4.27 shows candidate elements for the Project Management System. The User Interface package uses the Report Processing package. The Report Processing package uses the Data Management package.
2. Identify system realization elements.
   - Identify realization elements. We identify one collaboration, the Print Report collaboration that is responsible for implementing the Print Report use case.
   - Model the structural view. Figure 4.28 shows the Print Report collaboration that realizes the Print Report use case.

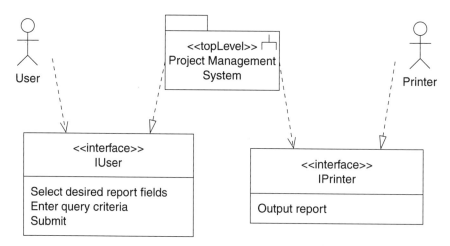

FIGURE 4.26.   System conceptualization—Specification element: Structural view.

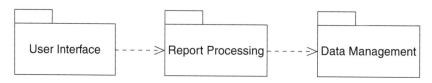

FIGURE 4.27.   System specification—Candidate elements: Structural view.

FIGURE 4.28.   System specification—Realization element.

3. Describe system realization elements, effectively analyzing and understanding system specification elements and what the system specification elements involve.

■ Identify conceptual elements. We identify five conceptual elements, including User Form, Print Report Manager, Report Fields, Report, and Print System. The User Form boundary class is responsible for providing an interface to the User actor. The Print Report Manager control class is responsible for managing the execution of the Print Report collaboration. The Report Fields entity class is responsible for housing the available report fields. The Report entity class is responsible for housing the report. The Print System boundary class is responsible for providing an interface to the Printer actor.

■ Model the structural and behavioral views. Figure 4.29 shows the

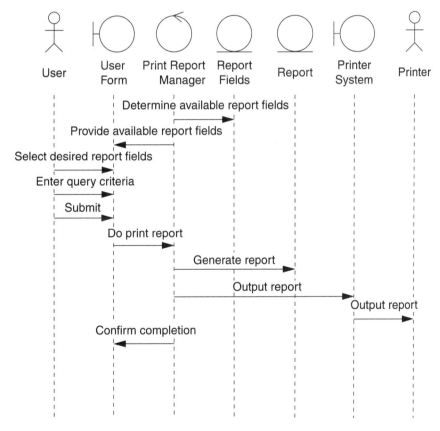

FIGURE 4.29. System specification— Realization element and conceptual elements: Behavioral view.

behavioral view of the Print Report collaboration in which conceptual elements are used to realize the use case. Figure 4.30 shows the corresponding structural view of the Print Report collaboration.

■ Reconcile the structural and behavioral views. For each class, we ensure that every incoming message has an associated operation, and there is a navigable relationship from the sender to the receiver.

4. Distribute system realization elements to system elements, effectively designing and understanding system realization elements, that is, how the system provides its services.

■ Map conceptual elements to candidate elements in order to refine the candidate elements and identify actual elements. We

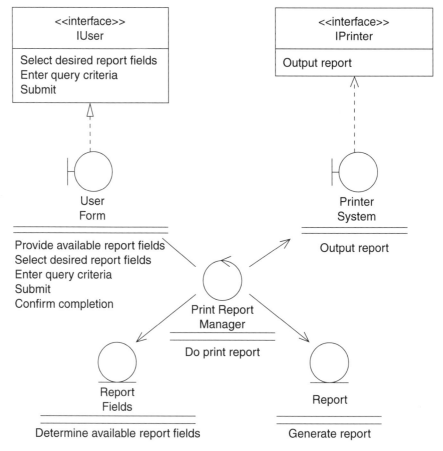

FIGURE 4.30. System specification. Realization element and conceptual elements: Structural view.

map the User Form class to be in the User Interface package, the Printer System class to be in the External Interfaces package, the Print Report Manager class to be in the Report Processing package, the Report Fields class and Report class to be in the Data Management subsystem. The External Interface package has been added and is used for interacting with external systems. The Data Management candidate package has been made an actual subsystem that realizes the IDataManagement interface.

■ Update the structural view with actual elements. Figure 4.31 shows actual elements for the Project Management System.

5. Describe system realization elements using system elements, effectively validating the design against the analysis of the system.

■ Update the structural and behavioral views using the actual ele-

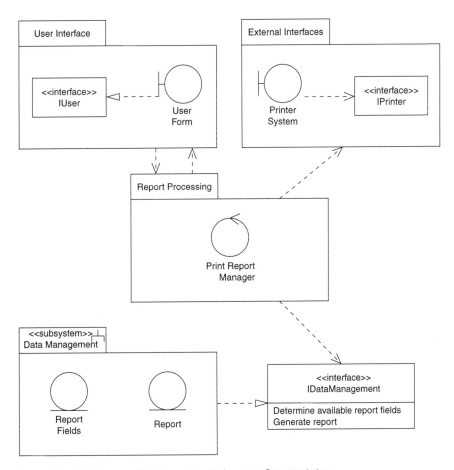

FIGURE 4.31. System specification— Actual elements: Structural view.

ments to which the conceptual elements were mapped. Figure 4.32 shows the behavioral view of the Print Report collaboration in which actual elements are used to realize the use case. Figure 4.33 shows the corresponding structural view of the Print Report collaboration.

- Reconcile the structural and behavioral views. For each class, we ensure that every incoming message has an associated operation, and there is a navigable relationship from the sender to the receiver.
- Validate that the actual element supports the structure and behavior of its conceptual element. For each actual class, we validate that it supports the necessary operations and has the necessary navigable relationships.

6. Unify system specification, effectively synchronizing and concluding

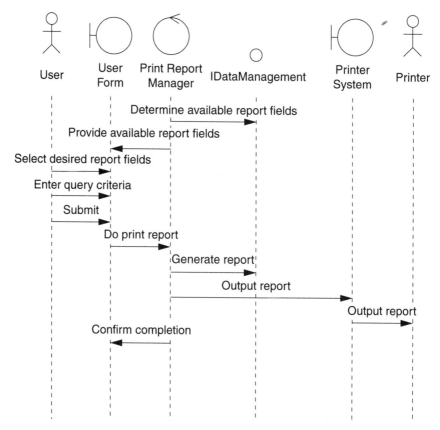

FIGURE 4.32.   System specification—Realization elements and actual elements: Behavioral view.

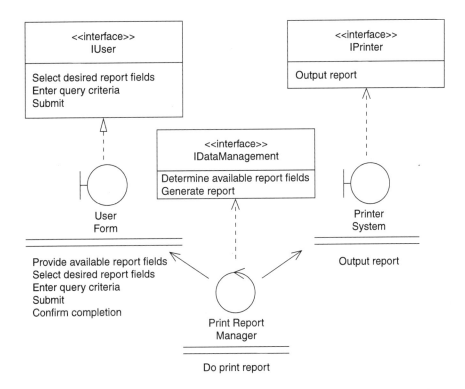

FIGURE 4.33.   System specification—Realization element and actual elements: Structural view.

system specification. At this point, we understand how the system will satisfy its requirements, what elements and their relationships collaborate to constitute the system, and how these elements interact to provide functionality to its users.

For system implementation, we apply the following steps:

1. Identify the system implementation element.
   - Identify the implementation element. We identify the Project Management System component that implements the Project Management System. We also identify the Printer component that implements the Printer interface.
   - Model the implementation view. Figure 4.34 shows the implementation view of the Project Management System.
2. Identify the system environment element.
   - Identify the environment element. We identify the Infrastructure node that supports the Project Management System component and the Printer component.

- Model the environment view. Figure 4.35 shows the environment view of the Project Management System.
3. Unify system implementation, effectively synchronizing and concluding system implementation. At this point, we understand how the system is packaged or implemented and how it resides in its environment.

Successive iterations would elaborate and refine the system model with more detail.

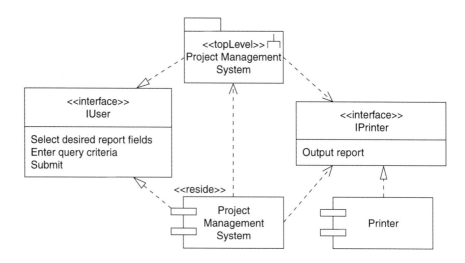

FIGURE 4.34.   System implementation—Implementation view

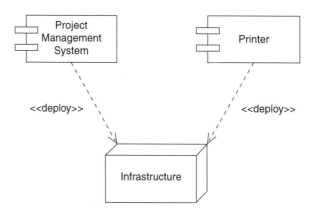

FIGURE 4.35.   System implementation—Environment view

Data Management Subsystem

For subsystem conceptualization, we apply the following steps:

1. Identify subsystem actors.
   - Identify actors. There are two actors involved: Data Management Client and Database. The Data Management Client actor wishes to use the Data Management subsystem. The Database actor is responsible for housing physical data.
   - Model the user view. Figure 4.36 shows the two subsystem actors.
2. Identify the subsystem.
   - Identify the subsystem. The subsystem under discussion is the Data Management subsystem, which is used for managing data.
   - Model the structural view. Figure 4.37 shows the Data Management subsystem.
3. Identify subsystem specification elements.
   - Identify specification elements. We are only interested in the Generate Report service, which involves generating a report.
   - Update the user view with specification elements. Figure 4.36 shows a Generate Report use case that the Data Management Client actor initiates and in which the Database actor participates.
   - Update the structural view with specification elements. Figure 4.37 shows the IDataManagement interface through which the Data Management Client actor communicates with the Data Management subsystem and the IDatabase interface through

FIGURE 4.36.   Subsystem conceptualization—User view.

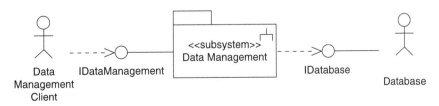

FIGURE 4.37.   Subsystem conceptualization—Structural view.

which the Data Management subsystem communicates with the Database actor.

4. Describe subsystem specification elements, effectively capturing the requirements of the subsystem.
   - Model the structural and behavioral views. Figure 4.38 shows the behavioral view of the Generate Report use case. Figure 4.39 shows the corresponding structural view of the Generate Report use case.

5. Unify subsystem conceptualization, effectively synchronizing and concluding subsystem conceptualization. At this point, we understand what requirements the subsystem must satisfy and what functionality it provides to its users.

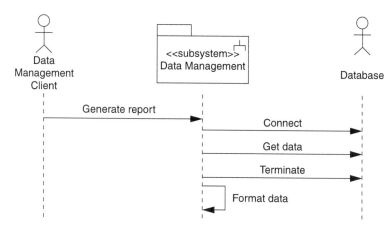

FIGURE 4.38.   Subsystem conceptualization. Specification element: Behavioral view.

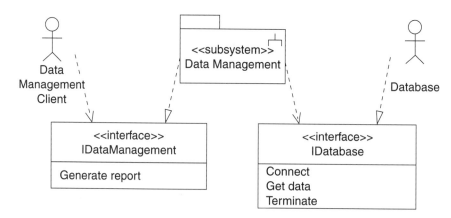

FIGURE 4.39.   Subsystem conceptualization. Specification element: Structural view.

For subsystem specification, we apply the following steps:

1. Identify subsystem elements.
   - Identify candidate elements. We identify one subsystem, the Database subsystem that is responsible for implementing the IDatabase interface through which the Data Management subsystem communicates with the Database actor.
   - Model the structural view. Figure 4.40 shows candidate elements for the Data Management subsystem.
2. Identify subsystem realization elements.
   - Identify realization elements. We identify one collaboration, the Generate Report collaboration that is responsible for implementing the Generate Report use case.
   - Model the structural view. Figure 4.41 shows the Generate Report collaboration that realizes the Generate Report use case.
3. Describe subsystem realization elements, effectively analyzing and understanding subsystem specification elements and what the subsystem specification elements involve.
   - Identify conceptual elements. We identify five conceptual elements: Data Management Client Boundary, Generate Report Manager, Report, Connection Manager, and Database System. The Data Management Client Boundary class is a boundary that is responsible for providing an interface to the Data Management Client actor. The Generate Report Manager control class is responsible for managing the execution of the Generate Report collaboration. The Report entity class is responsible for housing the report and was already identified at the system level of abstraction. The Connection Manager control class is responsible for managing the connection to the database. The Database Sys-

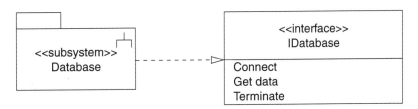

FIGURE 4.40. Subsystem specification—Candidate elements: Structural view.

FIGURE 4.41. Subsystem specification—Realization element.

tem boundary class is responsible for providing an interface to the Database actor.

- Model the structural and behavioral views. Figure 4.42 shows the behavioral view of the Generate Report collaboration in which conceptual elements are used to realize the use case. Figure 4.43 shows the corresponding structural view of the Generate Report collaboration.
- Reconcile the structural and behavioral views. Again, for each class, we ensure that every incoming message has an associated operation, and there is a navigable relationship from the sender to the receiver.

4. Distribute subsystem realization elements to subsystem elements, effectively designing and understanding subsystem realization elements, that is, how the subsystem provides its services.

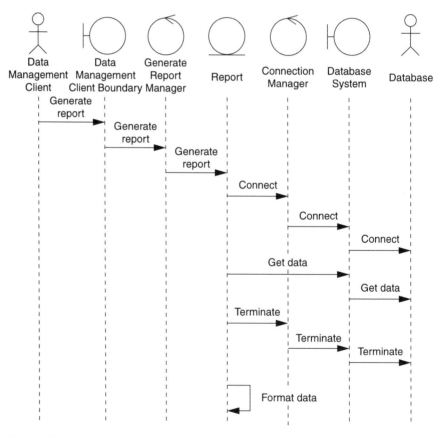

FIGURE 4.42. Subsystem specification—Realization element and conceptual elements: Behavioral view.

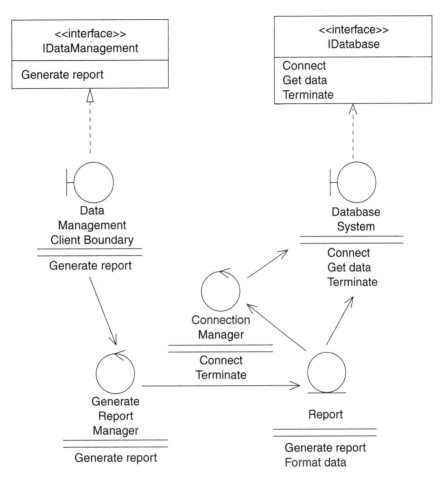

FIGURE 4.43. Subsystem specification—Realization element and conceptual elements:
Structural view.

- Map conceptual elements to candidate elements in order to refine the candidate elements and identify actual elements. We map the Data Management Client Boundary class to the IDataManagement interface because the boundary represents that interface, the Generate Report Manager class and the Connection Manger class to be in the Data Management subsystem, and the Database System class to be in the External Interfaces package.
- Update the structural view with actual elements. Figure 4.44 shows actual elements for the Data Management subsystem. Notice that the Report class has been updated with the "Format

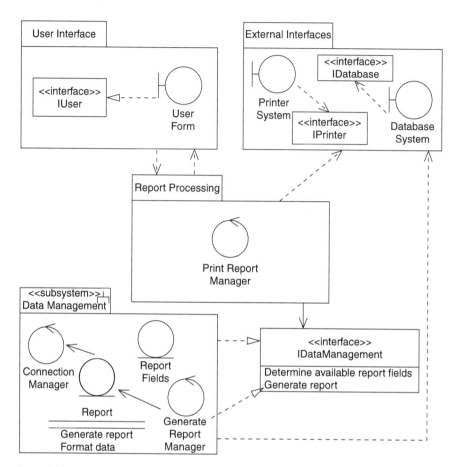

FIGURE 4.44. Subsystem specification—Actual elements: Structural view.

data" operation, and appropriate relationships have been added within the subsystem. Likewise, a dependency is added from the Data Management subsystem to the External Interfaces packages in order to access the Database System class. Notice that the candidate elements from Figure 4.40 were not incorporated into the actual elements.

5. Describe subsystem realization elements using subsystem elements, effectively validating the design against the analysis of the subsystem.

- Update the structural and behavioral views using the actual elements to which the conceptual elements were mapped. Figure 4.45 shows the behavioral view of the Generate Report collaboration in which actual elements are used to realize the use case.

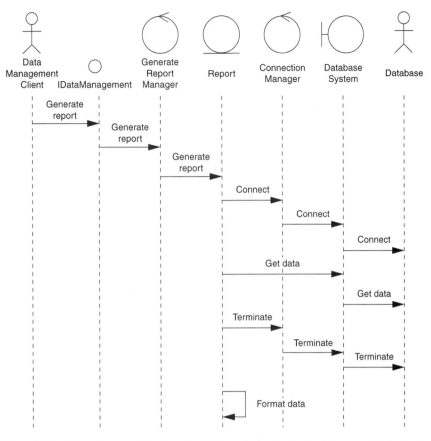

FIGURE 4.45.   Subsystem specification—Realization element and actual elements: Behavioral
view.

Figure 4.46 shows the corresponding structural view of the Print
Report collaboration.

- Reconcile the structural and behavioral views. Again, for each
  class, we ensure that every incoming message has an associated
  operation, and there is a navigable relationship from the sender
  to the receiver.
- Validate that the actual element supports the structure and behavior of its conceptual element. Again, for each actual class, we
  validate that it supports the necessary operations and has the
  necessary navigable relationships.

6. Unify subsystem specification, effectively synchronizing and concluding subsystem specification. At this point, we understand how
   the subsystem will satisfy its requirements, what elements and their

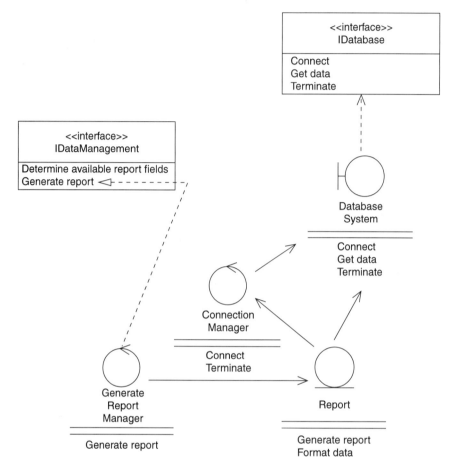

FIGURE 4.46. Subsystem specification—Realization element and actual elements: Structural view.

relationships collaborate to constitute the subsystem, and how these elements interact to provide functionality to its users.

For subsystem implementation, we apply the following steps:

1. Identify the subsystem implementation element.
   - Identify the implementation element. We identify the Data Management component that implements the Data Management subsystem.
   - Model the implementation view. Figure 4.47 shows the implementation view of the Data Management subsystem.

2. Identify the subsystem environment element.
    ■ Identify the environment element. We identify the Data Server
      node that supports the Data Management subsystem component.
    ■ Model the environment view. Figure 4.48 shows the environment
      view of the Data Management subsystem.

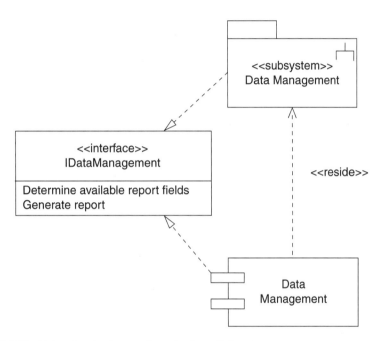

FIGURE 4.47.   Subsystem implementation—Implementation view.

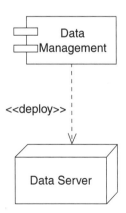

FIGURE 4.48.   Subsystem implementation—Environment view.

3. Unify subsystem implementation, effectively synchronizing and concluding subsystem implementation. At this point, we understand how the subsystem is packaged or implemented and how it resides in its environment.

Successive iterations would elaborate and refine the subsystem model for all subsystems with more detail.

Connection Manager Class

For class conceptualization, we apply the following steps:

1. Identify class actors.
    -   Identify actors. There are three actors involved: Connection Manager Client, Resource Locator, and Database. The Connection Manager Client actor wishes to use the Connection Manager class. The Resource Locator is responsible for locating resources. The Database actor is responsible for housing physical data and was already identified at the subsystem level of abstraction.
    -   Model the user view. Figure 4.49 shows the three class actors.
2. Identify the class.
    -   Identify the class. The class under discussion is the Connection Manager class, which is used for managing the connection to a database.
    -   Model the structural view. Figure 4.50 shows the Connection Manager class.
3. Identify class specification elements.
    -   Identify specification elements. We are only interested in the Connect service, which involves connecting to a database.
    -   Update the user view with specification elements. Figure 4.51 shows a Connect use case that the Connection Manager Client actor initiates and in which the Resource Locator actor and Database actor participate.

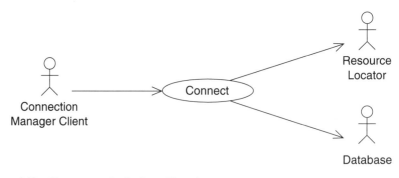

FIGURE 4.49.   Class conceptualization—User view.

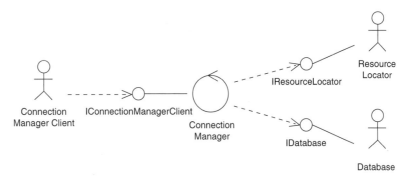

FIGURE 4.50.   Class conceptualization—Structural view.

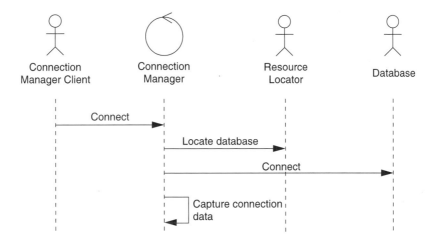

FIGURE 4.51.   Class conceptualization. Specification element: Behavioral view.

- Update the structural view with specification elements. Figure 4.52 shows the IConnectionManagerClient interface through which the Connection Manager Client actor communicates with the Connection Manager class and the IDatabase interface through which the Connection Manager class communicates with the Database actor and the I Resource Locator interface through which the Connection Manager class communicates with the Resource Locator.

4. Describe class specification elements, effectively capturing the requirements of the class.
    - Model the structural and behavioral views. Figure 4.51 shows the behavioral view of the Connect use case. Figure 4.52 shows the corresponding structural view of the Connect use case.

5. Unify class conceptualization, effectively synchronizing and con-
    cluding class conceptualization. At this point, we understand what
    requirements the class must satisfy and what functionality it pro-
    vides to its users.

For class specification, we apply the following steps:

1. Identify class elements.
    - Identify candidate elements. We identify one subsystem, the Re-
      source Locator subsystem that is responsible for implementing
      the IResourceLocator interface through which the Connection
      Manager class communicates with the Resource Locator actor.
    - Model the structural view. Figure 4.53 shows candidate elements
      for the Connect use case.
2. Identify class realization elements.
    - Identify realization elements. We identify one collaboration, the
      Connect collaboration that is responsible for implementing the
      Connect use case.

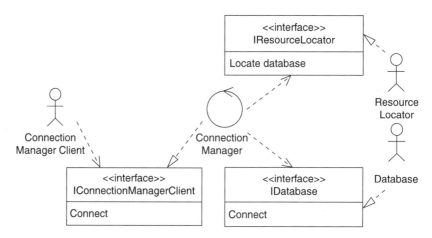

Figure 4.52.   Class conceptualization. Specification element: Structural view.

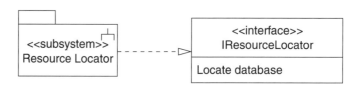

Figure 4.53.   Class specification—Candidate elements: Structural view.

- Model the structural view. Figure 4.54 shows the Connect collaboration that realizes the Connect use case.
3. Describe class realization elements, effectively analyzing and understanding class specification elements, what the class specification elements involve.
   - Identify conceptual elements. We identify five conceptual elements: Connection Manager Client Boundary, Connect Manager, Connection Data, Resource Locator System, and Database System. The Connection Manager Client Boundary class is a boundary that is responsible for providing an interface to the Connection Manager Client actor. The Connect Manager control class is responsible for managing the execution of the Connect collaboration. The Connection Data entity class is responsible for housing connection data. The Resource Locator boundary class is responsible for providing an interface to the Resource Locator actor. The Database System boundary class is responsible for providing an interface to the Database actor and was already identified at the subsystem level of abstraction.
   - Model the structural and behavioral views. Figure 4.55 shows the behavioral view of the Connect collaboration in which conceptual elements are used to realize the use case. Figure 4.56 shows the corresponding structural view of the Connect collaboration.

FIGURE 4.54.   Class specification—Realization element.

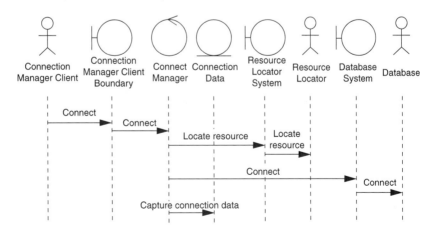

FIGURE 4.55.   Class specification—Realization element and conceptual elements: Behavioral view.

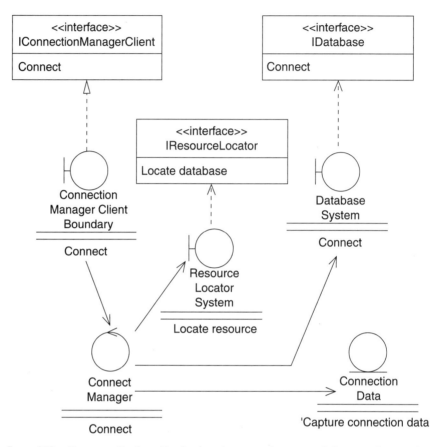

FIGURE 4.56. Class specification—Realization element and conceptual elements: Structural view.

- Reconcile the structural and behavioral views. Again, for each class, we ensure that every incoming message has an associated operation, and there is a navigable relationship from the sender to the receiver.

4. Distribute class realization elements to class elements, effectively designing and understanding class realization elements, how the class provides its services.

  - Map conceptual elements to candidate elements in order to refine the candidate elements and identify actual elements. We map the Connection Manager Client Boundary class to the IConnectionManagerClient interface because the boundary represents that interface, the Connect Manager class to the Connection Manager class because the Connect Manager class represents the Connect operation of the Connection Manager class, the Connection Data class to be in the Data Management subsystem, and the Resource Locator System class to be in the Resource Locator subsystem. The Resource Locator candidate subsystem package has been made an actual subsystem that realizes the IResourceLocator interface.

■ Update the structural view with actual elements. Figure 4.57 shows actual elements for the Data Management Class. Notice that a dependency is added from the Data Management subsystem to the IResourceLocator interface in order to access the Resource Locator System actor. Notice that the candidate elements from Figure 4.53 were incorporated into the actual elements.

5. Describe class realization elements using class elements, effectively validating the design against the analysis of the class.

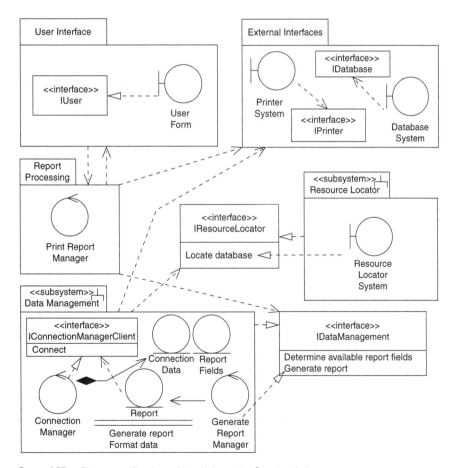

FIGURE 4.57.   Class specification—Actual elements: Structural view.

■ Update the structural and behavioral views using the actual elements to which the conceptual elements were mapped. Figure
   4.58 shows the behavioral view of the Connect collaboration in
   which actual elements are used to realize the use case. Figure
   4.59 shows the corresponding structural view of the Connect collaboration.
■ Reconcile the structural and behavioral views. Again, for each
   class, we ensure that every incoming message has an associated

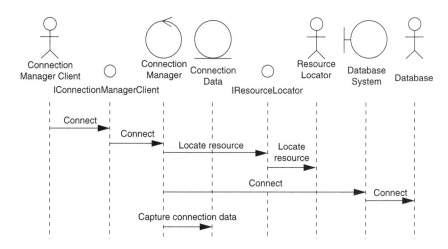

FIGURE 4.58.   Class specification—Realization element and actual elements: Behavioral view.

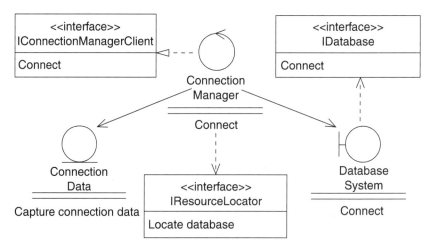

FIGURE 4.59.   Class specification—Realization element and actual elements: Structural view.

operation, and there is a navigable relationship from the sender to the receiver.

- Validate that the actual element supports the structure and behavior of its conceptual element. Again, for each actual class, we validate that it supports the necessary operations and has the necessary navigable relationships.

6. Unify class specification, effectively synchronizing and concluding class specification. At this point, we understand how the class will satisfy its requirements, what elements and their relationships collaborate to constitute the class, and how these elements interact to provide functionality to its users.

For class implementation, we apply the following steps:

1. Identify the class implementation element.
   - Identify the implementation element. We identify the Connection Manager component that implements the Connection Manager Class.
   - Model the implementation view. Figure 4.60 shows the implementation view of the Connection Manager class.
2. Identify the class environment element.
   - Identify the environment element. We identify the Data Server Processor node that supports the Connection Manager class.
   - Model the environment view. Figure 4.61 shows the environment view of the Connection Manger class.
3. Unify class implementation, effectively synchronizing and conclud-

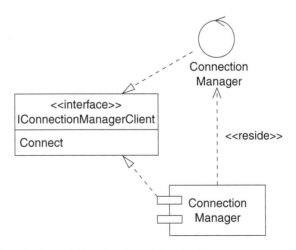

Figure 4.60.   Class implementation—Implementation view

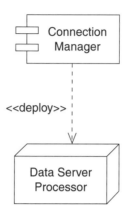

FIGURE 4.61.   Class implementation—Environment view

ing class implementation. At this point, we understand how the class is packaged or implemented and how it resides in its environment.

Successive iterations would elaborate and refine the class model for all classes with more detail.

4.5.   *Applying the Roadmap*

To apply the UML effectively, we must apply the roadmap to derive processes that are suitably lightweight or heavyweight (that is, as light or heavy on process) as necessary. The roadmap emphasizes checks and balances by indicating or suggesting what to model, why, and how to model it using the UML, traceability, and scalability between UML constructs. The roadmap also shows how they are holistically and cohesively integrated. Chapters 5–11 provide various essential rules, principles, and style guidelines for effectively applying the UML within the context of the roadmap, providing pragmatic descriptive and perspective information collated around the UML concepts.

As the roadmap is specifically derived from the UML via the UML sentence, it does not prescribe any particular process, and any specific methodology or process may be perceived as a traversal through the roadmap. A methodology or process specifically addresses or suggests who does what activities on what work products, including when, how, why, and where such activities should be done. However, the roadmap does not prescribe any process elements, but focuses on emphasizing what ought to be addressed when applying the UML, including the decision points and their relationships, providing a framework for a process or methodology. In turn, a process or methodology provides a framework for projects. Furthermore, traversal through the various decision points and relationships need not be sequential, but may be executed in parallel, were multiple efforts regarding the same system are carried out concurrently.

The roadmap is elaborated with various essential rules, principles, and style guidelines collated around the UML concepts throughout the remaining chapters, and may be leveraged for effectively applying the UML within the context of the roadmap. Essential rules for using the UML include pragmatic descriptive information concerning the UML modeling elements—addressing "what is . . ." questions using descriptive guidelines concerning the UML modeling elements. Essential principles for composing UML models include pragmatic descriptive information concerning UML models—addressing "what is . . ." questions using descriptive guidelines concerning UML models. Essential style guidelines for effectively applying the UML include pragmatic prescriptive guidelines concerning effectively applying the UML to compose UML models within the context of the roadmap—addressing "how to . . ." questions using prescriptive guidelines concerning the UML modeling elements.

4.5.1. HEAVYWEIGHT AND LIGHTWEIGHT APPROACHES

While a heavyweight approach involves a fairly significant number of rules and practices reified in numerous process elements and a lightweight approach involves very few rules and practices not reified at all or only implicitly reified in any process elements, the roadmap may be suitably scaled based on the desired level of formality or robustness and detail to be as lightweight or heavyweight as necessary with appropriate process elements, including workers, activities, work products, and heuristics. Undoubtedly, to maintain consistency within any project, there should exist standards and guidelines for the various applied process elements.

When scaling the roadmap toward a more lightweight approach, very few of the detailed roadmap steps are elaborated into activities and assigned to workers, and very few of the detailed roadmap models are elaborated into work products where most steps and models are removed from the roadmap.

When scaling the roadmap toward a more heavyweight approach, most of the detailed roadmap steps are elaborated into activities and assigned to workers, and most of the detailed roadmap models are elaborated into work products where other steps and models may be introduced.

Given both types of approaches, it is furthermore critical to consider what practices are leveraged within the context of the roadmap to mitigate risk throughout a use-case-driven, architecture-centric, iterative and incremental, and risk-confronting effort that is object oriented and component based, where successive iteration elaborates and refines the work of previous iterations with more detail; furthermore, traversal through the roadmap's various decision points and relationships need not be sequential, but may be executed in parallel, were multiple efforts regarding the same system are carried out concurrently.

4.5.2.   HEURISTICS

Having an understanding of the roadmap, we should consider— at least minimally if not exhaustively since an extensive elaboration of the application of the roadmap to a specific project would require an explicit project and is beyond the scope of this discussion— how the roadmap applies to various types of projects. Fundamentally, every constituent of the roadmap is optional and should only be applied if it adds value to the body of knowledge concerning the construct and facilitates achieving the overall objectives of the effort within the specific context of the effort. Those constituents of the roadmap that are applied constitute a roadmap instance.

Applying the roadmap to a new development project, characterized by the lack of an existing system, involves applying any portion of the roadmap as necessary at the onset of the project.

Applying the roadmap to a maintenance or evolution project (especially since the majority of the lifespan of a system is spent in maintenance), characterized by an existing system that is maintained and evolved via enhancement requests and defects to be remedied, involves incrementally applying any portions of the roadmap relevant to those parts of the existing system that are modified; and over time, resulting in more parts of the roadmap applied to more of the existing system.

Applying the roadmap to a package-based acquisition and implementation project (often referred to as commercial off-the-shelf software development, or COTS software development), characterized by selecting one or more packages and then assembling the system, rather than a development project of specifying and building or specifying, buying, and implementing components, involves applying the roadmap where use cases and interfaces are used to model the selection criteria for the packages to be sought after, and subsystems that realize the use cases and interfaces are used to model the selected package or packages from those packages available in the marketplace to be assembled. Furthermore, anything used to connect the selected packages with existing systems or customize the selected packages within a specific environment may involve new development and maintenance and evolution development as mentioned above. Generally, the roadmap may be used to select and assemble components (assemble before integrate), specify and implement components involving buy vs. build decisions (search then integrate), or specify and build components (construct and integrate).

Likewise, the roadmap may be applied to other types of systems in various domains as well, including non-software systems, where the elements of the roadmap are derived from the application domain.

CHAPTER 5

Use-Case (User) Modeling

This chapter provides essential rules, principles, and style guidelines for composing UML use-case or user models within the context of the roadmap, including use-case diagrams and their elements. Use-case modeling is concerned with modeling the functional dimension of a system—what functionality the system provides to its users—and is used for system, subsystem, and class conceptualization within the roadmap to capture in a conceptualization model what requirements the construct must satisfy and what functionality it provides to its users. A conceptualization model consists of use-case diagrams and their model elements. Our goal, in this chapter, is to gain more depth in understanding the UML notation and the roadmap concerning conceptualization models.

5.1. Use-Case Diagrams

A use-case diagram depicts the functionality of an entity using actors, use cases, and their relationships. An entity is a classifier, for example, a system, subsystem, or class.

5.1.1. ACTORS

An actor is a set of roles outside of an entity that users of the entity can play when interacting with the entity, including human users and other systems. An actor instance is a specific instance of an actor or a specific user that conforms to the actor and plays a specific role. An actor is depicted as a class stereotyped with the "actor" keyword or a "stick figure" icon.

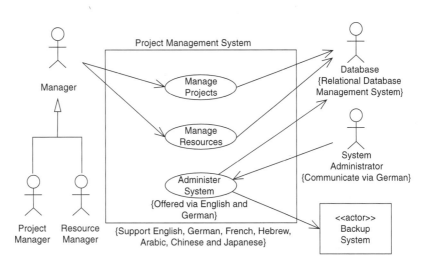

FIGURE 5.1. A Project Management System with actors and use cases.

Figure 5.1 shows a Project Management System with its actors and use cases, including four actors: Manager, System Administrator, Database, and Backup System. There are two types of managers, project managers and resource managers. The Manager actor is responsible for managing projects and resources. The System Administrator actor is responsible for administering the system. The Database actor is responsible for housing physical data. The Backup System actor is responsible for housing archived information.

An actor should be named using a noun phrase and described in a way that captures the actor's responsibilities and characteristics based on the context in which the actor resides. Likewise, capturing an actor's criteria for determining success is also very valuable since it provides insight as to how an actor will "measure" the feasibility of a system.

An actor is external to an entity. Actors define the boundary or context and scope of an entity, including its purpose and extent, by defining those elements that reside at the periphery and in the environment of the entity, those elements that depend on the entity, and those elements on which the entity depends. Actors define who interacts with the entity.

Figure 5.2, derived from Figure 5.1, shows the actors and their dependencies. If the Project Management System changes, the Manager actor and the System Administrator actor may be impacted and may require a change. If the Database actor or the Backup System actor change, the Project Management System may be impacted and may require a change.

An actor interacts with an entity via use cases, units of behavior or functionality, and interfaces. An actor plays one role per use case within

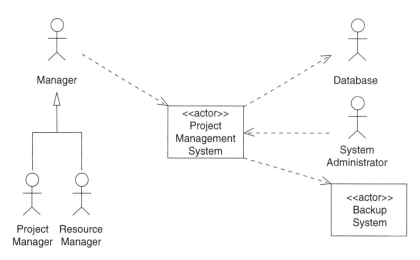

FIGURE 5.2.   Actors and their dependencies.

which it participates. An actor may use the functionality provided by an entity, including main functionality, in which case the actor is called a primary actor, and support or secondary maintenance functionality, in which case the actor is called a secondary actor, and an actor may provide functionality as a resource to the entity. An actor may receive information from an entity or provide information to the entity. An actor may be informed by the entity regarding occurrences within the entity or inform the entity of occurrence outside of the entity.

The Manager actor is a primary actor and the System Administrator actor is a secondary actor relative to the Project Management System.

Figure 5.1 indicates that the System Administrator actor communicates via German and that the Database actor is a Relational Database Management System (RDBMS).

5.1.2.   USE CASES

A use case is a unit of behavior or functionality provided by an entity as a service to actors. A use-case instance, called a scenario, is a specific use or performance of a use case. A use case is depicted as an ellipse containing the name of the use case. Use cases may be enclosed by a rectangle that represents the boundary of the containing entity.

Figure 5.1 shows a Project Management System with its actors and three use cases: Manage Projects, Manage Resources, and Administer System. The Project Management System offers project management, resources management, and administrative functionality. Project management functionality includes capabilities to maintain projects, activities, and tasks with their associated work products. Resource management functionality includes capabilities to maintain teams, people, and skills. Maintaining information about these elements includes capabilities to add, modify, or remove information. Administrative functionality includes capabilities to maintain the system by starting it up and shutting it down, and capabilities to maintain data by backing it up and restoring it. Other capabilities including publishing a schedule to a web site or via e-mail, and support for various languages, including English, German, French, Hebrew, Arabic, Chinese, and Japanese. Likewise, other business rules may be captured in the same manner as the support for various languages.

A use case should be named using a verb-noun phrase indicating what is achieved via the use case's sequence of actions from the perspective of its initiating actor and described in a way that captures its purpose. The description should include how the use case is started and ends; any conditions that must be satisfied when the use case starts (preconditions) or ends (postconditions); the sequences of exchanged messages and performed actions, including variant behavior sequences; the data or information exchanged; extension points; user interface and human factor considerations; business rules or constraints; and any nonfunctional characteristics. Each variant behavior sequence should be described, capturing where the sequence may be inserted into other sequences, what condition needs to be fulfilled for it to be inserted and performed, the actual sequence step, and how and where the sequence in which it is inserted resumes or how the use case ends. If constraints apply to a single use case, they may be captured as constraints of the use case itself. If constraints apply to multiple use cases, they may be captured in a note and attached to all of the use cases to which they apply. A use case should be described from the actor's perspective and describe what the entity does not how it does it given the participating actors. Declarative statements, such as "the system shall. . .", describing what the entity does may also be used with use cases. Use cases focus on the dialog between actors and an entity, while declarative states focus on what the entity does. The sequences of exchanged messages and performed actions may be expressed in round-trip form where the entity always responds to the user. This facilitates using the use case to derive observable results for validation and testing; that is, a use case may be viewed as a coin with two sides; one side treats the use case as a functional requirement, and the other side treats the use case for validation and testing of the functional requirement. Likewise, preconditions, postconditions, variant behavior sequence, and any other conditional behavior may be used to derive validation and testing criteria. A use case diagram may be regarded as a table of contents to the use cases and indicates what use cases exist; and the details of each use case may be regarded as the content behind the table of contents and indicates how the use cases execute between the entity and its actors.

Essential use cases are use cases that are void of any technology or implementation-dependent descriptions and are focused on the intention of the actors involved. Business use cases are business processes offered to business actors or customers by a system or business organization.

Behavior Sequences

A use case is exposed by an entity to actors and defines the functional or behavioral requirement of the entity, which the entity internally provides. The entity may have non-functional requirements that apply to it and all of its use cases, and a use case may have non-functional requirements that apply only to it. Non-functional requirements include usability, reliability, performance, and other such characteristics. Use cases define what functionality actors who interact with the entity require.

Figure 5.1 indicates that the Administer System use case offers its functionality via English and German.

A use case specifies an interaction or sequence of messages exchanged asynchronously using signals among actors, and a use case specifies a sequence of actions or atomic executable statements performed by the entity in response to messages. The behavior sequence of a use case is the sequence of steps (actions and interactions) of the use case, including the interaction with actors and sequence of actions performed by the entity. The messages should indicate what the entity is to do but not how it is to do it.

A use case includes variant behavior sequences. The overall behavior sequence of a use case may be iteratively elaborated from an outline and refined into a basic or normal sequence and variant or alternative sequences. The basic or normal behavior sequence includes what normally happens when the use case is performed. Variant behavior sequences include alternative, optional, exceptional, and any other variations of the normal behavior sequence. Behavior sequences are also called fragments, parts, flows and subflows, segments, and subsequences. Behavior sequences may be part of a use case or may be split apart from a use case and become their own use case. Furthermore, behavior subsequences may be nested as subsequences, and sub-subsequences, and so forth within use cases. The structure of a use case is defined as the identified behavior sequences of the use case, and the behavior of a use case is defined by the content of the identified behavior sequences of the use case. Use cases may be manipulated as a whole or via their individual behavior sequences or specific scenarios for further granularity; therefore, wherever a use case or collection of behavior sequences may be used, an individual behavior sequence may be used. A use case includes all of the individual behavior sequences associated with the use case, each individual behavior sequence may be used independently of the use case and the other individual behavior sequences, and when specific information and data is applied in an individual behavior sequence, it is called a specific scenario. A use case may have attributes and operations. Each operation is a single action from the behavior sequences defined in the use case. Furthermore, a use case may be a single operation. Uses cases may be used as a basis for planning, requirements, analysis, design, implementation, and validation.

There should always be a reason for identifying variant or alternative sequences or why such sequences are split apart from a use case. For example: Is the alternative too complex or localized to some part of the overall solution? Will it be implemented in future iterations? Does it require specialized expertise? Is it too risky? Must it be explicitly mitigated? And so forth. Likewise, change requests may be used to derive new use cases and impact existing use cases. Consider a use case for maintaining information: it may be elaborated into use cases that are used to create, read, update, and delete this information; this is often referred to as CRUD functionality, which is all grouped together under maintenance. Identifying distinct CRUD use cases should always be justified; otherwise these use cases should simply be grouped under a maintenance use case.

The various capabilities of a use case define different behavior sequences of the use case. Project management, resources management, and administrative functionality are different behavior sequences offered by the Project Management System. Capabilities to maintain projects, activities, and tasks are different behavior sequences offered within the project management functionality. Capabilities to maintain teams, people, and skills are different behavior sequences offered within the resource management functionality. Capabilities to add, modify, or remove information are different behavior sequences. Capabilities to maintain the system by starting it up and shutting it down, and capabilities to maintain data by backing it up and restoring it are different behavior sequences offered within the administrative functionality. Capabilities such as publishing a schedule to a web site or via e-mail are different behavior sequences offered by the Project Management System.

Extension Points

An extension point is a reference to one or more locations within a use case at which behavior may be inserted. Extension points are listed in a compartment labeled "extension points." An extension point is shown as a text string followed by a colon followed by a description of the locations of the extension point given in a suitable form. For example, a location may be specified as being "before," "after," or "in place of" a given step and so forth. A behavior sequence may also generally apply to a whole use, where the location may be specified as being "anywhere" in the use case.

Figure 5.3 shows various extension points associated with the Administer System use case and its related use cases. Behavior sequences may be inserted before and after starting up the system in the Startup use case, before and after shutting down the system in the Shutdown use case, before and after backing up the system in the Backup use case, and before and after restoring the system in the Restore use case.

Actors

A use case is initiated by an actor and may involve the participation of numerous other actors. If multiple actors can initiate the same use case, a more general actor is used in the place of the multiple actors and

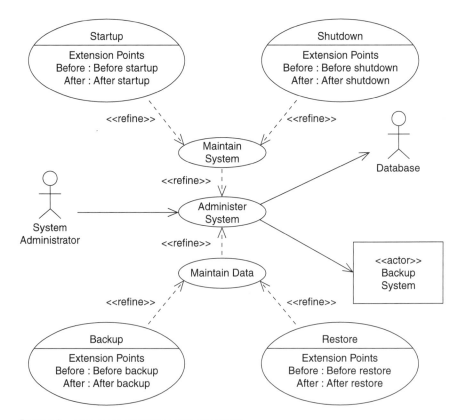

Figure 5.3.   Use cases and their extension points.

generalization relationships relate the multiple actors to the more general actor. A use case is complete in having a defined beginning and ending relative to the initiating actor; otherwise the use case is a fragment within another use case. A use case is observable and testable; otherwise there is no way to validate the use case. To fulfill their responsibilities, actors perform various tasks. Some tasks involve the entity, while others don't. A use case provides results of value to at least one of its actors by enabling that actor to use the entity to perform some tasks. Use cases capture those tasks in which the entity is involved. Use cases only identify what those tasks are but don't specify how the entity performs those tasks internally. Use cases for main functionality enable actors to achieve their objectives by performing tasks involving the entity to fulfill their responsibilities. Use cases for support or secondary maintenance functionality include startup, shutdown, backup, restore, and other types of general maintenance tasks involving the entity.

Figure 5.1 shows that the Manager actor initiates the Manage Projects use case and the Manage Resources use case in which the Database actor participates, and the System Administrator actor initiates the Administer System use case in which the Database and Backup System actors participate.

An explicit actor is one that is outside of the overall system and interacts with use cases at the system level of abstraction. An implicit actor is one that is inside the overall system, is a subsystem or class conforming to an actor, and interacts with uses cases at the subsystem and class levels of abstraction. Any number of subsystem levels may be used when modeling a system. Within the containment hierarchy, a super-ordinate use case is refined into subordinate use cases that cooperate to perform the super-ordinate use case. The super-ordinate use case specifies a service of an entity, and the subordinate use cases specify services of elements within the entity. However, the structure of the container entity is not revealed by the organization of use cases in levels of abstraction. Furthermore, the actors and interfaces of a super-ordinate use case are actors and interfaces of at least one subordinate use case.

Figure 5.3 shows how the Administer System use case is refined into a Maintain System use case and a Maintain Data use case, how the Maintain System use case is refined into a Startup use case and a Shutdown use case, and how the Maintain Data use case is refined into a Backup use case and a Restore use case. The Manager, System Administrator, Database, and Backup System actors are explicit actors.

Packages

Use cases may be organized and grouped into packages based on when they are delivered in terms of iterations, who will work on the use cases in terms of team members and resources, the actors that use the use cases, the other use cases to which they are related, and various other schemes and themes. For example, if a business rule applies to a single use case, it may be attached as a property of the use case itself; if a business rule applies to a multiple use cases, it may be placed in a note and attached to every use case to which it applies; if a business rule applies to multiple use cases and the use cases are all in the same containing package without any other use cases, it may be attached to the containing package and expressed as applying to all of its contained use cases, and if a business rule applies to a specific element, such as a classifier, it may be attached directly to the classifier.

5.1.3.   ACTOR RELATIONSHIPS

An actor may have associations, realizations, and generalizations.

Associations

An association relationship or communicate relationship between an actor and a use case or entity indicates that the actor communicates and participates in the use case and its realizations and that an instance of the actor playing one of the roles of the actor communicates with an instance of the use case or entity. A navigation arrow pointing from the actor to the use case or entity indicates that the actor initiates the interaction. A navigation arrow pointing from a use case or entity to an actor indicates that the use case or entity initiates the interaction. Multiplicity, as discussed in Chapter 6, may be used to indicate how many instances of an actor participate in one instance of a use case and how many instances of the use case are associated with one instance of the actor.

Figure 5.1 shows that the Manager actor initiates the Manage Projects use case and the Manage Resource use case, and the System Administrator actor initiates the Administer System use case, while the Database actor participates in the Manage Projects, Manage Resources, and Administer System use cases, and the Backup System actor participates in the Administer System use case.

Realizations

A realization relationship between an actor and an interface indicates that the actor offers the interface through which other elements may communicate with the actor.

Figure 5.4, which is derived from Figure 5.1 and is similar to Figure 5.2, shows the actors, the system, the interfaces they offer, and the interfaces they use or on which they depend. If the Project Management System's IManageProjects interface or IManageResources interface changes, the Manager actor may be impacted and may require a change. If the Project Management System's IAdministerSystem interface

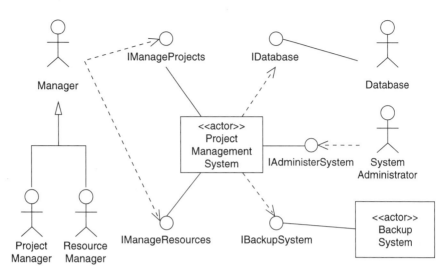

FIGURE 5.4.   Actors and their interfaces.

changes, the System Administrator actor may be impacted and may require a change. If the Database actor's IDatabase interface or the Backup
System actor's IBackupSystem interface change, the Project Management System may be impacted and may require a change. By depending
on interfaces rather than actors, as in Figure 5.2, we have a better understanding of what aspects of an actor must change in order to have
an impact on the various related actors and systems. Dependencies on
interfaces are more granular than dependencies on actors.

Generalizations

A generalization relationship between a more general actor and a more
specific actor indicates that the child actor inherits or receives the features of the parent actor, may add its own features, and instances of the
child actor may be substituted for instances of the parent actor. A parent
actor, called an abstract actor when it has child actors, groups common
roles, characteristics, and purposes of interacting with use cases for multiple child actors. An abstract actor may not have any actor instances. A
child actor, called a concrete actor when it does not have child actors,
groups specific roles, characteristics, and purposes of interacting with
use cases in addition to those it inherits or receives from its parent actors. A concrete actor may have actor instances.

Figure 5.1 shows that there are two types of managers, project managers and resource managers. The Manager actor is an abstract actor,
and the Project Manager and Resource Manager actors are concrete
actors.

5.1.4.   USE-CASE RELATIONSHIPS

A use case may have realizations, include and exclude relationships, and generalizations.

Realizations

A realization relationship between a use case and an interface indicates that the use case offers the interface through which other elements may communicate with the use case. The interface defines a subset of the operations used in the behavior sequences defined in the use case. Different interfaces offered by the same use case need not be disjoint.

Figure 5.5, which is derived from Figure 5.1 and is similar to Figures 5.2 and 5.4, shows the actors, the system's use cases, the interfaces they offer, and the interfaces they use or on which they depend. If the Project Management System's IManageProjects interface changes because the Manage Projects use case changes, the Manager actor may be impacted and may require a change. If the Project Management System's IManageResources interface changes because the Manage Resources use case changes, the Manager actor may be impacted and may require a change. If the Project Management System's IAdministerSystem interface changes because to the Administer System use case changes, the System Administrator actor may be impacted and may require a change. If the Database actor's IDatabase interface or the Backup System actor's IBackupSystem interface changes, the Project Management System may be impacted and may require a change. By using interfaces with use

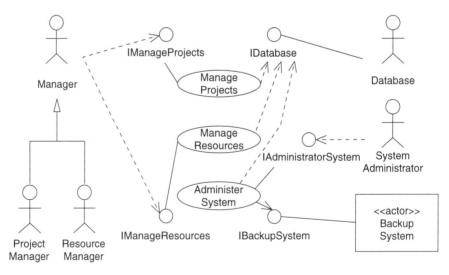

FIGURE 5.5.   Use cases and their interfaces.

cases rather than interfaces with actors and systems, as in Figure 5.4, we have a better understanding of what aspects of a system and its use cases must change in order to have an impact on the various related actors and systems. Dependencies on interfaces realized by use cases are more granular than dependencies on interfaces realized by a system.

Include Relationships

An include relationship from a base use case to an inclusion use case concerning the same system indicates that an instance of the base use case will contain the behavior specified by the inclusion use case. The base use case is responsible for defining the location at which to include the inclusion use case. The performance of the base use case and containment of the inclusion use case involves the performance of the base use case up to the inclusion point, performing the inclusion use case, and then continuing with the performance of the base use case. An include relationship is depicted as a dependency, a dashed arrow, from the base use case to the inclusion use case stereotyped with the "include" keyword. This relationship is used when the inclusion use case may be common to multiple base use cases or is factored out of the base use case and encapsulated so that it may be manipulated on its own as a unit. This information may be captured textually or using behavioral (dynamic) modeling techniques as discussed in Chapter 7.

Figure 5.6 shows that the Maintain Project, Maintain Activity, and Maintain Task use cases include the Find Project use case in order to find a project, activities within a project, or tasks within activities within a project to maintain. Figure 5.7 shows how a Project Manager actor interacts with the Maintain Project and Find Project use cases. Notices that the Maintain Project use case includes and performs the behavior of the Find Project use case, allowing the Project Manager actor to select a project, and then the Project Manager actor modifies or removes the selected project.

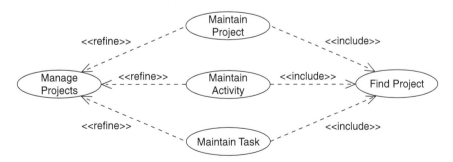

FIGURE 5.6.   Include relationships.

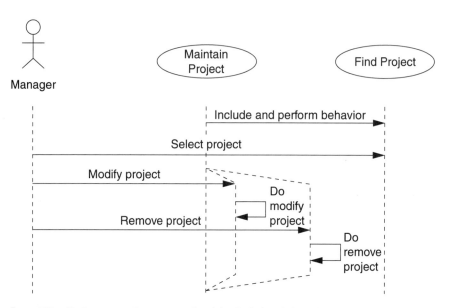

FIGURE 5.7.   Performance of a use case involving include relationships.

Extend Relationships

An extend relationship from an extension use case to a base use case concerning the same system indicates that an instance of the base use case may be augmented, subject to a condition, with behavior specified by the extension use case. The base use case is responsible for defining the extension points and their locations at which behavior sequences may be inserted. The extension use case is responsible for defining the behavior sequences that may be inserted. The extend relationship is responsible for defining the condition that must be satisfied in order to insert the behavior sequences from the extension use case into the base use case and defining the details of the insertion of the behavior sequences. The performance of the base use case and insertion of the extension use case involves the performance of the base use case up to the first extension point, testing the extension condition and inserting the extension use case's behavior sequences if the condition is satisfied, and then continuing the performance of the base use case intertwined with the inserted behavior sequences of the extension use case. When multiple extension points are used, only the first extension point may have multiple locations defined, and all other extension points must have only one location defined per extension point so that the location for inserting each behavior sequence is unambiguously defined and does not require inserting the same behavior sequence in multiple locations. An extend relationship is depicted as a dependency, a dashed arrow, from the extension use case to the base use case stereotyped with the "extend" keyword and followed by the condition for inserting the extension use case enclosed within square brackets followed by a comma-separated list of extension point names enclosed in parentheses. This relationship is used when the extension use case may be optional or exceptional to multiple base use cases.

Defined and named behavior sequences establish convenient locations for inserting other behavior sequences before and after. Defined and named behavior sequences are convenient for inserting into other behavior sequences. However, any location within a use case may be used to define an extension point; and any behavior sequence, so long as it can be identified, may be inserted into other use cases. This information may be captured textually or by using behavioral (dynamic) modeling techniques as discussed in Chapter 7.

Figures 5.8 and 5.9 demonstrate the use of one extension point with multiple locations. Figure 5.8 shows various extension points associated with the Maintain Project and Maintain Activity use cases. A behavior sequence may be inserted at the Activity Functions extension point in the Maintain Project use case after adding or modifying a project. A behavior sequence may be inserted at the Task Functions extension point in the Maintain Activity use case after adding or modifying an activity. Figure 5.9 shows how the Maintain Project, Maintain Activity, and Maintain Task use cases interact. Using the Activity Functions extension point in the Maintain Project use case, after adding or modifying a project, we may select the activity option, in which case the Maintain Activity use

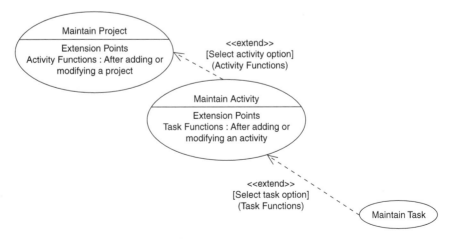

FIGURE 5.8.   Extend relationships with one extension point.

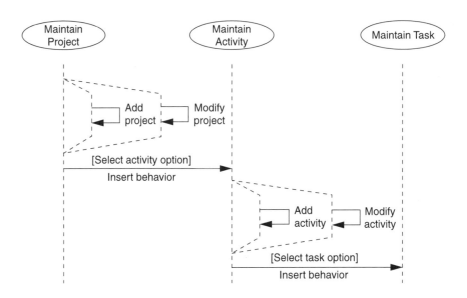

FIGURE 5.9.   Performance of a use case involving extend relationships with one
extension point.

case's Add Activity and Modify Activity behavior sequence are inserted
and performed. Using the Task Functions extension point in the Maintain Activity use case, after adding or modify an activity, we may select
the task option, in which case the basic or normal behavior sequence
and variant or alternative behavior sequences of the Maintain Task use
case are inserted and performed starting with the basic or normal behavior sequence.

Figures 5.10 and 5.11 demonstrate the use of one extension point with
multiple locations and one extension point with one location. Figure
5.10 shows various extension points associated with the Manage Projects
use case. A behavior sequences may be inserted at the Team and People
Functions extension point in the Manage Projects use case after adding
or modifying a project or activity. A behavior sequences may be inserted
at the Skill Functions extension point in the Manage Projects use case
after adding or modifying a task. Figure 5.11 shows how the Manage
Projects and Manage Resources use cases interact. Using the Team and
People Functions extension point in the Manage Projects use case, after
adding or modifying a project or activity, we may select to detail the
project, in which case the Manage Resources use case's Maintain Team
and Maintain People behavior sequences are inserted in one of two locations, and the Manage Resources use case's Maintain Skill behavior
sequence is inserted at the Skill Functions extension point. Once the

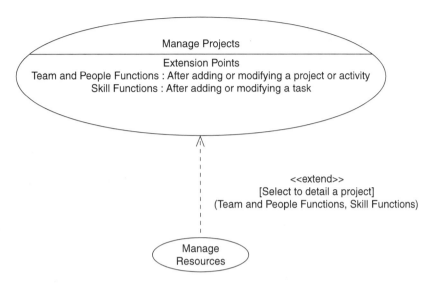

FIGURE 5.10.   Extend relationships with multiple extension points.

behavior sequences have been inserted, performance of the use case continues.

Generalizations

A generalization relationship between a more general use case and a more specific use case concerning the same system indicates that the child use case inherits or receives the features of the parent use case and may add its own features and define new behavior sequences. It may also modify and specialize behavior sequences it inherits or receives from the parent use case, and instances of the child use case may be substituted for instances of the parent use case. The features of a use case include its participating actors, attributes, operations, associations, behavior sequences, and extension points. A child use case may modify the content of the behavior sequences it receives, and intertwine its own behavior sequence with the behavior sequences it receives, but it may not modify the existence of the behavior sequences it receives form its parent use case; that is, the behavior sequences of the parent must still exist, but their content may be modified. Actors of a parent use case are actors of its child use case. A parent use case groups common structure, behavior, and purposes for multiple child use cases. A child use case groups specific structure, behavior, and purposes in addition to those it inherits or receives from its parent use case. This relationship is used when the more specific use case is similar to the more general use case

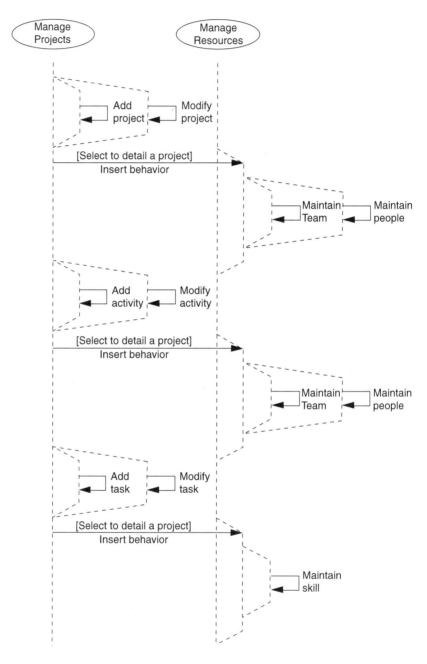

FIGURE 5.11. Performance of a use case involving extend relationships with multiple
extension points.

but requires specialization. This information may be captured textually or using behavioral (dynamic) modeling techniques as discussed in Chapter 7.

Figure 5.12 shows that the Manager actor may initiate publishing the project schedule by generating a web site using the Generate Web Site use case in which the Database and the Web Site Host actor participate and the behavior sequences from the Publish Project Schedule use case are used, or the Manager actor may initiate publishing the project schedule by sending e-mail using the Send E-mail use case, in which the Database and the E-mail System actor participate and the behavior sequences from the Publish Project Schedule use case are used. Figure 5.13 show the behavior sequence of the Publish Project Schedule use case. Figure 5.14 shows how the Generate WebSite use case intertwines its own behavior sequence with that of the Publish Project Schedule use case, and Figure 5.15 shows how the Send E-mail use case intertwines its own behavior sequence with that of the Publish Project Schedule use case.

A concrete use case is a use case that is complete in having a defined beginning and ending, is meaningful to the initiating actor, and may have use case instances on its own. An abstract use case is a use case that does not have to be complete, only exists for other use cases, and does not have use case instances on its own but only as it is used by other use cases. Inclusion and extension use cases are abstract use cases if they are not directly initiated by actors, while the concrete use cases reflect the main purpose of the entity.

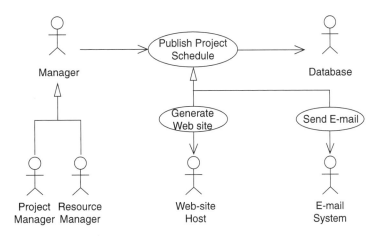

FIGURE 5.12.   Generalization relationships.

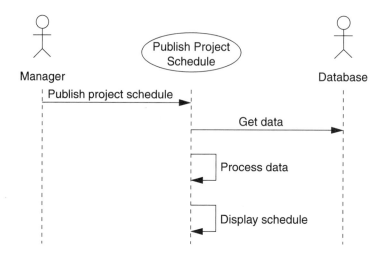

FIGURE 5.13.   Performance of a parent use case within a generalization relationship.

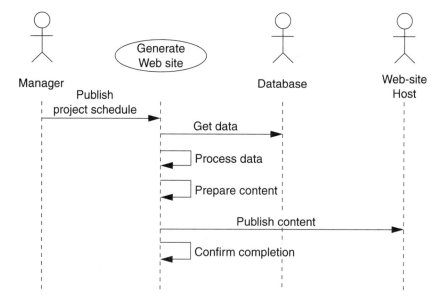

FIGURE 5.14.   Performance of a child use case within a generalization relationship.

Figure 5.12 shows that a project schedule may be published by generating a web site or sending e-mail. The Publish Project Schedule use case is an abstract use case, and the Generate Web Site and Send E-mail use cases are concrete use cases.

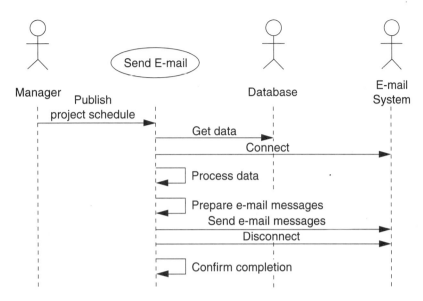

FIGURE 5.15.   Performance of another child use case within a generalization relationship.

5.2.   *Applying Use-Case Diagrams*

When modeling the conceptualization perspective of a construct (system, subsystem, or class) and determining what requirements the construct must satisfy and what functionality it should provide to its users, consider the guidelines above and herein which ought to be applied within a use-case-driven, architecture-centric, iterative and incremental, risk-confronting effort that is object oriented and component based. Successive iterations evolve, elaborate, and refine the work of previous iterations with more detail. Steps need not be sequential, but may be executed in parallel, where multiple efforts regarding the same system are carried out concurrently.

Within the specification perspective of the roadmap, specification elements include use cases, interfaces, and operations; and construct elements include any elements that may constitute the construct or system, including subsystems, packages, and classes which evolve from proposed candidate elements to accepted actual elements. Properties capture constraints and characteristics of elements.

Every constituent of the roadmap is optional and should only be applied if it adds value to the body of knowledge concerning the construct and facilitates achieving the overall objectives of the effort within the specific context of the effort. Those constituents of the roadmap that are applied constitute a roadmap instance. Reference the examples above and the Project Management System example used in Chapter 4 as the result of applying use-case modeling within the context of the roadmap.

5.2.1. The Construct

This section elaborates steps 1 through 5 concerning construct conceptualization of the Detailed and Notational Roadmap section of Chapter 4. The focus is on actors, the construct, and specification elements.

Actors

To identify construct actors, consider the various types of actors. Often, practitioners don't spend enough time identifying actors; however, this is critical because it begins to define the scope and extent of the construct. For each actor, model the user view using a use-case diagram (actor) to establish a placeholder for information about the actor.

To describe construct actors, for each actor, capture the actor's properties. This involves capturing any pertinent constraints and characteristics of the actor. An actor's properties include the actor's responsibilities and characteristics. Responsibilities define the purpose, obligation, or the rationale for the actor's existence given the context of the actor and how the actor addresses the needs, goals, and objectives of other actors that depend on it. Characteristics include any other relevant information pertaining to the actor. For actors who are humans, these characteristics include any relevant human factors due to the context of the actors. For actors who are systems, these characteristics include any non-functional properties due to the context of the actors. Progressively split and merge actors to decrease the coupling and increase the cohesion of their roles and responsibilities, apply generalization relationships between actors, and apply interfaces with actors. Often, practitioners don't spend enough time describing actors; however, this is critical because it defines the scope and extent of the construct.

The Construct

To identify the construct, consider focusing on a central construct. Review the descriptions of the actors and identify any relevant constructs that would enable the actors to fulfill their responsibilities. Often, practitioners presume that there is only one construct; however, there may be numerous constructs that may be identified. Progressively negotiate amongst stakeholders to identify one central construct on which to focus, then regard the other identified constructs as actors in relation to the construct on which focus is directed. For the construct, model the structural view using a class diagram (construct) to establish a placeholder for information about the construct.

To describe the construct, capture the construct's properties. This involves capturing any pertinent constraints and characteristics of the construct. The construct's properties include its responsibilities and characteristics. Responsibilities define the purposes, obligations, or the rationale for the construct's existence given the context of the construct and how the construct addresses the needs, goals, and objectives of actors that depend on it. Characteristics include any other relevant information pertaining to the construct. These characteristics include any relevant non-functional properties due to the context of the construct.

Specification Elements

To identify construct specification elements, consider the actors and the construct. For each actor, consider what tasks, similar to a to-do list, the actor performs to fulfill their responsibilities, and consider which of these tasks involve the construct. The tasks that involve the construct may be modeled as use cases, interfaces, or operations. An operation is processing offered by the construct, an interface is a collection of operations offered as a service by the construct, and a use case is a dialog between actors and the construct. An operation may be modeled as a use case with only one action in its behavior sequence. Each interface operation may also be modeled as a use case with only one action in its behavior sequence. Ensure that every use case provides results of value to at least one of its actors by enabling them to use the construct to perform some tasks that enable the actors to fulfill their responsibilities. Often, practitioners classify use cases as the goals of the actors. Use cases are not actor goals, but are units of functionality that allow actors to achieve their goals, which include fulfilling their responsibilities. Often, practitioners don't spend enough time identifying specification elements; however, this is critical because it begins to define the requirements of the construct. Often, the terms "high-level" requirement or construct "feature" focus on specifying more generically what the construct provides to its actors from the perspective of the construct or its actors, and the term "detailed" requirement focuses on specifying what the actor requires of the construct from the perspective of the actor.

For each actor, update the user view (actor and use cases) with specification elements in order to establish placeholders for information about the specification elements. For the construct, update the structural view (construct, use cases, interfaces, and operations) with specification elements in order to establish placeholders for information about the specification elements.

5.2.2.   REQUIREMENTS

This section elaborates step 6 concerning construct conceptualization of the Detailed and Notational Roadmap section of Chapter 4.

To describe construct specification elements, focus on effectively capturing the requirements of the construct by addressing the question of why it should have the requirements. For every use case, be able to identify "why" the construct should have the requirement—because it enables actors to fulfill their responsibilities.

Specification Element Properties

For each specification element, capture the specification element's properties based on its actor's properties and the construct's properties to ensure traceability between its actors and the construct and the specification element. This involves propagating any pertinent constraints and characteristics from the actors and the construct to the specification element.

Specification Elements

For each use case, focus on capturing the basic or normal behavior sequence then focus on capturing variant or alternative behavior sequences. First focus on specific alternative behavior sequences that may occur at specific locations within the basic or normal behavior sequence, and then focus on general alternative behavior sequences that may occur anywhere within the basic or normal behavior sequence. The behavior sequences may be iteratively elaborated from an outline and refined into a basic or normal behavior sequence and variant or alternative behavior sequences. The messages exchanged in the behavior sequences should indicate what the construct is to do but not how it is to do it.

Use cases may be manipulated as a whole or via their individual behavior sequences or specific scenarios for further granularity. Progressively identify, split, and merge behavior sequences to decrease the coupling and increase the cohesion of behavior sequences within the use cases. Progressively apply include relationships between behavior sequences to factor out and include behavior sequences that are common to multiple behavior sequences, apply extend relationships between behavior sequences to factor out and insert behavior sequences that are optional and exceptional, and apply generalization relationships between behavior sequences to factor out behavior sequences that are similar. Often, practitioners forcefully apply use-case relationships because they perceive that they are beginning to architect the construct; however, the architecture of the construct is not captured in the organization of the use cases but in the specification of the construct. These relation-

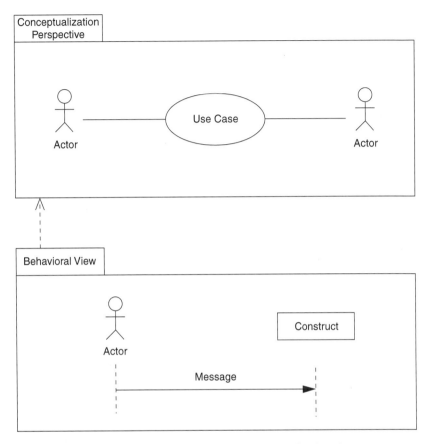

FIGURE 5.16.   The behavioral view of the description of the specification element.

ships may be used to manage alternative, optional, and exceptional behavior sequences, including any behavior sequences that are of high risk
or require management that is more explicit and manipulation as their
own units. Effectively applying these relationships involves using them
when discovering the relationships in the behavior sequences and using
the relationships to manage dependencies between behavior sequences.
If a relationship is applied, there must be an explicit reason as to why
the behavior sequence was extracted; otherwise, there is no justification
as to why it was extracted and it will only require more effort to manage
the relationship. Often, practitioners don't spend enough time describing specification elements; however, this is critical because it defines the
requirements of the construct.

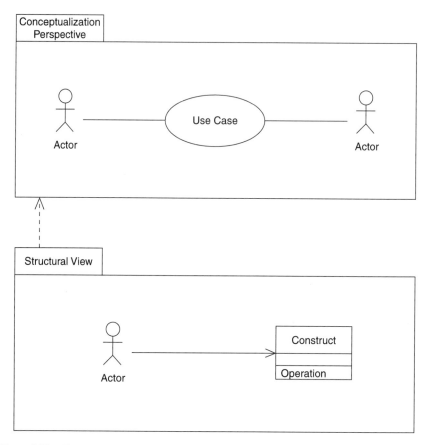

For each specification element, model the structural and behavioral views (actors, construct, interfaces, messages, and relationships) in order to describe the specification element as discussed in Chapters 6 and 7. For each specification element, reconcile the structural and behavioral views in order to ensure that the description of the specification element is consistent as discussed in Chapters 6 and 7. Figure 5.16 shows conceptually the behavioral view of the description of a specification element, and Figure 5.17 shows conceptually the structural view of the description of a specification element. Ensure that every exchanged message between a sender and receiver has an associated operation offered by the receiver and a navigable relationship from the sender to the receiver through which the message is communicated.

5.2.3. *UNIFICATION*

This section elaborates step 7 concerning construct conceptualization of the Detailed and Notational Roadmap section of Chapter 4.

To unify construct conceptualization, focus on effectively synchronizing and concluding construct conceptualization. Reconcile all of the elements used in construct conceptualization to ensure homogeneity and consistency between actors and their responsibilities, and between use cases and their behavior sequences. Reconcile the construct conceptualization at the current level of abstraction with the construct conceptualization at the next higher level of abstraction to ensure that the conceptualization perspective is consistent. This involves ensuring that the construct conceptualization at the current level of abstraction does not invalidate anything in the construct conceptualization at the next higher level of abstraction and that the construct conceptualization at the next higher level of abstraction is able to support everything in the construct conceptualization at the current level of abstraction.

CHAPTER 6

Structural (Static) Modeling

This chapter provides essential rules, principles, and style guidelines for composing UML structural or static models within the context of the roadmap, including class and object diagrams and their elements. Structural modeling is concerned with modeling the structural or static dimension of a system— the elements and their relationships that constitute a system—and is used for system, subsystem, and class specification within the roadmap to capture in a specification model how the construct will satisfy its requirements. Structural modeling is also used to determine which elements and their relationships collaborate to constitute the construct, and how these elements interact to provide functionality to end users. A specification model consists of class, object, sequence, collaboration, state, and activity diagrams and their model elements. Our goal, in this chapter, is to gain more depth in understanding the UML notation and the roadmap concerning the structural or static aspect of specification models.

6.1. Class Diagrams

A class diagram depicts the static structure of an entity using classifiers and relationships. An entity is a classifier, for example, a system, subsystem, or class.

6.1.1. CLASSIFIERS

A classifier is a concept that defines structural features and behavioral features, and has various types of relationships. A feature is a property encapsulated within a model element, an atomic constituent of a model. Structural features define the static features of a model element. Behavioral features define the dynamic features of a model element. A classifier may contain other classifiers. It owns its contents and defines a namespace, a part of a model in which a name may be uniquely defined and used. An element may access any contents of its own namespace or a containing namespace. Specific types of classifiers include classes, actors, use cases, data types, interfaces, components, nodes, subsystems, and artifacts.

A classifier is depicted as a vertex or node, including an icon or two-dimensional symbol that may contain other elements. Other information is depicted as strings or sequences of characters attached to nodes. A classifier is named using an optional stereotype or list of stereotypes followed by an optional visibility symbol followed by the classifier name string followed by an optional property. Not all details of a modeling element need to be depicted on a diagram, only those that are relevant to the purpose of the diagram.

A stereotype is used to classify (brand) or mark a model element so that it may be given a specific meaning. A stereotype is depicted as a text string keyword enclosed in guillemets («») or double-angle brackets preceding or above the name of the element. Multiple stereotypes may be applied to an elements depicted vertically one below the other or preceding each other. A user-defined icon may be used to signify a stereotype. The guillemets and the stereotype icon may be depicted simultaneously; however only one is required. The icon is placed in the upper right corner near the name of the element, or the entire base model element symbol is collapsed into an icon containing the element name or with the name above or below the icon, and other information contained by the base model element symbol is suppressed. When multiple stereotypes are used for an element, the icons are omitted.

A property is used to attach arbitrary information to a model element so that its specific meaning may be defined. A property consists of property strings or property specifications representing the constraints and characteristics of the element. A property is depicted as a comma-delimited list of text strings inside a pair of braces ([}) succeeding or below the name of the element. The text strings may be expressed in any natural or computer language or be tagged values. A constraint is a property string that is a semantic condition that must be maintained as true for the element. A tagged value is a property string that is a characteristic of an element expressed as a keyword-value pair depicted using the keyword followed by an equal sign followed by its value.

The visibility specifies the accessibility of the classifier relative to its container. The visibility symbol "+" means public and the classifier is accessible from outside of its container, "-" means private and the classifier is inaccessible from outside of its container, "#" means protected and the classifier is inaccessible from outside of its container but is accessible from more specialized classifiers as discussed in the generalization section, and "~" means package visibility and other elements in the same container package or nested subpackages to any level may access the classifier. There is no default visibility. Visibility may also be specified using the property keywords "public", "protected", "private", and "package".

Classes

A class is a set of objects with common structural features, behavioral features, and semantics. Structural features include properties or attributes and associations. Behavioral features include operations and methods. The most crucial aspect of a class is its semantics, the meaning of the class. A class may contain nested classes, associations, generalizations, use cases, constraints, dependencies, collaborations, data types, and interfaces. A class may have associations, generalizations, and realize interfaces.

A class is depicted as a solid outline rectangle with three standard compartments separated by horizontal lines. The top name compartment is required and contains the stereotype, visibility, name, and properties of the class; the middle list compartment is optional and contains a list of attributes; and the bottom list compartment is optional and contains a list of operations.

A class may be nested inside another class, indicating that it belongs to the namespace of the container class and may only be used within the containing class. A nested class is connected by a line with an "anchor" icon on the end connected to the containing or declaring class, a plus sign (+) within a circle drawn at the end attached to the container, called tree notation.

Figure 6.1 shows various classes, including Work Effort, Person, Date, Time, Date and Time Routines, and Work Effort Priority.

A list compartment holds a list of text strings and may have a name depicted centered at the top of the compartment. The items are depicted one to a line and may have a meaningful order. For the attributes compartment, the string "attributes" may be used. For the operations compartment, the string "operations" may be used. Other compartments may be used as necessary; each compartment need only show what is relevant to the diagram, and optional compartments may be suppressed. A stereotype or property may be used as an element, in which case it applies to all succeeding list elements until another stereotype or property appears. An ellipsis (. . .) may be depicted as the final element of a list to indicate that additional elements in the model meet the selection criteria but are not shown.

A class should be named using a noun phrase and described in a way that captures the class's role and purpose, responsibilities, attributes,

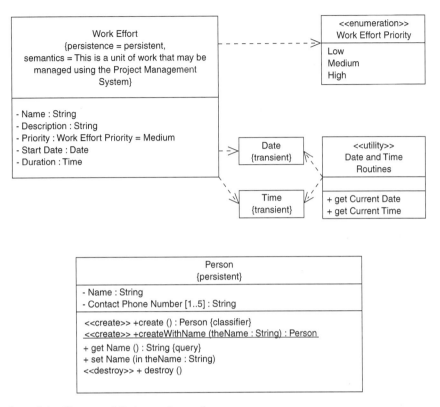

FIGURE 6.1.   Classes, attributes, and operations.

operations, and characteristics. A class's name should reflect that the
class is a single well-defined abstraction that plays various roles. A class
should have a small set of consistent and unique responsibilities, attributes, and operations. That is, no two classes have the same purpose. A
class's features do not sufficiently define the semantics of the class, but
only describe the class; to sufficiently define a class, there ought to be
sufficiently understandable semantics pertaining to the class within the
context in which it is used—that is, contextual semantics.

A class may be stereotyped with the "focus" keyword to denote that
the class defines core logic or control flow for one or more auxiliary
classes that support it. A class may be stereotyped with the "auxiliary"
keyword to denote that the class defines secondary logic or control flow
to support another more central or fundamental class. A focus class depends on its auxiliary classes.

The "semantics" property keyword specifies the meaning of a classifier, association, attribute, or operation. The "persistence" property keyword specifies whether a classifier, association, or attribute outlives the

process that created the element. The value of "persistent" denotes that it does outlive the process that created it; this may also be denoted using the "persistent" keyword. The default value of "transient" denotes that it does not outlive the process that created it; this may also be denoted using the "transient" keyword.

A classifier may be stereotyped with the "utility" keyword to denote that the element has no instances and all features are classifier-scoped. If a feature is shared by all instances of the classifier, it is said to be classifier-scoped and is shown by underlining the feature or by applying the "classifier" property keyword. If a feature is not shared by all instances of the classifier and each instance has its own value (as in an attribute) for the feature or the feature may be applied to an instance (as in an operation), it is said to be instance-scoped and is shown by not underlining the feature or by applying the "instance" property keyword.

A classifier may be stereotyped with the "enumeration" keyword to denote that the element is an enumerated data type. The enumerated set of possible values, an ordered list of enumerated literals, is placed in the second compartment. The enumerated set of possible operations defined on the literals are placed in the third compartment.

Figure 6.1 shows that instances of the Work Effort class are persistent and indicates that they are units of work that may be managed using the Project Management System, instances of the Person class are persistent, and instances of the Date and Time classes are transient.

Attributes

An attribute is an element of information or data that instances of a classifier may hold. A responsibility is implemented by any number of operations and any number of attributes. An attribute is shown as a text string in the middle compartment of the class rectangle.

The syntax for an attribute is "<<stereotype>> visibility name [multiplicity ordering] : type = initial-value {property}", where—

■ The visibility is optional and specifies the accessibility of the attribute relative to its container. There is no default visibility.
■ The multiplicity is optional and specifies how many instances of the attribute exist. Multiplicity is depicted as a literal integer value or a closed range depicted as "lower-bound .. upper-bound" and a single asterisk to denote an unlimited range. Both the lower-bound and upper-bound ought to be specified in order to indicate that they have both been considered. The default multiplicity for attributes is 1.
■ The ordering is optional and only meaningful if the multiplicity upper bound is greater than one. When absent, the values are unordered; the keyword "unordered" indicates that the values are unor-

dered, and the keyword "ordered" indicates that the values are
ordered.

■ The type is optional and specifies the type of the attribute. The UML
provides data types for Boolean true and false values, integers, real
numbers, and strings. Classifier names may also be used. The colon
is omitted if no type is specified.

■ The initial value is optional and specifies the initial value of the attribute. The equal symbol is omitted if no initial value is specified.

■ The stereotype or list of stereotypes and property are optional.

■ An attribute may be classifier-scoped and is shared by all instances
of the classifier, or it may be instance-scoped and each instances has
it its own values for the attribute.

Alternatively, an attribute may be expressed using pseudo-code or another language.

Figure 6.1 shows various attributes, including Name, Description, Priority, Start Date, and Duration for the Work Effort class; and Name and
Contact Phone Number for the Person class. Notice that the Work Effort
Priority enumeration class specifies the possible values for the Priority
attribute of the Work Effort class.

An attribute should be named using a noun phrase that is descriptive
and understandable, and the attribute should represent a single well-
defined abstraction. An attribute should be modeled as a separate class
if it has an independent identity and can be used independent of the
class that owns it, may be associated with other classes, has a complex
type, or holds complex types of data, requires its own relationships, or
may be an attribute of multiple classes. If it is modeled as a separate
class, the original class that contained it would have an association to
the attribute class. Attributes depend, via dependency relationships, on
the classes of their types. These dependencies are depicted from the class
having the attribute rather than from the attribute itself.

There are various property keywords that are usable with attributes.
The default "changeable" property keyword denotes that the attribute
may be modified after the instance is created and initialized. The "frozen" property keyword denotes that the attribute value may not be modified after the instance is created. The "addOnly" property keyword denotes that additional attribute values may be added after the instance is
created and initialized, but once a value is added, it may not be removed
or altered, assuming multiplicity is greater than one.

Operations

An operation is a specification of a service or processing that instances
of a classifier offer. A responsibility is implemented by any number of
operations and any number of attributes. A method is an implementa-

tion of a service or processing. A method may be associated with a procedure that defines a set of actions that model the method's computation or algorithm, when an operation is invoked, its method dispatches its associated procedure to execute. The method realizes the operation. An operation is shown as a text string in the bottom compartment of the class rectangle. A method may be shown within a note attached to the operation or modeled using a realization relationship.

The syntax for an operation is "<<stereotype>> visibility name (parameter list) : return-type {property}", where—

- The visibility is optional and specifies the accessibility of the operation relative to its container. There is no default visibility.
- The parameter list is an optional comma-separated list that specifies the formal parameters passed to the operation. The syntax for each parameter is "<<stereotype>> kind name : type = default-value {property}". The stereotype or list of stereotypes and property is optional. The kind is optional, "in" means that the parameter is input and may not be modified by the method, "out" means that the parameter is output and may be modified by the method to communicate information to the caller, "inout" means that the parameter is input and may be modified by the method. The default is "in". The type is optional and specifies the type of the parameter. The colon is omitted if no type is specified. The default value is optional and specifies the default value of the parameter. The equal symbol is omitted if no initial value is specified. The parentheses may be omitted if no parameter list is specified.
- The return type is optional and specifies the type of the return value. A comma-separated list of return types may be used where each return type has the same notation as the parameter list without a kind or default value. The colon and type or list of types may be omitted if nothing is returned. The colon is omitted if no type or list of types is specified. The parameter list and return type may be omitted together, but not separately.
- The stereotype or list of stereotypes and property is optional.
- An operation may be classifier-scoped and apply to the classifier, or it may be instance-scoped and apply to instances of the classifier. The method of an operation is shared by all instances.

Alternatively, an operation may be expressed using pseudo-code or another language.

Figure 6.1 shows various operations, including "get Current Date" and "get Current Time" for the Date and Time Routines utility class; and "create", "createWithName", "get Name", "set Name", and "destroy" for the Person class.

An operation should be named using a verb or verb-noun phrase that is descriptive and understandable, and the operation should represent a single well-defined service where the name should reflect the result of the operation from the perspective of the user of the operation. Operations are required to support the messages that a class receives and appear on interaction diagrams where one message may resolve into multiple operations. Supporting operations are also necessary, including creating and destroying objects of a class, copying object, and testing for the same object or object with equal attribute values. Operations depend, via dependency relationships, on the classes of their parameter types, on the classes of any objects that they create or destroy or that are used within their methods, and on the classes of their return types. Operations depend on other operations they may invoke in their methods. These dependencies are depicted from the class having the operation rather than from the operation itself. Likewise, where there are optional associations, associations with a lower-bound multiplicity of zero, an operation for determining if the link exists given an instance is required. A method realizing an operation has the same signature (name, types and parameters, and return type) as the operation and a body implementing the specification of the operation. Furthermore, operations should not simply pass various data elements within interactions, but should also pass objects in order to maintain an object-oriented focus. Likewise, if an operation receives too many data elements, then perhaps the data elements constitute a specific abstraction wherein the data elements may be treated as an object. This focus on object orientation must be tempered with pragmatic performance, scalability, and throughput considerations.

There are various stereotype keywords and property keywords that are usable with operations. The "create" stereotype keyword denotes that the operation creates instances of the classifier. The "destroy" stereotype keyword denotes that the operation destroys instances of the classifier. The "signal" stereotype keyword denotes that the operation is invoked via an asynchronous message. The "query" property keyword denotes that the operation may not modify the state or attributes of its classifier. The "concurrency" property keyword specifies how concurrent access to the operation is handled. If the tag value is "sequential," callers must coordinate simultaneous access. If the tag value is "guarded," multiple calls are allowed and the classifier blocks itself to handle simultaneous access sequentially. If the tag value is "concurrent," multiple calls are allowed and the classifier handles them simultaneously.

Types

A type is a set of instances to which a collection of operations and structural features (attributes and relationships) apply; it focuses on a role or a part a classifier or instances of a classifier may play in a particular situation without defining the physical implementation of the instances of the classifier. A type specifies its attributes and operations, but no methods, and cannot be instantiated nor nested. A role is a named specific behavior of a classifier participating in a particular context. A type is depicted as a class stereotyped with the "type" keyword.

Figure 6.2 shows an Employee type with a Schedule attribute and operations for setting an appointment and requesting the schedule.

Implementation Classes

An implementation class defines an implementation for behavioral features (operations and methods) and structural features (attributes and relationships). An implementation class physically implements its attributes and operations, and instances may have only one implementation class. An implementation class may realize any number of types. An implementation class is depicted as a class stereotyped with the "implementationClass" keyword. An undifferentiated class, non-implementation or implementation, has no stereotype.

Figure 6.3 shows a person implementation class related to various types and interfaces.

Interfaces

An interface is a characterization of the behavior of a classifier defining a service or contract as a collection of externally visible operations with-

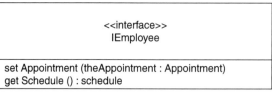

FIGURE 6.2. Types and interfaces.

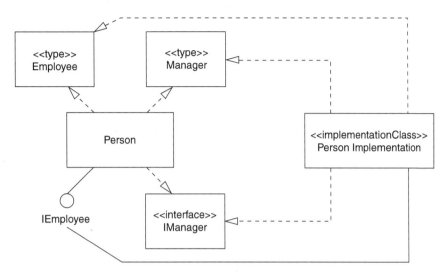

FIGURE 6.3.   Types, interfaces, implementation classes.

out any structural features. An interface does not specify any internal structure (attributes and relationships) or implementation (methods) and only specifies public operations, may have generalizations, and cannot be instantiated. Use generalizations when an element defines a default operation and method, and use interfaces when there is a default operation signature, but no default method.

An interface is depicted as a class stereotyped with the "interface" keyword. The attributes compartment may be omitted because it is always empty. The operations compartment contains a list of the operations specified by the interface. An interface may also be depicted as a small circle with the name of the interface placed near the symbol. The operations specified by the interface are not shown using the circle notation. The circle may be attached by a solid line to an element that supports the interface or provides an implementation for the operations the interface specifies.

Figure 6.2 shows two depictions of an Employee interface with operations for setting an appointment and requesting the schedule.

An interface partitions and characterizes logical groups of operations into collections that constitute a coherent service offered by a classifier. A classifier that realizes the interface offers the service by conforming to the interface, and supporting and implementing the operations of the interface. A classifier that conforms to an interface may be substituted for other classifiers that conform to the same interface. A classifier may offer several services by realizing multiple interfaces and several classifiers may realize the same interface. An interface may be the target of a relationship that other elements can navigate or traverse to reach the interface, but it may not have relationships it can navigate or traverse to reach other elements.

An interface should be named using a noun phrase and described in a way that captures the interface's purpose and responsibilities, operations, and characteristics. It is a common convention to name interfaces as "IX" or some other general form of a name where X is the name of the service that the element that realizes the interface provides; that is, the name is derived from the perspective of the element that realizes the interface. This is commonly used for elements that are active or may initiate control on their own volition. For example, if we perceive a car as being active, the car realizes an "IDrive" interface that a person uses to drive the car. Also, it is a common convention to name interfaces as "Xable" or some other general form of a name where X is the name of the service that the elements that use the interface utilize; that is, the name is derived from the perspective of the elements that use the interface. This is commonly used for elements that are passive or may not initiate control on their own volition. For example, a car realizes a "Drivable" interfaces that a person uses to drive the car. Either convention may be used; however, consistency is vital. A class's description should explain the role the interface facilitates. Consider ordering the operations of an interface in the order in which they are performed; this may be done using statechart diagrams and the externally visible states of the elements which realize the interface.

Each interface represents a seam within the entity in which it is used. It represents a "point" within the entity at which the entity may be pulled part, a "point" within the entity at which the entity may be extended by inserting other entities, and generally the means for reorganized the whole entity. It defines a service and decouples clients using the service from suppliers providing the service where clients may change without impacting suppliers and suppliers may change without impacting clients as long as clients and suppliers abide by the contract defined by the interface. An interface should be simple to understand, complete in providing all of the necessary and sufficient operations to specify a single service, understandable by clients and suppliers without having to delve into implementation details, and approachable in having enough supporting information to use or realize the interface without overwhelming practitioners attempting to apply the interface. As an extension point is a reference to one or more locations between two steps within a use case at which behavior maybe inserted, an interface is a reference to a service between clients and suppliers within an entity at which other clients and suppliers may be inserted.

Templates

A template or parameterized element is a descriptor of an element with one or more unbound parameters defining a family of elements; each actual element is specified by binding the parameters to actual values. A parameter is a variable that may be bound or given a value, and it may represent any referenceable element, including classifiers, attribute types, operations, and so forth. Partially instantiated templates are allowed.

A template classifier is depicted with a small dashed rectangle that is superimposed on the upper right-hand corner of the rectangle for the class (or to the symbol for another modeling element) containing a comma-separated formal parameter list or one formal parameter per line. The formal parameter list has the same notation as the parameter list for classifier operations without a kind. If the type of a parameter is omitted, it is assumed to be a classifier. The contents of the template classifier appear as normal in the classifier definition; however, they may use the formal parameters. The bound element name may be used anywhere an element name of the parameter's type may be used, including defining attributes and operation signatures. However, the parameter is only meaningful within the template and has no features, because the features are part of an actual element that is provided when the template is bound and the parameters are bound to actual element values. Parameterization may be applied to any modeling element.

When using generalization relationships and associations with templates, only a class can be a superclass or the target of a navigable association. A template may have one-way associations to other elements, and a template may be a subclass of an ordinary class to indicate that the classes formed by binding the template are subclasses of the given superclass. The bound element is fully specified by its template; therefore, its contents may not be explicitly extended in the application of the template, declaring new attributes or operations for the class is not allowed, but a bound class may be subclassed and the subclass may be extended as usual.

Figure 6.4 shows a parameterized package container from which two containers are created. The People package uses the "bind" dependency and may contain up to five people in the container. The other container package uses an alternative notation combining the "bind" dependency directly within the definition and may contain up to ten people in the container.

Structural Organization

The structural organization of a system involves packages, systems and subsystems, specification and realization elements, and a structural

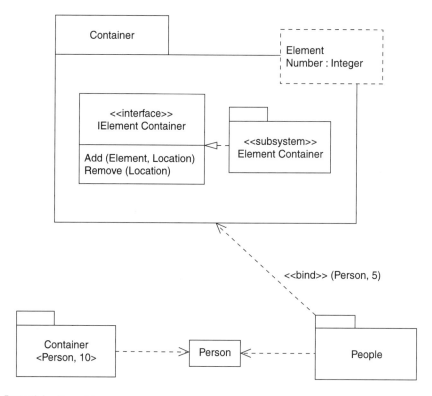

FIGURE 6.4.   Templates.

scheme to constitute the system's structure in order to establish the system's behavioral organization. See the Behavioral Organization section of Chapter 7 for more information.

Packages

A package is a general means for grouping and organizing elements. A package is depicted as a large rectangle with a small rectangle or "tab" attached to the left side of the top of the large rectangle.

Figure 6.5 shows various packages, including View Layer, Application Layer, Domain Layer, and Infrastructure Layer.

A package owns its contents and defines a namespace, a part of a model in which a name may be uniquely defined and used and are the basis for configuration management, storage, and access control. Packages may be nested and elements within a package see or have visibility all the way out through nested packages to the outermost package. An element may access any contents of its own namespace or a containing namespace. A reference to a class in a different package is denoted using

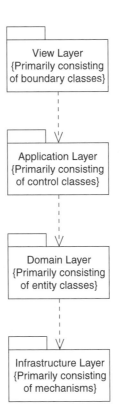

FIGURE 6.5. Packages.

a pathname, a series of names linked together and separated by a double colon (::) delimiter, where the chaining together of package names and the element name starting from the root of the system or from some other point selects the element. By default, an element shown within a package is assumed to be defined within that package, and a reference to an element defined in another package is shown using a pathname to the element. A package may have branching lines to contained elements that are depicted outside of the package with a plus sign (+) within a circle drawn at the end attached to the container, called tree notation using an "anchor" icon. A package may have dependencies and generalizations.

A package should be named using a noun phrase and described in a way that captures the package's role and purpose ("subject" or "theme"), contents (including classifiers, relationships, and other nested model elements), and characteristics. Packages are used to group related elements together. A package does not realize an interface, but provides an interface via its public elements. A package has independent existence in the specification perspective, but does not have independent existence in the implementation perspective; rather it is combined with other elements to form components. It is independent in the sense that its contents are encapsulated and only revealed through public elements. The contents of a package should be consistent and highly cohesive while loosely coupled to elements outside of the package. The non-public contents of a package may change freely so long as its public elements don't change.

The "facade" stereotype keyword denotes that the package only contains references to model elements owned by other package and is used to provide a public view of the model elements. The "framework" stereotype keyword denotes that the package mainly contains a collection of patterns defined as template collaborations with their supporting elements that specify a reusable architecture. When a framework applies to a specific application domain, it is often referred to as an application framework. The "stub" stereotype keyword denotes that the package is incompletely transferred; that is, it provides the public parts of another package, but nothing more.

The "model" stereotype keyword or a triangle icon denotes that the package is a model from a specific viewpoint and at a specific level of abstraction. The "systemModel" stereotype keyword or a triangle icon denotes that the package is a model pertaining to a specific system containing all of the models from different viewpoints and at different levels of abstraction. The "topLevel" stereotype keyword or a fork symbol icon denotes that the package is a system, and is the top-most package in a containment hierarchy, the outer limit for looking up names. The "subsystem" stereotype keyword or a fork symbol icon denotes that the package is a subsystem, and is the top of the subsystem containment hierarchy. The "instantiable" property keyword denotes that the subsystem may be instantiated. A subsystem instance is the execution time representation of a subsystem.

The "modelLibrary" stereotype keyword denotes that the package is a model library that contains model elements which are reused by other packages, but it does not extend the UML language using stereotypes and tag definitions. The "profile" stereotype keyword denotes that the package is a profile or specialized vocabulary for the UML that contains model elements that are customized for a specific domain or purpose using extension mechanisms, including stereotypes, tag definitions and constraints.

Figure 6.6 shows various packages and interfaces for the Project Management System.

Systems

A system is a behavioral unit that may be recursively decomposed into multiple subsystems and each subsystem may be fully decomposed into classes within a containment hierarchy. The functionality of a system or

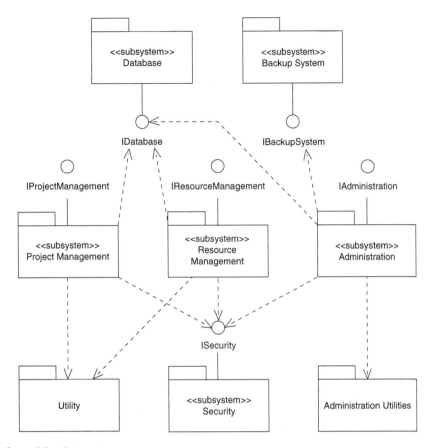

FIGURE 6.6. Subsystems.

subsystem is provided as a service to its users via some interface; the system or subsystem has responsibility for the service and conforms to or offers and provides the interface, and the parts of the system or subsystem have responsibility for implementing the service and realizing the interface.

A subsystem may have associations and offer interfaces. It may have operations, may specialize other subsystems similar to generalization relationships between packages, and may have its contents partitioned into specification elements and realization elements. Specification elements include use cases. Realization elements are those elements of the subsystem that realize the use cases or behavior sequences and operations. The subsystem may be instantiable once it is implemented as a component or subsystem instance; however, if the subsystem is non-instantiable, it serves as a specification unit for the behavior of its contained elements. Each element within a subsystem has its own visibility.

A subsystem package's large rectangle may have three compartments, one for operations, one for specification elements, and one for realization elements, delineated by dividing the rectangle with a vertical line, and then dividing the area to the left of this line into two compartments with a horizontal line. Operations are depicted in the upper left compartment, which is not labeled; specification elements are depicted in the bottom left compartment, which is labeled "Specification Elements"; and realization elements are depicted in the right compartment, which is labeled "Realization Elements". This general notation may be customized as necessary; compartments may be collapsed or suppressed if they are not relevant in a particular diagram; all contained elements may be depicted together in one non-labeled compartment; the contexts of a subsystem may be depicted with the tree notation using an "anchor" icon and labeling branches appropriately, or compartments may be rearranged.

A subsystem should be named using a noun phrase and described in a way that captures the subsystem's role and purpose ("subject" or "theme"), contents (including classifiers, relationships, and other nested model elements), and characteristics. Subsystems are used to encapsulate behavior inside packages and provide behavior or services via interfaces; the responsibilities for implementing the operations of the interfaces are distributed to contained elements. A subsystem formally realizes interfaces. A subsystem has independent existence in the specification perspective and the implementation perspective, and it retains its independent existence in the implementation perspective. It is independent in the sense that its contents are encapsulated and only revealed through interfaces with operations. A subsystem should represent a single logically consistent set of services. The contents of a subsystem may change freely so long as its interfaces don't change. A subsystem is a specification perspective representation of an implementation perspective component, and a component is an implementation perspective representation of a specification perspective subsystem.

Specification and Realization Elements

Any element may be used as a specification or realization element because a realization relationship indicates conformance of behavior, where the client supports at least all of the operations defined in the supplier without the necessity to support any structural features of the supplier (attributes and associations). When a realization element realizes a specification element, the realization element conforms to the role specified by the specification element. Subsystems within the realization compartment represent subordinate subsystems relative to the encompassing subsystem. Realization relationships are depicted between specification elements and realization elements within the package. A subsystem package or its elements may have realization relationships to specification elements that are external to the subsystem, including interfaces and operations. A subsystem may realize several interfaces, and an interface may be realized by several subsystems. Each operation of every interface offered by a subsystem must be offered by the subsystem itself, or at least one contained specification element must have a matching operation. Generally, system use cases, interfaces, and operations are realized by subsystems, classes, and collaborations; subsystem use cases, interfaces, and operations are realized by subsystems, classes, and collaborations; and class use cases, interfaces, and operations are realized by class operations.

Structural Scheme

The structural scheme of a system is the foundation for the system's behavioral scheme. The structural scheme constitutes the structural or static model view, which focuses on the static dimension of a system, the elements and their relationships that constitute a system. A layer, modeled as a package, groups elements at the same level of abstraction; it represents a horizontal slice through the architecture. A partition, modeled as a package, groups elements at the same level of abstraction or across layers; it represents a vertical slice through the architecture.

A entity may be logically partitioned and organized into layers or grouping of elements based on various criteria, including their visibility, volatility, generality, how users are organized, areas of competence and expertise within the development team, distribution considerations, security considerations, variability considerations, and so forth. The layering scheme shown in Figure 6.5 is commonly called a Four-Layer Architecture. It is very general and flexible because it separates the various concerns within an entity better to facilitate increasing cohesion and decreasing coupling. The View Layer package contains elements relevant to the user interface and system or device protocols for other systems that interact with the system. The Application Layer package contains elements relevant to interactions, transactions, or business processing. The Domain Layer package contains elements relevant to data and information. The Infrastructure Layer contains elements relevant to mechanisms.

Consider various issues when packaging elements: Are they are independently ordered, configured, developed, deployed, changed or replaceable, purchased or commercially available rather than constructed? Are they currently being reused or may they be reused in the future? Are they developed in parallel, and are they volatile or optional? Do they provide front-end functionality particular to an actor, back-end functionality, or a service within an entity? Do they have specific substitution or distribution requirements, encapsulate complex collaborations and interactions, require the expertise of specific team members, have specific security requirements, are existing products or services, and so forth? Likewise, optional elements and mandatory elements should not be placed into the same package or subsystem. These same issues generally apply to classes as well. Classes tend to have fine-grained responsibilities while subsystems have coarse-grained responsibilities, and both may be developed in parallel. The challenge of packaging and subsystems involves addressing the fundamental issues of complexity and change in order to increase cohesion and decrease coupling.

Figure 6.7 shows how the various packages and interfaces depicted in Figure 6.6 are used to provide the functionality discussed in Chapter 5 for the Project Management System. The Project Management subsystem realizes the Manage Projects use case, the Manage Resources collaboration realizes the Manage Resources use case, and the Administer System collaboration realizes the Administer System use case. Notice how actors communicate with the system via the interfaces of the use cases, and how the subsystems communicate with actors via the interfaces of the actors, delineating the boundary or scope of the system. Notice how interfaces are used in the Realization Elements compartment to seam or knit together how the various realization elements provide the behavior of the system.

The utilities used by the Project Management subsystem and Resource Management subsystem are decoupled from utilities used by the Administration subsystem. The utilities used by the Project Management subsystem and Resource Management subsystem are coupled in the Utility package as they most likely will be maintained together, and the utilities used by the Administration subsystem are maintained in the Administration Utilities package.

Because the Project Management subsystem solely realizes the Manage Projects use case, the IManageProjects interface of the Project Management subsystem is possibly the same interfaces as the IManageProjects interface of the Manage Projects use case.

The Database subsystem and Backup System subsystem represent means for communicating with their corresponding actors. The IDatabase interface realized by the Database subsystem need not be the same IDatabase interface realized by the Database actor, and the IBackupSystem interface realized by the Backup System subsystem need not be the same IBackupSystem interface realized by the Backup System actor. The subsystems may reveal only a subset of the overall operations offered by their corresponding actors, or the subsystems may provide some intermediate translation between the internal services they offer via their interfaces and the services offered by the corresponding actors. These subsystems shield the other elements within the system from external changes of the actors and their interfaces.

In Figure 6.6, the Project Management subsystem and Resource Management subsystem usc the IDatabase interface, and these relationships are preserved in Figure 6.7. However, in Figure 6.6, the Administration subsystem uses the IBackupSystem interface, but this relationship is not preserved in Figure 6.7. The decision whether to preserve or remove these relationships is based on whether the involved subsystems are always used together in every collaboration and whether the client subsystem ever directly realizes behavior that may require the supplier subsystem outside of the collaboration. Figure 6.7 presumes that the Administration subsystem will not be used outside of the Administer System collaboration in which the Backup System subsystem also participates, and the Administration subsystem does not directly realize any other behavior that may require the Backup System subsystem outside of the collaboration; therefore, the relationship is removed. Figure 6.7 presumes that the Resource Management subsystem may be used in other collaborations independently of the Database subsystem and may directly realize other behavior that may require the Database subsystem. Generally, it is better to retain the relationships between subsystems independent of their participating in collaborations in order to avoid the above presumptions.

6.1.2. RELATIONSHIPS

A relationship is a connection among concepts. Specific types of relationships include associations, generalizations, dependencies, use-case include relationships, and use-case extend relationships. A relationship may have a stereotype or list of stereotypes and properties.

A relationship is depicted as an arc or path made of a series of line segments connecting nodes. Other information is depicted as strings or sequences of characters. A relationship is named using the same notation as a classifier. Furthermore, the details of a relationship are often as important, if not more important, than elements the relationship relates.

Associations

An association is a structural relationship between classifiers, a set of links with common structural features, behavioral features, and semantics. An association end is an endpoint of an association, which connects the association to a classifier. A binary association involves two classifiers, and an n-ary association involves three or more classifiers. An association class is a class pertaining to the association.

Figure 6.8 focuses on the Team, Person, and Skill classes of the Project Management system. Figure 6.9 focuses on the Project, Activity, and Task classes. Figure 6.10 is similar to Figure 6.9, but uses graphical nesting to depict composition relationships. Figure 6.11 focuses on the relation-

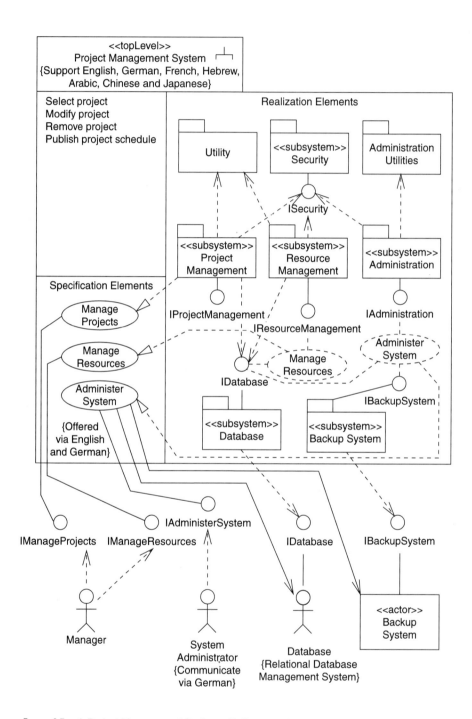

Figure 6.7. A Project Management System with its contents.

ships between the Person, Activity, and Task classes. Figure 6.12 refines and details the relationship between the Person and Skill classes.

An association should be named using a verb phrase and described in a way that captures the association's purpose and responsibilities, attributes, operations, and characteristics. Associations are the means through which objects communicate messages with one another. An association's features do not sufficiently define the semantics of the association, but only describe the association; to define an association sufficiently, there ought to be understandable semantics pertaining to the association within the context in which it is used—that is, contextual semantics.

There are various stereotype keywords and property keywords that are usable with associations. The "implicit" stereotype keywords denote that the association is not manifest, but is only conceptual. The "xor" property keyword denotes a set of elements that share a connection to one classifier, where only one of the elements may be instantiated.

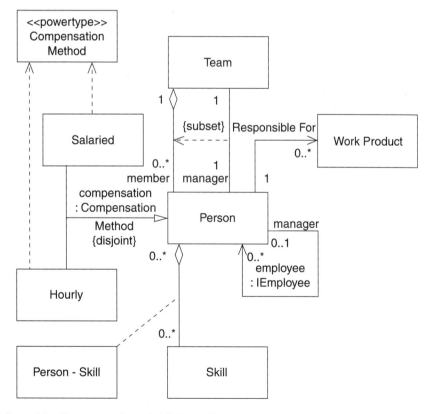

FIGURE 6.8.   Teams, people, and skills in the Project Management System.

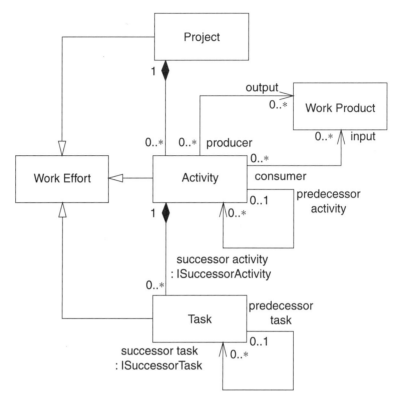

FIGURE 6.9.   Projects, activities, and tasks in the Project Management System.

Binary Associations

A binary association between two classifiers indicates a structural relationship between the classifiers. A binary association is depicted as an arc or a solid path made of a connected series of line segments connecting the classifiers. A binary association may be labeled with a name. The name is usually read from left to right and top to bottom. The name may have a small black solid triangle next to it, called a name-direction arrow, where the point of the triangle indicates the direction in which to read the name; but the arrow is purely descriptive and has no semantics associated with it.

Figure 6.8, via binary associations, shows that a single person is responsible for zero or more work products, and a work product must be the responsibility of only one person. A person playing the role of a manager manages employees using the IEmployee interface, where a manager may manage zero or more employees and an employee may have no more than one manager but need not have a manager.

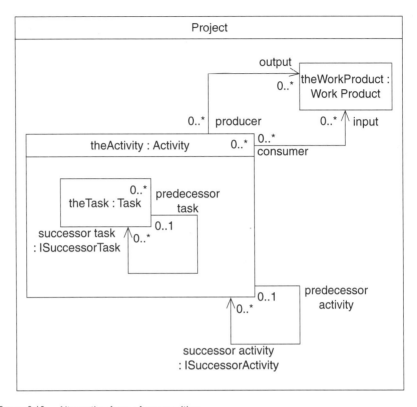

FIGURE 6.10.   Alternative form of composition.

Figure 6.9, via binary associations, shows that an activity involves any number of work products as input and any number of work products as output, and work products may be used with any number of activities as input or output. Activities are related where one predecessor activity may have any number of successor activities, and one successor activity may have zero or one predecessor activity. Tasks are related where one predecessor task may have any number of successor tasks, and one successor task may have zero or one predecessor task.

N-ary Associations

An *n*-ary association between three or more classifiers indicates a structural relationship between the classifiers. An *n*-ary association is depicted as a large diamond with an arc or a solid path made of a connected series of line segments from the diamond to each participating classifier. An *n*-ary association may be labeled with a name near the diamond. The name is read from left to right and top to bottom. The name may have a small black solid triangle next to it, called a name-

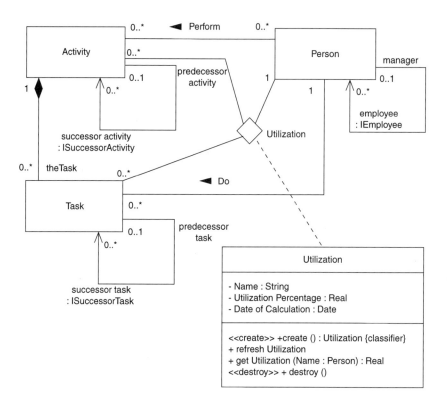

FIGURE 6.11.   People, activities, and tasks in the Project Management System.

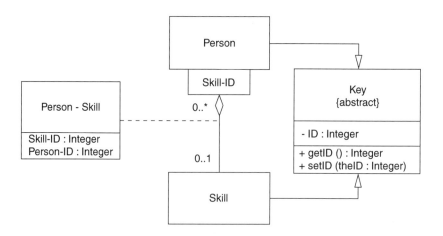

FIGURE 6.12.   People and skills in the Project Management System.

direction arrow, where the point of the triangle indicates the direction in which to read the name; but the arrow is purely descriptive and has no semantics associated with it. Qualifiers, aggregation, and composition may not be used with *n*-ary associations.

Figure 6.11 shows that a person will perform any number of activities, and an activity will be performed by any number of people. Also, a person will do any number of tasks, and each task will be done by a single person. The ternary association between people, activities, and tasks defines a person's utilization.

Association Classes

An association class is a class that represents an association; it defines the structural and behavioral features of the association. An association class is depicted as a class rectangle attached by a dashed line to its association path in a binary association, or to its association diamond in an *n*-ary association. The name in the class symbol and the name attached to the association are redundant and should be the same. Only one name need appear, and association names are optional.

Figure 6.8 shows a "Person–Skill" association class for the binary association between the Person class and the Skill class. Figure 6.11 shows a Utilization association class for the ternary Utilization association between the Person, Activity, and Task classes.

Association Ends

An association end is an end of an association connected to a classifier. The syntax for labeling an association end is "<<stereotype>> multiplicity visibility rolename: interface-specifier {property}", where—

- The visibility is optional and specifies the accessibility of the classifier at the association end by associated classifiers. There is no default visibility.
- The rolename is optional and specifies how the classifier participates in the association, the "face" it projects in the relationship. A role is a named specific behavior of a classifier participating in a particular context. A visibility symbol may be attached in front of a rolename to specify the visibility of the association traversing in the direction toward the rolename. Package visibility indicates that elements in the same package or nested subpackages to any level may reference the rolename. This type of role is known as a static role.
- The interface-specifier is optional and specifies the behavior expected of the classifier by other classifiers that participate in the association, that is, a classifier's responsibilities. The interface-specifier is depicted as a comma-separated list of interface specifiers. If no inter-

face specifiers are indicated, full access to the classifier is permitted. An interface-specifier may use interface and type names. The colon is omitted if no interface-specifier is used.

- The multiplicity is optional and specifies how many instances of the classifier may participate in the association when the associated classifiers are fixed. The multiplicity is depicted as a comma-separated sequence of integer intervals, including literal integer values. Closed ranges are depicted as "lower-bound .. upper-bound" and a single asterisk is used to denote an unlimited range. Both the lower-bound and upper-bound ought to be specified in order to indicate that they have both been considered. There is no default multiplicity for association ends; it is simply undefined.
- The stereotype or list of stereotypes and property is optional.

When multiple adornments are used on an association end, they are presented in the following order, from the end of the path attached to the classifier toward the opposite association end: qualifier, aggregation or composition symbol, and navigation arrow.

An association's rolenames should be specified because they sometimes convey more information than the name of the association alone. When rolenames are difficult to identify, consider why the association exists. Multiple associations between the same classifiers should be justified by the roles the classifiers play in relation to one another in the different associations. Rolenames are critical for self-referential or reflexive associations, associations between the same classifier, and to describe the purpose of the association.

Navigation may be used to indicate that the classifier is identifiable and referenceable from associated classifiers. Navigation is depicted as an arrow pointing at the classifier to indicate that navigation is supported toward the classifier attached to the arrow; otherwise the association is assumed to be bi-directional and navigable in all directions. When depicting bi-directional navigability, no navigation arrows are used; it is not the case that two arrows are used. There may not exist a navigable association from an interface, but there may exist a navigable association to an interface. Navigation provides insight into the access paths through the various classifiers from both an architectural and database perspective: that is, from an architectural perspective, what elements depend on other elements, and from a database perspective, what database relations may be traversed between database tables.

A list of attributes of the association, called a qualifier, may be used to partition the set of instances associated with an instance across an association. A qualifier is depicted as a small rectangle attached to the source end of an association. Instances of the source classifier, together with values for the qualifier attributes, uniquely select a partition from the set of target classifier instances on the other end of the association. Qualifier attributes have the same notation as classifier attributes, but no initial values and must be attributes of the association or target classifier. They are used to reduce the effective multiplicity of an association. That is, if the multiplicity of a classifier is more than one, a qualifier specifies a set of attributes and values that will return a subset of the instances on the other end of the association. A "0..1" indicates that a unique qualifier value may or may not select a target instance, "1" indicates that a unique qualifier value will select a unique target instance, and "*" means that a unique qualifier value will select a subset of the target instances similar to an index or key. Both the lower-bound and upper-bound ought to be specified in order to indicate that they have both been considered. Qualifier attributes must have a multiplicity of 1.

Figure 6.12 shows that a person with a Skill-ID attribute will either have that skill or not; as both people and skills are identifiable via the Key class that is abstract and cannot be instantiated on its own.

There are various stereotype keywords and property keywords that are usable with association ends. The default "unordered" property keyword denotes that links to the corresponding classifier form an unordered set when the multiplicity is greater than one. The "ordered" property keyword denotes that links to the corresponding classifier form an ordered set when the multiplicity is greater than one. The default "changeable" property keyword denotes that links to the corresponding classifier may be created or destroyed without restriction. The "frozen" property keyword denotes that links to the corresponding classifier may not be created or destroyed once instances at the opposite ends have been created and initialized. The "addOnly" property keyword denotes that links to the corresponding classifier may only be created once instances at the opposite ends have been created and initialized if the multiplicity is not fixed, but may not be deleted or moved.

An association end, link end, or association role end may be stereotyped with the "association" keyword to denote that the corresponding or attached element is visible via an actual association. An association end, link end, or association role end may be stereotyped with the "global" keyword to denote that the corresponding or attached element is visible because it is in a global scope, defined and accessible by any element. An association end, link end, or association role end may be stereotyped with the "local" keyword to denote that the corresponding or attached element is visible because it is in a local scope, defined and accessible within this context. An association end, link end, or association role end may be stereotyped with the "parameter" keyword to denote that the corresponding or attached element is visible because it is parameter, defined and passed into this context. An association end, link end, or association role end may be stereotyped with the "self" keyword to denote that the corresponding or attached element is visible because it is the element under discussion.

Aggregation Associations

An aggregation association between classifiers indicates a whole-part relationship between an aggregate, the whole, and its parts. At most only one end of a binary association may be an aggregate, and parts may be included in several aggregates. Likewise, a part cannot own its whole; that is, there cannot be any cycles among whole and part instances. An aggregation association is often called a "has-a" relationship because the whole has its parts, and may be read as a "has-a" (for instances) or "has-a-kind-of" (for classifiers). An aggregation association is depicted using a hollow diamond attached to the end of the path connected to the classifier that is the aggregate.

Figure 6.8, via aggregation associations, shows that a team has zero or more people, and a person may belong only to one team; and a person has zero or more skills, and multiple people may have the same skill.

Composition Associations

A composition association, also called composite aggregation, between classifiers is an aggregation association where the part may belong to at most one whole, called strong ownership, and the whole is responsible for destroying its parts when the whole is destroyed, called coincident lifetime. The whole is responsible for the life of the part. At most only one end of a binary association may be a composite. It propagates its dynamic semantics to its parts as if the parts are subordinate or are asymmetrically related to the whole, including when it is copied or destroyed. A composition association is often called a "contains-a" (for instances) or "contains-a-kind-of" (for classifiers) relationship because the whole contains its parts, and may be read as a "contains-a" (for instances) or "contains-a-kind-of" (for classifiers). A composition association is depicted using a filled diamond attached to the end of the path connected to the classifier that is the composite.

Alternately, composition may be depicted by graphically nesting elements. A nested element's multiplicity may be depicted in its upper right corner, and its rolename may be indicated in front of it its classifier name followed by a colon. Attributes are, in effect, composition relationships between a classifier and the classifiers of its attributes. This notation may be used for classes and objects, but on object diagrams, multiplicity is not shown and rolenames are shown on the links rather than in the rectangle symbols. A relationship drawn within the border of a composite is considered to be part of the composition such that instances of the relationship are within the same composite instance. A relationship drawn such that it breaks the boarder of the composite is not considered to be part of the composition such that instances of the relationship may be from the same or different composite instances.

A composition association should be used rather than an aggregation association when there is strong interdependence between the aggregate and the parts; that is, when the aggregate is incomplete without its parts and the aggregate is responsible for the lifetimes of its parts. The aggregate is known as a composite within a composition association.

Figure 6.9, via composition associations, shows that a project contains zero or more activities, an activity may belong only to one project contains zero or more tasks, and multiple tasks may belong only to one activity. Figure 6.10 demonstrates composition associations using graphical nesting for Figure 6.9.

A composite is responsible for the creation and destruction of its parts: if a composite is destroyed, it must destroy all of its parts. A composite may remove a part and give it to another composite, which then assumes responsibility for the part. When multiplicity on the composite end of an association is "0..1", the composite may remove the part and the part may assume responsibility for itself; otherwise it may not exist apart from a composite. Shareable aggregation denotes weak ownership where a part may be included in several aggregates, and the semantics of a shareable aggregation does not imply deletion of the parts when an aggregate referencing it is deleted.

Generalizations

A generalization is a taxonomic relationship between a more general element and a more specific element, indicating that the more specific element inherits or receives the structural features (attributes and relationships) and behavioral features (operations and methods) of the more general element. It may add its own more specialized structural and behavioral features and may override inherited features, implementations, or methods while maintaining the specifications or operations of the behavior provided by the more general element. It is fully consistent with the more general element, and instances of the more specific element may be substituted for instances of the more general element. Use generalizations when an element defines a default operation and method, and use interfaces when there is a default operation signature, but no default method. Generalizable elements include classifiers, associations, packages, models, subsystems, and collaborations. A generalization relationship is often called an "is-a-kind-of" relationship because the more specific element is a specialized type of the more general element, and may be read as an "is-a-kind-of". A generalization relationship is depicted as a solid-line path from the more specific element to the more general element, with a large hollow triangle at the end of the path connected to the more general element.

The more general element and the more specific element must be consistent with one another; that is, they must be of the same type of modeling element (types, interfaces, implementation classes, an so forth). The more general element is called the parent, supertype, superclass, or generalization (traversing the relationship toward the parent) and the more specific element is called the child, subtype, subclass, or specialization (traversing the relationship toward the child). Ancestors are non-immediate parents, and descendants are non-immediate children.

Subtyping involves using a generalization relationship between types. Subtyping indicates that the child is a subtype of its ancestors, it inherits the structure and behavior (operations and no methods) of its ancestors, and instances of the child may be substituted for instances of the parent. Subtyping supports polymorphism and allows clients of the parent to be more general and reusable by shielding them from changes in the children. Subclassing involves using a generalization relationship between classes. Subclassing indicates that the child is a subclass of its ancestors, it inherits the structure and behavior (operations and methods) of its ancestors, but the child is not explicitly a type of its ancestors, but is implicitly a type of its ancestors. Subclassing supports reusing implementations while realization relationships with interfaces supports reusing specifications. Changes to a parent class imply changes to its children. The objective in applying generalization relationship, subtyping and subclassing, is to generalize common features and specialize noncommon features.

A full descriptor is the full description of an instance; it is required to create the instance. A segment is a model element that is incrementally combined using generalization relationships to produce a full descriptor. Inheritance is the sharing mechanisms through which more specific elements acquire the characteristics of more general elements. Single inheritance involves only a single parent, and multiple inheritance involves at least two or more parents. The topmost appearance of an operation within a generalization hierarchy determines the signature for the operation; and descendant may override ancestor methods but not modify the operation specification. For classifiers, only public and protected features are inherited; private features are not inherited. For packages, only public or protected content is inherited, private content is not inherited. An ellipsis (. . .) may be depicted in place of a child to indicate that additional children in the model exist but are not shown.

A method realizing an operation or overriding an inherited operation has the same signature (name, types and parameters, and return type) as the operation and a body implementing the specification of the operation. Methods in descendants override and replace methods inherited from ancestors. The "abstract" property keyword denotes that the operation is not implemented and has no method, and an operation must be supplied by a descendant of the classifier or is inherited by an ancestor. The "leaf" property keyword denotes that the operation may not be overridden by a descendant of the classifier; otherwise, it may be overridden. The "root" property keyword denotes that the classifier must not inherit a declaration of the same operation; otherwise, a declaration of the same operation may be inherited. A classifier may not modify an inherited operation specification. When an operation is invoked on an object via a message sent to the object, the most specific or specialized method is invoked. This is called polymorphism, where the classifiers share an operation but provide their own unique methods, and when a message is received by an object, the method invoked is dependent on the classifier of the object.

Instances of a parent class may be divided into disjoint sets or partitions based on some discriminator. A discriminator may be used to indicate the basis for the partitioning of the parent into the children. Each partition represents an orthogonal dimension of specialization of the parent. The discriminator is the name of the partition of the children of the parent. The discriminator is shown as a text label near the generalization triangle. It may be followed by a colon and a powertype used to discriminate or partition the children. The subclasses are instances of the powertype. A classifier may be stereotyped with the "powertype" keyword to denote that the element is used as a discriminator in a generalization relationship.

Figure 6.8 shows that a person may be salaried or hourly based on their method of compensation; however, they cannot be both, as indicated using the "disjoint" property keyword on the generalization relationship. Note how the discriminator is used to establish this partitioning. Figure 6.9 shows that a project, activities, and tasks are all efforts of work, subclasses of the Work Effort class.

There are various stereotype keywords and property keywords that are usable with generalizations. The "implementation" stereotype keyword denotes that the child inherits the implementations of the parent, including attributes, operations, and methods, but does not make their interfaces public. The child does not guarantee to support the inherited features, thereby violating substitutability. This is often called private inheritance or implementation inheritance. The "overlapping" property keyword denotes that there may exist instances that instantiate two or more of the children. The "disjoint" property keyword denotes that there may not exist an instance that instantiates more than one of the children. The "complete" property keyword denotes that all children are specified.

The "incomplete" property keyword denotes that not all children are specified.

A generalizable element may use the "abstract" property keyword to denote that the elements may not have any instances, the "root" property keyword to denote that the element does not have any ancestors, and the "leaf" property keyword to denote that the element may not have any descendants. Otherwise, the generalizable element is considered concrete and may have instances.

Dependencies

A dependency is a non-structural relationship between elements, indicating that one or more client elements are dependent on and require the presence of one or more other supplier elements where clients may be affected by a change to the suppliers. A dependency is more temporary in comparison to an association. A dependency is often called a "uses" relationship because the client element uses the supplier element, and may be read as a "uses".

A dependency is depicted as a dashed arrow from the dependent client element to the independent supplier element, and it may also be named. Note that a dependency may be traversed in either direction, and the direction of the arrow does not limit traversal but only indicates the dependent and independent elements. A dependency may exist for a set of elements, depicted as one or more arrows with their tails on the clients connected to the tails of one or more arrows with their heads on the suppliers, where a small dot can be placed on the junction and a note should be attached to the junction point describing the dependency. A dependency may be stereotyped with various keywords to indicate the exact nature of the dependency, but this is often evident from the context in which the dependency is used.

A dependency stereotyped with the "instanceOf" keyword denotes that the source is an instance and that the target is a classifier.

A binding dependency stereotyped with the "bind" keyword denotes that the source model element is generated from the target template model element. A template element is not directly usable because it has unbound parameters, and it must be bound to actual values before it is used. The keyword is followed by a comma-separated list of actual parameters enclosed in parentheses. Alternatively, the source model element may use the target model element name directly within the source definition followed by a comma-separated list of actual parameters enclosed in greater-than and less-than symbols.

A permission dependency stereotyped with the "friend" keyword denotes that the source operation, class, or package may access the target operation, class, or package in a different package regardless of the target's declared visibility. It extends the visibility of the target to the source.

A permission dependency stereotyped with the "use" keyword denotes that the contents of the source package use the contents of the target package. The keyword is often suppressed because the meaning is evident form the context in which the dependency is used. The "import" and "access" keywords provide a more specific meaning. A permission dependency stereotyped with the "import" keyword denotes that the public contents of the target package are imported into the source package and may be directly accessed by name. An imported element may be assigned an alias to avoid name conflicts with other names in the source package and by default becomes private to the importing package, but may be assigned another visibility. A permission dependency stereotyped with the "access" keyword denotes that the public contents of the target package are accessible by the contents of the source package using pathnames.

The number of dependencies between packages impacts an entity's tolerance to change. The lower the number of dependencies between packages, the higher the cohesion of the contents of the packages and the lower the coupling between the packages. Furthermore, cross-dependent packages are less resilient because if either package changes, the other is impacted. A navigable association between a client and supplier that reside in different packages require that the package in which the client resides is dependent on the package in which the supplier resides. A package should only depend on other packages, representing specification perspective dependencies that are not propagated into the implementation perspective. A package or subsystem should only depend on the interfaces of subsystems not the subsystems themselves, representing specification perspective dependencies that also exist in the implementation perspective. This allows the actual subsystem to be a replaceable element. If multiple subsystems depend on a common set of elements, the elements may be placed into a package that is imported into the subsystems. Mandatory elements should not depend on optional elements because there is no guarantee they will be available.

An abstraction dependency stereotyped with the "refine" keyword denotes a historical or derivation connection between two elements with a mapping between them where the source is a fuller specification of the target. A description of the formal and computable mapping may be attached to the dependency in a note. An abstraction dependency stereotyped with the "realize" keyword denotes an implementation connection between two elements with a mapping between them where the source element supports the operations and signals of the target specification element. A description of the formal and possibly computable mapping may be attached to the dependency in a note. An abstraction dependency stereotyped with the "trace" keyword denotes a historical connection between two elements that represent the same concept at different levels of meaning. A description of the informal and rarely computable mapping may be attached to the dependency in a note. An abstraction dependency stereotyped with the "derive" keyword denotes a derivation connection between two elements with a mapping between them where the source may be computed from the target. A derived attribute is one that can be computed from other elements; it is shown by placing a slash (/) in front of the name of the element or used as a property keyword with a description of how it is derived. A description of the computation may be attached to the dependency or attribute in a note.

A flow relationship stereotyped with the "become" keyword denotes that the source element becomes the target element at a different point in time and space with possibly new values, states, and roles. A flow relationship stereotyped with the "copy" keyword denotes that the target element is a copy of the source element. The source and target are different instances, each with the same values, state, roles, and distinct identity.

A usage dependency stereotyped with the "call" keyword denotes that the source class or operation invokes the target class or operation. A usage dependency stereotyped with the "create" keyword denotes that the source classifier creates instance of the target classifier. A usage dependency stereotyped with the "instantiate" keyword denotes that operations on the source classifier create instances of the target classifier. A usage dependency stereotyped with the "send" keyword denotes that the source operation or classifier sends the target signal to some unspecified target. A signal is an asynchronous message or stimulus. A classifier may be stereotyped with the "signal" keyword to denote that the element is an asynchronous message that may be received by a classifier, in which case its parameters are depicted in the attributes compartment, and its access operations are depicted in the operations compartment. Signal classes may be used in generalization relationship where an occurrence of a subevent triggers any transition that depends on the event or any of its ancestors.

A use-case extend relationship stereotyped with the "extend" keyword denotes that the source use case may extend the target use case. A use-case include relationship stereotyped with the "include" keyword denotes that the source includes the target use case.

A dependency stereotyped with the "powertype" keyword denotes that the target is the powertype of the source generalizations. This is the type of the attributes or rolenames used as a discriminator in the generalization. Its values enumerate the partitions for the generalization.

A dependency stereotyped with the "modelLibrary" keyword denotes that the source package that is stereotyped as a profile shares the model elements in the target package that is not stereotyped as a profile. A dependency stereotyped with the "appliedProfile" keyword denotes that the target package that is stereotyped as a profile applies transitively to the model elements in the source package.

Figure 6.8 shows that a team may have one manager, and a single person may play the role of a manager for only a single team; furthermore, the person must be a member of the team as indicated using the "subset" property keyword on the dependency between this relationship and the aggregation relationship between the Team class and the Person class.

Realizations

A realization relationship between a specification element and a realization element indicating that the realization element provides an implementation for the specification element. This is often called interface inheritance. A realization relationship is often called an "implements" relationship because the realization element implements the specification element, and may be read as a "implements". A realization relationship is depicted using a dependency stereotyped with the "realize" keyword drawn from the implementing source element to the specifying target element or a dashed line with a solid triangle arrowhead attached to the specifying target element. When the specifying element is an interface that is depicted as a small circle with the name of the interface placed near the symbol, the realization relationship is depicted as a solid line from the implementing element to the interface. The realizing element is said to realize or implement the specifying element. Any element may be used as a specification or realization element because a realization relationship indicates conformance of behavior, where the client supports at least all of the operations defined in the supplier without the necessity to support any structural features of the supplier (attributes and associations).

6.2.   Object Diagrams

An object diagram depicts the static structure of an entity at a particular time using classifier instances and relationship instances. An entity is a classifier, for example, a system, subsystem, or class.

6.2.1.   CLASSIFIER INSTANCES

A classifier instance is a specific concept with a unique identity, a set of operations that apply to it, and a state. Objects, use-case instances, data values, component instances, node instances, and subsystem instances are specific types of classifier instances. The stereotype or list of stereotypes and properties of a classifier instance's classifier apply to the classifier instance.

Objects

An object is an instance of a class. A class defines the structural and behavioral characteristics of its objects. An object defines values for its structural features, attribute values and specific relationships or links, and shares the behavioral features of its class. The state of an object is defined by the values of the object's structural features, what an object knows. The behavior of an object is defined by the behavior of its class, what an object can do. The most crucial aspect of an object is that it has its own identity. No two objects are the same, even if they have the same values for their structural features.

An object is depicted as a solid-outline rectangle with two standard compartments separated by horizontal lines. The top name compartment is required and contains the object name followed by a colon followed by a comma-separated list of the object's class names fully underlined. The object name and its class names are optional and the colon is only present if the object's classes are specified; the second list compartment is optional and contains a list of attributes and their values. It is a common convention to name objects as "aX", "anX", "theX", or some other general form of a name where X is the name of the classifier of the object, especially for simple examples. Other compartments may be used as necessary, each compartment need only show what is relevant to the diagram, and optional compartments may be suppressed.

Figure 6.13 is derived from Figure 6.11, but focuses on Project, Activity, and Task objects. Figure 6.13 shows that Nora manages Phillip, Jack, Jill, Andy, and Si, who are all people. The Scope and Requirements activity involves the Scope and Requirements tasks; the Analysis and Design activity involves the Analysis and Design tasks; the Implementation activity involves the Code, Test, and Deploy tasks. The Scope and Requirements activity is the predecessor to the Analysis and Design activity, and the Analysis and Design activity is the predecessor to the Implementation activity. The Requirements task is the predecessor to the Scope task. The Design task is the successor to the Analysis task. The Code, Test, and Deploy tasks are successively related. Phillip performs the whole Scope and Requirements activity by doing all of its tasks. Jack and Jill perform the Analysis and Design activity by splitting tasks. Andy and Si perform the Implementation activity, but Si does all of is tasks and Andy does not do any tasks. Notice how the Implementation activity is shown as a composite object.

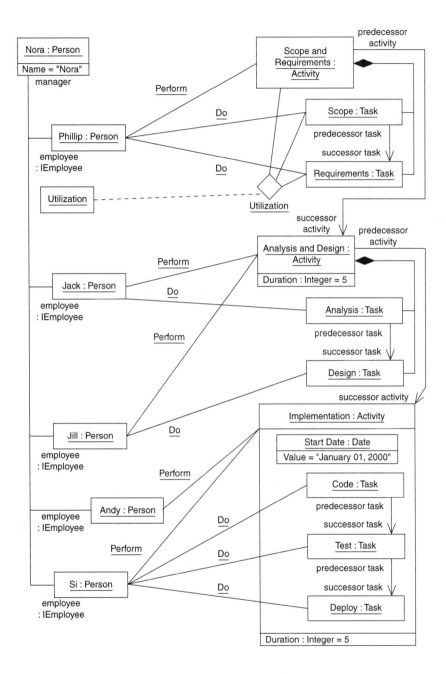

FIGURE 6.13. People, activity, and task instances in the Project Management System.

Classes may be added and detached from an object, in which case, the features of the object dynamically change. An object may have or conform to any number of types since a type is a role that an object may adopt and play, and then abandon. An object may have only one implementation class since an implementation class specifies the physical implementation of the object.

To show the presence of an object in a particular state of its class, follow the name of the object with a comma-separated list of the object's state names enclosed within square brackets. A multiobject is a collection of objects. A multiobject is depicted as two rectangles in which the top rectangle is shifted slightly vertically and horizontally to suggest a stack of rectangles. Multiobjects are also used on class diagrams as multiobject classes using the class notation.

A classifier may be stereotyped with the "process" keyword to denote that the classifier is active and has a heavy-weight flow of control; it is a physical construct that occupies a memory or address space composed of multiple threads, similar to a program in memory. A classifier may be stereotyped with the "thread" keyword to denote that the classifier is active and has a light-weight flow of control; it is a path of execution or control that executes within a memory space, similar to an independent task concurrently executing with other tasks in memory. A process or thread may have active objects and is an implementation distinction. An active class or object owns a thread of control and may initiate control activity. An active element is shown as a rectangle with a heavy border. Alternatively, the property keyword "active" may also be used to indicate an active element. A passive element does not initiate control, but it may communicate with other objects in the course of processing a request that it has received. An active element passes control to a passive element, thus making the passive element become active such that it can handle the request.

Attribute Values

An attribute value is a value for an attribute of an instance. An attribute value is shown as a text string in the second compartment of the object rectangle.

The syntax for an attribute value is "name [index] : type = value", where—

- The index is optional and specifies the instance of the attribute. The index is depicted as a literal integer value. The square brackets are omitted if no index is specified and the index is assumed one.
- The type is optional and specifies the type of the attribute which must match its classifier definition. The colon is omitted if no type is specified.

- The value specifies the value of the attribute.
- An attribute shown for an object may be classifier-scoped or instance-scoped based on the attribute definition.

6.2.2. RELATIONSHIP INSTANCES

A relationship instance is a specific connection among specific concepts. Links are specific types of relationship instances. The stereotype or list of stereotypes and properties of a relationship instance's relationship apply to the relationship instance.

Links

A link is an instance of an association. A link end, similar to an association end, is an endpoint of a link, which connects the link to an instance. A binary link, similar to a binary association, involves two instances, and an *n*-ary link, similar to an *n*-ary association, involves three or more instances. A link object, similar to an association object, is an object pertaining to the link. If a link's association has a related association class, the link has a corresponding link object.

Figure 6.14 is similar to Figure 6.12, but focuses on Person and Skill objects. Figure 6.14 shows that Andy and Phillip can do analysis, but Nora cannot.

A link may have its association name depicted near the path fully underlined, but links do not have instance names as they take their identity from the instances that they relate.

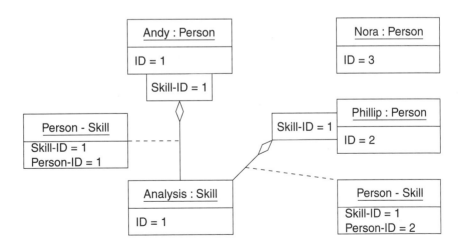

FIGURE 6.14.   People and skill instances in the Project Management System.

Binary Links

A binary link between two instances indicates a structural relationship between the instances. A binary link is depicted as an arc or a solid path made of a connected series of line segments connecting the instances.

N-ary Links

An *n*-ary link between three or more instances indicates a structural relationship between the instances. An *n*-ary link is depicted as a large diamond with an arc or a solid path made of a connected series of line segments from the diamond to each participating instance. Qualifiers, aggregation, and composition may not be used with *n*-ary links.

Link Objects

A link object is an object that represents a link; it defines the values for its structural features and shares the behavioral features of its association class. A link object is depicted as an object rectangle attached by a dashed line to its link path in a binary link, or to its link diamond in an *n*-ary link. The name in the object symbol and the name attached to the link are redundant and should be the same, only one name need appear, and link names are optional. Classes may be added and detached from a link, in which case, the features of the link dynamically change; however, one of the classes must always be an association class.

Link Ends

A link end is an end of a link connected to a instance. Visibility, role-names, interface specifiers, navigation, aggregation, composition, and values for qualifiers may be shown for links, but generalization relationships and multiplicity are not shown. When multiple adornments are used on a link end, they are presented in the following order, from the end of the path attached to the instance toward the opposite link end: qualifier values, aggregation or composition symbol, and navigation arrow.

6.3. Applying Class and Object Diagrams

When modeling the specification perspective of a construct (system, subsystem, or class) and how the construct will satisfy its requirements, what elements and their relationships collaborate to constitute the construct, and how these elements interact to provide functionality to its users, consider the guidelines above and herein which ought to be applied within a use-case-driven, architecture-centric, iterative and incremental, and risk-confronting effort that is object oriented and component based. Successive iterations evolve, elaborate, and refine the work of previous iterations with more detail. Steps need not be sequential, but may be executed in parallel, where multiple efforts regarding the same system are carried out concurrently.

Within the specification perspective of the roadmap, specification elements include use cases, interfaces, and operations; realization elements include subsystems, classes, and collaborations; and construct elements include any elements that may constitute the construct or system, including subsystems, packages, and classes which evolve from proposed candidate elements to accepted actual elements. Properties capture constraints and characteristics of elements.

Every constituent of the roadmap is optional and should only be applied if it adds value to the body of knowledge concerning the construct and facilitates achieving the overall objectives of the effort within the specific context of the effort. Those constituents of the roadmap that are applied constitute a roadmap instance. Reference the examples above and the Project Management System example used in Chapter 4 as the result of applying structural and behavioral modeling within the context of the roadmap.

Different workers should be leveraged throughout the specification perspective steps. An architect or technical leader is responsible for identifying, describing, and mapping between mechanisms. A system designer is responsible for using and incorporating mechanisms. An architect or technical leader often identifies construct elements, describes construct elements, identifies construct realization elements, distributes construct realization elements to construct elements, and unifies the construct specification. A system designer often describes construct realization elements using conceptual elements and describes construct realization elements using construct elements.

6.3.1. CONCEPTUAL ELEMENTS

Conceptual elements include boundary, control, and entity classes. A boundary class represents means of input or output through which to interact with actors; it is a user interface for interacting with human actors or a system or device protocol for interacting with non-human actors. A boundary class is depicted as a class stereotyped with the "boundary" keyword or an icon consisting of a circle with a vertical line connected to it via a horizontal line on its left side. A control class represents processing by which input is processed into output; it is a an interaction, transaction, or process that is not done by the class, but coordinated and managed by the class in delegating responsibility for the processing to other elements. A control class is depicted as a class stereotyped with the "control" keyword or an icon consisting of a circle with a small arrow pointing counterclockwise attached at the top of the circle. An entity class represents passive data and information that is input, processed, and output. Entity classes may be derived from the context process discipline and its resulting business, context, or domain model. An entity class is depicted as a class stereotyped with the "entity" keyword or an icon consisting of a circle with a small horizontal line attached at the bottom of the circle.

The use of conceptual elements establishes a conceptual solution, an abstract solution void of real constraints. The conceptual solution evolves into an actual system via the evaluation of candidate solutions that integrate the elements of the conceptual solution. A candidate solution is a proposed solution whose elements are known as candidate elements, and an actual solution is a proposed solution that has been justified via the conceptual solution, with consideration of real constraints, and whose elements are known as actual elements.

6.3.2. Mechanisms

Mechanisms are specific patterns, that is, solutions to problems within a given context, that facilitate solving the problem. For example, mechanisms include means for error detection and handling, security management, interfacing with legacy systems, information exchange, transaction management, resource management, communication and distribution, persistence, and other capabilities. A conceptual mechanism is an implementation independent solution. A logical mechanism, a refinement of a conceptual mechanism, is a solution that assumes some implementation environment detail, but not a specific implementation. A physical mechanism, a refinement of a logical mechanism, is a specific solution implementation.

Figure 6.15 shows conceptually how candidate, conceptual, and actual elements are related and how conceptual, logical, and physical mechanisms are related. The incorporation of conceptual elements into candidate elements results in the actual elements of the construct.

6.3.3. The Construct

This section elaborates steps 1 through 3 concerning construct specification of the Detailed and Notational Roadmap section of Chapter 4. Focus on candidate elements and realization elements.

Candidate Elements

To identify construct elements, identify candidate elements. Review the specification elements and the construct, and identify candidate logical

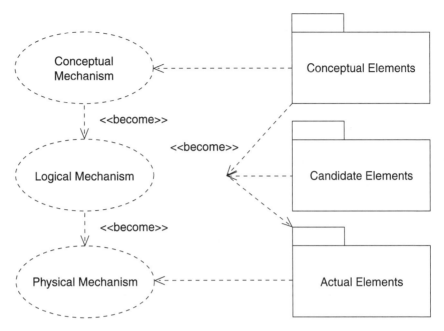

FIGURE 6.15.   Candidate, conceptual, and actual elements with conceptual, logical, and
physical mechanisms.

structural "chunks," or units, by speculatively partitioning and layering
the construct. "Chunks," or units, include any elements that may constitute the construct, including subsystems, packages, and classes. The
term "chunk" (or "unit") is purposely used to emphasize that this involves
relying on experience, brainstorming, contemplating, pondering, and so
forth; furthermore, consider using a generic pattern such as the Four
Layer Architecture to seed the specification of the construct. Progressively apply "use" dependency relationships between "chunks," or units,
speculatively to relate the candidate elements. Often, practitioners aren't
sure what criteria to use as the basis for partitioning and layering. Virtually any criteria may be used; however, it should be stable so as to
provide a solid foundation. For example, if the problem domain is stable,
domain-related criteria and abstractions are viable; if the problem domain is unstable and the solution domain is more stable, technology-
related criteria and abstractions are viable. This does not imply and
should not be interpreted as retrofitting a solution to a problem, but
erecting a solution atop of a stable foundation. Actors, use cases, and
technology-based criteria are commonly used. Often, practitioners don't
spend any time identifying candidate elements or relationships and presume they are immediately identifying actual elements and relationships; however, this may be problematic, depending on their presump-

tions, and is highly dependent on their experience. Often, practitioners spend too much time identifying candidate elements or relationships, and because so much time and effort is invested in identifying these elements, they often become regarded as actual elements and relationships, which again is problematic, depending on the basis used for identifying candidate elements. Focus on identifying packages and their dependencies. Even though other types of candidate elements are possible, by focusing on packages, these "chunks," or units, form a "sketch" and remain less formal than subsystems and classes as they are only candidate elements, and the expended effort to formalize them into subsystems and classes may be wasted. For the construct, model the structural view using a class diagram (subsystems, packages, classes, and relationships) to establish placeholders for information about the construct elements. Figure 6.16 shows conceptually the structural view of the construct.

Identify conceptual mechanisms. This involves identifying or recognizing, and naming, a need for a capability. Review the specification elements and the construct, and identify what common problems require common solutions. Use conceptual mechanisms as placeholders for complex behaviors and technologies required to support the specification elements while avoiding being hindered by describing the behaviors and technologies.

To describe construct elements, for each candidate element, capture the candidate element's properties based on the construct's properties to ensure traceability between the construct and the candidate element. This involves propagating any pertinent constraints and characteristics from the construct to the candidate elements. A candidate element's properties include its responsibilities and characteristics. Responsibili-

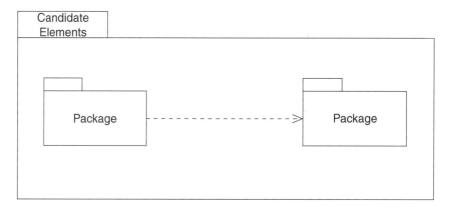

FIGURE 6.16.   Construct candidate elements.

ties define the purposes, obligations, or the rationale for the candidate element's existence given the context of the candidate element and how the candidate element addresses the needs, goals, and objectives of other candidate elements that depend on it. Characteristics include any other relevant information pertaining to the candidate element. These characteristics include any relevant non-functional properties due to the context of the candidate element.

Describe conceptual mechanisms. This involves capturing any pertinent constraints and characteristics of the conceptual mechanisms. A conceptual mechanism's properties include any functional and non-functional properties that are relevant to the mechanism. For each conceptual mechanism, focus on capturing the requirements of the mechanism.

Realization Elements

To identify construct realization elements, consider the specification elements. For each specification element, consider how it is realized by elements that constitute the construct. A whole use case, part of a use case or a behavior sequence, whole interface, part of an interface or an interface operation, or a construct operation may be realized by a single element, multiple non-collaborating and non-interacting elements, or multiple collaborating and interacting elements. Review the construct's actual elements to determine if there already exists an actual element that may be assigned responsibility for realizing the specification element; however, if there is no obvious element, avoid prematurely assigning responsibility to an actual element, but identify a collaboration responsible for realizing the specification element. Focus on identifying collaborations. Even though other types of elements may realize the specification element, if collaborations remain the focus, responsibility for the realization of the specification element is not prematurely assigned to an actual element. For the construct, model the structural view using a class diagram (subsystems, classes, and collaborations) to establish placeholders for information about the realizations of the specification element. Figure 6.17 shows conceptually the realization element for a specification element.

6.3.4. *ANALYSIS*

This section elaborates step 4 concerning construct specification of the Detailed and Notational Roadmap section of Chapter 4. Focus on conceptual elements and mechanisms.

To describe construct realization elements, focus on effectively analyzing and understanding construct specification elements, and what the

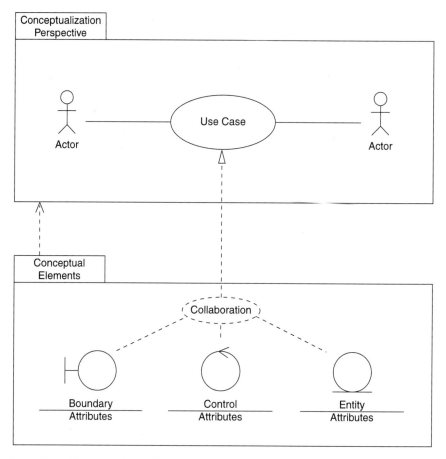

FIGURE 6.17.   The conceptualization perspective and conceptual elements.

construct specification elements involve, by addressing the question of what the construct should do.

Conceptual Elements

Focus on realization element properties, conceptual elements, and conceptual element properties.

Realization Element Properties

For each realization element, capture the realization element's properties based on its specification element's properties to ensure traceability between the specification element and the realization element. This involves propagating any pertinent constraints and characteristics from the specification element to the realization element. A realization element's properties include its responsibilities and characteristics. Responsibilities define the purposes, obligations, or the rationale for the realization element's existence given the context of the realization element and how the realization element addresses the needs, goals, and objectives of other realization elements that depend on it. Characteristics include any other relevant information pertaining to the realization element. These characteristics include any relevant non-functional properties due to the context of the realization element.

Conceptual Elements

For each realization element, identify conceptual elements and review its associated specification element description (which was captured in the conceptualization perspective), identifying conceptual elements that participate in realizing the specification element. For each specification element, focus on the normal behavior sequence, then focus on the variant or alternative behavior sequences until no new conceptual elements are identified. For every use-case actor-pair, identify one or more boundary classes responsible for facilitating communication between the construct and the actor. For boundary classes associated with actors who are humans, these classes may be named with a Form suffix as in LoginForm or another such suffix. For boundary classes associated with actors who are systems, these classes may be named with a System suffix as in DatabaseSystem or another such suffix. For every use-case or behavior sequence, identify one or more control classes responsible for facilitating the performance of the use-case or behavior sequence. For every use-case or behavior sequence, identify zero or more entity classes responsible for maintaining information used in the performance of the use-case or behavior sequence. The use of suffixes helps communicate the purpose of each class. Focus on identifying classes and their attributes. At the system level of abstraction, boundary classes evolve into system interfaces or operations of system interfaces; control classes evolve into active system parts, including subsystems and classes, which may initiate control activity; and entity classes evolve into passive system parts, including packages and classes, which do not initiate control activity on their own behalf, but may communicate with other elements in the course of processing a request that was received. At the subsystem level of abstraction, boundary classes evolve into subsystem interfaces or operations of subsystem interfaces; control classes evolve into active subsystem parts, including enclosed subsystems and classes; and entity classes evolve into passive subsystem parts, including packages and classes. At the class level of abstraction, boundary classes evolve into class operation specifications, control classes evolve into class operation implementations or methods, and entity classes evolve into class attributes. Progressively apply classifiers and relationships, using instances and object diagrams to explore and refine class diagrams. Figure 6.17 shows the conceptual elements for a realization element.

For each realization element, model the structural and behavioral views (conceptual elements, messages, and relationships) in order to describe the realization element. For each realization element, reconcile the structural and behavioral views in order to ensure that the description of the realization element is consistent as discussed in Chapter 7, which focuses on identifying associations and operations. Figure 6.18 shows conceptually that the behavioral view of a realization element is derived from the conceptual elements and the behavioral view of the description of a specification element. Actors are modeled in the behavioral view of a realization element in order to provide context for the realization element. Figure 6.19 shows conceptually that the structural view of a realization element is derived from the behavioral view of the realization element. Ensure that every exchanged message between a sender and receiver has an associated operation offered by the receiver and a navigable relationship from the sender to the receiver through which the message is communicated. Actors are not modeled in the structural view of a realization element, relationships between actors and other elements are not modeled in the structural view of a realization element, but operations due to the communication with the actors are modeled in the structural view of a realization element in order to capture the communication.

Conceptual Element Properties

For each conceptual element, capture the conceptual element's properties based on its realization element's properties to ensure traceability between the realization element and the conceptual element. This involves propagating any pertinent constraints and characteristics from the realization element to the conceptual elements. A conceptual element's properties include its responsibilities and characteristics. Responsibilities define the purposes, obligations, or rationale for the conceptual element's existence given the context of the conceptual element and how the conceptual element addresses the needs, goals, and objectives of other conceptual elements that depend on it. Characteristics include any other relevant information pertaining to the conceptual element. These characteristics include any relevant non-functional properties due to the context of the conceptual element.

Mechanisms

For each conceptual element, consider the conceptual element's use of conceptual mechanisms. This involves capturing any additional relevant

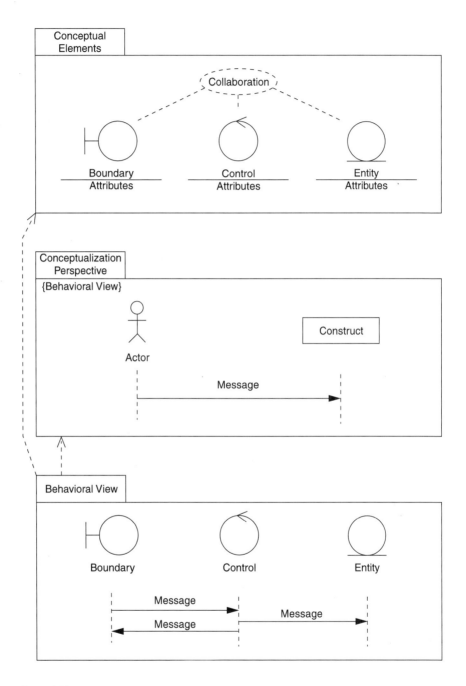

FIGURE 6.18.   Conceptual elements, the behavioral view of the description of the specification
element from the conceptualization perspective, and the behavioral view of the
realization element.

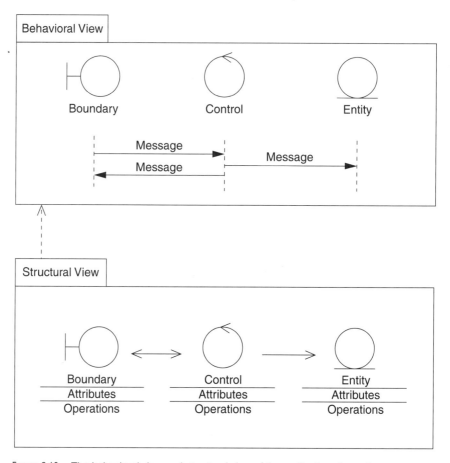

FIGURE 6.19.   The behavioral view and structural view of the realization element.

constraints and characteristics of the conceptual mechanisms by virtue of the use of the conceptual mechanisms.

6.3.5.   DESIGN

This section elaborates step 5 concerning construct specification of the Detailed and Notational Roadmap section of Chapter 4. Focus on actual elements and mechanisms.

To distribute construct realization elements to construct elements, focus on effectively designing and understanding construct realization element,—how the construct provides its services—by addressing the question of how the construct will do what it should do.

Actual Elements

Focus on conceptual, candidate, and actual elements and properties.

Conceptual, Candidate, and Actual Elements

Map conceptual elements to candidate elements in order to refine the candidate elements and identify actual elements. This involves balancing various issues. For each conceptual element, review the responsibilities and characteristics of the conceptual element; review the responsibilities and characteristics of the various candidate elements; and progressively identify, split, and merge conceptual elements and candidate elements to decrease the coupling and increase the cohesion of their responsibilities in order to map the conceptual elements into the candidate elements and identify actual elements. This involves identifying actual elements using the candidate elements and the conceptual elements by addressing the fundamental issues of complexity and change within the real constraints imposed by the context of the problem and solution—that is, balancing the functional and non-functional requirements to identify a set of actual elements that will sufficiently address the various criteria and issues.

Cohesion, Coupling, Complexity, and Change

Cohesion is a measure of relatedness, how parts of a whole are logically related to each other. The higher the cohesion of a collection of parts, the more likely that change and the impact of change will be localized to those parts within the whole. Coupling is a measure of dependence, the strength of the connections or dependencies between wholes, where each whole is a collection of parts. The looser the coupling among wholes, the more likely that change and the impact of change will be localized to each whole collection of parts and not ripple to effect other wholes. The fundamental forces of complexity and change intertwine and manifest themselves at two extremes, at one extreme, having non-highly cohesive elements that are tightly coupled, and at another extreme, having highly cohesive elements that are loosely coupled. Stability focuses on steadiness and consistency. Flexibility focuses on elasticity. Complexity may be regarded as a function of the number of elements, their relationships, and the degree of effort required to understand how they are combined spatially and temporally while considering their uniqueness and redundancy. Volatility may be regarded as how widespread and rampant change is across these elements and relationships. By looking at each individual element, the more volatility, the more instability. By looking at the conglomeration of all of the elements, we can see that stability is not the summation of the volatility of each individual element, but rather is a indication of how accommodating or resilient the whole is in the face of volatility, and how much volatility is necessary to require that the whole change. That is, if any or a minimal amount of volatility requires the whole to change, the whole is not stable; however, if only a significant amount of volatility would require the whole to change, the whole is more stable. Furthermore, the more change the whole can accommodate, the more stable it is because a significant amount of effort is required by the elements to impose change on the change. It is for this reason that adaptability is less desirable than evolution, because adapting involves reacting to change, but evolution involves reacting to change and learning to adapt to future change better. Likewise, this allows for the localization of risk. Finding the pivot point between the two extremes involves balancing the coupling and cohesion of the elements, their complexity, the impact of change, and other functional and non-functional criteria via mapping conceptual elements to candidate elements in order to refine the candidate elements and identify actual elements. To evolve readily, a construct ought to be simple, flexible, and dynamic, but not loose and chaotic nor rigid and stagnant.

The use of classes, types, packages, subsystems, interfaces, and dependencies is crucial for addressing these issues, particularly, the use of interfaces as seams or "points" within the construct at which the construct may be pulled part, extended by inserting other constructs, and generally reorganized. Interfaces define services and decouple clients using the services from suppliers providing the services such that clients may change without impacting suppliers and suppliers may change without impacting clients as long as clients and suppliers abide by the contract defined by the interface. Just as an extension point is a reference to one or more locations between two steps within a use case at which behavior maybe inserted, an interface is a reference to a service between clients and suppliers within an entity at which other clients and suppliers may be inserted. The number of dependencies between packages is an indication of the construct's tolerance for change. The lower the number of dependencies between packages, the higher the cohesion of the contents of the packages and the lower the coupling between the packages. Figure 6.20 shows conceptually that the actual elements of a construct are derived from the structural view of the realization element and the candidate elements.

Actual Elements

A conceptual element may remain a class because it is a well-defined abstraction, merge with other classes because they have similar responsibilities, split into multiple classes because it has dissimilar responsibilities, or become a package because it has more complex responsibili-

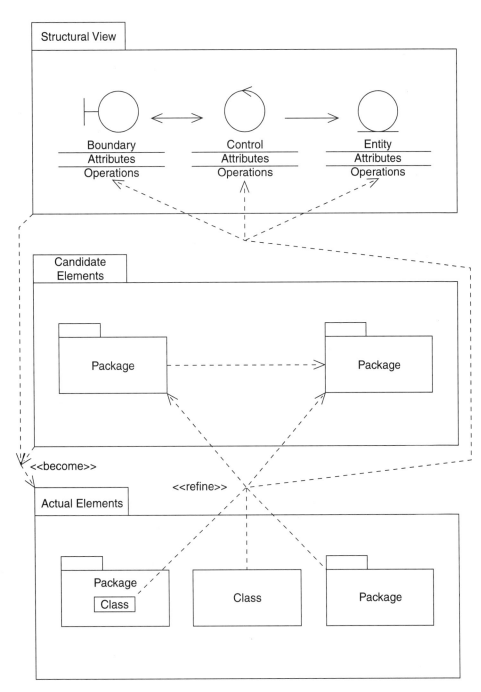

FIGURE 6.20.   The structural view of the realization element, construct candidate elements, and construct actual elements.

ties, part of a package, a subsystem, part of a subsystem, part of another class, or be removed and its responsibilities assigned to another element.

Figure 6.21 shows a class with a navigable association used by clients that becomes part of a package where the class and applicable operations must have public visibility within the package, and the class's clients depend on the package.

A candidate element may remain an element, merge with other similar elements, split into multiple dissimilar elements, become part of another element, or be removed. Progressively identify, split, and merge packages to decrease their coupling and increase their cohesion. For each package, review the purpose and characteristics of the package, and consider whether it should become a subsystem.

Figure 6.21 shows a class with a navigable association used by clients that becomes part of a package, and the package with a dependency relationship used by clients becomes a subsystem where the class has private visibility within the subsystem, the subsystem offers an interface with the applicable operations, the class realizes the operations, and the class's clients depend on the subsystem's interface.

Figure 6.22 shows a package with a dependency relationship used by clients that becomes a subsystem where the subsystem offers an interface with the applicable operations, and the package's clients depend on the interface.

Figure 6.23 shows a circular dependency or cycle where two elements or packages depend on one another; circular dependencies involving more than two elements may also be treated similarly. If either element changes, the other element may be impacted; thus, both elements are in effect treated as one element. If the elements are classes, such cycles are not as critical so long as both classes are in the same package; however, for packages, it is more critical because both packages must in effect be treated as one package. Extract the contents from each element that the other element depends on and create a new element upon which both of the original elements depend. For more flexibility, both elements may be made subsystems such that interfaces are introduced upon which the other element may depend. If either element changes, the other element is only impacted if the offered interface changes. Dependencies on interfaces are more granular and offer better change control than dependencies on elements. As an interface is a contract offered by a suppler to clients, the two interfaces may be combined and offered by an intermediating subsystem upon which the other elements depend. The two elements are encapsulated modules with active elements, often called capsules. The intermediating subsystem, often called a connector, establishes an explicit communication path via its offered interfaces, often called ports. The collaboration and interaction that occurs in this context is often known as a protocol and may be modeled as a collaboration

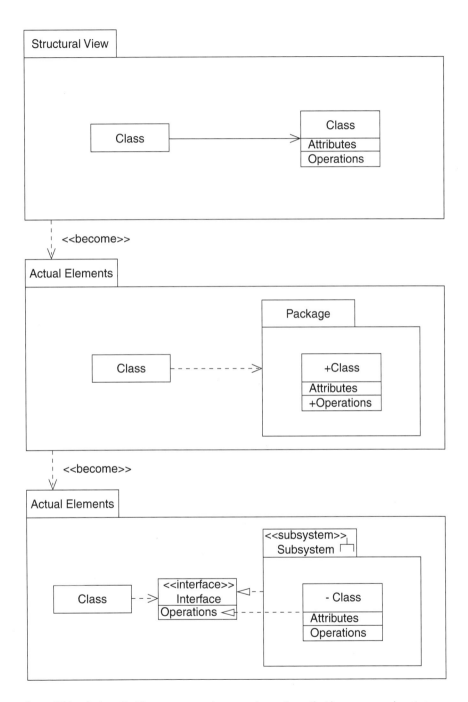

FIGURE 6.21.   A class that becomes a package, and a package that becomes a subsystem.

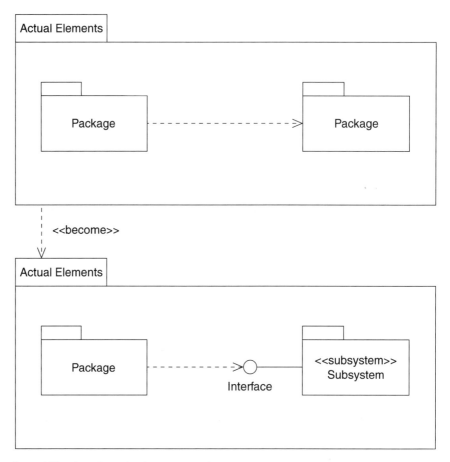

Figure 6.22.   A package that becomes a subsystem.

that is realized by the intermediating subsystem in which the elements participate. The use of protocols and elements that support protocols allows even greater flexibility and resilience than simply applying interfaces; that is, as elements change, if they support the same protocol, they may be integrated.

Progressively identify, split, and merge subsystems to decrease the coupling and increase the cohesion of their responsibilities. For each subsystem, review the responsibilities and characteristics of the subsystem and identify, split, and merge interfaces to decrease the coupling and increase the cohesion of their responsibilities. Progressively identify, split, and merge actual elements to decrease the coupling and increase the cohesion of their responsibilities. Progressively identify active elements from control classes. Each control class may require one or more

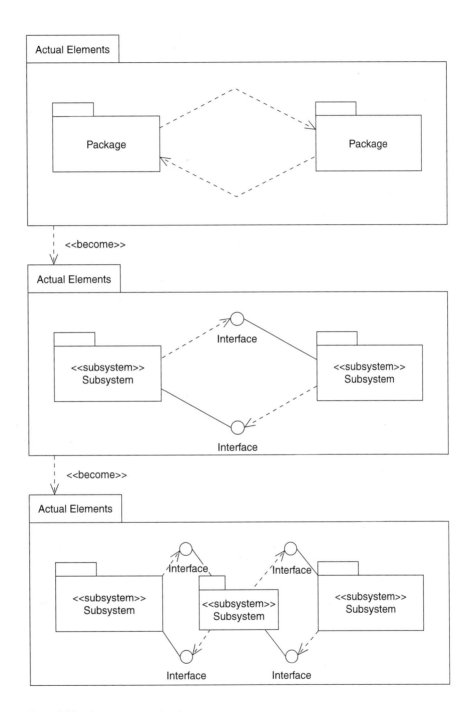

FIGURE 6.23. Circular dependencies.

threads of control, possibly for each concurrently performed behavior sequence. Progressively apply classifiers and relationships, using instances and object diagrams to explore and refine class diagrams. For the construct, update the structural view (subsystems, packages, classes, interfaces, and relationships) with actual elements.

Actual Element Properties

For each actual element, capture the actual element's properties based on its candidate element's properties and its conceptual element's properties to ensure traceability between the candidate element and the conceptual element and the actual element. This involves propagating any pertinent constraints and characteristics from the candidate element and the conceptual element to the actual element. An actual element's properties include its responsibilities and characteristics. Responsibilities define the purposes, obligations, or the rationale for the actual element's existence given the context of the actual element and how the actual element addresses the needs, goals, and objectives of other actual elements that depend on it. Characteristics include any other relevant information pertaining to the actual element. These characteristics include any relevant non-functional properties due to the context of the actual element.

Mechanisms

Identify logical mechanisms. This involves identifying various options for satisfying the capabilities required of the conceptual mechanisms. For each conceptual mechanism, identify what options ought to be explored in addressing the conceptual mechanism. Use logical mechanism as placeholders for options to satisfy the conceptual mechanisms while avoiding making premature implementation decisions. Map conceptual mechanisms to logical mechanisms. This involves capturing the evolution of conceptual mechanisms to logical mechanisms. Describe logical mechanisms. This involves determining the feasibility of the various options by demonstration, including implementing and validating or prototyping the various mechanisms. A logical mechanism's properties include any functional and non-functional properties that are relevant to the mechanism. For each logical mechanism, focus on capturing the advantages and disadvantages of the mechanism.

6.3.6. VALIDATION

This section elaborates step 6 concerning construct specification of the Detailed and Notational Roadmap section of Chapter 4. Focus on actual and conceptual elements and mechanisms.

To describe construct realization elements using construct elements, focus on effectively validating the design against the analysis of the construct.

Actual and Conceptual Elements

For each realization element, update the structural and behavioral views (actual elements, messages, and relationships) based on the actual elements to which the conceptual elements were mapped. Figure 6.24 shows conceptually that the behavioral view of a realization element must be fulfilled and satisfied by the actual elements. Notice that the interface receives a message and sends a message; the actual element that conforms to the interface must be capable of receiving the indicated message, and satisfy the criteria of sending the originating message. Figure 6.25 shows conceptually that the structural view of a realization element must be fulfilled and satisfied by the actual elements. Thus, both the structural view and behavioral view of a realization element, shown in Figure 6.19, are fulfilled; and because these were derived from the behavioral view of the description of a specification element, shown in Figure 6.18, the specification element is fulfilled by the construct, shown in Figure 6.17. This establishes closure backwards through Figures 6.19, 6.18, and 6.17 to the conceptualization perspective.

For each actual element, validate that the actual element supports the structure and behavior of its conceptual element. If this check identifies inconsistencies or conflicts, balance the two sets of information by changing the information appropriately to resolve the issues. Likewise, focus on simplifying the structural and behavioral views. If a class with a navigable association used by clients was mapped to a package as in Figure 6.21, ensure that the class and applicable operations have public visibility within the package, and the class's clients depend on the package. If a class with a navigable association used by clients was mapped to a package, and the package with a dependency relationship used by clients was mapped to a subsystem as in Figure 6.21, ensure that the subsystem offers an interface with the applicable operations and that the class's clients depend on the subsystem's interface; and then replace the occurrence of the class in the structural and behavioral views with the interface. If a package with a dependency relationship used by clients was mapped to a subsystem, ensure that the subsystem offers an interface with the applicable operations, and the package's clients depend on the interface. If multiple collaborating and interacting source elements are mapped to the same target element, any realization information pertaining to their collaboration and interaction may be used in the specification of the target element; that is, their behavior sequence remains intact, but resides inside the target element as shown in Figure 6.26. Furthermore, navigable associations to interfaces are replaced

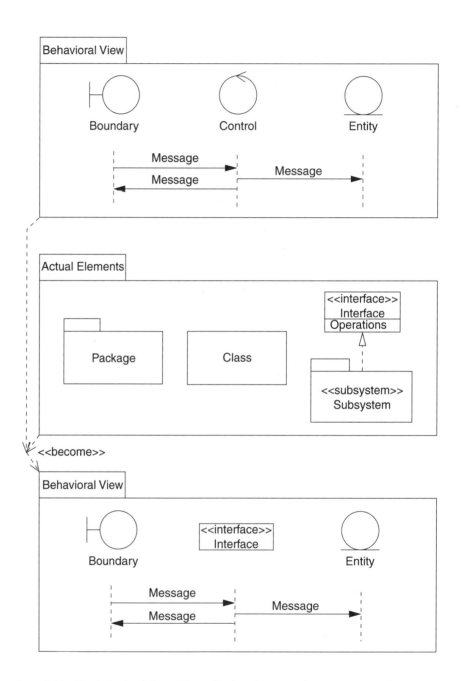

FIGURE 6.24.   The behavioral view of the realization element and construct actual elements.

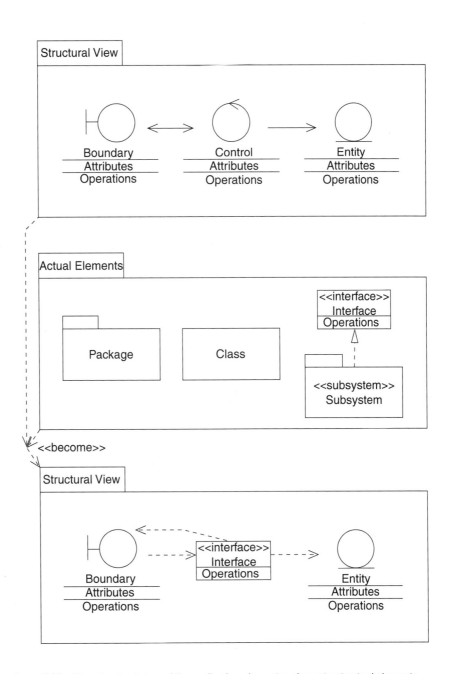

FIGURE 6.25.   The structural view of the realization element and construct actual elements.

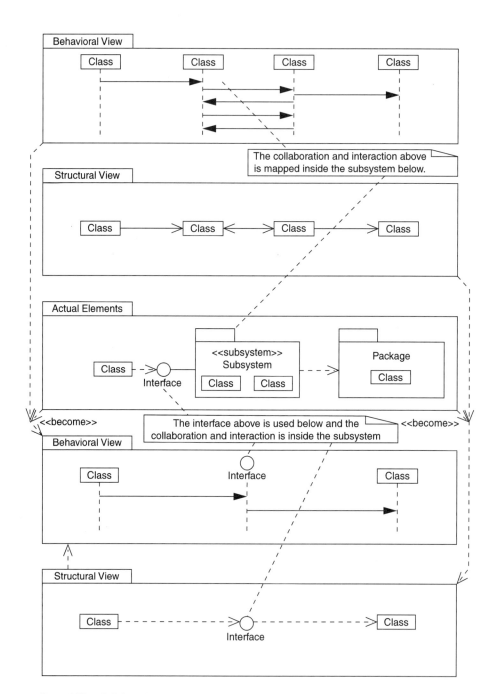

FIGURE 6.26.   Collaborations and interactions mapped inside subsystems.

with dependencies on the interfaces, and navigable associations from interfaces are replaced with dependencies from the interfaces.

For each actual element, validate that the actual element's properties are consistent with its conceptual element's properties. If this check identifies inconsistencies or conflicts, balance the two sets of information by changing the information appropriately to resolve the issues. Often, practitioners don't spend the time to describe construct realization elements using construct elements; however, this validates the distribution of construct realization elements to construct elements and ensures that the construct will satisfy the construct realization elements. Otherwise, such inconsistencies and conflicts are detected as the construct is made or being used. This results in building the construct without validating the design against the analysis of the construct, in which case, inconsistencies and conflicts are detected in testing or while the construct is being used.

Mechanisms

Identify physical mechanisms. This involves identifying the exact mechanisms to be used. For each logical mechanism, identify what implementations ought to be provided in satisfying the conceptual mechanism. Use physical mechanisms as placeholders for implementation decisions and standards. Map logical mechanisms to physical mechanisms. This involves capturing the evolution of logical mechanisms to physical mechanisms. Describe physical mechanisms. This involves capturing the details of physical mechanisms. A physical mechanism's properties include any functional and non-functional properties that are relevant to the mechanism. For each physical mechanism, focus on capturing how the mechanism is implemented and applied. A mechanism is modeled as a collaboration; it may be implemented by one or more collaborating actual elements, or it may be implemented as a service offered by an actual element. If a mechanism is implemented by one or more collaborating actual elements, model the structural or static aspect of the collaboration and the behavioral or dynamic aspect of the collaboration where the collaboration includes the various ways in which the mechanism may be applied; this may involve modeling one specification-level collaboration for the mechanism or many instance-level collaborations for each way the mechanism may be applied. If a mechanism is implemented as a service offered by an actual element, model the service as an interface, and model the various ways in which the mechanism may be applied by modeling the structural or static aspect and the behavioral or dynamic aspect of the collaboration necessary in using the service; this may involve modeling one specification-level collaboration for the mechanism or many instance-level collaborations for each way the mechanism be applied. For each actual element, incorporate the actual element's use of physical mechanisms. This involves applying physical mechanisms.

6.3.7. Unification

This section elaborates step 7 concerning construct specification of the Detailed and Notational Roadmap section of Chapter 4.

To unify construct specification, focus on effectively synchronizing and concluding construct specification. Reconcile all of the elements used in construct specification to ensure homogeneity and consistency. Reconcile the construct specification at the current level of abstraction with the construct specification at the next higher level of abstraction to ensure that the specification perspective is consistent. This involves en- suring that the construct specification at the current level of abstraction does not invalidate anything in the construct specification at the next higher level of abstraction and that the construct specification at the next higher level of abstraction is able to support everything in the con- struct specification at the current level of abstraction.

CHAPTER 7

Behavioral (Dynamic) Modeling

This chapter provides essential rules, principles, and style guidelines for composing UML behavioral or dynamic models within the context of the roadmap, including sequence, collaboration, state, and activity diagrams and their elements. Behavioral modeling is concerned with modeling the behavioral or dynamic dimension of a system—how the elements that collaborate to constitute a system interact to provide the functionality of the system—and is used for system, subsystem, and class specification within the roadmap to capture in a specification model how the construct will satisfy its requirements, what elements and their relationships collaborate to constitute the construct, and how these elements interact to provide functionality to its users. A specification model consists of class, object, sequence, collaboration, state, and activity diagrams and their model elements. Our goal, in this chapter, is to gain more depth in understanding the UML notation and the roadmap concerning the behavioral or dynamic aspect of specification models.

7.1. Sequence Diagrams

A sequence diagram depicts the dynamic behavior of an entity via a temporal focus on an interaction, how the elements that collaborate to constitute an entity interact over time to provide the functionality of the entity, using classifier roles and messages or using instances and stimuli. This type of role is known as a dynamic role. Sequence diagrams are also known as interaction diagrams; they capture patterns of collaboration and interaction among participating elements. A sequence diagram is used to depict one or more interactions within a single collaboration. An entity is a classifier, for example, a system, subsystem, or class.

Classifiers interact to accomplish a purpose by exchanging messages in order to convey information with the expectation that action will ensue, and instances interact to accomplish a purpose by exchanging stimuli in order to convey information with the expectation that action will ensue. An interaction involves communicating elements interacting or reciprocally acting on one another with focus on the elements and their communication. Communication is achieved via messages that specify stimuli and indicate the kind of communication, sender, receiver, what is communicated, and the dispatching procedure. A stimulus is a communication conforming to a message. A stimulus is an instance of a message, just as an object is an instance of a class. An event is a specification of an observable occurrence, including sending a message or stimulus and including receiving a message or stimulus. An action is an executable statement that is part of a computation, including actions for sending a message or stimulus, and including responding to the reception of a message or stimulus. A procedure or action sequence is a collection of actions modeling a computation involving sequential, conditional, and repetitive logic where composite or complex actions made of primitive or simpler actions manipulate data, communicate data via data flows using pins (connection points for inputting and outputting data values), and are sequenced via control flows. A procedure may be associated with an expression to model how the expression is evaluated or associated with a method to model how the method is executed. Generally, wherever an action may be used, a procedure or collection of actions may be used. An operation is a specification of a service or processing, and a method is an implementation of a service or processing composed of an action sequence or procedure. The ensemble of instances and links that collaborate form a collaboration instance set, and the stimuli they exchange form an interaction instance set.

A sequence diagram is used to depict one or more interactions within a single collaboration. An interaction has a generic and instance form. A generic-form interaction describes two or more possible sequences of interaction. An instance-form interaction, also called an individual behavior sequence or specific scenario, describes one actual sequence of interaction consistent with its generic-form interaction. A generic-form and instance-form sequence diagram depicts an interaction among classifiers or instances that conform to the classifier roles in the interaction, messages or stimuli that conform to the messages in the interaction, and additional classifiers or instances as necessary. A generic-form sequence diagram describes two or more possible sequences of interaction, but an instance-form sequence diagram describes one actual sequence of interaction.

A sequence diagram has two dimensions. The vertical dimension represents time where time proceeds down the page. The horizontal dimension represents the different classifier roles or instances that participate in an interaction. There is no significance to the horizontal ordering of the elements. Various labels, including timing constraints and descriptions, may be shown either in the margin or near the elements that they label.

7.1.1. CLASSIFIER ROLES

A role is a named specific behavior of an element participating in a particular context; it is a specific placeholder or part played by a participant in a collaboration and interaction, and it specifies a usage of an element. A classifier defines the features and properties of its instances, and a classifier role defines a specific usage of a classifier or instance, or descendants and specializations of the classifier. An instance conforms to its classifier and must conform to a classifier role in order for it to participate in the place of that classifier role within a collaboration or interaction. An instance conforms to its role if it supports the structural and behavioral features required of its role within a collaboration or interaction. A classifier role is depicted using the notation for a classifier, including adornments, but the name string is depicted as a forward slash followed by the classifier rolename followed by a colon followed by a classifier name or a comma-separated list of classifier names to which participants must conform.

Figure 7.1 shows a generic-form interaction of how the Project Management System is started using actor classifier roles:

1. A system administrator initiates the process.
2. The Project Management System starts the database, restores data into the database from the backup system, and informs the manager that the system is ready.
3. The database system prepares itself and starts any redundant databases for use in case the primary database fails during processing.
4. The backup system restores the data into the database.

A classifier role should be named using a noun phrase and described in a way that captures the classifier role's purpose and responsibilities, structural features, behavioral features, and characteristics. A classifier role's name should reflect a single well-defined abstraction within a given role. The features and characteristics of a classifier role define the criteria that an instance must satisfy in order for it to conform to the role and participate in the place of that classifier role within a collaboration or interaction.

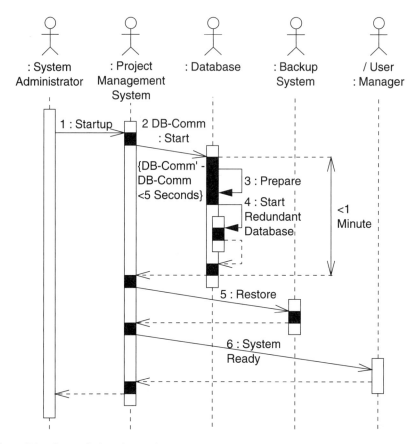

FIGURE 7.1. A generic-form interaction among actors.

The "destroyed" property keyword specifies that the classifier role or association role exists at the beginning for of the interaction but is destroyed prior to completion of the interaction. The "new" property keyword specifies that the classifier role or association role is created during the interaction and still exists at the completion of the interaction. The "transient" property keyword specifies that the classifier role or association role is created during the interaction but is destroyed prior to completion of the interaction.

7.1.2.   INTERACTIONS

An interaction is a pattern of communication or set of partially ordered messages, each specifying one communication, meaningful for a purpose—the behavioral or dynamic aspect of interacting or communicating elements. An interaction is defined in the context of a collaboration. A interaction executes when classifiers or instances are bound to the roles defined by the interaction, and the pattern of communication is executed.

Figure 7.2 shows a generic-form interaction of how a project is removed from the Project Management System using classifier roles:

1. A manager initiates the process via a manager form or user interface.
2. The form communicates the request to a controller for managing the process or interaction.
3. The controller requests confirmation from the manager via the form.
4. If the manager cancels the request, the form indicates that nothing is done.
5. If the manger continues with the request, the form confirms the

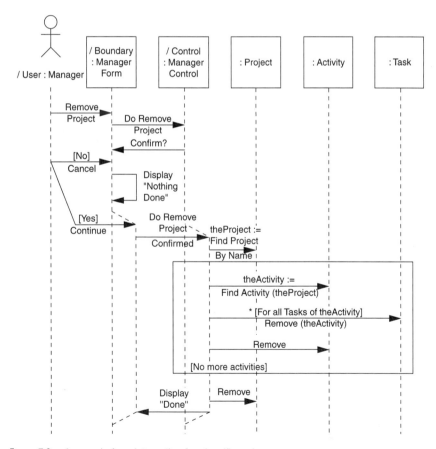

FIGURE 7.2.   A generic-form interaction for classifier roles.

request to the controller, and the controller finds the project and the project's activities, deletes all the tasks associated with each activity, deletes each activity, removes the project, and requests that the form confirm completion to the manager.

Figures 7.3–7.6 are related to Figure 7.2 and show how a project is removed from the Project Management System. Figure 7.3 shows a generic-form interaction using instances conforming to classifier roles. Figures 7.4–7.6 are concerned with projects consisting of three activities, where two activities have two tasks and one activity has three tasks. Figure 7.4 shows an instance-form interaction using classifier roles. Figure 7.5 shows an instance-form interaction using instances conforming to classifier roles. Figure 7.6 shows an instance-form interaction using instances conforming to classifier roles for a specific project. These fig-

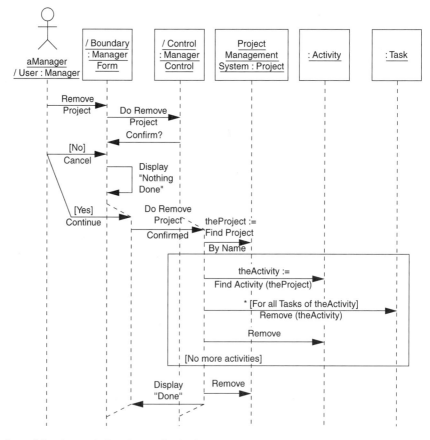

FIGURE 7.3.   A generic-form interaction for instances.

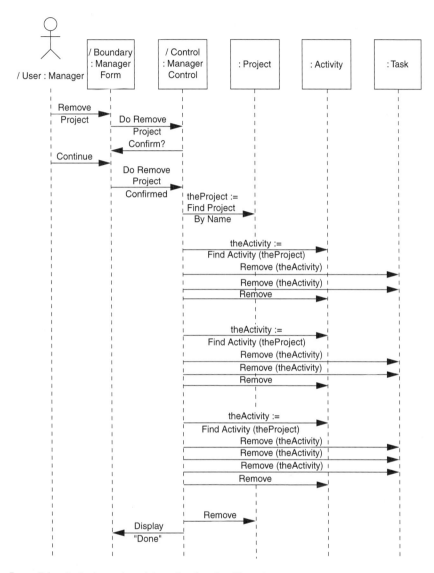

FIGURE 7.4.   An instance-form interaction for classifier roles.

ures demonstrate the use of classifier roles, lifelines, activations, messages, stimuli, branching, iterations, and timing constraints.

7.1.3. *LIFELINES*

A lifeline represents the existence of an element over time. A lifeline is depicted as a vertical dashed line from a classifier role or instance. If an

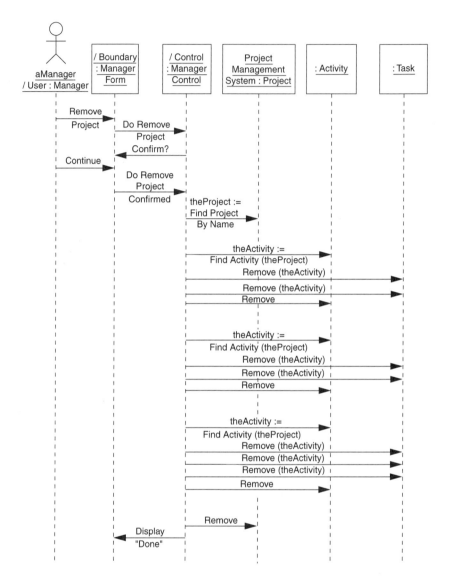

Figure 7.5.   An instance-form interaction for instances.

element exists when the interaction starts, the lifeline starts before the first message or stimulus. If an element exists when the interaction ends, the lifeline continues beyond the last message or stimulus. If an element is created during the interaction, the message or stimulus that creates the element is drawn with its arrowhead to the element. If an element is destroyed during the interaction, the message or stimulus that de-

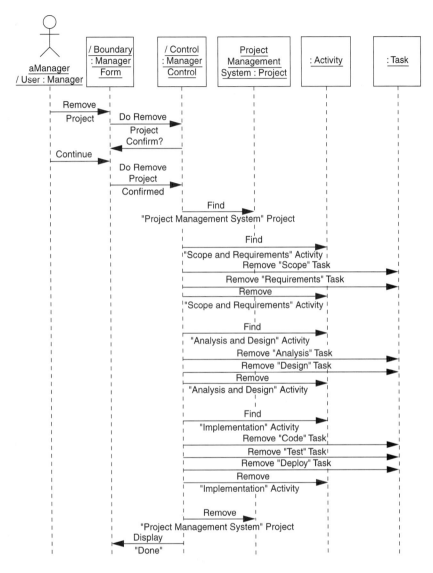

FIGURE 7.6.   An instance-form interaction for an individual behavior sequence or specific scenario.

stroys the element is drawn with its arrowhead to the element's lifeline or indicated with a return arrow from the element, and the destruction is marked with a large "X" symbol. A lifeline may split into two or more concurrent lifelines to show conditionality, where each separate track represents a conditional branch in the interaction, and the lifelines may subsequently merge together again. A lifeline may represent an entire set of classifier roles where the diagram represents a high-level view.

7.1.4. ACTIVATIONS

An activation, also known as a focus of control, represents the period during which an element is performing an action or procedure, capturing the duration of the performance of the action in time and the control relationship between the activation and its callers. An activation is depicted as a tall thin rectangle on a lifeline whose top is aligned with its initiation time and whose bottom is aligned with its completion time. The action or procedure being performed may be labeled in text next to the activation symbol, in the left margin, or on the incoming message or stimulus. To show direct computation, where an element is performing an action or procedure, versus indirect computation, where a nested element is performing an action or procedure, each element may have an activation; otherwise, the entire lifeline may be shown as an activation for all nested elements or all activations may be omitted and only lifelines shown. To show a live activation, where an element is not performing an action or procedure but control resides in something that is called by the element, an ordinary double line is used. To show a computing activation, where an element is performing an action or procedure, the ordinary double line may be shaded. Recursive calls where an element communicates with itself may be shown by staking up an activation symbol slightly to the right of the first activation symbol, and nesting may occur to any arbitrary depth.

Figure 7.1 uses live activations and computing activations to show which actors are processing requests among the Project Management System, Database, and Backup System actors. The Database actor also recursively calls itself to start a redundant database.

7.1.5. MESSAGES AND STIMULI

A message is a specification of a communication between classifier roles, and a stimulus is an instance of a communication between instances. A message or stimulus is depicted as a horizontal solid arrow from the lifeline or activation of the sender to the lifeline or activation of the receiver. An element may communicate with itself where a message or stimulus is sent from the element to itself, called a self-referential or reflexive message or stimulus. A self-referential message or stimulus is depicted as a horizontal solid arrow from the lifeline or activation of the element that loops back to the same lifeline or activation; the arrow starts and finishes on the same lifeline or activation where the sending point is above the receiving point.

For sequence diagrams, the syntax for a message or stimulus that invokes an operation (or raises a signal) is "[guard] *[iteration-specification] sequence-number name : return-list := operation-or-signal (argument-list)", where—

- The guard condition is optional and specifies a condition that must be satisfied to enable the communication to be sent. The square brackets are omitted if no guard condition is specified.
- The iteration-specification is optional and specifies the number of times the message is sent. An asterisk without a specified iteration and without square brackets indicates that the message is repeatedly sent an unspecified number of times. The asterisk and square brackets are omitted if no iteration-specification is used.
- The sequence-number is optional and specifies the sequence of the communication in the overall interaction. The colon following the sequence-number is omitted if no sequence number is specified.
- The name is optional and specifies a reference to the communication.
- The return-list is an optional comma-separated list that specifies the names of the values returned by the operation. These identifiers may be used as actual parameters in subsequent messages. The identifiers must match the order, number, and types specified in the formal return list of the operation. The return-list and assignment operation (:=) is omitted if the operation does not return any values.
- The argument-list is an optional comma-separated list that specifies the actual parameters passed to the operation. The actual parameters must match the order, number, and types specified in the formal parameter list of the operation. The parentheses may be omitted if there are no arguments.

Alternatively, a communication may be expressed using pseudo-code or another language.

The message arrowhead indicates the type of communication. A filled solid arrowhead indicates an operation call or other nested flow of control where the entire nested sequence is completed before the outer level sequence resumes. A stick arrowhead indicates an asynchronous message or stimulus, called a signal, without nesting of control where the sender dispatches the communication and immediately continues with its next step. It is assumed that every call has a paired return and may be depicted as a dashed arrow with stick arrowhead. Within a non-concurrent system, the filled solid arrowhead denotes an ordinary passing of control. Within a concurrent system, the filled solid arrowhead denotes the sending of a signal between concurrently active elements while the sender waits for the nested sequence of behavior to complete before continuing, and a stick arrowhead denotes the sending of a signal between concurrently active elements while the sender immediately continues with the next step. For parallel processing and asynchronous communication, returns should be shown explicitly.

In UML 1.3, a filled solid arrowhead indicates an operation call or other nested flow of control where the entire nested sequence is completed before the outer level sequence resumes; a stick arrowhead indicates a flat flow of control where each arrow shows the progression to the next step in the sequence; and a half-stick arrowhead indicates an asynchronous message or stimulus—this is only used for backward compatibility.

A message or stimulus that is shown horizontally indicates that it is atomic and nothing else can happen during the transmission of the message or stimulus. A message or stimulus that is shown slanted downwards so that the arrowhead is below the arrow tail indicates that time is required for the communication to be transmitted and something may happen during that time, including a message or stimulus in the opposite direction. Figure 7.1 shows that communication among the actors requires time; for example, the start message sent from the Project Management System actor to the Database actor must occur in under five seconds, and the Database actor must perform its processing in under one minute.

Multiple messages or stimuli leaving a single point indicate branching if messages or stimuli have mutually exclusive guard conditions or indicate concurrency if messages or stimuli have mutually inclusive guard conditions.

A set of messages or stimuli may be enclosed and marked as an iteration. An iteration specification may be specified at the top of the iteration. A continuation condition for the iteration may be specified at the bottom of the iteration. An iteration specification may also be specified in a constraint expression that is attached to the messages or stimuli within the iteration. Figure 7.2 shows that a Manager actor may choose to cancel or continue the remove project processing. Once a project is selected and the operation is confirmed, all of the activities are removed with their associated tasks until no more activities remain, as indicated by enclosing the messages inside the rectangle.

A timing constraint may be shown in the left margin aligned with a message or stimulus or near the tail of a communication. The timing constraint is an expression that may use the name of messages or stimuli where the send-time is expressed by "name.sendTime ()" and the receive-time is expressed by "name.receiveTime ()". The name itself may be used to denote the time at which the message or stimulus is started, and the name with a prime sign appended may be used to denote the time at which the transition is ended. Other time functions may be invented and used as necessary.

Figure 7.7 shows how a schedule controller manages a schedule, including creating, populating, storing, and destroying the schedule.

7.2. Collaboration Diagrams

A collaboration diagram depicts the dynamic behavior of an entity via a spatial and temporal focus on a collaboration and interaction and shows how the elements that collaborate to constitute an entity interact over time and are related in space to provide the functionality of the entity, using classifier roles, association roles, and messages or using instances, links, and stimuli. This type of role is known as a dynamic role. Collaboration diagrams are also known as interaction diagrams; they capture patterns of collaboration and interaction among participating elements. A collaboration diagram is used to depict collaborations with zero or more interactions. An entity is a classifier, for example, a system, subsystem, or class.

A collaboration of classifiers interact to accomplish a purpose by exchanging messages via associations in order to convey information with the expectation that action will ensue, and a collaboration of instances interact to accomplish a purpose by exchanging stimuli via links in order to convey information with the expectation that action will ensue. These associations or links are optional if the receiver is already accessible within the current context, is a local or global variable, or the sender is the receiver as in a self-referential communication. A collaboration in-

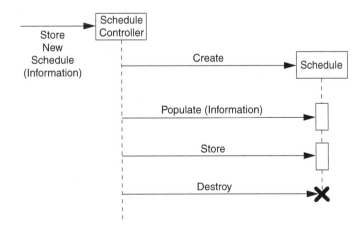

FIGURE 7.7.   An interaction between two Schedule-related classifiers.

volves an ensemble of participating elements collaborating or cooperatively working together with focus on the elements and their relationships. Communication is achieved via messages that specify stimuli and indicate the kind of communication, sender, receiver; what is communicated; and the dispatching procedure. A message is communicated via an association. A stimulus is a communication conforming to a message. A stimulus is an instance of a message, similar to an object being an instance of a class. A stimulus is communicated via a link. An event is a specification of an observable occurrence, including sending a message or stimulus, and including receiving a message or stimulus. An action is an executable statement that is part of a computation, including actions for sending a message or stimulus, and including responding to the reception of a message or stimulus. A procedure or action sequence is a collection of actions modeling a computation involving sequential, conditional, and repetitive logic where composite or complete actions made of primitive or simpler actions manipulate data, communicate data via data flows using pins (connection points for inputting and outputting data values), and are sequenced via control flows. A procedure may be associated with an expression to model how the expression is evaluated or associated with a method to model how the method is executed. Generally, wherever an action may be used, a procedure or collection of actions may be used. An operation is a specification of a service or processing, and a method is an implementation of a service or processing composed of an action sequence or procedure. The ensemble of instances and links that collaborate form a collaboration instance set, and the stimuli they exchange form an interaction instance set.

A collaboration diagram is used to depict a collaboration with zero or more interactions. A collaboration has a specification and instance level. A specification-level collaboration describes classifier roles, association roles, and their messages. An instance-level collaboration describes instances, links, and their stimuli conforming to the classifier roles, association roles, and messages of its specification-level collaboration. A specification-level collaboration diagram depicts a collaboration among classifier roles, association roles, messages, and additional classifiers and associations as necessary. An instance-level collaboration diagram depicts a collaboration among instances that conform to classifier roles, links that conform to association roles, stimuli that conform to messages, and additional instances and links as necessary.

7.2.1. Association Roles

A role is a named specific behavior of an element participating in a particular context; it is a specific placeholder or part played by a participant in a collaboration and interaction, and it specifies a usage of an element.

An association defines the features and properties of its links, and an association role defines a specific usage of an association or link, or descendants and specializations of the association. A link conforms to its association and must conform to an association role in order for it to participate in the place of that association role within a collaboration or interaction. A link conforms to its role if it supports the structural and behavioral features required of its role within a collaboration or interaction. An association role is depicted using the notation for an association, including adornments, but the name follows the same syntax as for a classifier rolename.

Figure 7.8, related to Figure 7.1, shows a specification-level collaboration for a generic-form interaction of how the Project Management System is started using actor classifier roles.

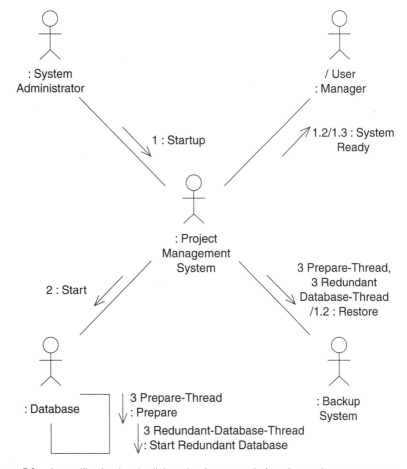

FIGURE 7.8.   A specification-level collaboration for a generic-form interaction among actors.

An association role should be named using a verb phrase and described in a way that captures the association role's purpose and responsibilities, structural features, behavioral features, and characteristics. Association roles are the means through which classifier roles communicate with one another.

The "destroyed" property keyword specifies that the classifier role or association role exists at the beginning of the interaction but is destroyed prior to completion of the interaction. The "new" property keyword specifies that the classifier role or association role is created during the interaction and still exists at the completion of the interaction. The "transient" property keyword specifies that the classifier role or association role is created during the interaction but is destroyed prior to completion of the interaction.

An association end, link end, or association role end may be stereotyped with the "association" keyword to denote that the corresponding or attached element is visible via an actual association. An association end, link end, or association role end may be stereotyped with the "global" keyword to denote that the corresponding or attached element is visible because it is in a global scope, defined and accessible by any element. An association end, link end, or association role end may be stereotyped with the "local" keyword to denote that the corresponding or attached element is visible because it is in a local scope, defined and accessible within this context. An association end, link end, or association role end may be stereotyped with the "parameter" keyword to denote that the corresponding or attached element is visible because it is parameter, defined and passed into this context. An association end, link end, or association role end may be stereotyped with the "self" keyword to denote that the corresponding or attached element is visible because it is the element under discussion, the element to which the collaboration pertains.

7.2.2. COLLABORATIONS

A context is a set of participating elements and their relationships meaningful for a purpose—the structural or static aspect of collaborating or participating elements. A collaboration is an interaction within a context. A collaboration owns zero or more interactions. A collaboration executes when instances and links are bound to the roles defined by the collaboration, and the pattern of communication is executed.

Figure 7.9, related to Figure 7.2, shows a specification-level collaboration for a generic-form interaction of how a project is removed from the Project Management System using classifier roles. Figures 7.10–7.13 are related to Figures 7.3–7.6 and show how a project is removed from the Project Management System. Figure 7.10, related to Figure 7.3,

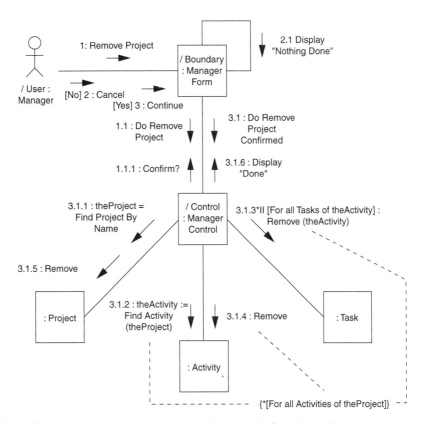

FIGURE 7.9.   A specification-level collaboration for a generic-form interaction.

shows an instance-level collaboration for a generic-form interaction using instances conforming to classifier roles. Figures 7.11–7.13 are concerned with projects consisting of three activities, where two activities have two tasks and one activity has three tasks. Figure 7.11, related to Figure 7.4, shows a specification-level collaboration for an instance-form interaction using classifier roles. Figure 7.12, related to Figure 7.5, shows an instance-level collaboration for an instance-form interaction using instances conforming to classifier roles. Figure 7.13, related to Figure 7.6, shows an instance-level collaboration for an instance-form interaction using instances conforming to classifier roles for a specific project. These figures demonstrate the use of classifier roles, association roles, messages, stimuli, nesting, concurrency, branching, and iterations.

The structural or static aspect of a collaboration may be captured using class diagrams that describe classifier roles, association roles, and additional classifiers and associations. The behavioral or dynamic aspect of a collaboration may be captured using interaction diagrams that de-

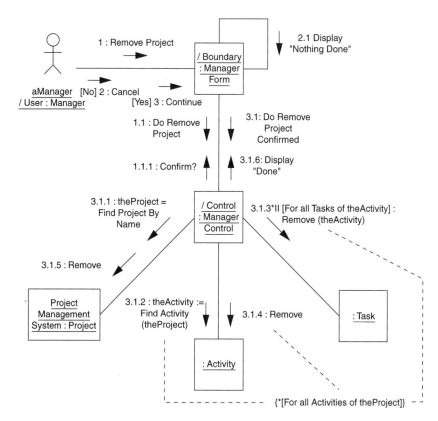

Figure 7.10.   An instance-level collaboration for a generic-form interaction.

scribe interactions among classifier roles, association roles, and additional classifiers and associations. When a collaboration is used or applied, classifier roles and association roles are played by elements that apply or instantiate the collaboration, and the additional classifiers and associations are only used within the context of the collaboration.

7.2.3.   Messages and Stimuli

A message or stimulus is depicted as an arrow placed near an association role or link. The relationship is used for transportation of the communication and the arrow points along the line in the direction of the receiving classifier role or instance. A self-referential message or stimulus is depicted as a message on a self-referential association or link.

For collaboration diagrams, the syntax for a message or stimulus that invokes an operation (or raises a signal) is "predecessor [guard] sequence-expression return-list := operation-or-signal (argument-list)" where—

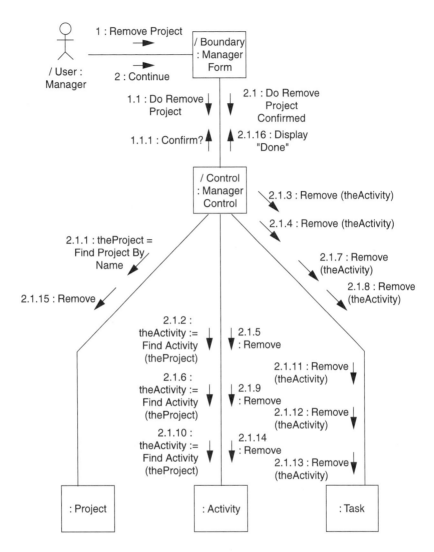

FIGURE 7.11. A specification-level collaboration for an instance-form interaction.

- The predecessor is an optional comma-separated list that specifies the sequence numbers that must have occurred in order to enable the communication. The list is followed by a forward slash (/). Each sequence number must match the sequence number of another message. Numerically proceeding sequence numbers are implicit predecessors and need not be explicitly listed. The forward slash is omitted if no predecessors are specified.

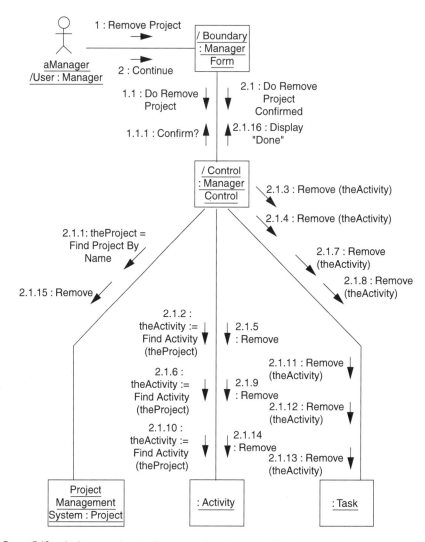

FIGURE 7.12.   An instance-level collaboration for a instance-form interaction.

- The guard condition is optional and specifies a condition that must be satisfied to enable the communication to be sent. The square brackets are omitted if no guard condition is specified.
- The sequence-expression is optional and specifies nesting, concurrency, branching, and iteration control. The syntax for a sequence-expression is "sequence-number sequence-name *‖[recurrence-clause] name :",where—
  - The sequence-number is required and specifies the sequence of

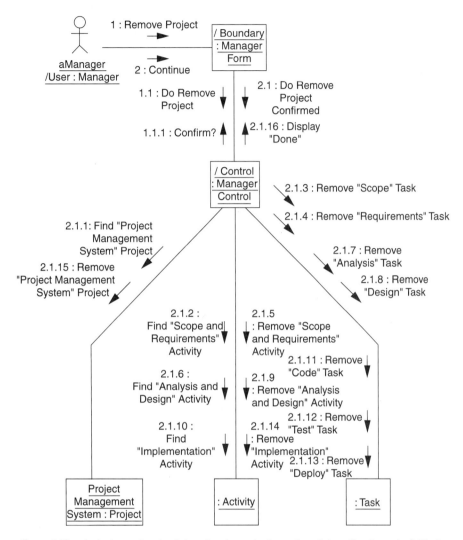

FIGURE 7.13. An instance-level collaboration for an instance-form interaction for an individual behavior sequence or specific scenario.

the communication in the next higher level of nesting. It starts at 1 and increments by 1. Communications that differ in one integer are sequentially related at the same level of nesting when associated with the same classifier role; that is, within activation 1, communication 1.1 precedes communication 1.2, communication 1.2 precedes communication 1.3, and so forth—representing the nesting of control via the dot notation. Nesting is also used to show conditionality, similar to the splitting of a lifeline on a sequence diagram, where communication 1.1.1 only occurs if the condition on communication 1.1 is satisfied and communication 1.1 only occurs if the condition on communication 1 is satisfied. If control is concurrent, nesting does not occur; that is, communication 1 and 2 are concurrent if these communications are associated with different classifier roles. Other numbering schemes may be used, but they must be defined in the context in which they are used. For example, the numerical sequence 1, 2, 3, etc., may be used independent of nesting using the dot notation.

■ The sequence-name is optional and specifies the thread of control. Communications that differ in the final name are concurrent at the same level of nesting; that is, within activation 1, communications 1.1a and 1.1b are concurrent via threads a and b. All threads of control are concurrent within a nesting level.

■ The asterisk (*) indicates that the recurrence clause is an iteration specification in which communications are executed sequentially within the nesting level. The recurrence clause indicates the number of times the communication is sent. An asterisk followed by a double vertical line (*||) indicates that the recurrence clause is an iteration specification in which communications are executed concurrently. An asterisk or asterisk followed by a double vertical line without square brackets indicates that the communication is repeatedly sent an unspecified number of times. The asterisk, double vertical lines, and square brackets are omitted if no recurrence clause is specified. An iteration specification may also be specified in a constraint expression that is attached to the communications within the iteration.

■ Square brackets alone indicate that the recurrence clause is a condition specification. The execution of the communication is contingent on the truth of the condition. The square brackets are omitted if no condition is specified.

■ Sequence-expressions are concatenated together in a dot-separated list at each level of nesting. The sequence number and sequence name are concatenated, but each nesting level specifies its own recurrence clause within its enclosing context.

■ The name is optional and specifies a reference to the communication.

■ The trailing colon is omitted if the sequence expression is omitted.

■ The return list is an optional comma-separated list that specifies the names of the values returned by the operation. These identifiers may be used as actual parameters in subsequent communications. The identifiers must match the order, number, and types specified in the

formal return list of the operation. The return list and assignment
operation (: =) is omitted if the operation does not return any values.
- The argument list is an optional comma-separated list that specifies
the actual parameters passed to the operation. The actual parameters
must match the order, number, and types specified in the formal parameter list of the operation. The parentheses may be omitted if there
are no arguments.

Alternatively, a communication may be expressed using pseudo-code
or another language.

Figure 7.8 shows the following sequence of messages: 1, 2, 3 Prepare-
Thread and 3 Redundant-Database-Thread concurrently, 1.2 after the
threads complete, and 1.3 after 1.2 completes. Figure 7.9 shows the following sequence of messages: 1, 1.1, and 1.1.1 followed by 2 and 2.1 or 3,
where the manager cancels the request, or 3, 3.1, 3.1.1, 3.1.2, 3.1.3, which
is an iteration to remove the tasks associated with the activity, 3.14, 3.1.5,
and 3.1.6, where the manager continues with the request; and messages
3.1.2, 3.1.3, and 3.14 are repeated for all activities of the project.

The message or stimulus arrowhead indicates the type of communication and follows the same notation used in sequence diagrams. Timing
constraints may be used following the same notation as in sequence
diagrams.

The argument and return names may be expressed as data tokens.
Data tokens are shown as small circles labeled with the argument expression or return value name with a small arrow pointing along the
message or stimulus for an argument or opposite the message or stimulus for a return value.

The use or application of a collaboration is depicted as a dashed ellipse. A collaboration may be labeled with a name in the collaboration
symbol. A collaboration may be left anonymous if it is attached to an
element via a realization relationship, as a collaboration may realize an
operation, use case or behavior sequence, or a class to define its static
structure. A dashed line is drawn from the collaboration symbol to each
of the symbols denoting elements that participate in the collaboration.
Each dashed line may be labeled with the role of the participant; alternatively each participant may be labeled to indicate the role it plays. A
role corresponds to an element within the context of the collaboration,
where the role is a parameter that is bound to the specific element to
which the role is attached on each occurrence or use of the collaboration. A collaboration instance set is depicted as a dashed ellipse with the
name of the collaboration underlined. The static structure of a collaboration may be shown within the collaboration icon, the dashed ellipse.
A collaboration may be labeled with the string "representedOperation"
followed by a colon followed by the operation the collaboration realizes.

A collaboration may be labeled with the string "representedClassifier" followed by a colon followed by the classifier the collaboration realizes.

Figure 7.14, related to Figures 7.2 and 7.9, shows a collaboration among classifiers for removing a project, and Figure 7.15, related to Figures 7.6 and 7.13, shows the same collaboration among instances for removing a project using a collaboration instance set.

7.2.4. Behavioral Organization

The behavioral organization of a system involves roles, classifiers, relationships, instances, and a structural scheme to constitute the system's

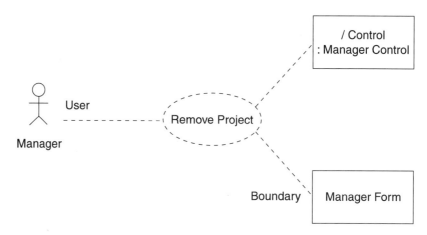

FIGURE 7.14. A collaboration among classifiers for removing a project.

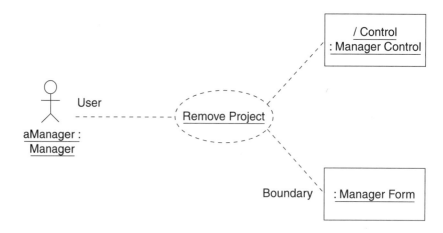

FIGURE 7.15. A collaboration among instances for removing a project.

behavioral organization, which is established atop of the system's structural organization. See the Structural Organization section of Chapter 6 for more information.

Roles, Classifiers, Relationships, and Instances

A classifier or association conforming to or playing the role defined by a classifier role or association role is depicted using the notation for a classifier or association, including adornments (with association end adornments for association roles), but the name is depicted as a forward slash followed by the classifier or association rolename followed by a colon followed by the classifier or association name; all names are optional and the forward slash is present if the classifier or association rolename is specified and the colon is present if the classifier or association name is specified. Figure 7.14 shows that a Manager actor plays the classifier role of User, a Manager Form class plays the classifier role of Boundary, and a Manager Control class plays the classifier role of Control.

An instance or link conforming to or playing the role defined by a classifier role or association role is depicted using the notation for an instance or link, including adornments (with link end adornments for links), where the name is depicted as the instance or link name followed by a forward slash followed by the classifier or association rolename followed by a colon followed by a comma-separated list of the instance's or link's classifier or association names fully underlined; all names are optional and the forward slash is present if the classifier or association rolename is specified and the colon is present if the instance's or link's comma-separated list of classifier or association names is specified. Figure 7.15 shows that the aManager actor instance plays the classifier role of User, and two anonymous instances play the classifier roles of Boundary and Control.

The multiplicity of an association end may be reduced in a collaboration; that is, the upper- and the lower-bounds of the association end roles may be within those of the corresponding participating association end. An association may be traversed in some, but not necessarily all, allowed directions within a collaboration; therefore, the collaboration may constrain the traversal of the actual association end. An association may not, however, be used for traversal within a collaboration in a direction that is not allowed according to the association end participating in the collaboration. A subset or all of the qualifiers of an association end may be used by an association end role. The changeability and ordering of an association end may be strengthened in a association end role; that is, it may be used in a more restricted way than is defined by the association end.

When multiobjects are used, a message or stimulus to the multiobject symbol indicates a message or stimulus to the set of instances, and a message to a simple instance symbol indicates a message or stimulus to an individual instance that is part of the set. Typically a selection stimulus to a multiobject returns a reference to an individual instance, to which the original sender then sends a stimulus. The instance from the set is shown as a normal instance symbol, but it may be attached to the multiobject symbol using a composition link to indicate that it is part of the set. The target rolename of the multiobject symbol has a many indicator (*) to imply many individual links.

Behavioral Scheme

The behavioral scheme of a system is established on top of the system's structural scheme. The behavioral scheme constitutes the behavioral or dynamic model view, which focuses on the dynamic dimension of a system, how the elements that collaborate to constitute a system interact to provide the functionality of the system.

A generalization relationship between a more general collaboration and a more specific collaboration concerning the same system indicates that the child collaborations inherits or receives the features of the parent collaboration, may add its own features and define new sequences of communication or interactions and new roles, modify and specialize sequences of communication it inherits or receives from the parent collaboration, and modify and specialize roles it inherits or receives from the parent collaboration. The features of a collaboration include its participating roles and sequences of communication or interactions. A child collaboration may modify the content of the sequences of communication it receives by inserting new messages or stimuli, and intertwine its own messages or stimuli with the sequences of communication it receives. Roles of a parent collaboration are roles of its child collaboration. A child collaboration may add new roles and replace existing roles with specializations of them. The specialized roles may have new features and replace or override features of their parents. The base classifiers of the specialized roles need not be specializations of the base classifiers of the parent's roles, but must only contain all the required features.

Figure 7.16 shows that a Manager actor may initiate publishing the project schedule by generating a web site using the Generate Web site use case, where the behavior sequences from the Publish Project Schedule use case are used; or a Manager actor may initiate publishing the project schedule by sending e-mail using the Send E-mail use case, where the behavior sequences from the Publish Project Schedule use case are used. These use cases are realized by corresponding collaborations. Notice that an External Target classifier playing the role of Target participates in the Publish Project Schedule collaboration, and as

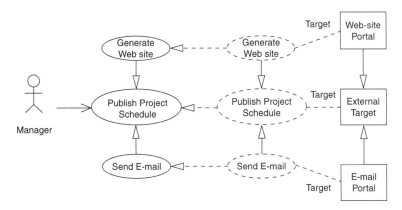

FIGURE 7.16.   Generalization relationships.

the collaborations are specialized for generating a web site or sending e-mail, the role is also appropriately specialized.

Within the containment hierarchy of a system, a super-ordinate collaboration is refined into subordinate collaborations that cooperate to perform the super-ordinate collaboration. The super-ordinate collaboration specifies the realization of a service of an entity, and the subordinate collaborations specify the realization of services by elements within the entity. However, the structure of the container entity is not revealed by the organization of collaborations in levels of abstraction. Furthermore, the roles of a super-ordinate collaboration are roles of at least one subordinate collaboration, where at least one role must participate in multiple subordinate collaborations such that the multiple collaborations compose the super-ordinate collaboration wherein the subordinate roles are merged into one super-ordinate role. If a role is renamed in a super-ordinate collaboration, the original name of the role in the subordinate collaboration is shown within curly brackets after the name used within the super-ordinate collaboration. When a collaboration is defined in terms of other collaborations, this may be depicted using dashed ellipses showing the contents of the collaborations and the relationships between elements of each collaboration via dependencies, or simply using separate collaboration diagrams. A dependency stereotyped with the "usedCollaboration" keyword may be shown from the super-ordinate collaboration to the subordinate collaboration.

Figure 7.17 shows how various elements, including collaborations and subsystems, realize various use cases. Notice how the B-Sys role of the Restore collaboration is renamed in the super-ordinate Administer System collaboration as the Backup System role. Use cases may be realized by collaborations among participating elements as in the Admin-

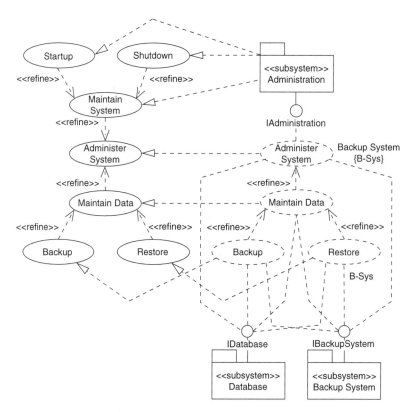

FIGURE 7.17. Collaborations for the Project Management System.

ister System collaboration or by elements directly as in the Administration subsystem.

Figure 7.18 shows how the Backup collaboration is defined in terms of two Connect collaborations, two Disconnect collaborations, and one Transfer Content collaboration. In the first Connect collaboration, the Backup Manager classifier plays the From role and the IDatabase interface plays the To role. In the second Connect collaboration, the Backup Manager classifier plays the From role and the IBackupSystem interface plays the To role. In the Transfer Content collaboration, the IDatabase interface plays the Sender role, the IBackupSystem interface plays the Receiver role, and the Project classifier plays the Content role. In the first Disconnect collaboration, the Backup Manger classifier plays the First Party role and the IDatabase interface plays the Second Party role. In the second Disconnect collaboration, the Backup Manger classifier plays the First Party role and the IBackupSystem interface plays the Second Party role.

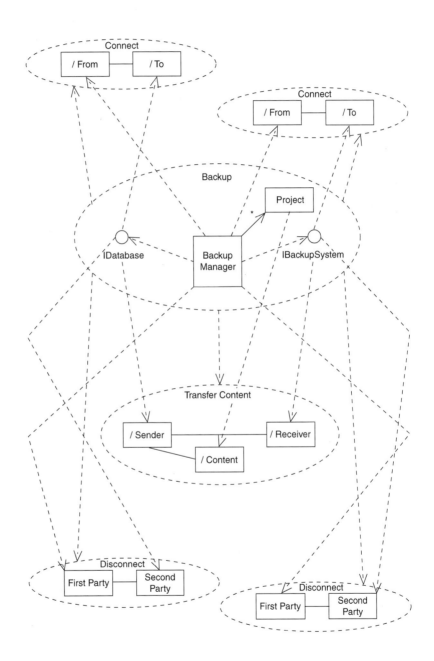

Figure 7.18. Collaborations defined in terms of other collaborations.

Within a centralized control structure, one or a few classifier roles guide an interaction. Within a decentralized control structure, an interaction is more evenly distributed across classifier roles. A centralized control structure captures the knowledge of performing an interaction within one or a few classifiers, thus increasing the cohesion and decreasing the coupling of multiple interaction behavior sequences. This encapsulates behavior sequences to form abstractions of behavior that may be more easily reused, changed, and have new behavior sequences inserted into them; this is the objective of applying collaborations.

Figure 7.19, related to Figure 7.7, shows a collaboration and interaction of how a schedule controller manages a schedule, including creating, populating, storing, and destroying it. Figure 7.20 is derived from Figures 7.19 or 7.7. Every exchanged message from the Schedule Controller class to the Schedule class has an associated operation offered by the Schedule class and a navigable association from the Schedule Con-

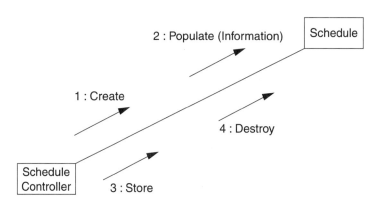

FIGURE 7.19.   A collaboration between two Schedule-related classifiers.

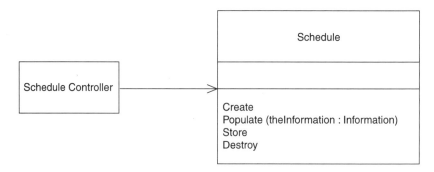

FIGURE 7.20.   A class diagram for two Schedule-related classifiers.

troller class to the Schedule class through which the communication occurs. From an interaction, the association, its navigation, and operations on the target class are derived.

7.3.   *Statechart Diagrams*

A state diagram depicts the dynamic behavior of an entity, the status conditions and responses and actions of elements that constitute the entity due to events, using states and transitions. State diagrams are also known as statechart diagrams or state machines. An entity is a classifier, for example, a system, subsystem, or class.

7.3.1.   STATES

Each instance has a lifecycle in which it is created, passes through or transitions between various states, and is destroyed. The state of an instance is the condition or situation of the instance during its life during which it satisfies some condition. The state of an instance is defined by the values of the instance's structural features. A simple state is not decomposed into subordinate states or substates. A composite state is decomposed into subordinate states or substates.

A state is depicted as a rectangle with rounded corners and three compartments separated by horizontal lines. A name tab is optional and contains the name of the state; it is shown as a rectangle resting on the inside or outside of the top-side of the state. The top name compartment is optional and contains the name of the state; the name compartment and name tab should not be used simultaneously. The middle internal transitions compartment is optional and contains a list of actions or activities performed while an entity is in the state. The bottom nested state diagram compartment is optional and contains a state diagram, in which case the state is known as a composite state.

Figure 7.21 shows the lifecycle of the Project Management System. This figure demonstrates the use of states, transitions, events, and actions.

A state should be named using a phrase that is descriptive of what the entity is waiting for or what is happening during the state. A state is not a point in time, but a period during which the state machine is waiting for something to happen or to be doing something. States may often be determined by considering the various values that attributes of a classifier may have and the various associations that an instance of a classifier may have.

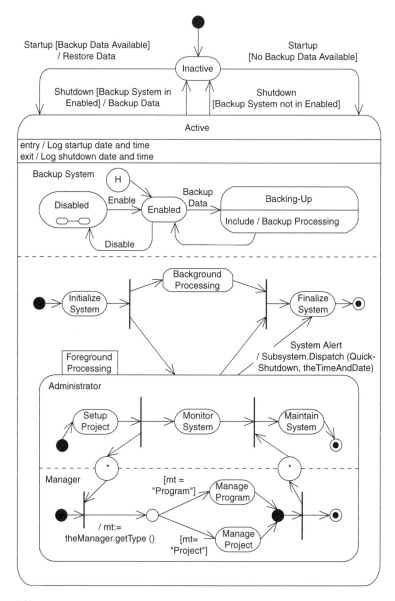

FIGURE 7.21.   A state machine for the Project Management System.

Internal Transitions

The middle internal transitions compartment of a state is optional and contains a list of actions or activities performed while an entity is in the state.

The syntax for internal transitions is "action label [guard] / action expression", where—

- The action label is optional and identifies the conditions or circumstances under which the action expression is performed.
- The guard condition is optional and specifies a condition that must be satisfied to enable the action label. The square brackets are omitted if no guard condition is specified.
- The "entry" action label indicates that the action expression is a procedure that is performed upon entry to the state.
- The "exit" action label indicates that the action expression is a procedure that is performed upon exit from the state.
- The "do" action label indicates that the action expression is an ongoing activity that is performed when the entity is in the state.
- The "include" action label indicates that the action expression invokes a submachine, a statechart within a composite state.
- The action label may otherwise be an event.
- The action expression is optional and identifies the action or procedure executed if the internal transition fires.

Composite States

The bottom nested state diagram compartment of a state is optional and contains a state diagram, in which case the state is known as a composite state. The nested state diagram defines an activity within the composite state. The composite state may have mutually exclusive disjoint substates or may have two or more concurrent substates called regions. The compartment is tiled into multiple regions using dashed lines, where each region is a concurrent substate with an optional name and its own nested state diagram with disjoint states. The concurrent states may also use a tab notation for the name. The third compartment may be hidden and represented using a special "composite" icon in the lower right-hand corner consisting of two horizontally placed and connected states. Other compartments may be used as necessary; each compartment need only show what is relevant to the diagram, and optional compartments may be suppressed.

Figure 7.21 shows that the Project Management System may be inactive or active. When the Project Management System enters or exits the Active state, it logs the startup or shutdown date and time. The Backup System may be disabled, enabled, or busy in the Backing-Up state. The Project Management System is initialized, commences with background and foreground processing, then finalizes itself precursor to shutting down.

Initial and Final States

A newly created instance enters its initial state, also called a pseudostate, as an instance never is in that state and only transitions from the state. An initial state is depicted as a small solid filled circle, and the default transition originating from the initial state may be labeled with the event that creates the instance and may have an action; otherwise, it must be unlabeled.

An instance that transitions to its final state, also called a pseudostate, is terminated or destroyed. A final state is depicted as a circle surrounding a small solid filled circle (a bull's-eye), and the transition to the final state may be labeled with the event that destroys the instance but is usually displayed as an unlabeled transition.

Each region of a composite state may have an initial state and final states; one and only one initial state must be used for each region, and zero or more final states may be used for each region. A transition to a composite state represents a transition to the initial states of its regions, and a transition to a final state represents the completion of an activity in the enclosing region. Completion of all concurrent regions represents the completion of activity by the enclosing state.

7.3.2. TRANSITIONS

A transition between states indicates how an instance changes state due to an event. An event is an occurrence, for example, receiving a message or stimulus, that may trigger a state transition. An action is an executable statement that is part of a computation, including actions for sending a message or stimulus, and including responding to the reception of a message or stimulus. A procedure or action sequence is a collection of actions modeling a computation involving sequential, conditional, and repetitive logic where composite or complex actions made of primitive or simpler actions manipulate data, communicate data via data flows using pins (connection points for inputting and outputting data values), and are sequenced via control flows. A procedure may be associated with an expression to model how the expression is evaluated or associated with a method to model how the method is executed. Generally, wherever an action may be used, a procedure or collection of actions may be used.

A transition is depicted as a solid line originating from a source state and terminating to a target state. The syntax for transitions is the same notation as for internal transitions; however, if no action label is specified, the transition is fired once the internals of the state are handled, that is, once any activities, including "do" and "include" internal transitions complete. The forward slash (/) is omitted if no action expression is specified. An instance in the first state will enter the second state and perform the specific action, which should take a negligible amount of time such that an instance always has a current state, when the specified event occurs provided that the specified guard condition is satisfied. The transition is said to fire on such a change of state. If an event does not trigger a transition, it is ignored; and if an event triggers multiple transitions, only one will fire where the one with the highest priority is selected; otherwise, an arbitrary one is selected. The guard may involve tests of concurrent states of a state machine using the keywords "in" or "not in" followed by a state name or qualified nested state pathnames, a series of names of nested states inside one another linked together and separated by a double colon (::) delimiter where the chaining together of names and the element name starting from the topmost state selects the target state. Actions may be expressed in terms of structural and behavioral features of the element owning the state machine as well as any of the parameters passed by the triggering event. The corresponding action executes entirely before any other actions are considered; this is known as run-to-completion semantics.

A transition may be given a name preceding the transition label that may be used in timing constraint. Timing constraints are expressions that may use the name of transition where the send time is expressed by "name.sendTime ()" and the receive time is expressed by "name.receiveTime ()". The name itself may be used to denote the time at which the transition is started, and the name with a prime sign appended may be used to denote the time at which the transition ends. A default or automatic transition is one with no transition label and is immediately triggered after the state and its internal transitions have completed.

Figure 7.21 shows that when the Project Management System is started, if there is backup data available, it restores the data; and when the Project Management System is shut down if the Backup System is in the Enabled state, the data is backed up.

Events

An event is an occurrence, for example, receiving a message or stimulus, that may trigger a state transition.

The syntax for events is "event name (parameter list)",where—

- The parameter list is an optional comma-separated list that specifies the formal parameters passed to the event. An event is associated with an operation, and the parameter list must match the operation's parameter list. The parentheses may be omitted if no parameter list is specified. Events have the same notation as operations.
- The "after" event label followed by a time expression indicates that the action expression is performed after the time elapses after entry to the state.

- The "when" event label followed by Boolean expression indicates that the action expression is performed when the Boolean expression becomes true.

There are various stereotype keywords that are usable with events. The "create" stereotype keyword denotes that the event creates the classifier enclosing the state machine; this may only be applied at the topmost level of a state machine. The "destroy" stereotype keyword denotes that the event destroys the classifier enclosing the state machine.

A classifier may be stereotyped with the "signal" keyword to denote that the element is an asynchronous message that may be received by a classifier, in which case its parameters are depicted in the attributes compartment, and its access operations are depicted in the operations compartment. Signal classes may be used in a generalization relationship where an occurrence of a subevent triggers any transition that depends on the event or any of its ancestors.

Actions

An action is an executable statement that is part of a computation, including actions for sending a message or stimulus and responding to the reception of a message or stimulus. A procedure or action sequence is a collection of actions modeling a computation involving sequential, conditional, and repetitive logic where composite or complex actions made of primitive or simpler actions manipulate data, communicate data via data flows using pins (connection points for inputting and outputting data values), and are sequenced via control flows. A procedure may be associated with an expression to model how the expression is evaluated or associated with a method to model who the method is executed. Generally, wherever an action may be used, a procedure or collection of actions may be used.

A create action creates an instance of a classifier. A destroy action destroys an instance of a classifier. A terminate action denotes an instance of a classifier via self-destruction where an instance destroys itself. An uninterpreted action is an action that has semantics not expressed in the UML. A call action invokes an operation synchronously or asynchronously and may require a reply. A call event is the reception of a request to synchronously invoke a specific operation due to a synchronous call action. A send action sends a signal to a receiver or set of receivers asynchronously and without waiting for a reply. A signal event is the reception of a request to invoke a specific operation asynchronously due to an asynchronous call action or a send action. A return action returns a value from a sender to its caller. An exception is a raised signal. A change event occurs when an explicit Boolean expression become true as a result of a change in the values of the structural features of an instance. A time event occurs when a specific deadline has expired. An unlabeled transitions is an implicit "action complete" event that triggers once the contents of the state are completed.

Complex or Concurrent Transitions

A complex or concurrent transition is the synchronization or splitting of control into concurrent threads without necessarily having concurrent substates. A concurrent transition is depicted as a short heavy bar. If the bar has one or more incoming transitions to the bar, it represents a synchronization of control and the outgoing transition fires after the incoming transitions have fired. This is a join used to merge transitions. If the bar has one or more outgoing transitions from the bar, it represents a splitting of control and the outgoing transitions fire concurrently after the incoming transition has fired. This is a fork used to split transitions. A transition string may appear near the short heavy bar and each transition does not have its own transition string. Figure 7.21 shows that after the Project Management System is initialized, background and foreground processing occur concurrently.

A transition to the boundary of a composite state is a transition to the composite state's initial state or a complex transition to the initial states of each of its concurrent regions. An initial state must be used for each region. A transition from the boundary of a composite state applies to each of the composite state's regions at any depth of nesting; that is, the transition is "inherited" by the nested states. Inherited transitions may be overridden by the presence of nested transitions with the same trigger. The target of a transition may be a state within a composite state region at any depth. All entry actions are performed for any states entered to reach the target state. The source of a transition may be a state within a composite state region at any depth. All exit actions are performed for any states forcibly terminated to leave the source state.

Figure 7.21 shows that when the Foreground Processing state is entered, two substate regions are triggered, Administrator and Manager. Any time this state is occupied, a System Alert event may occur that forces this state to be exited and the Finalize System state to be active.

A synch state is used in conjunction with forks and joins to synchronize concurrent regions. Synchronization involves ensuring that one region leaves a particular state before another region can enter a particular state. The firing of an outgoing transition from a synch state may be limited by the difference between the number of times outgoing and incoming transitions have fired. A sync state is shown as a small circle with the upper bound specified as a positive integer inside it or a star ("*") for an unlimited number of synchronizations drawn on the boundary between regions when possible.

Figure 7.21 shows that the Manger substate region may not enter the Manage Program or Manage Project states until the Setup Project state completes and enables the synch state. Likewise, the Administrator substate regions may not enter the Maintain System state until the Manager substate region completes and enables the synch state.

A shallow history state indicator within a state region indicates that an instance resumes the state it last had within the composite region; and a deep history state indicator within a state region indicates that an instance resumes the state it last had at any depth within the composite region. A region may have both shallow and deep history indicators. History states may have any number of incoming transitions but may only have one outgoing unlabeled transition identifying the default "previous state" if the region has never been entered. A shallow history state indicator is shown as a small circle containing an "H"; and a deep history state indicator is shown as a small circle containing an "H*". Figure 7.21 shows that the Backup System will resume its previous state and enter the Enabled state the first time the Active state is entered.

As nested states may be suppressed, transitions to suppressed nested states are drawn to stubs. A stub state indicates a transition connected to a suppressed internal state. A stub state is shown as a small line (bar) inside the boundary of its enclosing state. Incoming transitions to a stub state may have events; however, outgoing transitions from a stub state are not shown as they are owned by the stubbed or suppressed state.

Compound Transitions

A compound transition is a chain of transitions that may be executed in the context of a single run-to-completion step. It is used to share or factor a set of transitions called factored transitions where distinct transitions may come together and continue via a common path or where a transition splits into separate mutually exclusive non-concurrent paths. Two or more transitions from different non-concurrent states incoming to a common junction point indicates that the incoming transitions share the outgoing path from the junction point. Two or more guarded transitions from the same junction point indicate that the outgoing transitions split from the junction point where the guards are mutually exclusive. All possible outcomes should be considered; otherwise, the keyword "else" may be applied as a guard condition to at most one outgoing transition which is triggered if all the other guard conditions on the other transitions are false. A static branch junction point involves evaluating all of the outgoing guards before any transition is taken while the conditions on the incoming transitions are "and-ed" together. A static branch junction point is shown as a small black circle or it may be shown as a diamond shape as discussed within the context of activity diagrams. A dynamic choice junction point involves evaluating all of the outgoing guards before any transition is taken while the conditions on the incoming transitions are "and-ed" together, where the evaluation of the guard conditions may be a function of some calculations performed in the actions of the incoming transitions. A dynamic choice junction point is shown as a small white circle. Alternatively, a junction point may be represented by a diamond shape. Figure 7.21 shows a dynamic choice junction point for managing programs or projects within the Manger substate region within the Foreground Processing state.

7.3.3. SUBMACHINES

A submachine state is a normal state with an "include" declaration within its internal transitions compartment that invokes a state machine defined elsewhere. The submachine state may have various stub states of the included submachine. In this case, the notation for stub ends includes a label specifying the name or pathname of the corresponding substates within the invoked submachine. Figure 7.21 shows that the Backing-Up state includes the Backup Processing submachine.

Figure 7.22, related to Figures 7.7 and 7.19, shows the lifecycle of instances of the Schedule class. Notice that communications to a Schedule class object, from Figures 7.7 and 7.19, correlate to events received by the Schedule class object, durations between communications and durations for handling communications correlate to states of the Schedule class object, and the sequences of communication correlate to transitions between the different states of the Schedule class object.

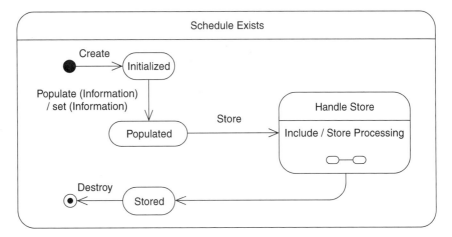

FIGURE 7.22.   A state machine for a Schedule-related classifier.

7.4. *Activity Diagrams*

An activity diagram, a variation of a state diagram, depicts the dynamic behavior of an entity, the activities or workflow (flow of work) and responsibilities of elements that constitute an entity, using action states and flows. Activity diagrams are also known as activity graphs. An entity is a classifier, for example, a system, subsystem, or class.

Once activity diagrams are produced using action states and flows, swimlanes may be introduced to assign responsibility of the action states and decisions to classifiers or instances. This is valuable in improving our understanding of the interaction, who has responsibility for the various parts of the interaction, and identifying efficiencies and inefficiencies when multiple classifiers or instances must interact.

7.4.1. Action States

An action state is a state with an action and at least one outgoing transition that is triggered upon completion of the action. An action state is depicted as a shape with straight top and bottom and with convex arcs on the two sides containing the action expression of the state. An action state may take a non-negligible amount of time and thus may be interrupted. A transition leaving an action state does not include an event, as it is trigged by the completion of the action, but may include a guard condition and an action expression. An action state may not have internal transitions or outgoing transitions triggered by explicit events. An action state need not be unique within a diagram. Action states may be nested to form activities that take a non-negligible amount of time, and may be used in ordinary state diagrams.

Figure 7.23 shows various action states for the Project Management System as it interacts with the database. This figure demonstrates the use of action states, object flows, and control or transition flows.

Figure 7.23 shows that the Project Management System will initialize itself, and in parallel, possibly restore its associated database, and commence with background and foreground processing in parallel.

An action state should be named using a phrase that is descriptive of what is happening during the action state. An action state is not a point in time, but a period during which the state machine is doing something.

A subactivity state (also known as an activity state) is a normal action state that invokes an activity graph. A subactivity state is depicted as an action state with an icon in the lower right-hand corner consisting of two horizontally placed and connected states. This notation may be used with any UML construct that supports "nested" structures where the icon

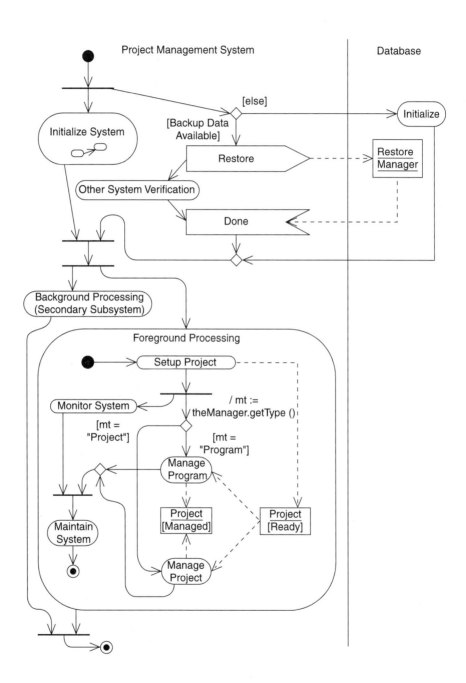

FIGURE 7.23.   An activity graph for the Project Management System.

must suggest the type of nested structure. A subactivity state need not be unique within a diagram. Figure 7.23 shows that the Initialize System action state is a subactivity state.

A call state is a normal action state that invokes an operation. A call state is depicted as an action state with the name of the operation in the symbol followed by the name of the classifier that hosts the operation in parentheses under it. A call state need not be unique within a diagram. Figure 7.23 shows that the Background Processing action state is hosted by the Secondary Subsystem classifier.

7.4.2. SWIMLANES

A swimlane is a region of responsibility for action and subactivity states, but not call states. A swimlane is depicted as a visual region separated from neighboring swimlanes by vertical solid lines on both sides. Each action or subactivity state is assigned to one swimlane and transitions may cross swimlanes. A swimlane may be labeled at the top with who or what classifier or instance has responsibility for the contents within the swimlane. Figure 7.23 shows two swimlanes, including one for the Project Management System and one for the Database.

7.4.3. FLOWS

An object flow determines the instances input to and output from action states. An object flow is depicted as a dashed arrow drawn from an action state to an output instance or drawn from an input instance to an action state. The same instance may be used with multiple action states. A transition or control flow may be omitted when an object flow specifies a redundant ordering; that is, when an action state produces an output that is input to a subsequent action state, the object flow implies a control or transition flow. One instance may have transitions to and from all of the relevant action states that pertain to the instance. However, for greater clarity, the instance may be depicted multiple times where each occurrence of the instance represents a different point during the instance's life, and the state of the instance at each point may be placed in brackets following the name of the instance.

Figure 7.23 shows a Project class object twice in the Project Management System swimlane; one occurrence specifies that it is "ready" and is the output from the Setup Project action state, and the second occurrence specifies that it is "managed" and is the output from the Manage Program or Manage Project action states.

A decision involves different possible transitions that depend on various conditions. A decision may be depicted by labeling multiple output transitions of an action state with different guard conditions. A decision may be depicted using the traditional diamond shape, with one incoming transition and with two or more outgoing transitions, each labeled with a distinct guard condition with no event trigger. All possible outcomes should be considered; otherwise, the keyword "else" may be applied as a guard condition to at most one outgoing transition, which is triggered if all the other guard conditions on the other transitions are false. A merging of decision branches back together may be depicted using the traditional diamond shape, in which case it is called a merge, with two or more incoming transitions and one outgoing transition. The outgoing transition from a merge may not have a trigger or guard condition. A set of decisions may be chained together, where only the first incoming transition may contain an event trigger, while all other transitions may have guard conditions. Figure 7.23 shows a decision in the Foreground Processing action state determining if a project or program is being managed.

There are various control icons or explicit symbols that are usable for specifying certain kinds of information associated with transitions. A signal receipt control icon represents the receipt of a signal. A signal receipt control icon is depicted as a concave pentagon that looks like a rectangle with a triangular notch on either side containing the signature of the signal inside the symbol. An unlabeled transition from the previous action state is drawn to the symbol and an unlabeled transition to the next action state is drawn from the symbol. An object flow may be drawn from the sender instance, the instance that sends the signal, to the notch. A signal sending control icon represents the sending of a signal. A signal sending control icon is depicted as a convex pentagon that looks like a rectangle with a triangular point on either side containing the signature of the signal inside the symbol. An unlabeled transition from the previous action state is drawn to the symbol and an unlabeled transition to the next action state is drawn from the symbol. An object flow may be drawn from the point on the pentagon to the receiver instance, the instance that receives the signal.

Figure 7.23 shows that the Project Management System sends a Restore signal via the sending control icon to the Restore Manager object in the Database, and the Project Management System receives a Done signal via the receipt control icon from the Restore Manager object in the Database.

An event is lost if it is not handled immediately. A state may defer events if they occur during the state and not used to trigger a transition. A deferrable event is shown by listing it within the state followed by a slash and the "defer" keyword. If the event occurs, it is saved and recurs when a transition is fired from the state, at which time it must be accepted or lost. Events may be deferred across multiple states. Because action states are not interruptible for event processing, both deferred and underfeed events that occur during the state are deferred until the state completes.

Synch states may be omitted in activity diagrams when the synch state has one incoming transition and one outgoing transition, and an unlimited bound. An action state or subactivity state may have a multiplicity shown in the upper right corner of the state indicating the number of concurrent invocations. A complex or concurrent transition in an activity diagram may use guards in the splitting of control forks indicating that regions initiated by a fork might not start, and therefore are not required to complete at the corresponding join.

Figure 7.24, related to Figures 7.7 and 7.19, shows various action states for a Schedule class object. Notice that communications to a Schedule class object correlate to action states that indicate the actions taken in response to the received communications.

7.5. Applying Sequence, Collaboration, Statechart, and Activity Diagrams

When modeling the specification perspective of a construct (system, subsystem, or class) and how the construct will satisfy its requirements, what elements and their relationships collaborate to constitute the construct, and how these elements interact to provide functionality to its

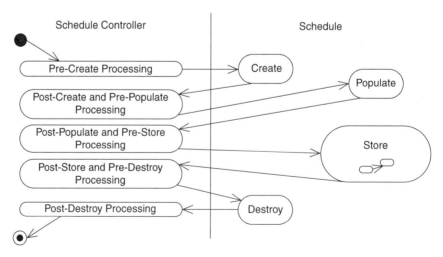

FIGURE 7.24.   An activity graph for two Schedule-related classifiers.

users, consider the guidelines above and herein which ought to be applied within a use-case-driven, architecture-centric, iterative and incremental, and risk-confronting effort that is object oriented and component based. Successive iterations evolve, elaborate, and refine the work of previous iterations with more detail. Steps need not be sequential, but may be executed in parallel, where multiple efforts regarding the same system are carried out concurrently.

Every constituent of the roadmap is optional and should only be applied if it adds value to the body of knowledge concerning the construct and facilitates achieving the overall objectives of the effort within the specific context of the effort. Those constituents of the roadmap that are applied constitute a roadmap instance. Reference the examples above and the Project Management System example used in Chapter 4 as the result of applying structural and behavioral modeling within the context of the roadmap.

When modeling and reconciling the structural and behavioral views, progressively apply sequence, collaboration, state, and activity diagrams while focusing on effectively emphasizing particular qualities of a model. Generally, messages and stimuli in interaction diagrams correlate to events in state diagrams, durations between messages and stimuli and durations for handling messages and stimuli in interaction diagrams correlate to states in state diagrams, the sequences of messages and stimuli in interaction diagrams correlate to transitions between the different states in state diagrams, and the responses to messages and stimuli correlate to action states in activity diagrams.

7.5.1. SEQUENCE DIAGRAMS

Use sequence diagrams to emphasize interactions via a temporal focus, including modeling classifier roles and their interactions. Progressively apply classifier roles, lifelines, messages, and stimuli for generic and instance forms of sequence diagrams while then applying other sequence diagram modeling elements. Sequence diagrams are useful for visualizing patterns of interaction and visualizing the overall performance of behavior sequences.

Figure 7.25 shows a simple sequence diagram of an interaction between a client and supplier.

7.5.2. COLLABORATION DIAGRAMS

Use collaboration diagrams to emphasize collaborations and interactions via a spatial and temporal focus, including modeling classifier roles, association roles, and their interactions. Progressively apply classifier roles, association roles, messages, and stimuli for specification and instance levels of collaboration diagrams while then applying other col-

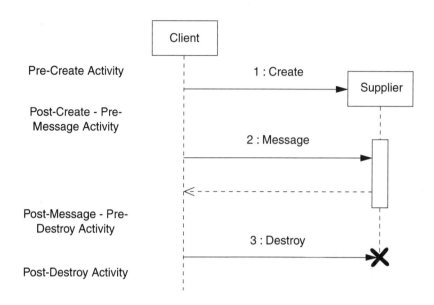

FIGURE 7.25.   A sequence diagram for an interaction between a client and a supplier.

laboration diagram modeling elements. Collaboration diagrams are useful for visualizing patterns of collaboration and visualizing the impact on a given element as it interacts with other elements. Collaboration diagrams are essentially equivalent to overlaying an interaction from a sequence diagram atop of a ensemble of elements from a class diagram.

Figure 7.26, related to Figure 7.25, shows a simple collaboration diagram of a collaboration and interaction between a client and supplier. Figure 7.27 is derived from Figures 7.26 or 7.25. Every exchanged message from the Client class to the Supplier class has an associated operation offered by the Supplier class and a navigable association from the Client class to the Supplier class through which the communication occurs. From an interaction, the association, its navigation, and operations on the target class are derived. From an application perspective, associations and navigations show dependencies between application elements or classifiers. From a data perspective, associations and navigation show access paths through the data elements or database tables where each database table represents a classifier and each row represents an instance of a classifier.

7.5.3.   STATE DIAGRAMS

Use state diagrams to emphasize the status conditions and responses of elements due to events, including modeling states and their transitions.

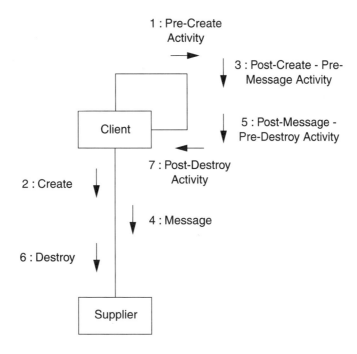

FIGURE 7.26. A collaboration diagram for a collaboration between a client and a supplier.

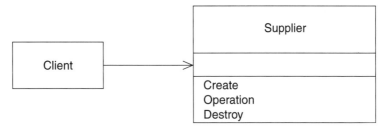

FIGURE 7.27. A class diagram derived from a collaboration and interaction between a client and a supplier.

Progressively apply states, transitions, events, and actions. State diagrams are useful for understanding how an element responds to stimuli from an external perspective, that is, how the element will respond to a sequence of communications. The nesting of states corresponds to the nesting of classifiers; that is, where there is a classifier nested inside another, its state diagrams may be nested inside the state diagram of its container.

Figure 7.28, related to Figures 7.25 and 7.26, shows the lifecycle of instances of the Supplier class. Notice that communications to a Supplier class object, from Figures 7.25 and 7.26, correlate to events received by the Supplier class object; durations between communications and durations for handling communications correlate to states of the Supplier class object; and the sequences of communication correlate to transitions between the different states of the Supplier class object.

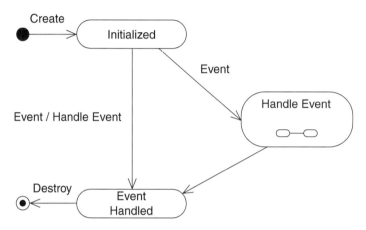

FIGURE 7.28.   A state diagram for a collaborating and interacting supplier.

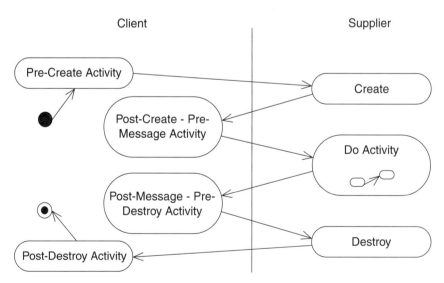

FIGURE 7.29.   An activity diagram for a collaboration and interaction between a client and a supplier.

7.5.4. ACTIVITY DIAGRAMS

Use activity diagrams to emphasize the activities of elements, including modeling action states and flows. Progressively apply action states, object flows, and control or transition flows. Activity diagrams are useful for understanding how an element responds to external stimuli from an internal perspective, that is, how the element internally responds to a communication. The nesting of action states corresponds to the nesting of classifiers; that is, where there is a classifier nested inside another, its activity diagrams may be nested inside the activity diagram of its container.

Figure 7.29, related to Figures 7.25 and 7.26, shows various action states for a Supplier class object. Notice that communications to a Supplier class object correlate to action states that indicate the actions taken in response to the received communications.

CHAPTER 8

Component (Implementation) Modeling

This chapter provides essential rules, principles, and style guidelines for composing UML component or implementation models within the context of the roadmap, including component diagrams and their elements. Component modeling is concerned with modeling the implementation dimension of a system—how a system is implemented—and is used for system, subsystem, and class implementation within the roadmap to capture in an implementation model how the construct is packaged or implemented and how it resides in its environment. An implementation model consists of component and deployment diagrams and their model elements. Our goal, in this chapter, is to gain more depth in understanding the UML notation and the roadmap concerning the implementation aspect of implementation models.

8.1 Component Diagrams

A component diagram depicts the implementation of an entity using components and their relationships, that is, its implementation-time configuration. Generally, a component diagram only has a type form and not an instance form; however, "degenerate" deployment diagrams are used to show component instances. An entity is a classifier, for example, a system, subsystem, or class. Both component and deployment diagrams are called implementation diagrams.

8.1.1. ARTIFACTS

An artifact is a physical element of information that is produced or consumed by a software development process, including models, source files, object files, executable files, scripts, and so forth. An artifact is depicted as a stereotyped classifier. An artifact may have features. An artifact should be named using a noun phrase and described in a way that captures the artifact's characteristics.

A classifier may be stereotyped with the "document" keyword to denote that the element is not a source file or executable file artifact, a subclass of file. A classifier may be stereotyped with the "executable" keyword to denote that the element is an executable file artifact, a subclass of file. A classifier may be stereotyped with the "file" keyword to denote that the element is a physical file artifact in the context of the system. A classifier may be stereotyped with the "library" keyword to denote that the element is a static or dynamic library artifact, subclass of file. A classifier may be stereotyped with the "source" keyword to denote that the element may be compiled into an executable file artifact, a subclass of file. A classifier may be stereotyped with the "table" keyword to denote that the element is a database table artifact.

Figure 8.1 shows a generic source file artifact for the Project Management System, and Figure 8.2 shows a specific source file artifact for the Project Management System. Figure 8.3 shows a generic file artifact within the Project Management System, and Figure 8.4 shows a specific file artifact within the Project Management System.

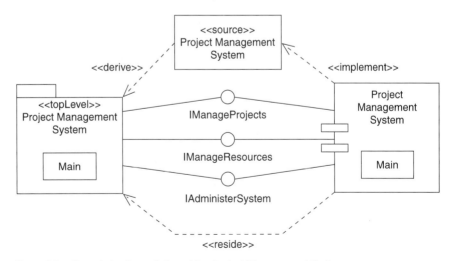

FIGURE 8.1. Generic implementation of the Project Management System.

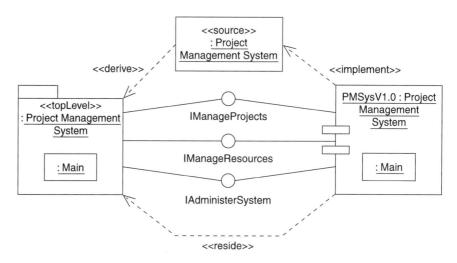

FIGURE 8.2.   Specific implementation of the Project Management System.

8.1.2.   COMPONENTS

A component is a modular, deployable, and replaceable physical implementation that has identity during execution time. A component is depicted as a rectangle with two small rectangles protruding from its side.
A component realizes and exposes interfaces to which it conforms. A
component encapsulates the implementation of classifiers that reside on
the component. A single element may reside in multiple components;
that is, each component requires it to be resident. Active elements constitute the active parts of a component. A component does not have its
own features but is a container for its elements. A component should be
named using a noun phrase and described in a way that captures the
component's characteristics.

Figure 8.1 shows a generic Project Management System component,
and Figure 8.2 shows a specific Project Management System component
named "PMSysV1.0". Figure 8.3 shows generic components within the
Project Management System, including components for project management, resource management, administration, security functionality,
and database functionality. Figure 8.4 shows specific components within
the Project Management System, including a project management component named "PMSysV1.0", a resource management component
named "RMSysV1.0", a security library component named "Security-
Lib", and a database component named "DB-Lib".

There are various property keywords that are usable with classifiers.
The "location" property keyword used with a non-component denotes

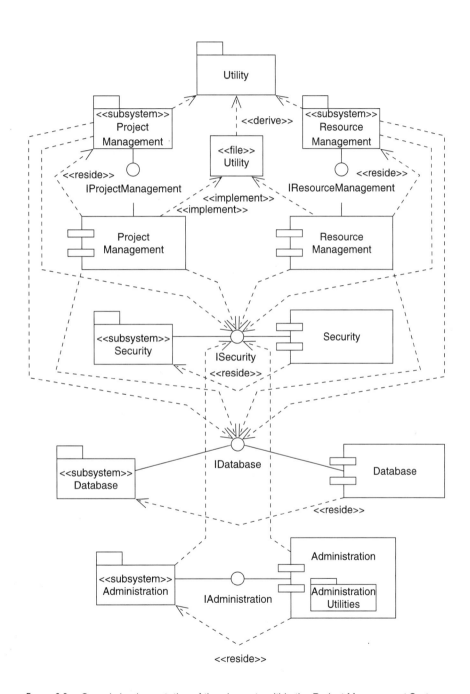

FIGURE 8.3. Generic implementation of the elements within the Project Management System.

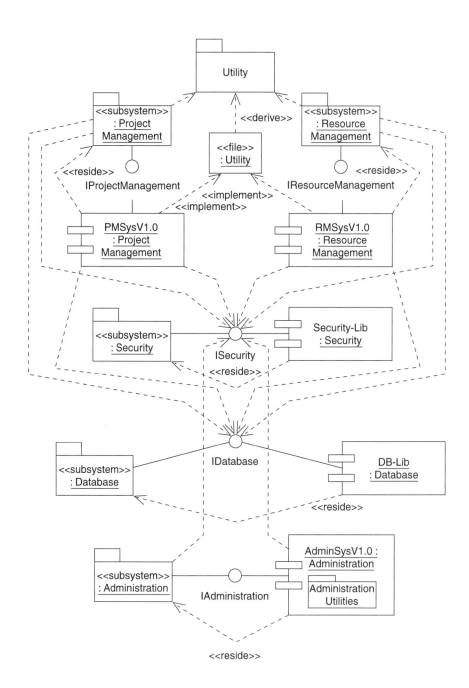

FIGURE 8.4.   Specific implementation of the elements within the Project Management System.

the component on which the classifier resides. The "location" property keyword used with a component denotes the node that supports the component.

8.1.3. COMPONENT RELATIONSHIPS

A component may have dependency relationships on classifiers, including other components, or may have composition relationships with the elements that reside on the component. A dependency may be stereotyped with the "reside" keyword to specify that the target element resides on the source component. This does not indicate ownership but residence. The visibility of a resident element may be shown using the notation discussed in Chapter 6. A dependency may be stereotyped with the "implement" keyword to specify that the target artifact element is implemented by the source component, while it in turn is derived from one or more classifiers. A dependency may be stereotyped with the "derive" keyword to specify that the source artifact is derived or may be computed from the target classifier.

Figures 8.1 and 8.2 show that the Project Management System component implements the source file artifact that is derived from the Project Management System "topLevel" package that resides on the component.

Figures 8.3 and 8.4 show the Utility file artifact that is derived from the Utility package and is implemented on the Project Management and Resource Management components. The Security subsystem package resides on the Security component, the Database subsystem package resides on the Database component, and the Administration subsystem package resides on the Administration components on which the Administration Utilities package also resides.

A static dependency, such as a compiler dependency where one component requires the presence of another component in order for it to be compiled from a source file into an executable file, may be shown as a dependency between a client component and a source component and may be further stereotyped to indicate its implementation-specific nature. Figures 8.3 and 8.4 show that the Project Management and Resource Management subsystem packages depend on the Utility package.

A component may realize interfaces that it exposes and to which it conforms. The interfaces represent the services provided by the elements that reside on the component. A calling dependency, where one component calls another components or uses its services, may be shown as a dependency between a client component and the interface of a source component and may be further stereotyped to indicate its precise nature. Figures 8.3 and 8.4 show how various elements use the interfaces of other elements.

8.2.   *Applying Component Diagrams*

When modeling the implementation perspective of a construct (system, subsystem, or class) and how the construct is packaged or implemented and how it resides in its environment, consider the guidelines above and herein which ought to be applied within a use-case-driven, architecture-centric, iterative and incremental, and risk-confronting effort that is object oriented and component based. Successive iterations evolve, elaborate, and refine the work of previous iterations with more detail. Steps need not be sequential but may be executed in parallel, where multiple efforts regarding the same system are carried out concurrently.

Within the implementation perspective of the roadmap, specification elements include use cases, interfaces, and operations; construct elements include any elements that may constitute the construct or system, including subsystems, packages, and classes which evolve from proposed candidate elements to accepted actual elements; implementation elements are components; and environment elements are nodes. Properties capture constraints and characteristics of elements.

Every constituent of the roadmap is optional and should only be applied if it adds value to the body of knowledge concerning the construct and facilitates achieving the overall objectives of the effort within the specific context of the effort. The constituents of the roadmap that are applied constitute a roadmap instance. Reference the examples above and the Project Management System example used in Chapter 4 as the result of applying component and deployment modeling within the context of the roadmap.

8.2.1.   *The Construct*

This section elaborates step 1 concerning construct implementation of the Detailed and Notational Roadmap section of Chapter 4.

To identify the construct implementation element, focus on identifying one implementation element, then focus on identifying any related implementation elements that further describe the implementation element. For the construct, model the implementation view using a component diagram (component, interfaces, and relationships) to establish a placeholder for information about the implementation of the construct. Progressively apply artifacts, components, and relationships while considering the implementation technology, tools, and environment. Figure 8.5 shows conceptually that the implementation view of a construct is derived from the actual elements of the construct.

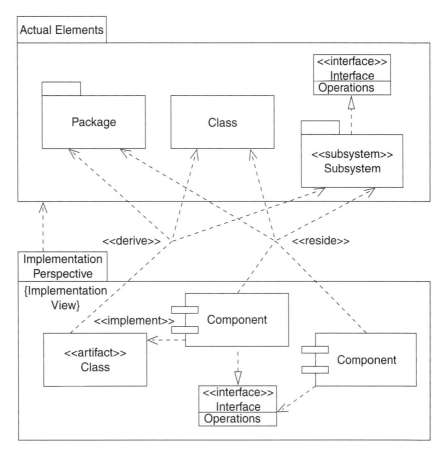

FIGURE 8.5.   The implementation view.

8.2.2.   IMPLEMENTATION

This section elaborates step 2 concerning construct implementation of the Detailed and Notational Roadmap section of Chapter 4.

To describe the construct implementation element, focus on effectively capturing the implementation of the construct.

For the implementation element, capture the implementation element's properties based on the construct's properties to ensure traceability between the construct and the implementation element. This involves propagating any pertinent constraints and characteristics from the construct to the implementation element. The implementation element's properties include its characteristics, any relevant information pertaining to the implementation element. These characteristics include any relevant non-functional properties due to the context of the implementation element.

For each specification element of the implementation element, validate that the specification element's properties are consistent with the construct's specification element's properties. If this check identifies inconsistencies or conflicts, balance the two sets of information by changing the information appropriately to resolve the issues. Often, practitioners don't spend enough time to describe the construct implementation element; however, this validates the construct implementation element to ensure that the construct implementation element will satisfy the construct specification. Otherwise, such inconsistencies and conflicts are detected as the construct is made or being used. This results in building the construct without validating the implementation of the construct against the specification of the construct; in which case, inconsistencies and conflicts are detected in testing or while the construct is being used.

8.2.3.   UNIFICATION

This section elaborates step 5 concerning construct implementation of the Detailed and Notational Roadmap section of Chapter 4.

To unify construct implementation, focus on effectively synchronizing and concluding construct implementation. Reconcile all of the elements used in construct implementation to ensure homogeneity and consistency. Reconcile the construct implementation at the current level of abstraction with the construct implementation at the next higher level of abstraction to ensure that the implementation perspective is consistent. This involves ensuring that the construct implementation at the current level of abstraction does not invalidate anything in the construct implementation at the next higher level of abstraction and that the construct implementation at the next higher level of abstraction is able to support everything in the construct implementation at the current level of abstraction.

CHAPTER 9

Deployment (Environment) Modeling

This chapter provides essential rules, principles, and style guidelines for composing UML deployment or environment models within the context of the roadmap, including deployment diagrams and their elements. Deployment modeling is concerned with the environment dimension of a system—how the implementation or implemented system resides in its environment—and is used for system, subsystem, and class implementation within the roadmap to capture in an implementation model how the construct is packaged or implemented and how it resides in its environment. An implementation model consists of component and deployment diagrams and their model elements. Our goal, in this chapter, is to gain more depth in understanding the UML notation and the roadmap concerning the environment aspect of implementation models.

9.1. Deployment Diagrams

A deployment diagram depicts how an implementation or implemented entity resides in its environment using nodes and their relationships, that is, its run-time configuration. Generally, a component that does not exist at run-time because it is compiled away does not appear on a deployment diagram. An entity is a classifier, for example, a system, subsystem, or class. Both component and deployment diagrams are called implementation diagrams.

9.1.1. Nodes

A node is a resource in the execution environment on which components reside. A node is depicted as a three-dimensional cube figure. A node should be named using a noun phrase and described in a way that captures the node's characteristics.

Figure 9.1 shows a generic node for the Project Management System, and Figure 9.2 shows a specific node for the Project Management System named "2001-Infrastructure". Figure 9.3 shows generic nodes on which components within the Project Management System are deployed, including desktop clients (project manager, resource mange, and system administrator), an enterprise application server, an enterprise services node, a database server, and an internal network. Figure 9.4 shows specific nodes on which components within the Project Management System are deployed, including a system administrator desktop client named "Admin00", a database server named "DB-USA", and various anonymous nodes.

9.1.2. Node Relationships

A node may contain components; that is, the components live or execute on the node. A dependency may be stereotyped with the "deploy" key-

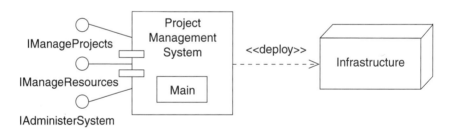

FIGURE 9.1.   Generic deployment of the Project Management System.

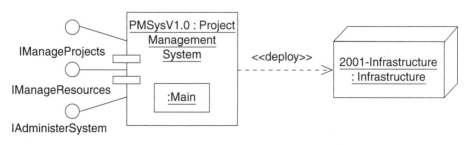

FIGURE 9.2.   Specific deployment of the Project Management System.

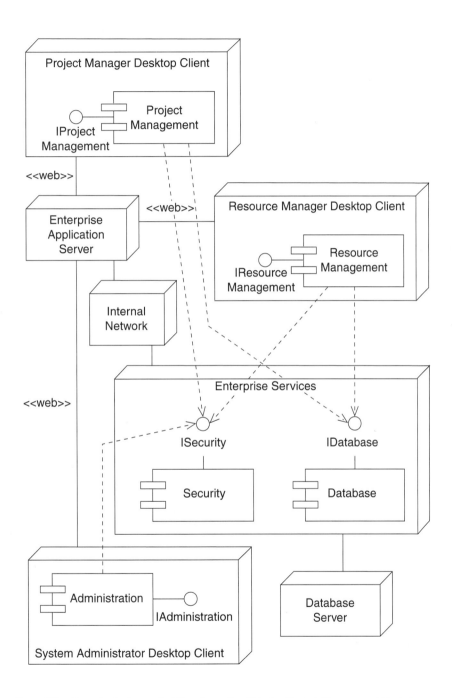

FIGURE 9.3.   Generic deployment of the elements within the Project Management System.

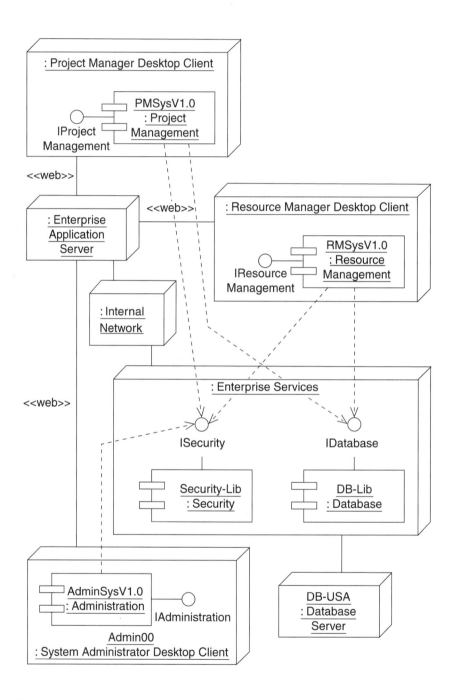

FIGURE 9.4.   Specific deployment of the elements within the Project Management System.

word to specify that the target node may contain or support the source component and that the source component may be deployed on the target node.

Figures 9.1 and 9.2 show that the Project Management System is deployed on the node.

Figures 9.3 and 9.4 show that the Project Manager component is deployed on the Project Management Desktop Client node, the Resource Manager component is deployed on the Resource Manager Desktop Client node, the Administration component is deployed on the System Administrator Desktop Client node, and the Security and Database components are deployed on the Enterprise Services node.

A node may be connected to other nodes using communication associations that provide a communication path between the nodes through which the components on the nodes may communicate with one anther. The communication association may be stereotyped to indicate the nature of the communication path. An association should be named using a noun phrase and described in a way that captures the association's characteristics.

Figures 9.3 and 9.4 show that the desktop clients are connected to the Enterprise Application Server node via the "web," while the Application Services node is connected to the Enterprise Application Server node via the Internal Network node and also directly connected to the Database Server node.

9.2. *Applying Deployment Diagrams*

When modeling the implementation perspective of a construct (system, subsystem, or class) and how the construct is packaged or implemented and how it resides in its environment, consider the guidelines above and herein which ought to be applied within a use-case-driven, architecture-centric, iterative and incremental, and risk-confronting effort that is object oriented and component based. Successive iterations evolve, elaborate, and refine the work of previous iterations with more detail. Steps need not be sequential but may be executed in parallel, where multiple efforts regarding the same system are carried out concurrently.

Within the implementation perspective of the roadmap, specification elements include use cases, interfaces, and operations; construct elements include any elements that may constitute the construct or system, including subsystems, packages, and classes which evolve from proposed candidate elements to accepted actual elements; implementation elements are components; and environment elements are nodes. Properties capture constraints and characteristics of elements.

Every constituent of the roadmap is optional and should only be applied if it adds value to the body of knowledge concerning the construct and facilitates achieving the overall objectives of the effort within the specific context of the effort. Those constituents of the roadmap that are applied constitute a roadmap instance. Reference the examples above and the Project Management System example used in Chapter 4 as the result of applying component and deployment modeling within the context of the roadmap.

9.2.1. THE CONSTRUCT

This section elaborates step 3 concerning construct implementation of the Detailed and Notational Roadmap section of Chapter 4.

To identify the construct environment element, focus on identifying one environment element, then focus on identifying any related environment elements that further describe the environment element. For the construct, model the environment view using a deployment diagram (node and relationships) to establish a placeholder for information about the environment of the construct. Progressively apply nodes and relationships while considering the implementation technology, tools, and environment. Figure 9.5 shows conceptually that the environment view of a construct is derived form the implementation view of the construct.

9.2.2. DEPLOYMENT

This section elaborates step 4 concerning construct implementation of the Detailed and Notational Roadmap section of Chapter 4.

To describe the construct environment element, focus on effectively capturing the environment of the construct.

For the environment element, capture the environment element's properties based on the construct's properties to ensure traceability between the construct and the environment element. This involves propagating any pertinent constraints and characteristics from the construct to the environment element. The environment element's properties include its characteristics, any relevant information pertaining to the environment element. These characteristics include any relevant nonfunctional properties due to the context of the environment element.

For the environment element, validate that the environment element's properties are consistent with the implementation element's properties. If this check identifies inconsistencies or conflicts, balance the two sets of information by changing the information appropriately to resolve the issues. Often, practitioners don't spend enough time to describe the construct environment element; however, this validates the construct envi-

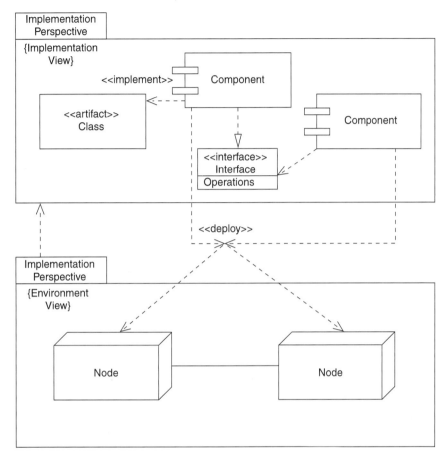

FIGURE 9.5. The environment view.

ronment element to ensure that the construct environment element will satisfy the construct implementation element. Otherwise, such inconsistencies and conflicts are detected as the construct is made or being used. This results in deploying the construct without validating the environment of the construct against the implementation of the construct; in which case, inconsistencies and conflicts are detected in testing or while the construct is being used.

9.2.3.   UNIFICATION

This section elaborates step 5 concerning construct implementation of the Detailed and Notational Roadmap section of Chapter 4.

To unify construct implementation, focus on effectively synchronizing and concluding construct implementation. Reconcile all of the elements used in construct implementation to ensure homogeneity and consistency. Reconcile the construct implementation at the current level of abstraction with the construct implementation at the next higher level of abstraction to ensure that the implementation perspective is consistent. This involves ensuring that the construct implementation at the current level of abstraction does not invalidate anything in the construct implementation at the next higher level of abstraction and that the construct implementation at the next higher level of abstraction is able to support everything in the construct implementation at the current level of abstraction.

10

Extension Mechanisms

This chapter provides an introduction to using extension mechanisms in composing UML models. Our goal in this chapter is to gain an introductory understanding of how to extend the UML.

10.1. Architecture of the Unified Modeling Language (UML)

The UML is defined within a conceptual framework for modeling called a four-layer metamodeling architecture that consists of four distinct layers or levels of abstraction wherein the UML is defined in a circular or recursive manner, in which a subset of the language notation and semantics is used to specify the language itself. Within this framework, a concept is depicted as a vertex or node, including an icon or two-dimensional symbol that may contain other elements, and a relationship among concepts is depicted as an arc or path made of a series of line segments connecting the nodes. Other information is depicted as strings or sequences of characters within or attached to these symbols.

This conceptual framework for modeling may be understood by considering how computer programs and programming languages are related. There are many different programming languages (C, C + +, Java, C#, Smalltalk, and so forth), and each particular program is developed using a specific programming language. All of these languages support various declarative constructs for declaring data, procedural constructs for defining the sequential, conditional, and repetitive logic that manipulates data, and the notions of input, data or declarative constructs, processing or procedural constructs, and output. These concepts may be partitioned into various models based on their level of abstraction. Programming language concepts are defined in a model called a metamodel. Each particular programming language is defined in a model that utilizes and specializes the concepts within the metamodel. Each program implemented in a programming language may be defined in a model called a user model that utilizes and instantiates the concepts within the model of the appropriate programming language. This scheme of a metamodel representing programming language concepts, models representing programming languages, and user models representing programs exemplifies the architecture of the UML within this conceptual framework.

10.1.1. The Four-Layer Metamodeling Architecture

The four-layer metamodeling architecture is composed of the following four layers or levels of abstraction as shown in Figure 10.1:

- The meta-metamodel, or M3-level, layer formalizes the notion of a concept and defines a language for specifying metamodels.
- The metamodel, or M2-level, layer, an instance of the meta-metamodel layer, formalizes paradigm concepts and defines a language for specifying models. For the UML, this includes concepts from the object-oriented and component-based paradigms, which are called metaobjects or metaelements. Figure 10.1 shows that the M2 Metamodel package uses the M3 Meta-metamodel package. Figure 10.2 shows a fragment of the actual UML metamodel with various foundational concepts, including Class, Attribute, Operation, Method, AttributeLink, Object, and their relationships. AttributeLink defines a "slot" that holds a value for an attribute of an instance object.
- The model, or M1-level, layer, an instance of the metamodel layer, formalizes concepts and defines a language for communicating expressions regarding a give domain or subject. These are type-level models of the type-instance dichotomy and include classifiers, associations, messages, and so forth. Each M1-level model element is an instance of one or more M2-level model elements via stereotyping or branding. Figure 10.1 shows that the M1 Model package uses the M2 Metamodel package. Figure 10.2 shows that the M1 Model package uses the M2 Model package, Person is an instance of Class, Name is an instance of Attribute, and setName is an instance of Operation.
- The user (object or data) model, or M0-level, layer, an instance of the model layer, formalizes specific expressions regarding a give domain or subject. These are instance-level models of the type-instance dichotomy and include instances, links, stimuli, and so forth. Each M0-level model element is an instance of one or more M1-level model elements via classification and is an instance of one or more M2-level model elements via stereotyping. Figure 10.1 shows that the M0 User

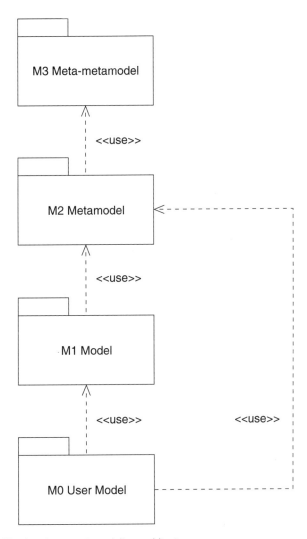

FIGURE 10.1.   The four-layer metamodeling architecture.

Model package uses the M1 Model package and the M2 Model package. Figure 10.2 shows that the M0 Model package uses the M1 Model package and the M2 Model package; aPerson is an instance of Person via classification and an instance of Object via stereotyping; and "Nora" is an instance of Name via classification and an instance of AttributeLink via stereotyping. Classifier roles and association roles are between type-like elements of the M1-level layer and instance-like elements of the M0-level layer. Similar to an instance, a role identifies a distinct occurrence of a classifier. Similar to a type, a

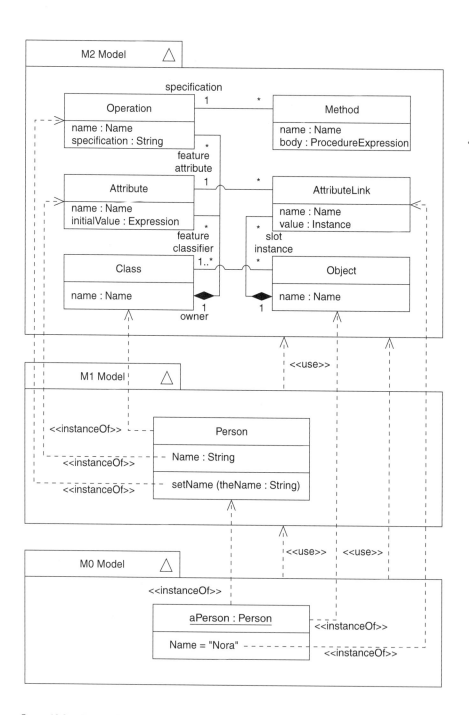

FIGURE 10.2.   Example M2-, M1-, and M0-level layers.

role describes an element that may have many distinct instances. A role is a distinguishable use of a classifier as part of a general description that may be used to create many instances.

A model is a description of a system and context from a specific viewpoint and at a specific level of abstraction. A model element is an abstraction that is a constituent of a model. A metamodel is a model of another model. Within this framework, the "meta" notion is used to signify a relationship between a set of non-metaconcepts or non-metaelements (or simply, concepts and elements) in a more elaborate non-metamodel and their metaconcepts or metaelements in a more compact and higher-level metamodel, where the non-metaconcepts receive the characteristics from their metaconcepts, have their own values for their characteristics or features, and must satisfy the rules specified by their metaconcepts. The "meta" notion is not a property of a model, but of the role a model plays in relation to another model such that this notion is recursively applied where a meta-metamodel relates to a metamodel the same way that a metamodel relates to a model and the same way that a model relates to a user model.

Abstraction or abstracting involves formulating metaconcepts from a set of non-metaconcepts. Manifestation or manifesting involves exemplifying or instantiating non-metaconcepts from metaconcepts. Instantiation has three variant forms within this framework, including classifying, stereotyping, and extending. Classifying involves instantiating an M0-level model element from M1-level model elements, stereotyping involves instantiating an M1-level model element from M2-level model elements or instantiating an M0-level model element from M2-level model elements, and extending involves applying generalization relationships within the same modeling layer. M0-level model elements are manifestations of M1-level model elements via classification and manifestations of M2-level model elements via stereotyping, and M1-level model elements are manifestations of M2-level model elements via stereotyping.

Figure 10.2 shows that Person is a manifestation of Class via stereotyping, Name is a manifestation of Attribute via stereotyping, setName is a manifestation of Operation via stereotyping, aPerson is a manifestation of Person via classification and a manifestation of Object via stereotyping, and "Nora" is a manifestation of Name via classification and a manifestation of AttributeLink via stereotyping.

As a language is a means to express and communicate information, this framework provides an infrastructure for capturing data at the M0-level layer, information at the M1-level layer, and knowledge at the M2-level layer, where each layer provides the context for the layer below it. For example, "12" is an element of data at the M0-level layer, "12 hours" is an element of information at the M1-level layer, and "Time" is an element of knowledge at the M2-level layer.

The recursive nature of this framework enables it to provide a simple and powerful infrastructure composed of various levels of abstraction for managing the complexity and precision involved in defining languages while allowing languages to evolve over time across these levels. A language is defined to have the necessary, sufficient, and consistent collection of concepts with the appropriate precision of semantics, syntax, and guidelines. Something is necessary if it is required; sufficient if it, by itself, is enough to satisfy a given purpose; and consistent if it does not have contradictory suppositions or conflicting imperative expressions that have contradictory consequences.

10.1.2. THE UNIFIED MODELING LANGUAGE (UML) METAMODEL

The UML metamodel is organized as a collection of logical packages as shown in Figure 10.3.

- The Foundation package defines structural or static modeling concepts, often called the language infrastructure, and consists of the following logical packages:
  - The Data Types package defines data types used within the UML metamodel.
  - The Core package defines the most fundamental concepts of the Foundation package, including abstract non-instantiable concepts, such as Classifier, and concrete instantiable concepts, such as Class, Attribute, Operation, and Association.
  - The Extension Mechanisms package defines the concepts for customizing and extending the UML, including stereotypes, constraints, tag definitions, and tagged values.
- The Behavioral Elements package defines behavioral or dynamic modeling concepts, often called the language superstructure, and consists of the following logical packages:
  - The Common Behavior package defines the most fundamental concepts of the Behavioral Elements package, including Signal, Procedure, Stimulus, and Instance.
  - The Collaborations package defines concepts related to collaborations and interactions.
  - The Use Cases package defines concepts related to use cases.
  - The State Machines package defines concepts related to state machines.
  - The Activity Graphs package defines concepts related to activity graphs.
  - The Actions package defines concepts related to actions and pro-

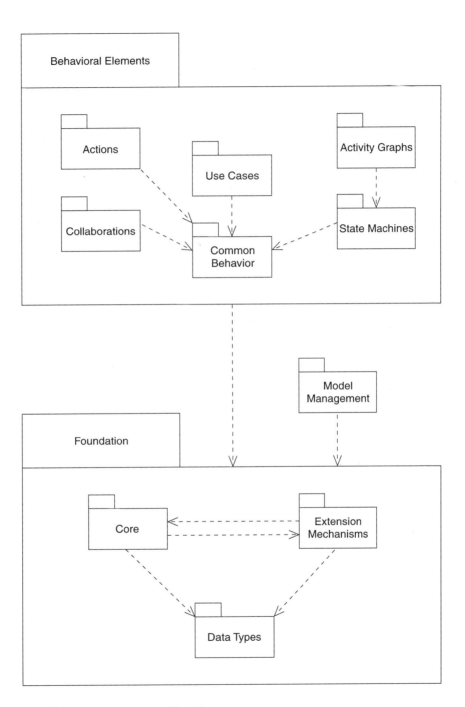

FIGURE 10.3.   The UML metamodel architecture.

cedures and how they execute. It defines the semantics of an action language, a language for executing modeled actions and procedures, but does not define its syntax. A model of an action or procedure is known as an action model.

- The Model Management package defines grouping units, including Model, Package, and Subsystem.

The extension mechanisms of the UML define a means for customizing and extending the UML by specializing the language for different types of systems (software and non-software), domains (business versus software), and methods or processes. A semantic variation point is a point of variation in the semantics of a metamodel allowing an intentional degree of freedom for the interpretation of the metamodel semantics that may be required in different domains when applying the language; that is, semantic variation points allow for different semantic interpretations. The extension mechanisms, including stereotypes and properties (tag definitions and constraints), allow for refining the standard semantics in a strictly additive manner, where the additional semantics do not contradict or conflict with the standard semantics, they only refine the standard semantics based on semantic variations and different semantic interpretations, but not arbitrary semantic extensions. These mechanisms enable the UML to evolve based on problem domains, solution domains, and processes by specializing the language rather than by redefining the language to satisfy the emerging needs of its users.

10.2. Stereotypes

A stereotype is a mechanism for classifying or branding a model element and introducing a new type of modeling element.

10.2.1. DECLARATION

When introducing a new type of modeling element, the new declared and user-defined stereotype is a metaelement that is based on an existing UML metaelement, called its base class, and appears in the model layer but conceptually belongs in the metamodel layer. A user-defined stereotype may have one or more base classes or base elements. The stereotype is a virtual subclasses of one or more UML metaclasses with new properties, including tag definitions that capture metaattributes and constraints that capture additional semantics. The base class must be a UML metamodel element such as Model, Package, Subsystem, Class, Association, and so forth, and not a user-level modeling element. All stereotype definitions must be contained either directly or transitively in a profile package.

A stereotype is declared using the class notation (or symbol for the metamodel base element as a solid-outline rectangle with three compartments separated by horizontal lines. The top name compartment is required and contains the "stereotype" keyword enclosed in guillemets («») or double-angle brackets preceding or above the name of the stereotype being declared, followed by the stereotype name string followed by an optional property; the middle list compartment is optional and contains a list of tag definitions; and the bottom list compartment is optional and contains a list of constraints. The contents of the property may be specified in the middle and bottom list compartments. A stereotype may also specify a geometrical icon to be used for presenting elements branded by the stereotype.

Figure 10.4 shows various stereotype declarations, including Work Effort, Project, Work Product, Activity, Task, Activity Relationship, Task Relationship, Produce, and Consume.

A list compartment holds a list of text strings and may have a name depicted centered at the top of the compartment. The items are depicted one to a line and may have a meaningful order. For the tags compartment, the string "Tags" may be used. For the constraints compartment, the string "Constraints" may be used. Other compartments may be used as necessary, each compartment need only show what is relevant to the diagram, and optional compartments may be suppressed.

Figure 10.4 show the tags compartment and the constraints compartment for the various stereotype declarations.

A package stereotyped with the "metamodel" keyword or a triangle icon denotes that the package is a model that is an abstraction of another model, that is, a model of another model where every element of the first model is an instance of elements in the second model. A classifier stereotyped with the "metaclass" keyword denotes that the classifier is a model element that is an abstraction of other model elements; that is, instances of the classifier are classes. A classifier stereotyped with the "stereotype" keyword denotes that the classifier is a stereotype whose name may be used as a stereotype name of other model elements. A dependency stereotyped with the "stereotype" keyword denotes that the source model level element, the stereotype, depends on its metaelement, the UML base class.

Figure 10.4 shows that the base class of the Work Product stereotype is the abstract GeneralizableElement metaclass; it shows that the Class metaclass is the base class for the Project, Work Product, Activity, and Task stereotypes and that these stereotypes apply to classes; and it shows

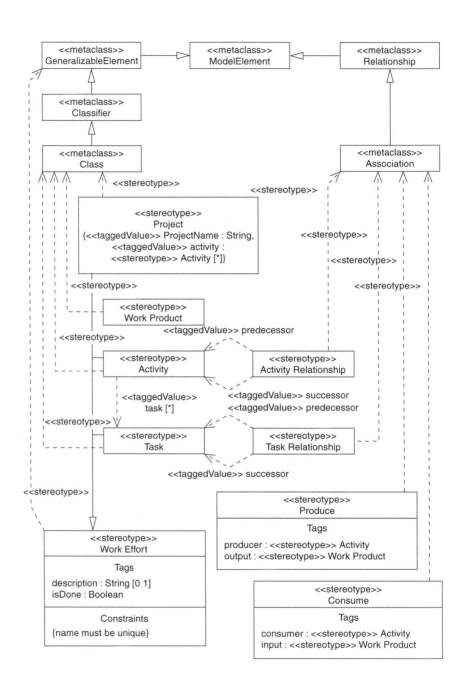

Figure 10.4. Stereotype declarations.

that the Association metaclass is the base class for the Activity Relationship, Task Relationship, Produce, and Consume stereotypes and that these stereotypes apply to associations.

Alternatively, stereotypes may be expressed using a stereotype specification table where each row represents one stereotype and has the following optional columns:

- The Stereotype column specifies the name of the stereotype.
- The Base Class column specifies the stereotype's base class UML metamodel element.
- The Parent column specifies the direct parent of the stereotype; otherwise "N/A" is used.
- The Tags column specifies a list of tags of the tagged values that may be associated with the stereotype or "N/A" if none are defined.
- The Constraints column specifies a list of constraints associated with the stereotype.
- The Description column specifies an informal description and explanatory comments for the stereotype.

Figure 10.5 shows how the information in Figure 10.4 may be represented using a stereotype specification table. This example places the

Stereotype Specification Table				
Stereotype	Base Class	Parent	Tags	Constraints
Work Effort	Generalizable Element	N/A	description isDone	name must be unique
Project	Class	Work Effort	ProjectName activity	N/A
Activity	Class	Work Effort	task	N/A
Task	Class	Work Effort	N/A	N/A
Work Product	Class	N/A	N/A	N/A
Activity Relationship	Association	N/A	predecessor successor	N/A
Task Relationship	Association	N/A	predecessor successor	N/A
Produce	Association	N/A	producer output	N/A
Consume	Association	N/A	consumer input	N/A

FIGURE 10.5. Stereotype declarations using a stereotype specification table.

table in a note; however, such a table need not be placed in a note but may simply accompany a model.

A more specific stereotype may have a generalization relationship to a more general stereotype, where it inherits all of the properties from its more general stereotype, including the more general stereotype's base class. The base class of the more specific stereotype may be refined to be a more specific base class of the more general stereotype's base class; that is, the base class of a stereotype must be the same or a subclass of the base class of its parent stereotype. If a more specific stereotype has multiple more general stereotypes, all of these more general stereotypes must be derived from a single common stereotype, and the base class of the more specific stereotype is the base class of the most specific parent stereotype or one of its subclasses.

Figure 10.5 shows that the base class of the Work Product stereotype is the abstract GeneralizableElement metaclass, and the Class metaclass is the base class for the Project, Work Product, Activity, and Task stereotypes that is more specific than the GeneralizableElement metaclass.

10.2.2.   APPLICATION

When applying a stereotype, the branded or classified model element receives or inherits the properties of the stereotype, including its attributes, associations, parent classes, and constraints. The model element bears the stereotype, must observe and satisfy the constraints attached to the stereotype and have those constraints attached to it, and must have associated tagged values specified by the tag definitions belonging to the stereotype and have those tags attached to it. The base class of the model element is the base class of the most specific parent or one of its subclasses. If a model element does not satisfy its constraints, the model is invalid and said to be ill formed or not well formed. Furthermore, model elements may be branded by zero or more stereotypes.

A model element is branded or marked by a stereotype by using the symbol for the metamodel base class element with a keyword string preceding or above the name of the element. The keyword string consists of zero or more stereotype names, where each name is enclosed in guillemets («») or double-angle brackets. The guillemets and the stereotype icon may be depicted simultaneously; however only one is required. The icon is placed in the upper right corner near the name of the element, or the entire base model element symbol is collapsed into an icon containing the element name or with the name above or below the icon, and other information contained by the base model element symbol is suppressed. When multiple stereotypes are used for an element, the icons are omitted.

Figure 10.6 shows how the stereotype declarations of Figure 10.4 and 10.5 may be applied to define an M1-level layer model, including a pro-

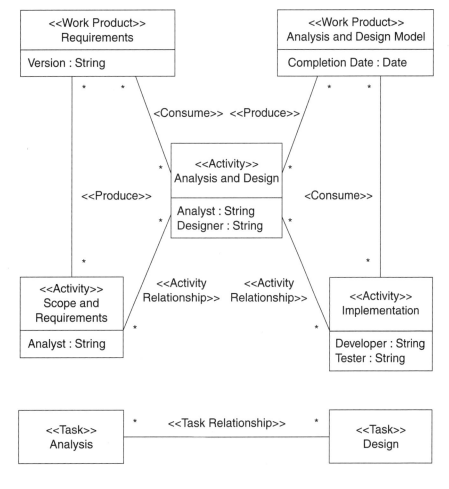

Figure 10.6. Stereotype application at the M1-level layer model.

ject, work products, activities, and tasks. Figure 10.7 shows an M0-level layer model based on the M1-level layer model of Figure 10.6, including a specific project, work products, activities, and tasks.

Within a list compartment, where text string items are depicted as a list, possibly with a meaningful order, a stereotype keyword string may be used as an element, in which case it applies to all succeeding list elements until another stereotype keyword string replaces it. An empty stereotype keyword string nullifies it. A stereotype keyword string attached to an individual list element augments or modifies the general stereotype keyword string but does not supersede the general stereotype keyword string. An ellipsis (. . .) may be depicted as the final element of a list to indicate that additional elements in the model meet the selection criteria but are not shown.

A note is a notational item containing textual information, similar to a comment in programming. A note is depicted as a rectangle with a bent upper right corner. A note may be attached to zero or more elements by dashed lines. If the contents of a note apply to a single element, the note may be attached to the element. If the contents of a note apply to multiple elements, the note may be attached to every element to which its contents apply. For example, if a note expresses a business rule that applies to a single use case, it may be attached to that single use case. If a note expresses a business rule that applies to multiple use cases, it may be attached to each use case; thus, when the rule changes, it need only be changed once for all of the use cases. If a note expresses a business rule that applies to multiple use cases and the use cases are all in the same containing package without any other use cases, it may be attached to the containing package and expressed as applying to all of its contained use cases. A note stereotyped with the "requirement" keyword denotes that the note specifies a feature, property, or behavior of the element to which it is attached. A note stereotyped with the "responsibility" keyword denotes that the note specifies a contract or obligation of the element to which it is attached to other elements.

A note stereotyped with the "invariant" keyword denotes that the note specifies a constraint whose conditions must hold true over time for the attached set of classifiers or relationships and their instances. A note stereotyped with the "precondition" keyword denotes that the note specifies a constraint whose conditions must hold true for invocation of the operation to which it is attached. A note stereotyped with the "postcondition" keyword denotes that the note specifies a constraint whose conditions must hold true after the invocation of the operation to which it is attached. A note stereotyped with the "stateInvariant" keyword denotes that the note specifies a constraint whose conditions must hold true for the associated state of a state machine for a classifier and instances of the classifier when an instance is in that state.

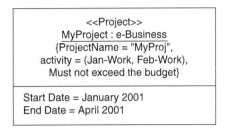

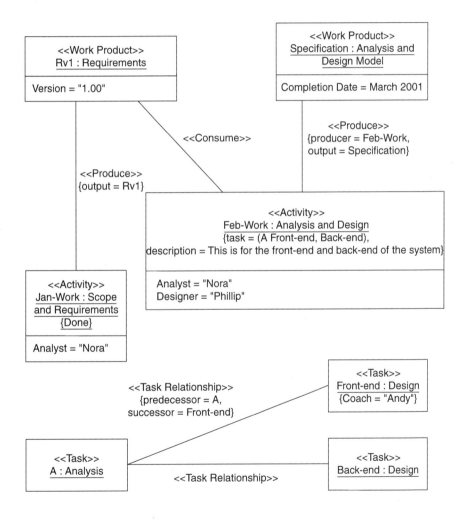

FIGURE 10.7. Stereotype application at the M0-level layer model.

10.3.   Properties

A property is a characteristic of a model element. A property consists of property strings or property specifications representing the characteristics of the element. A property is depicted as a comma-delimited list of text strings inside a pair of braces ({}) succeeding or below the name of the element. The text strings may be expressed in any natural or computer language or be tagged values. All properties must be contained either directly or transitively in a profile package.

For properties associated with two symbols or paths, the property is shown as a dashed arrow from one element to the other element labeled by the property, where the direction of the arrow may be relevant to the property. For properties associated with three or more symbols, the property with braces is placed in a note symbol and attached to each of the symbols by a dashed line. For properties associated with three or more paths, the property may be attached to a dashed line crossing all of the paths. Notes may be used with properties where a note has a stereotype; the "constraint" keyword or a more specific stereotype or its contents may be placed inside a pair of braces ({}), to indicate that it is a constraint and its contents are part of the model. Otherwise the note is just part of a diagram.

Within a list compartment, where text string items are depicted as a list, possibly with a meaningful order, a property may be used as an element, in which case it applies to all succeeding list elements until another property replaces it. An empty property nullifies it. A property attached to an individual list element augments or modifies the general property but does not supersede the general property. An ellipsis (. . .) may be depicted as the final element of a list to indicate that additional elements in the model meet the selection criteria but are not shown.

Properties should be defined in conjunction with a stereotype definition; however, for backward compatibility with UML 1.3, it is possible to have arbitrary properties not associated with any stereotype definition. Properties must not conflict with the UML metamodel.

10.3.1.   Constraints

A constraint is a property string that is a semantic condition or proposition that must be maintained as true for a model element. A constraint specifies new semantics for a model element. A constraint is shown as a text string in the bottom compartment of a stereotype declaration rectangle or as a property when applied to a model element. The text string may be expressed in any natural or computer language. Figure 10.4

shows a constraints compartment for the Work Effort stereotype declaration, and Figure 10.7 shows a constraint for the MyProject project.

10.3.2. Tag Definitions and Tagged Values

A tag definition is a property string that specifies a property of a model element. A tag definition specifies a new property similar to a meta-attribute definition attached to a model element.

A tag definition is shown as a text string in the middle compartment of a stereotype declaration rectangle. The syntax for a tag definition is "name : type [multiplicity]", where—

- The type specifies the type of the tag. The UML provides data types for Boolean true and false values, Integer, Real, and String. The type may be either the name of a UML data type or the name of a UML metaclass or a stereotype where the metaclass or stereotype is referenced. The syntax for a type that references a metaclass is "<<metaclass>> metaclass-name". The syntax for a type that references a stereotype is "<<stereotype>> stereotype-name". The default type is "String", which is effectively not typed. A pathname, a series of names linked together and separated by a double colon (::) delimiter, where the chaining together of package names and the element name starting from the root of the system or from some other point selects the element, starting with "UML", may be used to specify the metaclass. The string "reference to" may precede the metaclass reference.
- The multiplicity is optional and specifies the number of values that the tag may have. Multiplicity is depicted as a literal integer value or a closed range depicted as "lower-bound .. upper-bound," and a single asterisk is used to denote an unlimited range. When omitted, it is assumed to be 1. A tag with a lower-bound of zero indicates that it is optional.

Figure 10.4 shows a tags compartment for the Work Effort stereotype declaration, and Figure 10.7 shows the use of the various tags.

Alternatively, tag definitions may be expressed using a tag specification table where each row represents on tag and has the following optional columns:

- The Tag column specifies the name of the tag.
- The Stereotype column specifies the stereotype that owns the tag or with which the tag may be associated; otherwise "N/A" is used if it is a standalone tag that may be applied to any element.
- The Type column specifies the type of the values that may be associated with the tag.

- The Multiplicity column specifies the maximum number of values that may be associated with one tag instance.
- The Description column specifies an informal description and explanatory comments for the tag.

Figure 10.8 shows how the information in Figure 10.4 may be represented using a tag specification table. This example places the table in a note; however, such a table need not be placed in a note but may simply accompany a model.

When a tag definition references other model elements, it may be shown in the middle compartment of a stereotype declaration rectangle, as a property string stereotyped using the "taggedValue" keyword with the stereotype declaration, or graphically represented using a depen-

Tag Specification Table			
Tag	Stereotype	Type	Multiplicity
description	Work Effort	UML::Datatypes::String	0.1
isDone	Work Effort	UML::Datatypes::Boolean	1
ProjectName	Project	UML::Datatypes::String	1
activity	Project	Activity	*
task	Activity	Task	*
predecessor	Activity Relationship	Activity	1
successor	Activity Relationship	Activity	1
predecessor	Task Relationship	Task	1
successor	Task Relationship	Task	1
producer	Produce	Activity	1
output	Produce	Work Product	1
consumer	Consume	Activity	1
input	Consume	Work Product	1
Coach	N/A	UML::Datatypes::String	*

FIGURE 10.8.   Tag definitions using a tag specification table.

dency stereotyped with the "taggedValue" keyword from the stereotype to the referenced element. When a taggedValue dependency is used, the colon followed by the type is not depicted, but the name and multiplicity are depicted. Figure 10.4 shows the tags for the Work Effort stereotype using the middle compartment of the stereotype, the tags for the Project stereotype using the property, and the tag for the Activity stereotype using a dependency.

A tagged value is a property string that specifies a value for a property of a model element. A tagged value specifies an actual value for a property of an individual model element. A tagged value is shown as a keyword-value pair using the property keyword or a metamodel attribute followed by an equal sign followed by its value when applied to a model element. The keyword is called a tag. Metamodel attributes and arbitrary tags may be used as tag keywords. If the type of a tag is Boolean, then the default value is true if the equal symbol and value is omitted. That is, to specify a value of true, include the keyword, and to specify a value of false, omit the name completely. Boolean properties often have names such as "isX", where X is the tag name, in which case "{isX = true}" is equivalent to "{X}". Figure 10.4 shows an isDone tag associated with the Work Effort stereotype. Figure 10.7 shows that only the Jan-Work activity is done and all other activities have a value of False for the isDone tag.

The "documentation" property keyword specifies a comment, description, or explanation of the element to which it is attached. The "derived" property keyword specifies that model element to which it is attached can be completely derived from other model elements and is therefore logically redundant.

10.4. Profiles

A profile is a stereotyped package that contains model elements that are customized for a specific domain or purpose using stereotypes, tag definitions, and constraints, including any other supporting or required modeling elements. A profile refines the standard semantics by adding further constraints and interpretations that capture domain-specific semantics and modeling elements, but it does not add any new foundational concepts.

The "profile" stereotype keyword denotes that a package is a profile. The "applicableSubset" property keyword may be used with profiles to list the metaelements that are used by the associated profile. The value of the "applicableSubset" tag is a set of strings where each string represents the name of an applicable metaelement. The use of applicable subsets does not exclude the use of any metaelements, but identifies which metaelements are referenced from the associated profile. The absence of an applicable subset tag means that the whole UML metamodel is applicable. Because a profile is a specialization of the UML, a profile package may have a generalization relationship to a package named "UML". Figure 10.9 shows various profiles, including e-Business, Business Strategy, Creative Design, and Technology.

The "modelLibrary" stereotype keyword denotes that the package is a model library that contains model elements which are reused by other packages, but it does not extend the UML language using stereotypes, tag definitions, and constraints. Figure 10.9 shows a Digital Economy model library.

A profile package may have generalization, import, and access relationships with other packages. In the current version of the UML, no formal or robust mechanisms are defined to verify that a combination

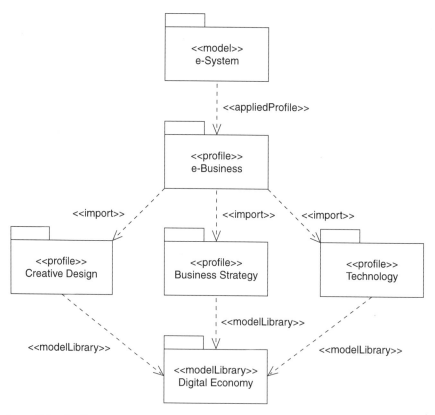

FIGURE 10.9.   Profiles.

of profiles is mutually consistent; that is, they are compatible and their constraints do not contradict. A more specific profile may have a generalization relationship to a more general profile; that is, the more specific profile is fully consistent with the more general profile, receives the stereotypes, tag definitions, and constraints of the more general profile, and it may refine the contents of the more general profiles. When applying generalization relationships, the subset of UML defined as applicable to a profile is not inherited by specializing profiles, while other relationships to model libraries are inherited. A profile may have access and import dependency relationships to other profiles; that is, the elements of the client profile have access or use elements of the supplier profile. Figure 10.9 shows that the e-Business profile imports the Business Strategy, Creative Design, and Technology profiles.

A dependency stereotyped with the "modelLibrary" keyword denotes that the source or client package that is stereotyped as a profile shares the model elements in the target or supplier package that is not stereotyped as a profile. A dependency stereotyped with the "appliedProfile" keyword denotes that the target or supplier package that is stereotyped as a profile applies transitively to the model elements in the source or client package; that is, the element in the client package have access to the elements in the supplier package. Figure 10.9 shows that the Business Strategy, Creative Design, and Technology profiles use the Digital Economy model library, and that the e-System model uses the e-Business profile.

CHAPTER 11

The Object Constraint Language (OCL)

This chapter provides an introduction to using the Object Constraint Language (OCL) in composing UML models. Our goal in this chapter is to gain an introductory understanding of how to use the OCL.

11.1. What is the Object Constraint Language (OCL)?

Within the UML, expressions, linguistic formulas that yield values when evaluated, are depicted as strings in a particular language (pseudo-code or another language). The UML assumes that the name of a class or simple data type maps into a classifier reference, but the syntax and semantics of complicated language-dependent expressions are outside the scope of the UML. The UML metamodel unitizes the Object Constraint Language (OCL) to capture constraints specifying the semantic conditions that must be maintained as true for model elements, and the OCL may be used for user (object or data) models to define constraints.

The OCL is a formal or robust, easily readable and writeable, non-programming, implementation-independent language for expressing typed, pure and side-effect-free, precise, and unambiguous constraints, including expressions specifying invariants attached to model elements (classifiers, relationships, stereotypes, operations, attributes, and so forth), preconditions and postconditions attached to operations and methods, guard conditions, navigation between model elements, general rules in the form of conditions and restrictions attached to model elements, and any expression in a UML model.

Because the OCL is a pure and side-effect-free language, the evaluation of an OCL expression may not alter the state of the model or system to which it pertains, but when the expression is evaluated, it simply returns a value and does not change anything in the model. As a non-programming language, but rather a constraint specification language, the OCL does not support program logic specification and only allows the invocation of query operations.

An OCL expression is said to be well formed if it satisfies the conformance rules of the language; an element is said to be well formed if it satisfies the invariants associated with it and its classifier; and a model is said to be well formed if all of its elements are well formed. Each classifier defined in a UML model is a distinct OCL type, and the evaluation of an OCL expression is instantaneous for a model such that the states of the elements in the model cannot change during evaluation.

11.2. Expressions

An expression is a linguistic formula or procedure that yields a value when evaluated. An expression is written and evaluated in the context of a model element, an instance of a specific classifier type. The "context" keyword specifies the context of the expression (called a context declaration), the contextual instance or model element to which the expression applies, and another keyword is used to denote the specific type of expression. An expression may be shown in a stereotyped note attached to the contextual element, in which case there is no need for an explicit context declaration, but a context declaration is used if the expression is not attached to any element.

An expression is evaluated from left to right, where each sub-expression results in a specific object of a specific type. The result may be an object or a group of objects, called a collection. Based on the type or class of the result, another feature or property may be applied to the result to derive the next value. Each expression uses basic values and types, collection values and types, and may reference model elements and their features. The "self" keyword is optional and refers to the contextual instance, an instance of the classifier to which the expression is attached, and from where the expression starts or is evaluated.

For operations in expressions, the following precedence order is used (from highest to lowest) where parentheses may be used to change the precedence order as parentheses are evaluated from innermost to outermost:

1. @pre keyword;
2. dot (".") and arrow ("->") operations;
3. unary ("not") and unary minus ("-");
4. multiplication ("*") and division ("/");
5. addition (" + ") and binary subtraction ("-");
6. "if-then-else-endif" keywords;
7. logical comparison operators ("", "", " = ", and " = ");
8. equal (" = ") and not-equal ("");
9. logical "and", "or", and "xor";
10. and logical "implies".

The OCL uses infix operators where "a + b" is conceptually equivalent to "a. + (b)" or invoking the " + " operation on "a" with the parameter "b". A type may define operator operations with the correct signature for " + ", "-", "*", "/", "<", ">", "<>", "<=", ">=", "and", "or", and "xor" with exactly one parameter and a return type of Boolean for logical operators or of the appropriate type for the other operators. The following OCL keywords are reserved and may not be used in expressions: "if", "then", "else", "endif", "not", "let", "or", "and", "xor", "implies", "endpackage", "package", "context", "def", "inv", "pre", "post", and "in".

Comments may be expressed as two successive dashes (minus signs) with everything immediately following the two dashes up to and including the end-of-line being a comment.

If a query or element within an OCL expression is undefined, the complete expression is undefined. However, if an expression results in the Boolean value of True, True Or-ed with anything remains True; and if an expression results in the Boolean value of False, False And-ed with anything remains False.

11.2.1. INVARIANTS

An invariant is a constraint whose conditions must hold true over time for the attached set of classifiers or relationships and their instances. An invariant is shown as a note stereotyped with the "invariant" keyword or within a context declaration using the "inv" keyword.

The syntax for the context declaration is "context instance-name : type-name inv invariant-name : expression" where—

- The instance-name is optional and specifies a name used in the expression to reference the contextual instance. The colon following the instance-name is omitted if no instance-name is specified. When no instance-name is specified, the "self" keyword may be used to refer to the contextual instance.
- The type-name specifies the classifier type of the contextual instance.

- The invariant-name is optional and specifies a name for the invariant such that it maybe referenced by name. The colon following the invariant-name is not optional and must be specified even if no invariant-name is specified.
- The expression is required and specifies the constraint that must be true for all instance of the classifier type at any point in time. The type of the expression is Boolean, true or false.
- Any number of invariants may be specified using the syntax "inv invariant-name : expression".

When an invariant is inherited by a more specific model element from a more general model element via a generalization relationship, the more specific model element may strengthen the invariant.

Figure 11.1 shows various constraints associated with the Person class. Notice the invariant that a person's last name and first name be nonempty may be attached directly to the Person class, shown as a note stereotyped with the "invariant" keyword and attached to the Person class, or shown within a context declaration using the "inv" keyword.

11.2.2. PRECONDITIONS AND POSTCONDITIONS

A precondition is a constraint whose conditions must hold true for invocation of the operation to which it is attached. A precondition is shown as a note stereotyped with the "precondition" keyword or within a context declaration using the "pre" keyword. A postcondition is a constraint whose conditions must hold true after the invocation of the operation to which it is attached. A postcondition is shown as a note stereotyped with the "postcondition" keyword or within a context declaration using the "post" keyword.

The syntax for the context declaration is "context type-name :: operation-name (parameter list) : return-type pre precondition-name : precondition-expression post postcondition-name : postcondition-expression", where—

- As no instance name is used, the "self" keyword may be used to refer to the contextual instance, an instance of the classifier type which owns the operation or method as a feature.
- The type-name specifies the classifier type of the contextual instance.
- The operation-name specifies the operation of the classifier type to which the expressions apply.
- The parameter list is an optional comma-separated list that specifies the formal parameters passed to the operation. The syntax for each parameter is "parameter-name : type". The parentheses may not be omitted and are mandatory even if no parameter list is specified.

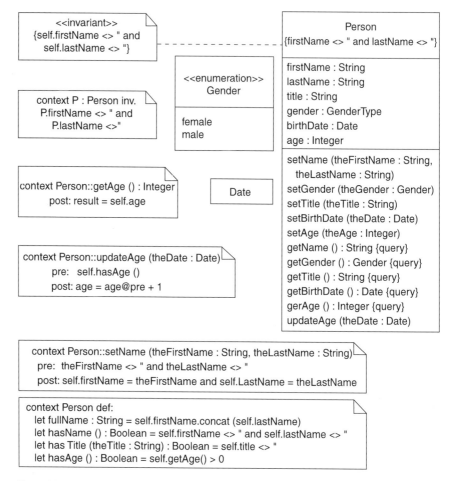

FIGURE 11.1.   Invariants, preconditions, and postconditions.

- The return type is optional and specifies the type of the return value. The colon is omitted if no type is returned. The parameter list and return type may be omitted together, but not separately.
- The precondition-name is optional and specifies a name for the precondition such that it maybe be referenced by name. The colon following the precondition-name is not optional and must be specified even if no precondition-name is specified.
- The precondition-expression is required if the "pre" keyword is specified, and it indicates the constraint that must hold true for invocation of the operation. Parameters in the parameter list may be used in the expression.

- The postcondition-name is optional and specifies a name for the postcondition such that it maybe referenced by name. The colon following the postcondition-name is not optional and must be specified even if no postcondition-name is specified.
- The postcondition-expression is required if the "post" keyword is specified, and it indicates the constraint that must hold true after the invocation of the operation. Parameters in the parameter list may be used in the expression. The "result" keyword denotes the result of the operation.
- Any number of preconditions and postconditions may be specified using the syntax "pre precondition-name : precondition-expression" for preconditions and the syntax "post postcondition-name : postcondition-expression" for postconditions.

Within a postcondition, an expression may refer to the value of a feature or property upon completion of the operation, or the value of a feature or property at the start of the operation. To refer to the value of a property upon completion of the operation, the property name is used. To refer to the value of a property at the start of the operation, the property name is appended with the string "@pre". This string may be postfixed to properties of object instances, including attributes and operations. The value of a property of an object that has been destroyed results in undefined, and the value of a property of an object that has been created during execution of the operation results in undefined.

Figure 11.1 shows various preconditions and postconditions for the getAge, updateAge, and setName operations for the Person class. Notice how the "@pre" string is used in the updateAge operation to ensure that the age has been incremented by one.

When a precondition or postcondition is inherited by a more specific model element from a more general model element via a generalization relationship, the more specific model element may weaken the precondition and may strengthen the postcondition.

11.2.3. PACKAGE STATEMENTS

Invariant, precondition, and postcondition constraints may be enclosed in package statements to specify the classifiers in the specific package to which they pertain. Any number of package statements may be stored together.

The syntax for a package statement is "package pathname OCL-expression endpackage", where the pathname is a series of names linked together and separated by a double colon (::) delimiter, where the chaining together of package names starting from the root of the system or from some other point selects the package in which the classifiers to which the OCL expression pertain reside. Any number of OCL expressions may be used in a single package statement.

11.2.4. *LET EXPRESSIONS AND DEFINITION CONSTRAINTS*

A let expression defines an attribute or operation which may be used in a constraint. The defined attribute or operation is only known within the specific context in which it is defined, including being defined in an invariant or precondition or postcondition.

The syntax for a let expression defining an attribute is "let attribute-name : type-name = OCL-expression". The type-name specifies the type of the result of evaluating the OCL-expression.

The syntax for a let expression defining an operation is "let operation-name (parameter list) : type-name = OCL-expression". The parameter list is an optional comma-separated list that specifies the formal parameters passed to the operation. The syntax for each parameter is "parameter-name : type". The parentheses may not be omitted and are mandatory even if no parameter list is specified. The type-name specifies the type of the result of evaluating the OCL-expression, the type of the return value.

A definition constraint enables let expressions to be defined and re-used. A definition constraint is shown as a note stereotyped with the "definition" keyword or within a context declaration using the "def" keyword. A definition constraint must be attached to a classifier and may only contain let expressions. The defined attributes and operations are essentially pseudo-attribute and pseudo-operations of the classifier to which they are attached. They are used within OCL expressions, they must be unique, and they may not conflict with the names of the attributes, association ends, and operation of the classifier to which they are attached. Figure 11.1 shows a definition constraint for the Person class wherein the fullName is a pseudo-attribute and hasName, hasTitle, and hasAge are pseudo-operations.

11.3. Properties

Figure 11.2 shows various classes within a Project Management system. The "subset" property keyword indicates that a person must be a member of the team on which that person is the manager. The "xor" property keyword indicates that a spending account may be associated with a person or a team but not both.

The constraint that when a team and project are associated with one

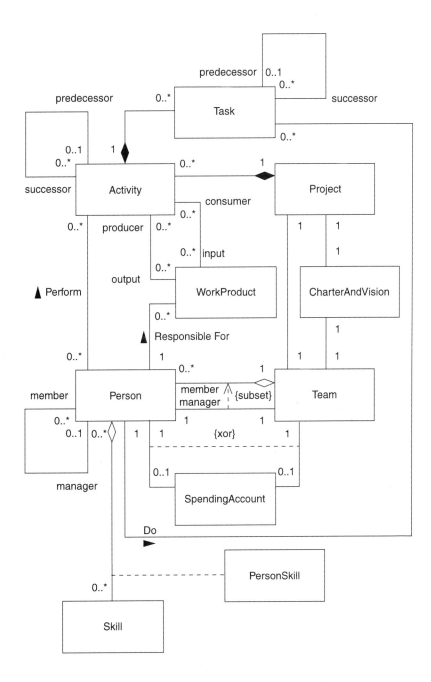

FIGURE 11.2. Teams, people, skills, projects, activities, and tasks in a Project Management System.

another, they must be associated with the same charter and vision is significant; however, it is not expressed in Figure 11.2. For example, Figure 11.3 is derived from and consistent with Figure 11.2; however, a team and project are associated with one another, but they are associated with different charters and visions, thus violating the rule. Figure 11.4 is derived from and consistent with Figure 11.2, and is consistent with the constraint that when a team and project are associated with one another, they must be associated with the same charter and vision. Therefore, it is desirable to capture the constraint in an OCL expression such that it may be enforced in the UML model of Figure 11.2.

An expression may reference model elements and their features, including classifiers or associations (acting as types or association classes) and their attributes, side-effect-free operations, and association ends.

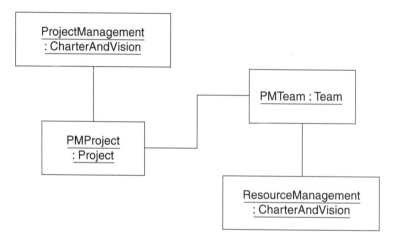

FIGURE 11.3.   Teams, projects, and charters and visions not adhering to a constraint.

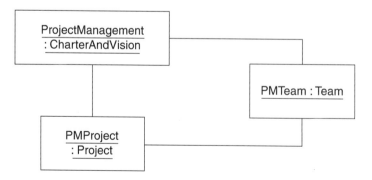

FIGURE 11.4.   Teams, projects, and charters and visions adhering to a constraint.

Side-effect-free operations must have the isQuery attribute of the operation set to True or the "query" property keyword denoting that the operation may not modify the state or attributes of its classifier. A property is an attribute, side-effect-free operation or method, or an association end.

11.3.1. CLASSIFIERS AND INSTANCES

To refer to a property of an object, the syntax is simply the property name, or the "self" keyword followed by a dot followed by the name of the property. As "self" is a reference to an object, "self.property" is the value of the property on the object self.

The syntax for referencing an attribute is the name of the attribute. The syntax for referencing an operation is the name of the operation followed by parentheses containing an optional comma-separated list that specifies the actual parameters passed to the operation. If the operation does not take any parameters, the parentheses with an empty argument list are mandatory.

Figure 11.5 shows various equivalent constraints within the context of the CharterAndVision class for expressing the significant rule that when a team and project are associated with one another, they must be associated with the same charter and vision. Notice that there are a multitude of expressions to capture the same constraint; however, these constraints only enforce the semantic rule on the CharterAndVision class. Figure 11.6 shows constraints that enforce this semantic rule on all of the classes involved, including the Team, Project, and CharterAndVision classes.

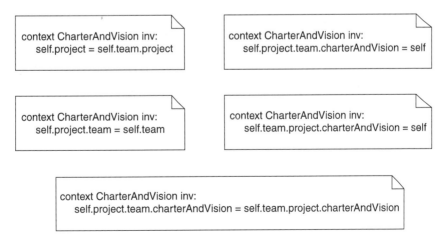

FIGURE 11.5.   Various constraints for teams, projects, and charters and visions.

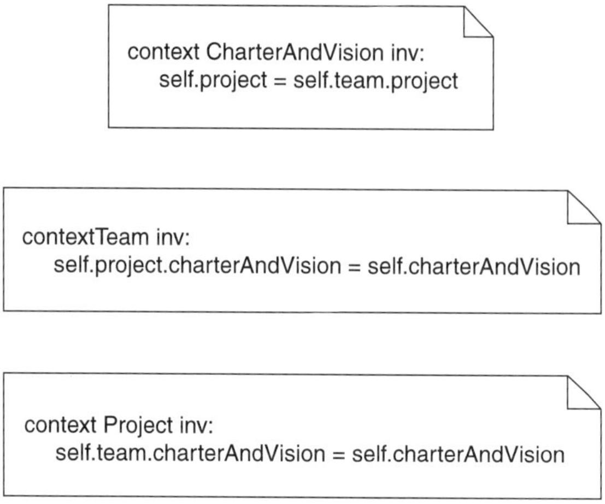

```
context CharterAndVision inv:
    self.project = self.team.project
```

```
contextTeam inv:
    self.project.charterAndVision = self.charterAndVision
```

```
context Project inv:
    self.team.charterAndVision = self.charterAndVision
```

FIGURE 11.6.   Constraints for teams, projects, and charters and visions.

11.3.2.   ASSOCIATIONS AND LINKS

The syntax for referencing associated objects, navigating an association, to the set of object on the other side of the association is the rolename of the target class. If the multiplicity on the association end has a maximum of one, the result is an object. If the multiply on the association end has no maximum of one, the result is a Set collection of objects of the target class, a collection of unique and unordered objects. If the association end is adorned with the "ordered" property, the result is a Sequence collection of object of the target class, an order set of objects. By default, navigation results in a Set collection, and even if the multiplicity on the association end has a maximum of one, it behaves as a Set collection containing the single object. While a dot followed by the name of a property is used to refer to the property of an object, an arrow "->" or minus symbol followed by a greater-than symbol is used to refer to a property of a collection. The use of the dot indicates that the sub-expression is used as an object, and the use of the arrow indicates that the sub-expression is used as a collection of objects. If an association end does not have a rolename, the name of the classifier type at the association end, starting with a lowercase character, is used as the role-name; and if the result is ambiguous such as with a reflexive association, the rolename is mandatory.

Figure 11.7 shows how the association between the Team class and Person class may be navigated to ensure that the person who is playing the role of the manager has the title of "Manager".

The syntax for referencing an association class is the name of the

```
context Team inv:
    self.manager.title = 'Manager'
```

```
context Person
    inv:      self.age > 0
    inv:      self.gender = Gender::female or self.gender = Gender::male
    inv:      self.firstName <>"
    inv:      self.lastName <>"
    inv:      self.title = 'Manager' or self.title = 'Architect' or self.title = 'Developer'
```

FIGURE 11.7.   Team and person constraints.

association class starting with a lowercase character following a dot rather than arrow. Because an association class does not have a rolename, the use of the class name is similar to a rolename as described above, and results in a Set of objects of the association class. When using the association class name within a reflexive association, the direction in which the association is navigated must be specified, where the rolename of the direction in which the association is to be navigated is added in square brackets following the association class name. This qualified version is allowed for non-recursive associations as well but is mandatory for recursive associations. The syntax for referencing an associated class from an association class is the dot followed by the rolename at the association end or the class name starting with a lowercase character, and always results in exactly one object.

The syntax for referencing through qualified associations to another associated class or an association class is the name of the target class starting with a lowercase character or rolename of the target class followed by the qualifier values separated by commas in square brackets or no qualifier values and no brackets, in which case the result will be all of the associated objects. It is not permissible to partially specify the qualifier attribute values.

11.3.3.   CLASSIFIER- AND INSTANCE-SCOPED PROPERTIES

To refer to a property of a classifier, a classifier-scoped property, rather than a property of an object, an instance-scoped property, the syntax is the classifier name followed by a dot followed by the name of the property. The "allInstances" property returns a Set of all objects of the classifier. Rather than use this property, it is recommended to model the overall contextual system explicitly as an object and navigate from it to its containing instances. Furthermore, for Integer, Real, and String types, this property is not defined because the meaning for an Integer to exist is problematic and the evaluation of the expression Integer.allInstances results in an infinite set.

11.4   *The Standard Object Constraint Language (OCL) Types*

An expression may use predefined standard types, including basic values and types and collection values and types. Figure 11.8 shows the standard OCL types.

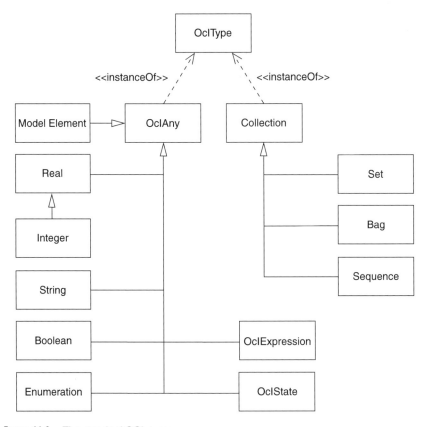

FIGURE 11.8.   The standard OCL types.

An OCL expression is said to be well formed if it satisfies the conformance rules of the language, that is, where the types used in the expression conform; otherwise the expression contains a type conformance error and is considered invalid. A type T1 conforms to a type T2 if an instance of type T1 may be substituted at each place where an instance of T2 is expected. Each type conforms to each of its supertypes transitively. For collections, a collection of element type T1 conforms to a collection of element type T2 when type T1 conforms to type T2, and the types of collections conform; that is, the type of collection of element type T1 conforms to the type of collection of element type T2, but different types of collections of the same element type don't conform to one another unless the types of collections conform. For example, a Set of element type T1 conforms to a Collection of element type T1 because the Set type conforms to the Collection type, a Set of element type T1 conforms to a Set of element type T2 if type T1 conforms to type T2, and a Set of element type T1 conforms to a Collection of element type T2 if type T1 conforms to type T2 and because the Set type conforms to the Collection type. Fundamentally, the collection type and element type must conform. Figure 11.8 shows that instances of the Set, Bag, and Sequence types conform to or are a subtype of instances of the Collection type, and instances of the Integer type conform to or are a subtype of instances of the Real type.

11.4.1. BASIC TYPES

The OCL provides various predefined basic types with appropriate values and operations. The OCL also provides various predefined fundamental or supplementary types, including OclType, OclAny, and OclExpression.

OclType Type

The OCL type OclType is the type of all OCL predefined types and types defined in a UML model. OclType allows limited meta-level access to a model. Figure 11.9 summarizes the features available for the OclType type, where T represents the instance on which the feature is applied.

OclAny Type

The OCL type OclAny is the supertype of all OCL predefined types and types defined in a model. The predefined OCL collection types are not subtypes of OclAny. The oclAsType operation allows retyping or casting of an object, possibly to reference overridden properties of supertypes. Figure 11.9 summarizes the features available for the OclAny type, where O represents the instance on which the feature is applied. The OclState OCL

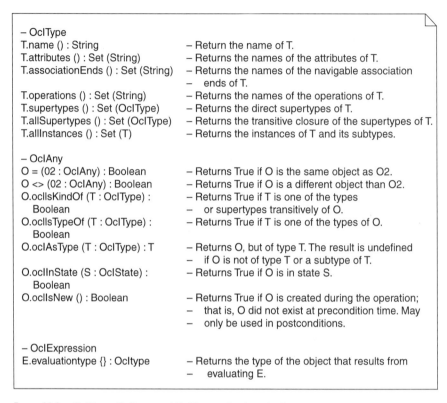

Figure 11.9. OclType, OclAny, and OclExpression type features.

type is used only with the oclInState operation; it has no properties, and any fully qualified state name may be used as a value for the type.

OclExpression Type

The OCL type OclExpression is the type of each OCL expression. Figure 11.9 summarizes the features available for the OclExpression type, where O represents the instance on which the feature is applied.

Real Type

The Real OCL type represents the mathematical concept of real numbers. Because the Integer type is a subtype of the Real type, an integer number may be substituted for a real number. Figure 11.10 summarizes the features available for the Real type, where R represents the instance on which the feature is applied.

R = (R2 : Real) : Boolean	– Returns True if R is equal to R2.
R <> (R2 : Real) : Boolean	– Returns True if R is not equal to R2.
R < (R2 : Real) : Boolean	– Returns True if R is less than R2.
R > (R2 : Real) : Boolean	– Returns True if R is greater to R2.
R <= (R2 : Real) : Boolean	– Returns True if R is less than or equal to R2.
R >= (R2 : Real) : Boolean	– Returns True if R is greater than or equal to R2.
–R : Real	– Returns the negative value of R.
R + (R2 : Real) : Real	– Returns the value of adding R and R2.
R – (R2 : Real) : Real	– Returns the value of subtracting R2 from R.
R * (R2 : Real) : Real	– Returns the value of multiplying R and R2.
R / (R2 : Real) : Real	– Returns the value of dividing R by R2.
R.abs () : Real	– Returns the absolute value of R.
R.floor () : Integer	– Returns the largest integer that is less than or equal to R.
R.round () : Integer	– Returns the integer that is closest to R; x.5 and higher – returns the next higher integer.
R.max (R2 : Real) : Real	– Returns the maximum of R and R2.
R.min (R2 : Real) : Real	– Returns the minimum of R and R2.

Figure 11.10.   Real type features.

Integer Type

The Integer OCL type, a subclass of the Real type, represents the mathematical concept of integer. Figure 11.11 summarizes the features available for the Integer type, where I represents the instance on which the feature is applied.

I = (I2 : Integer) : Boolean	– Returns True if I is equal to I2.
–I : Integer	– Returns the negative value of I.
I + (I2 : Integer) : Integer	– Returns the value of adding I and I2.
I – (I2 : Integer) : Integer	– Returns the value of subtracting I2 from I.
I * (I2 : Integer) : Integer	– Returns the value of multiplying I and I2.
I / (I2 : Integer) : Integer	– Returns the value of dividing I by I2.
I.abs () : Integer	– Returns the absolute value of I.
I.div (I2 : Integer) : Integer	– Returns the number of times that I2 fits completely – within I.
I.mod (I2 : Integer) : Integer	– Returns the value of I modulo I2, the remainder after – the number of times that I2 fits completely within I.
I.max (I2 : Integer) : Integer	– Returns the maximum of I and I2.
I.min (I2 : Integer) : Integer	– Returns the minimum of I and I2.

Figure 11.11.   Integer type features.

String Type

The String OCL type represents a sequence of ASCII characters. As a literal, a string is enclosed in single quotes. Figure 11.12 summarizes the features available for the String type, where S represents the instance on which the feature is applied.

Boolean Type

The Boolean OCL type represents the values true and false. The syntax for referring to the Boolean values is "True", "true", "False", or "false". Figure 11.13 summarizes the features available for the Boolean type, where B represents the instance on which the feature is applied.

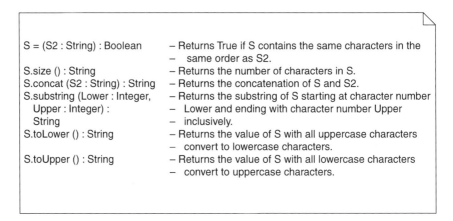

```
S = (S2 : String) : Boolean          – Returns True if S contains the same characters in the
                                      –   same order as S2.
S.size () : String                    – Returns the number of characters in S.
S.concat (S2 : String) : String       – Returns the concatenation of S and S2.
S.substring (Lower : Integer,         – Returns the substring of S starting at character number
   Upper : Integer) :                 –   Lower and ending with character number Upper
   String                             –   inclusively.
S.toLower () : String                 – Returns the value of S with all uppercase characters
                                      –   convert to lowercase characters.
S.toUpper () : String                 – Returns the value of S with all lowercase characters
                                      –   convert to uppercase characters.
```

Figure 11.12.   String type features.

```
B = (B2 : Boolean) : Boolean          – Returns True if B is the same as B2.
not B : Boolean                       – Returns True if B is False.
B and (B2 : Boolean) : Boolean        – Returns True if both B and B2 is True.
B or (B2 : Boolean) : Boolean         – Returns True if either B or B2 is True.
B xor (B2 : Boolean) : Boolean        – Returns True if either B or B2 is True, but not both.
B implies (B2 : Boolean) : Boolean    – Returns True if B is False, or if B is True and B2 is True.

if B then (E1 : OclExpression)        – Returns the result of evaluating E1 if B is True;
   else (E2 : OclExpression)          –   otherwise, returns the result of evaluating E2.
   endif : E1.evaluationType ()
```

Figure 11.13.   Boolean type features.

Enumeration Types

The Enumeration OCL type represents an enumeration defined in a model. The syntax for referring to the value of an enumeration is "enumeration-name::value". Figure 11.14 summarizes the features available for the Enumeration type, where E represents the instance on which the feature is applied.

11.4.2. COLLECTION TYPES

The OCL provides various predefined collection types, types of groups of objects, with appropriate values and operations. A collection operation never changes the collection, its isQuery property is always true, but it projects the results into a new collection. A single navigation results in a Set collection, a combined navigation results in a Bag collection, and navigation over an association end adorned with the "ordered" property results in a Sequence collection. The only way to get a collection is by a literal, navigation, or an operation on a collection that results in a new collection. Collections of collections are flattened automatically in the OCL.

As a literal, a collection is shown using the type of the collection: "Set", "Bag", or "Sequence", followed by curly brackets surrounding a comma-separated list of the zero or more elements of the collection. A sequence of consecutive Integers may be depicted as an interval specification, "lower-bound .. upper-bound" and includes the boundary integers.

Collection Type

The Collection OCL type is the abstract supertype of all OCL predefined collection types. An element represents an object in a collection, and if an object occurs twice in a collection, there are two elements. Figure 11.15 summarizes the features available for the Collection type, where C represents the instance on which the feature is applied.

Set Type

The Set OCL type represents the mathematical concept of set, a collection which may not contain duplicate elements and is unordered. Figure

```
E = (E2 : Enumeration) : Boolean      – Returns True if E is the same as E2.
E <> (E2 : Enumeration) : Boolean     – Returns True if E is not the same as E2.
```

FIGURE 11.14. Enumeration type features.

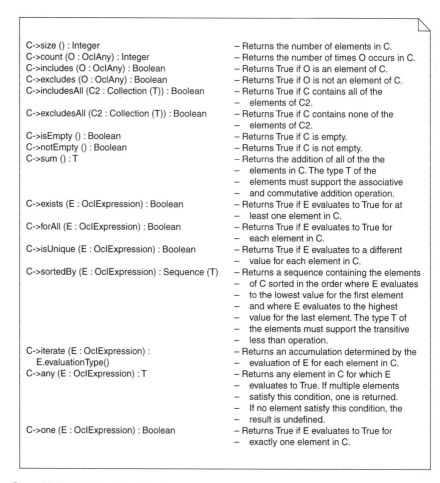

C->size () : Integer	– Returns the number of elements in C.
C->count (O : OclAny) : Integer	– Returns the number of times O occurs in C.
C->includes (O : OclAny) : Boolean	– Returns True if O is an element of C.
C->excludes (O : OclAny) : Boolean	– Returns True if O is not an element of C.
C->includesAll (C2 : Collection (T)) : Boolean	– Returns True if C contains all of the – elements of C2.
C->excludesAll (C2 : Collection (T)) : Boolean	– Returns True if C contains none of the – elements of C2.
C->isEmpty () : Boolean	– Returns True if C is empty.
C->notEmpty () : Boolean	– Returns True if C is not empty.
C->sum () : T	– Returns the addition of all of the the – elements in C. The type T of the – elements must support the associative – and commutative addition operation.
C->exists (E : OclExpression) : Boolean	– Returns True if E evaluates to True for at – least one element in C.
C->forAll (E : OclExpression) : Boolean	– Returns True if E evaluates to True for – each element in C.
C->isUnique (E : OclExpression) : Boolean	– Returns True if E evaluates to a different – value for each element in C.
C->sortedBy (E : OclExpression) : Sequence (T)	– Returns a sequence containing the elements – of C sorted in the order where E evaluates – to the lowest value for the first element – and where E evaluates to the highest – value for the last element. The type T of – the elements must support the transitive – less than operation.
C->iterate (E : OclExpression) : E.evaluationType()	– Returns an accumulation determined by the – evaluation of E for each element in C.
C->any (E : OclExpression) : T	– Returns any element in C for which E – evaluates to True. If multiple elements – satisfy this condition, one is returned. – If no element satisfy this condition, the – result is undefined.
C->one (E : OclExpression) : Boolean	– Returns True if E evaluates to True for – exactly one element in C.

Figure 11.15.   Collection type features.

11.16 summarizes the features available for the Set type, where S represents the instance on which the feature is applied. Use sets for non-ordered but unique collections of elements.

Bag Type

The Bag OCL type represents a collection which may contain duplicate elements and is unordered; one object may be an element of a bag multiple times. Figure 11.17 summarizes the features available for the Bag type, where B represents the instance on which the feature is applied. Use bags for non-ordered and non-unique collections of elements.

S->union (S2 : Set (T)) : Set (T)	– Returns the union of S and S2.
S->union (B : Bag (T)) : Bag (T)	– Returns the union of S and B.
S->intersection (S2 : Set (T)) : Set (T)	– Returns the intersection of S and S2.
S->intersection (B : Bag (T)) : Set (T)	– Returns the intersection of S and B.
S – (S2 : Set (T)) : Set (T)	– Returns the set of elements of S that are – not in S2.
S->including (O : T) : Set (T)	– Returns the set of elements of S plus O.
S->excluding (O : T) : Set (T)	– Returns the set of elements of S without O.
S->symmetricDifference (S2 : Set (T)) : Set (T)	– Returns the set of elements in S or S2, but – not both.
S->select (E : OclExpression) : Set (T)	– Returns the set of elements of S for which – E evaluates to True.
S->reject (E : OclExpression) : Set (T)	– Returns the set of elements of S for which – E evaluates to False.
S->collect (E : OclExpression) : Bag (E.evaluation Type ())	– Returns the bag of elements that results – from applying E to every memeber of S.
S->count (O : T) : Integer	– Returns the number of occurrence of O in S.
S->asSequence () : Sequence (T)	– Returns a sequence containing all of the – elements of S in an undefined order.
S->asBag () : Bag (T)	– Returns a bag containing all of the – elements of S.
S = (S2 : Set) : Boolean	– Returns True if S and S2 contain the – same elements.

Figure 11.16.   Set type features.

Sequence Type

The Sequence OCL type represents a collection which may contain duplicate elements and is ordered, one object may be an element of a sequence multiple times. Figure 11.18 summarizes the features available for the Sequence type, where Q represents the instance on which the feature is applied. Use sequences for ordered and non-unique collections of elements.

Collection Operations

The collection operations iterate over a collection of elements; evaluate an expression for each element; and based on the operation, the element may be projected into a new collection or a value that results from applying an expression to the elements may be projected into a new collection or an overall value of True or False results.

The Select, Reject, forAll, Exists, and Collect Operations

The select and reject operations results in a subset of the collection of elements for which a Boolean expression evaluates to True or False, re-

B->union (B2 : Bag (T)) : Bag (T)	– Returns the union of B and B2.
B->union (S : Set (T)) : Bag (T)	– Returns the union of B and S.
B->intersection (B2 : Bag (T)) : Bag (T)	– Returns the intersection of B and B2.
B->intersection (S : Set (T)) : Set (T)	– Returns the intersection of B and S.
B->including (O : T) : Bag (T)	– Returns the bag of elements of B plus O.
B->excluding (O : T) : Bag (T)	– Returns the bag of elements of B apart
	– from all occurrences of O.
B->select (E : OclExpression) : Bag (T)	– Returns the bag of elements of B for which
	– E evaluates to True.
B->reject (E : OclExpression) : Bag (T)	– Returns the bag of elements of B for which
	– E evaluates to False.
B->collect (E : OclExpression) :	– Returns the bag of elements that results
Bag (E.evaluationType ())	– from applying E to every member of B.
B->count (O : T) : Integer	– Returns the number of occurrence of O in B.
B->asSequence () : Sequence (T)	– Returns a sequence containing all of the
	– elements of B in an undefined order.
B->asSet () : Set (T)	– Returns a set containing all of the
	– elements of B with duplicates removed.
B = (B2 : Bag) : Boolean	– Returns True if B and B2 contain the
	– same elements the same number
	– of times.

Figure 11.17.   Bag type features.

spectively. The forAll operation results in True if an expression evaluates to True for all of the elements of the collection. The exists operation results in True if an expression evaluates to True for at least one element of the collection. The collect operation results in a collection of elements resulting from evaluating an expression for each element of the collection.

The syntax for the OCL expression used in the collection operations of select, reject, forAll, exists, and collect is "variable-name : type-name | OCL-expression" where—

- The variable-name is an optional iterator that specifies a name used in the expression to reference each element from the collection; that is, the variable iterates over the collection. The colon, type-name, and vertical bar following the variable-name are omitted if no variable-name is specified. The forAll operation has an extended syntax where multiple variable-names may be used separated by commas, where each iterator will iterate over the complete collection, effectively resulting in the Cartesian product of the collection with itself.
- The type-name specifies the classifier type of the elements in the col-

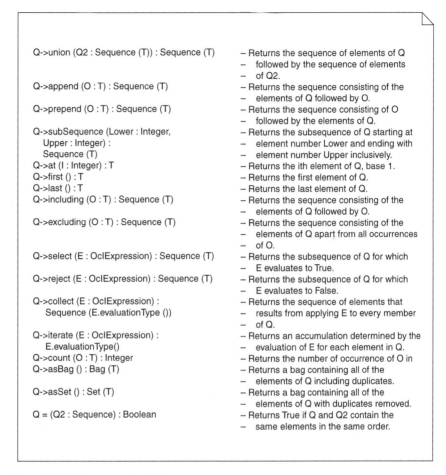

FIGURE 11.18. Sequence type features.

lection. The colon preceding the type-name is omitted if no type-name is specified.

■ The expression is required and specifies the constraint appropriately used by the collection operation.

When a property is applied to a collection of objects, it will automatically be interpreted as a collect operation over the members of the collection with the specified property; that is, "collection.property-name" is equivalent to collection->collect (property-name)", where the property may be an attribute or an operation which may include parameters.

Figure 11.19 shows constraints for expressing that if a person has a manger that manager is a different person; if a task has a predecessor

context Person inv:
    self.manager->notEmpty() implies self<>self.manager

context Task inv:
    self.predecessor->notEmpty() implies self<>self.predecessor

context Activity inv:
    self.predecessor->notEmpty() implies self<>self.predecessor

Figure 11.19. Constraints for people, tasks, and activities.

task, that predecessor task is a different task.; and if an activity has a predecessor activity, that predecessor activity is a different activity. Notice how the notEmpty operation is used to determine if a corresponding object exists, and how the implies operation is used to evaluate the constraint if a corresponding object exists.

Figure 11.20 shows how the "xor" property keyword as shown in Figure 11.2, used to indicate that a spending account may be associated with a person or a team, but not both, may be expressed using an OCL expression. Figure 11.21 shows how the "subset" property keyword as shown in Figure 11.2, used to indicate that a person must be a member of the team on which that person is the manager, may be expressed using an OCL expression.

Figure 11.22 shows different, but equivalent, ways to express the semantic rule that all members of a team must have a title of "Manager" "Architect," or "Developer".

Figure 11.23 shows that all activities must produce at least one work product, and that a person may not be associated with the same skill more than once; that is, no two PersonSkill objects referencing the same person may reference the same skill.

Figure 11.24 shows different, but equivalent, ways to express the semantic rule that all people on the same team must have the same man-

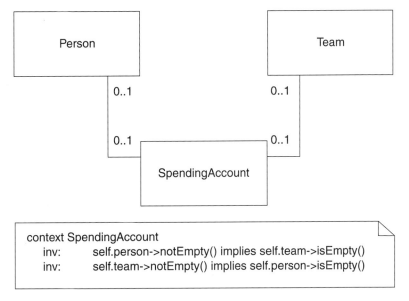

FIGURE 11.20. Alternative for the "xor" property keyword using an OCL expression.

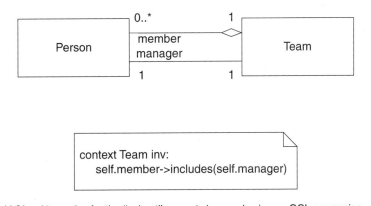

FIGURE 11.21. Alternative for the "subset" property keyword using an OCL expression.

ager. Notice that the forAll operation using two variables may be expressed as a forAll operation nested inside another forAll operation.

The Iterate Operation

The iterate operation iterates over a collection of elements and builds one accumulation value by evaluating an expression for each element.

The syntax for the OCL expression used in the iterate operation is "variable-name : variable-type-name; accumulator-name : accumulator-type-name = accumulator-initial-value | OCL-expression" where—

```
context Team inv:
    self.member->collect(title)->asSet()-
    Set{'Manager', 'Architect', 'Developer'}->isEmpty()
```

```
context Team inv:
    self.member->collect(P | P.title)->asSet()-
    Set{'Manager', 'Architect', 'Developer'}->isEmpty()
```

```
context Team inv:
    self.member->collect(P : Person | P.title)->asSet()-
    Set{'Manager', 'Architect', 'Developer'}->isEmpty()
```

```
context Team inv:
    self.member.title->asSet()-Set{'Manager', 'Architect', 'Developer'}->isEmpty()
```

FIGURE 11.22.   The collect operation.

```
context Activity inv:
    Activity.allInstances->forAll(A : Activity | A workProduct[output]->notEmpty()
```

```
context PersonSkill inv:
PersonSkill.allInstances->forAll(ps1, ps2 : PersonSkill | ps1<>ps2 implies
ps1.person=ps2.person implies ps1.skill<>ps2.skill)
```

FIGURE 11.23.   The allInstances operation.

- The variable-name is an iterator that specifies a name used in the expression to reference each element from the collection; that is, the variable iterates over the collection.
- The variable-type-name specifies the classifier type of the elements in the collection.
- The accumulator-name is an accumulator that specifies a name used in the expression to reference the result of the iterate operation.
- The accumulator-type-name specifies the type of result of the iterate operation.

- The accumulator-initial-value specifies an initial value for the accumulator.
- As the variable-name iterates over the collection and the expression is evaluated for each element, after each evaluation of the expression, its value is assigned to the accumulator.

When iterator names are not used within collection operations, properties must be unambiguously resolved. If a property may be associated with multiple iterators, it must be resolved via the introduction of an iterator or the expression is considered incorrect.

Figure 11.25 shows how to use the iterate operation to express the same constraints shown in Figure 11.22

11.5. The Standard Object Constraint Language (OCL) Package

The OCL is defined in a standard package named UML_OCL. The UML_OCL package contains all of the predefined OCL types and their

```
context Team inv:
    self.member->forAll(p1, p2 | p1<>p2 implies p1.team=p2.team implies
    p1.team.manager=p2.team.manager)
```

```
context Team inv:
    self.member->forAll(p1 | self.member->forAll(p2 | p1<>p2 implies
    p1.team=p2.team implies p1.team.manager=p2.team.manager))
```

FIGURE 11.24.   The forAll operation.

```
context Team inv:
    self.member->iterate(P : Person; Acc : Bag = Bag{} | Acc->including(P.title))
    ->asSet()-Set{'Manager', 'Architect', 'Developer'}->isEmpty()
```

FIGURE 11.25.   The iterate operation.

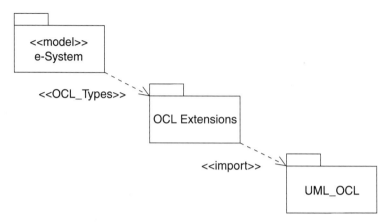

FIGURE 11.26.   The standard OCL package.

features, and is used by all packages in any model that uses OCL constraints in order to evaluate OCL expressions. Figure 11.26 shows the standard OCL package being extended.

A package may import the UML_OCL package and extend the OCL types with new features. At the minimum, all of the predefined OCL types with all of their features must be defined, and the user-defined package must be a proper extension to the standard OCL package. A dependency stereotyped with the "OCL_Types" keyword is used to denote that the source package uses the target package containing extended OCL types rather than the standard package.

References

Herein are references to notable resources on the World Wide Web and various books. Visit the World Wide Web resources for links to other resources.

WORLD WIDE WEB RESOURCES

2U Consortium. <http://www.2uworks.org>
Action Semantics Consortium. <http://www.umlactionsemantics.org>
Sinan Si Alhir. <http://home.earthlink.net/~salhir>
Cetus Team's links. <http://www.cetus-links.org>
The Object Constraint Language (OCL). <http://www.klasse.nl/ocl/index.htm>
The Object Management Group (OMG). <http://www.omg.org> and <http://www.omg.org/uml>
The Object Management Group (OMG) UML Revision Task Force (RTF). <http://www.celigent.com/omg/umlrtf>
The Precise UML (pUML) Group. <http://www.cs.york.ac.uk/puml>
Rational Software Corporation. <http://www.rational.com> and <http://www.rational.com/uml>
U2 Partners. <http://www.u2-partners.org>
UML Forum. <http://www.uml-forum.com>

BOOKS

Alhir, Sinan Si. UML in a Nutshell : A Desktop Quick Reference (Nutshell Handbook). Sebastpol: O'Reilly & Associates, 1998.
Alhir, Sinan Si. The unified modeling language (UML). In John J. Marciniak (ed.): Encyclopedia of Software Engineering, Second Edition. New York: John Wiley & Sons, 2001.

Alhir, Sinan Si. The unified process (UP). In John J. Marciniak (ed.): Encyclopedia of Software Engineering, Second Edition. New York: John Wiley & Sons, 2001.

Beck, Kent. Extreme Programming Explained: Embrace Change. Reading, MA: Addison Wesley Longman, 1999.

Booch, Grady. Object-Oriented Analysis and Design with Applications. Addison Wesley Longman, 1999.

Booch, Grady. Object Solutions: Managing the Object-Oriented Project. Reading, MA: Addison Wesley Longman, 1995.

Booch, Grady, and Ed Eykholt (eds.). The Best of Booch: Designing Strategies for Object Technology. Chatsworth, CA: SIGS Books, 1996.

Booch, Grady, James Rumbaugh, and Ivar Jacobson. The Unified Modeling Language User Guide. Reading, MA: Addison-Wesley, 1999.

Carlson, David. Modeling XML Applications with UML: Practical e-Business Applications. Reading, MA: Addison Wesley Longman, 2001.

Conallen, Jim. Building Web Applications with UML. Reading, MA: Addison Wesley Longman, 2000.

Douglass, Bruce Powel. Doing Hard Time. Reading, MA: Addison Wesley Longman, 1999.

Douglass, Bruce Powel. Real-Time UML. Reading, MA: Addison Wesley Longman, 1999.

D'Souza, Desmond Francis, and Alan Cameron Wills. Objects, Components, and Frameworks with UML: The Catalysis Approach. Reading, MA: Addison Wesley Longman, 1998.

Eriksson, Hans-Erik, and Magnus Penker. Business Modeling With UML: Business Patterns at Work. New York: John Wiley & Sons, 1998.

Eriksson, Hans-Erik, and Magnus Penker. UML Toolkit. New York: John Wiley & Sons, 1997.

Firesmith, Donald G., and Edward M. Eykholt. Dictionary of Object Technology: The Definitive Desk Reference. Cambridge University Press, 1995.

Fowler, Martin, and Kendall Scott. UML Distilled: A Brief Guide to the Standard Object Modeling Language. Reading, MA: Addison Wesley Longman, 1999.

Henderson-Sellers, Brian, and Bhuvan Unhelkar. Open Modeling with UML. Reading, MA: Addison Wesley Longman, 2000.

Jacobson, Ivar. Object-Oriented Software Engineering: A Use Case Driven Approach. Addison Wesley Longman, 1992.

Jacobson, Ivar. The Road to the Unified Software Development Process. Cambridge University Press, 2000.

Jacobson, Ivar, Grady Booch, and James Rumbaugh. The Unified Software Development Process. Reading, MA: Addison Wesley Longman, 1999.

Jacobson, Ivar, Maria Ericsson, and Agneta Jacobson. The Object Advantage: Business Process Reengineering with Object Technology. Reading, MA: Addison Wesley Longman, 1995.

Jacobson, Ivar, Martin Griss, and Patrik Jonsson. Software Reuse: Architecture, Process and Organization for Business Success. Reading, MA: Addison Wesley Longman, 1997.

Kruchten, Philippe. The Rational Unified Process: An Introduction, Second Edition. Reading, MA: Addison Wesley Longman, 2000.

Larman, Craig. Applying UML and Patterns: An Introduction to Object-Oriented Analysis and Design and the Unified Process. Prentice Hall PTR, 2001.

Leffingwell, Dean, and Don Widrig. Managing Software Requirements: A Unified Approach. Reading, MA: Addison Wesley Longman, 1999.

Nailburg, Eric J., and Robert A. Maksimchuck. UML for Database Design. Reading, MA: Addison Wesley Longman, 2001.

The Object Management Group (OMG). OMG Unified Modeling Language Specification (Action Semantics) (version 1.4). The Object Management Group (OMG), 2001.

Odell, James J., Advanced Object-Oriented Analysis and Design Using UML. Cambridge University Press, 1998.

Oestereich, Bernd, Developing Software with UML: Object-Oriented Analysis and Design in Practice. Reading, MA: Addison Wesley Longman, 1999.

Page-Jones Meilir, Fundamentals of Object-Oriented Design in UML. Reading, MA: Addison Wesley Longman, 1999.

Rosenberg, Doug, and Kendall Scott. Applying Use Case Driven Object Modeling with UML : An Annotated E-Commerce Example. Reading, MA: Addison Wesley Longman, 2001.

Rosenberg, Doug, and Kendall Scott. Use Case Driven Object Modeling with UML: A Practical Approach. Reading, MA: Addison Wesley Longman, 1999.

Royce, Walker. Software Project Management: A Unified Framework. Reading, MA: Addison Wesley Longman, 1998.

Rumbaugh, James. OMT Insights. Chatsworth, CA: SIGS Books & Multimedia, 1996.

Rumbaugh, James, Michael Blaha, William Premerlani, Frederick Eddy, and William Lorenson. Object-Oriented Modeling and Design. Prentice Hall, 1990.

Rumbaugh, James, Ivar Jacobson, and Grady Booch. The Unified Modeling Language Reference Manual. Reading, MA: Addison Wesley Longman, 1999.

Scott, Kendall. UML Explained. Addison Wesley Longman, 2001.

Scott, Kendall. The Unified Process Explained. Addison Wesley Longman, 2001.

Stevens, Perdita, and Rob Pooley. Using UML: Software Engineering with Objects and Components. Addison Wesley Longman, 1999.

Warmer, Jos, and Anneke Kleppe. The Object Constraint Language: Precise Modeling with UML. Reading, MA: Addison Wesley Longman, 1999.

Index

A

Abstract programming language, 143
Abstract use case, 203
Abstraction, 2, 26, 61–63, 347
    encapsulated, 63–65
    general, 61
    levels of, *see* Levels of abstraction
    specific, 61
Abstraction dependency, 245
Access dependency, 113
Action, 94, 104, 278, 312
    call, 312
    create, 312
    destroy, 312
    return, 312
    send, 312
    terminate, 312
    transition, 313–314
    uninterpreted, 312
Action model, 9, 350
Action Semantics, 9
Action sequence, 278
Action state, 108
    activity diagram, 316–318
Actions package, 348, 350
Activation, 99
    sequence diagram, 285–286
Active element, 249
Active object, 69
Activity, 44
Activity diagram, 32, 108–111, 138,
    315–318
    action state, 316–318

    applying, 325
    flow, 318–320
    swimlane, 318
Activity graph, 108, 316
    see also Activity diagram
Activity Graphs package, 348, 349
Activity state, 316
Actor, 87, 186
    Backup System, 187
    construct, 206
    Database, 187
    explicit, 193
    implicit, 193
    instance, 186
    manager, 187
    primary, 188
    Project Management System, 187
    secondary, 188
    System Administrator, 187
    use case, 192–194
    use-case diagram, 182–188
Actor relationship
    association, 194
    generalization, 195
    realization, 194–195
    use-case diagram, 194–195
Actual element
    design, 263–270
    validation, 270–275
Actual element properties, 270
Actual solution, 143
Aggregation association, 79–80
    relationship, 240

Agile methodology, *see* Lightweight
    methodology
allInstances operation, 388
Alphabet, 13
Analysis, 257–260
    conceptual elements, 258–261
    mechanisms, 260, 262
Analysis domain, 23
Analysis iteration phase, 42–43, 44
Analysis process discipline, 137
Ancestors, 65, 242
Anchor icon, *see* Tree notation
Application, stereotype, 354–356
Application domain, 23
Approach, 3
Architect, 50–51, 253
Architectural elements, 25
Architectural pattern, 115
Architectural view, 18, 23, 30–31
Architecture, 5, 24–26
Artifact, 327
    component diagram, 326–327
Assembly languages, 29
Association, 72–76
    actor relationship, 194
    association class, 237
    association end, 237–238
    binary association, 234–235
    n-ary association, 235, 237
    property, 374
    relationship, 231–240
Association class, 73–74
    association, 237
Association end, 74–76
    association, 237
Association role, 96
    collaboration diagram,
        290–292
Asynchronous message, 288
Attribute, 67, 112
    class, 216
Attribute value, object, 250–251
Attributes compartment, 67
Auxiliary class, 216–217

B

Backup System actor, 187
Backup System subsystem, 230
Bag collection, 381
Bag OCL type, 382
Base class, 350
Base use case, 197
Basic type, 377–381
    Boolean OCL type, 380
    Enumeration OCL type, 381
    Integer OCL type, 379
    OclAny type, 377
    OclExpression type, 378
    OclType type, 377–378
    Real OCL type, 378
    String OCL type, 380
Beck, Kent, xvi
Behavior, 24, 119
Behavior sequence, 4, 88, 190
    use case, 190–191
Behavioral aspect, 25
Behavioral (dynamic) concepts, 93–111
    see also Activity diagram
    see also Collaboration diagram
    see also Sequence diagram
    see also State diagram
Behavioral Elements package, 348, 349
Behavioral feature, 67, 212–213
Behavioral (dynamic) modeling, 31,
    277–325
    see also Activity diagram
    see also Collaboration diagram
    see also Sequence diagram
    see also Statechart diagram
Behavioral organization
    behavioral scheme, 302–306
    classifier, 301–302
    collaboration diagram, 300–306
    instance, 301–302
    relationship, 301–302
    role, 301–302
    see also Structural organization
Behavioral pattern, 115
Behavioral scheme

behavioral organization, 302–306
see also Structural scheme
Binary association, 73
    association, 234–235
Binary link, 76, 77
    link, 252
Binding dependency, 244
"Black box" description, 38
Booch, Grady, xv, 2, 3, 7
Booch's '93 method, 3
Book references, 391
Boolean OCL type, 380
Bound element, 223
Boundary class, 142, 253
Boundary concept, 140–141
Braces, 21–22
Business domain, 23
Business system, 137
Business use cases, 185

C

Call action, 312
Call event, 312
Call state, 318
Calling dependency, 331
Candidate elements, 263
    construct, 254–257
Candidate solution, 143
Capsules, 266
Cartesian product, 130–132
Change, 1, 263
Change event, 312–313
Changeable attribute, 217
Characteristics, 206
Checks, 54–55
Child collaboration, 302
Child use case, 201
Children, 65
Chunks, 255
Class, 67–68, 96
    attribute, 216–217
    classifier, 214–219
    operation, 217–219
Class conceptualization model, 131

Class diagram, 31, 66–86, 212–247,
    255–257
    applying, 252–276
    classifier, 212–231
    relationship, 231–247
Class example, Connection Manager,
    174–182
Class implementation model, 131
Class name, 69
Class role, 96–97
Class specification model, 131
Classification, 63, 347
Classifier, 67
    behavioral organization, 301–302
    class, 214–219
    class diagram, 212–231
    implementation class, 220
    interface, 220–222
    property, 373
    structural organization, 223–224
    template, 223
    type, 219–220
Classifier instance object, 247–249
    object diagram, 247–251
Classifier role, sequence diagram,
    279–280
Classifier-scoped, 216
Classifier-scoped property, 376
Cohesion, 63, 263
Coincident lifetime, 240
Collaborating system, 124–125
Collaboration, 17, 40, 93–95
    child, 302
    collaboration diagram, 293
    instance-level, 101
    interaction and, 95
    parent, 302
    specification-level, 101
    super-ordinate, 303
Collaboration diagram, 32, 95, 101–104,
    289–306
    applying, 321–323
    association role, 290–292
    behavioral organization, 300–306

collaboration, 292–293
   message, 294–300
   stimulus, 294–300
Collaboration instance set, 97
Collaboration package, 348, 349
Collaboration symbol, 96
Collect operation, 383–387, 388
Collection, 365
Collection OCL type, 381
Collection operation, 383–390
Collection type, 381–389
   Bag OCL type, 382
   collect operation, 383–387, 388
   Collection OCL type, 381
   collection operation, 383–390
   Exists operation, 383–387
   forAll operation, 383–387, 389
   iterate operation, 387–389
   reject operation, 383–387
   select operation, 383–387
   Sequence OCL type, 383
   Set OCL type, 381–382
Colon, 16
Comment, 366
   see also Note
Common Behavior package, 348, 349
Communication, 278
Compartment, 67–68, 120
Completeness, 50
Complex transition, 313
   transition, 313–314
Complexity, 1, 263
Component, 90
   component diagram, 328, 331
Component-based paradigm, 5
Component diagram, 32, 90, 326–331
   applying, 332–334
   artifact, 327
   component, 328, 331
   component relationship, 331
   construct, 332
   implementation, 333–334
Component (implementation) modeling,
   30, 326–334
   see also Component diagram

Component relationship, component
   diagram, 331
Composite aggregation, 80–81
   see also Composition association
Composite state, 307
   state, 309
Composition association, 80–81
   relationship, 240–241
Compound transition, 314–315
Computer assisted software engineering
   (CASE) tools, 30
Computing activation, 286
Concept, 13–14, 343
Conception development cycle, 40
Conceptual element, 140–144, 253–254,
   263
   analysis, 257–261
   boundary, 140–141
   conceptual element properties, 260
   control, 141
   entity, 141–142
   at levels of abstraction, 142–143
   realization element properties, 258–
      259
   validation, 271–275
Conceptual element properties, 260
Conceptual framework for modeling
   see Four-layer metamodeling
      architecture
Conceptual mechanism, 145, 254
Conceptual programming language, 143
Conceptual solution, 143
Conceptualization perspective, 34–35,
   135–136
Concrete use case, 203
Concurrent transition, 111, 313–314
Conditionality, 285
Connection Manager Class example,
   174–182
Connector, 266
Constraint, 22, 119–120, 144–145, 213
   property, 358–359
Construct, 206–207
   actor, 206
   candidate elements, 254–257

component diagram, 332
deployment diagram, 340
realization elements, 257
specification elements, 207
Construct actor, 206
Constructing systems, 2
Construction development phase, 41
Consultant, xviii
Contains-a relationship, 240
Contains-a-kind-of relationship, 240
Context, 40
Context declaration, 365
Context modeling iteration phase, 42, 45
Context modeling process discipline, 137
Contextual iteration cycle, 46
Contract, 24
Control class, 142, 253
Control concept, 141
Control icon
    signal receipt, 319
    signal sending, 319
Core iteration phases, 43
Core package, 348, 349
Coupling, 63–64, 263–264
Create action, 312
Creational pattern, 115
CRUD functionality, 191
Cunningham, Ward, xvi

D

Dashed ellipse, 299
Data Management Subsystem example,
    165–174
Data model, *see* User model
Data Types package, 348, 349
Database actor, 187
Database subsystem, 230
Database table artifact, 327
Decision, 110–111, 318–319
Decision point, 131
Declaration, stereotype, 350–354
Declarative statements, 189
Deep history state indicator, 314
Deferrable event, 319
Defined behavior sequence, 199

Definition constraint, expression, 370
Dependency, 20, 83–85, 112
    abstraction, 2, 27, 61–62, 347
    access, 113
    binding, 244
    calling, 331
    import, 112
    permission, 244–245
    relationship, 244–247
    static, 331
    usage, 246
Deployment, deployment diagram,
    340–341
Deployment diagram, 32, 91–94, 336–339
    applying, 339–342
    construct, 340
    deployment, 340–341
    node, 336
    node relationship, 336–339
Deployment iteration phase, 43, 45
Deployment (environment) modeling, 30,
    336–342
    see also Deployment diagram
Deployment process discipline, 138
Derived attribute, 246
Descendants, 65, 242
Design, 262–270
    actual elements, 263–270
Design domain, 23
Design iteration phase, 43, 45
Design process discipline, 137–138
Destroy action, 312
Destroyed classifier, 280
Detailed roadmap, 123, 140
Development cycle
    cessation, 40
    conception, 40
    evolution, 40
    and phases, 40–41
Diagram, 14, 16, 23, 31–33
    activity, *see* Activity diagram
    class, *see* Class diagram
    collaboration, *see* Collaboration
        diagram
    component, *see* Component diagram

deployment, *see* Deployment diagram

implementation, *see* Implementation diagram

interaction, *see* Interaction diagram

object, *see* Object diagram

sequence, *see* Sequence diagram

state, *see* State diagram

statechart, *see* Statechart diagram

use-case, *see* Use-case diagram

Diagram fragments, 14

Dichotomy, 38
   specification-implementation, 38
   static-dynamic, 38
   type-instance, 38

Discriminator, 243

Documenting systems, 2

Documents, 17–18

Domain, 23

Double colon delimiter, 20

Dynamic aspect, 25

Dynamic choice junction point, 315

Dynamic (behavioral) concepts, 93–111

Dynamic library artifact, 327

Dynamic (behavioral) modeling, 30, 277–325

Dynamic role, 277

E

Elaboration development phase, 41

Elements, 20

Ellipsis, 214

Emergent methodology, *see* Lightweight methodology

Empirical methodology, *see* Lightweight methodology

Empty property, 358

Encapsulated abstraction, 64

Encapsulation, 63–65

Entity class, 142, 254

Entity concept, 141–142

Enumerated set, 216

Enumeration OCL type, 381

Environment (deployment) modeling, 30, 336–342

Essential use cases, 190

Event, 95, 104, 278, 311
   call, 312
   change, 312–313
   deferrable, 319
   signal, 312
   time, 313
   transition, 311–312

Evolution development cycle, 40

Executable file artifact, 327

Exists operation, 384–386

Explicit actor, 193

Explicit interface, 125

Expression, 366–370
   definition constraint, 370
   invariant, 367
   let expression, 370
   package statement, 369–370
   postcondition, 369
   precondition, 368–369

Extend relationship, use-case relationship, 198–202

Extending, 347

Extension mechanism, 38, 343–363
   see also Profile
   see also Property
   see also Stereotype

Extension Mechanisms package, 348, 349

Extension point, use case, 191–192

Extension use case, 198

eXtreme Programming (XP), xvi

eXtreme Programming (XP) practices, 10

F

Facade, 116

Factored transition, 314

False, 361

Feature, 212
   behavioral, 67, 212–213
   private, 242
   protected, 242
   public, 242
   structural, 67, 212

Feedback, 3–4
Final state, 310
    state, 310
First-generation methods, 7
Fitness criteria, 143
Flexibility, 263
Flow, 109–110, 190
    activity diagram, 318–320
    object, 109–110
    subflows, 190
    workflow, 44
Flow relationship, 246
Focus class, 215
Focus of control, 99, 286
forAll operation, 384–387, 388, 389
Fork symbol icon, 24
Foundation package, 348, 349
Four-Layer Architecture, 229
Four-layer metamodeling architecture,
    343, 344–348
Fragmentation period, 7
Fragments, 190
Framework, 117
Frozen attribute, 217
Full descriptor, 242
Functional requirement, 144
Fundamental principles of language, 12

G
General abstraction, 62
General roadmap, 135–139
Generalization, 65–66, 80
    actor relationship, 196
    relationship, 241–244
    use-case relationship, 201–204
Generalization relationship, 80–83
Generic-form interaction, 99, 278
Global scope, 239
Goals, 57
Graphs, 14
Guard condition, 287
Guide to Applying the UML, xv
    approach, xvii–xx
    audience, xvii
    goals, xvi–xvii

organization and content, xx–xxii
    overview, xv–xvi
Guidelines, 12
Guillemet, 21

H
Has-a relationship, 79, 239
Has-a-kind-of relationship, 79, 239
Heavyweight approach, xviii, 57–58
    roadmap, 182–183
    see also Roadmap
Heavyweight methodology, 10
    see also Heavyweight approach
Heuristics, 46–52
    roadmap, 184–185
Higher-level programming languages, 29
History state, 314

I
Icons, 20
Implementation, xix
    component diagram, 332–334
Implementation class, 71
    classifier, 220
Implementation diagram, 32, 326
    see also Component diagram
    see also Deployment diagram
Implementation domain, 23
Implementation hiding, 64
Implementation inheritance, 243
Implementation iteration phase, 43, 45
Implementation model, 326
Implementation (component) modeling,
    30, 326–334
Implementation perspective, 35, 136
Implementation process discipline, 138
Implicit actor, 193
Import dependency, 112
Inception development phase, 40
Include relationship, use-case
    relationship, 197
Inclusion use case, 197
Individual behavior sequence, 99, 278
Industrialization period, 9
Information hiding, 64

Information system, 137
Inheritance, 82–83, 242
    implementation, 243
    interface, 247
    private, 243
    see also Generalization
Initial state, 310
Instability, 263
Instance, 38
    behavioral organization, 301
    property, 373
    see also Classifier instance
Instance-form interaction, 99, 278
Instance-level collaboration, 101
Instance-scoped property, 375–376
Instantiation, 26, 61, 347
Integer OCL type, 379
Interacting system, 124
Interaction, 17, 40
    collaboration and, 95
    generic-form, 99, 278
    Instance-form, 99, 278
    sequence diagram, 281–282
Interaction diagram, 32, 277–278
    see also Collaboration diagram
    see also Sequence diagram
Interaction instance set, 96
Interface, 24, 72, 196
    classifier, 220–222
Interface inheritance, 247
Interface specifier, 74–75, 237–238
Internal transition, state, 309
Invariant, 119
    expression, 367
Is-a-kind-of relationship, 241
Iterate operation, 387–389
Iteration, 3–4
Iteration cycle
    contextual, 46
    and phases, 43–44
Iteration phase details, 44–46

J
Jacobson, Ivar, xv, 2, 3, 7
Jeffries, Ron, xvi

Junction point, 314–315
    dynamic choice, 314–315
    static branch, 314–315

K
Keywords, reserved, 366

L
Label, 17, 279
Language, xviii, 12–22, 348
    alphabets, 13
    documents, 18
    fundamental principles, 12
    guidelines, 12
    paragraphs, 14–17
    sections, 17
    semantics, 12
    sentences, 14
    syntax, 12
    words, 13
Layer, 229
    of abstraction, *see* Levels of
        abstraction
    see also Package
Let expression, 370
Levels of abstraction, 36–37, 130
    conceptual elements at, 142–143
    perspective and, 135–137
Lifecycle, 307
    cessation development cycle, 40
    conception development cycle, 40
    evolution development cycle, 40
    see also Development cycle
Lifeline, 99
    sequence diagram, 282–289
Lightweight approach, xviii, 58–59
    roadmap, 182–183
    see also Roadmap
Lightweight methodology, 10–11
    see also Lightweight approach
Linear approach, 47–48
Link, 76–78, 96
    binary link, 76, 252
    link end, 78, 252

link object, 76, 252
n-ary link, 76, 252
property, 374–376
relationship instance, 251–252
Link end, 78
link, 252
Link object, 76
link, 252
List compartment, 67, 214
Live activation, 286
Local scope, 239
Localization, 63–64
Logical mechanism, 144–146, 254
Lower-level programming languages, 29–30

M

M0-level, *see* User model
M1-level, *see* Model
M2-level, *see* Metamodel
M3-level, *see* Meta-metamodel
Machine language programs, 29
Main functionality, 188
Management iteration phase, 42
Manager actor, 186–187
Manifestation, 26, 61, 347
Mechanism, 117, 144–146, 254, 270
analysis, 260, 262
conceptual, 145, 254
extension, 38, 343–363
logical, 145, 254
physical, 145–146, 254
validation, 275, 276
Merge, 111, 319
Message, 17, 94, 95, 99, 100, 286
asynchronous, 287–288
collaboration diagram, 293–297
reflexive, 286
self-referential, 102, 286
sequence diagram, 287–288
Message arrowhead, 100
Meta-metamodel layer, 344
Metadata Interchange, XML (XMI), 9
Metaelement, 344

Metamodel, 343–345, 347
Metaobject, 344
Method, 67, 218
see also Process
Methodology, xvi, 39–40
processes and, *see* Processes and methodologies
Unified Modeling Language, 3–5
Methodology iteration phase, 42, 45
Model, 2, 18, 23, 26–30, 347
Model element, 27, 347
Model library, 362
Model Management package, 350
Modeling, 12–60
see also Context
see also Language
see also Modeling mechanisms
see also Process
see also System
Modeling languages, 7
Modeling mechanisms, 33–38
dichotomies, 37–38
extension mechanisms, 38
levels of abstraction, 36–37
perspectives, 34–36
Modularity, 64–65
Multiobject, 69, 96, 249
Multiplicity, 75, 216

N

N-ary association, 73
association, 235–237
N-ary link, 76, 79
link, 252
Name, 16
Name-direction arrow, 16, 228
Name string, 96
Named behavior sequence, 199
Namespace, 14
Navigation, 75, 238
Navigation arrow, 15, 89
Nested class, 214
Nesting, 102
New classifier, 279, 280

Node, 91–92
  deployment diagram, 336
Node relationship, deployment diagram,
  336, 339
Non-functional requirement, 144, 190
Notational adornments, 16
Notational roadmap, 123, 140
Note, 18–19, 22, 356
notEmpty operation, 386

O

Object, 68–69, 96, 111–112
  attribute value, 250–251
  classifier instance, 247–248
Object Constraint Language (OCL),
  364–390
  basic type, *see* Basic type
  collection type, *see* Collection type
  defined, 364–365
  expression, *see* Expression
  standard package, 389–390
  standard types, 376–389
Object Constraint Language (OCL)
  Specification, 9
Object diagram, 31–32, 66–86, 247–250
  applying, 252–276
  classifier instance, 247–248
  relationship instance, 252
Object flow, 109–111
Object Management Group (OMG), xv, 2
Object Management Group's (OMG)
  Object Analysis and Design Task
  Force, 8
Object model, *see* User model
Object Modeling Technique (OMT), 3
Object-oriented paradigm, 5
Object orientation, 60–122
  principles, 60–66
Object-Oriented Software Engineering
  (OOSE), 3
Object-oriented systems, 111–122
OCL, *see* Object Constraint Language
  entries
OclAny type, 377–378

OclExpression type, 378
OclType type, 377
OMG, *see* Object Management Group
  entries
OMT (Object Modeling Technique), 3
OOSE (Object-Oriented Software
  Engineering), 3
Operation, 67–68, 119, 278
  class, 217–218
Operation call, 288
Operations compartment, 67–68
Ordering, 216–217

P

Package, 19–20, 112–114
  structural organization, 223–226
  use case, 193–194
Package statement, expression, 369–370
Paradigm, 34
  component-based, 5
  Object-oriented, 5
Paragraphs, 14–17
Parameter list, 218
Parameterization, *see* Template
Parameterized element, 114
Parent collaboration, 302
Parent use case, 201
Parentheses, 365–366
Parents, 65
Partition, 229
  see also Package
Parts, 190
PAS (Publicly Available Specification), 9
Passive element, 249
Passive object, 69
Pathname, 20, 114
Paths, 13
Pattern, 115–117
  architectural, 115
  behavioral, 115
  creational, 115
  structural, 115
Permission dependency, 245
Persistence, 215–216

Perspective, 34–35, 130–131
    levels of abstraction and, 135–137
Physical file artifact, 327
Physical mechanism, 146, 254
Physical system, *see* System
Plus sign notation, 20
Polymorphism, 66, 243
Postcondition, 120
    expression, 367–369
Powertype, 243
Precedence order, 365–366
Precondition, 120
    expression, 367–369
Predecessor, 294–295
Primary actor, 188
Primitive element level, 37
Primitive elements, 23
Private feature, 242
Private inheritance, 242
Problem, 33–34
Problem domain, 23
Problem requirements, 138
Problem solving, 33–34
Procedure, 278
Process, xviii, 39
    Unified Modeling Language, 3–5
Process coach, *see* Process manager
Process discipline, 137–140
    analysis, 137
    context modeling, 137–138
    deployment, 138, 140
    design, 137–138
    implementation, 137–138
    requirements, 137–138
    validation, 137–138
Process elements, 39, 52
Process framework, 39
Process instance, 10, 39–40
Process iteration phase, 42, 45
Process manager, 49–51
Processes and methodologies, 39–52
    value of, 52–60
Profiles, 361–363
Program, 39

Programming language, 343
Project, 39
Project Management System, 121, 122
    actor, 187–188
    example, 154–164
Project manager, 49–51, 187
Properties, 20–21, 358–361, 370–376
    association, 374
    classifier, 373
    classifier-scoped property, 375–376
    constraint, 358–359
    instance, 373
    Instance-scoped property, 375–376
    link, 374–375
    tag definition, 359–361
    tagged value, 361
Protected feature, 242
Protocol, 124, 267–268
Proxy, 116
Pseudostate, 109, 310
Public feature, 242
Publicly Available Specification (PAS), 9

Q
Qualifier, 13, 239
Quality, 50

R
Rational Software Corporation, xv, 2
Real OCL type, 378
Realization
    actor relationship, 194–195
    relationship, 247
    use-case relationship, 196–197
Realization element, 118, 120
    construct, 256
    structural organization, 229
Realization element properties,
    conceptual elements, 258–259
Realization perspective, 35
Realization relationship, 85–86
Receiver, 124
Recipe, 53–54
Recursive calls, 286

References, 391–394
Reflexive message, 286
Regions, 309
Regression testing, 4
Reject operation, 383–384
Relationship, 13, 67, 89
    aggregation association, 240
    association, 231–240
    behavioral organization, 301
    class diagram, 234–247
    composition associations, 240–241
    dependencies, 244–247
    generalizations, 241–244
    realizations, 247
Relationship instance link, 251
    object diagram, 251
Requirements, 118, 208–211
    functional, 143–144
    Non-functional, 144, 190
    problem, 138
    process discipline, 137–140
    specification element properties, 208
    specification elements, 208–210
Requirements iteration phase, 42, 45
Requirements process discipline, 137
Reserved keywords, 366
Resident element, 331
Resource managers, 187
Responsibility, 118, 206
Return action, 312
Return type, 218
Revision period, 8–9
Revision task force (RTF), 8
Risks, 5
Roadmap, xvi, xvii, xviii, 11, 56–60,
    123–185
    applying, 182–185
    conceptualization, 147–149
    Connection Manager Class example,
        174–182
    construction, 145–154
    Data Management Subsystem
        example, 165–174
    detailed, 123, 140

examples, 154–182
general, 135–140
heavyweight approach, 183–184
heuristics, 184–185
implementation, 152–154
lightweight approach, 183–184
notational, 123, 140
Project Management System
    example, 154–164
specification, 150–152
Roadmap space, 123, 130–135
    example, 132–135
Role, 69, 74–75, 96, 99–100, 220, 345,
    347
    association, 95, 96
    behavioral organization, 301–302
    class, 95, 96–97
    classifier, sequence diagram, 279–280
    dynamic, 277
Rolename, 74, 238
Rumbaugh, James, xv, 2, 3, 7

S
Scalability, 55–56, 134–135
Scenario, 4, 88, 188
Second-generation methods, 7
Secondary actor, 188
Secondary maintenance functionality,
    188
Sections, 17–18
Segment, 190, 242
Select operation, 383–387
Selector, 14
Self-referential message, 102, 286
Semantic variation point, 350
Semantics, 12
Send action, 312
Sender, 124
Sentences, 14
Sequence collection, 374
Sequence diagram, 32, 95, 99–101,
    272–289
    activation, 286
    applying, 321

classifier role, 279–280
interaction, 281–283
lifeline, 283–285
message, 286–289
stimulus, 286–289
Sequence numbers, 102
Sequence OCL type, 383
Sequential approach, 48–49
Service, 24, 64, 119, 124–125
Service realizations, 126–127
Set collection, 374
Set OCL type, 381–382
Shallow history state indicator, 314
Shareable aggregation, 241
Signal, 246, 287
Signal event, 312
Signal receipt control icon, 319
Signal sending control icon, 319
Simple state, 307
Skills, 112
Society of objects, 111–112
Socratic method, xviii
Solution, 33–34, 115
Solution domain, 23
Solution specification, 138
Space, 23
see also Domain
Specialization, 82
see also Generalization
Specific abstraction, 62
Specific scenario, 99, 278
Specification, 2
Specification element properties, requirements, 208
Specification elements, 118, 120, 122
construct, 206–207
requirements, 208–210
structural organization, 229
Specification-implementation dichotomy, 38
Specification-level collaboration, 101
Specification model, 277
Specification perspective, 35, 136–137

Specification-realization dichotomy, *see* Specification-implementation dichotomy
Stability, 263
Stages, 40
Standardization period, 8
State, 104–105
composite, 309
final, 310
history, 314
initial, 310
internal transition, 308–309
simple, 307
statechart diagram, 307–310
stub, 314
subactivity, 316–318
State diagram, 32, 104–108
State Machines package, 348, 349
Statechart diagram, 104, 307–315
applying, 323
state, 307–310
submachines, 315
transition, 310–315
see also State diagram
Static aspect, 25
Static branch junction point, 314
Static (structural) concepts, 66–94
Static dependency, 331
Static-dynamic dichotomy, 38
Static library artifact, 327
Static (structural) modeling, 30, 212–276
Stereotype, 20–21, 213, 350–356
application, 354–356
declaration, 350–354
Stereotyping, 347
Stimulus, 17, 95, 99–100, 278, 286–287
collaboration diagram, 294–299
sequence diagram, 287–288
String, 13, 364
String OCL type, 380
Strong ownership, 240
Structural aspect, 25–26

Structural (static) concepts, 66–94
  see also Class diagram
  see also Component diagram
  see also Deployment diagram
  see also Object diagram
  see also Use-case diagram
Structural feature, 67, 212
Structural (static) modeling, 30, 212–276
  see also Class diagram
  see also Object diagram
Structural organization
  classifier, 223
  package, 224–226
  realization elements, 228–229
  specification elements, 228–229
  structural scheme, 229–231
  system, 226–228
Structural pattern, 115
Structural scheme
  structural organization, 229–231
  see also Behavioral scheme
Structural view, 207
Stub state, 314
Subactivity state, 316, 318
Subclass, 82
Subclassing, 242
Subflows, 190
Submachine, statechart diagram, 315
Subordinate systems, 23–24
Subordinate use case, 193
Subsequences, 190
Subsystem, 23–24, 118, 120–122, *see also*
  System
Subsystem conceptualization model, 131
Subsystem example, Data Management,
  165–174
Subsystem implementation model, 131
Subsystem level, 36–37
Subsystem specification model, 131
Subtype, 82
Subtyping, 242
Suitability, 55
Super-ordinate collaboration, 303
Super-ordinate use case, 193

Superclass, 82
Supertype, 82
Support iteration phase, 42, 45
Supporting iteration phases, 43
Swimlane, 109
  activity diagram, 318
Synchronization (synch state), 313, 320
Syntax, 12
System, xix, 23–25, 117–118
  structural organization, 227–228
System Administrator actor, 187, 188
System conceptualization model, 130, 131
System designer, 253
System example, Project Management,
  154–164
System generation, 40
System implementation model, 131
System level, 36
System release, 42
System specification model, 131
Systems development, 1, 54–56

T

Tag, 361
Tag definition, property, 359–361
Tagged value, 21
  property, 361
Task, 44, 193
Technical leader, 253
Technique, 44
Template, 114–115
  classifier, 223
Template class, 114
Template element, 114
Terminate action, 312
Text strings, 21
Three Amigos, xv, 2, 8
Three Extremoes, xvi, 10
Time boxing, 49
Time event, 313
Timing constraint, 288
Tools, xviii
Traceability, 55, 129
Transience, 216

Transient classifier, 280
Transition, 105–108, 310
    action, 312–313
    complex transition, 313–314
    compound transition, 314–315
    concurrent transition, 313–314
    event, 311–312
    statechart diagram, 310–315
Transition development phase, 41
Transition string, 313
Tree notation, 20, 131–132
Triangle icon, 27
True, 361
Type, 38, 69–71
    classifier, 219–220
Type-instance dichotomy, 38

U

UML, *see also* Unified Modeling
    Language
UML Example Profiles, 9
UML metamodel, 348–350
UML Model Interchange, 9
UML Notation Guide, 9
UML Partners Consortium, 3, 8
UML Semantics, 9
UML sentence, 123, 124–129
    defined, 128
Unification, 211, 276, 334, 341–342
Unified Modeling Language (UML),
    xv–xvi
    architecture, 343–350
    defined, 1–3
    effectively and successfully applying,
        9–11
    evolution, 6
    goals, 3
    history, 5–9
    introduction, 1–11
    process or methodology and, 3–5
    see also UML *entries*
Unified Process (UP), xvi, 10
Uninterpreted action, 312
Units, 254–255

Universal language, xix
UP (Unified Process), xvi, 10
Usage dependency, 246
Use case, 4–5, 87–89, 188
    actor, 192–193
    behavior sequences, 190–191
    extension points, 191–192
    package, 193–94
    use-case diagram, 188–194
Use-case diagram, 31, 87–89, 186–204
    actor, 186–188
    actor relationship, 194–195
    applying, 205–211
    use case, 188–194
    use-case relationship, 196–204
Use-case extend relationship, 246
Use-case instance, 88
Use-case (user) modeling, 30, 31, 186–211
    see also Use-case diagram
Use-case relationship
    extend relationship, 198–202
    generalization, 201–204
    include relationship, 197
    realization, 196–197
    use-case diagram, 196–204
Use Cases package, 348, 349
User model, 344–345
User (use-case) modeling, 30, 186–211
User view, 207

V

Validation, 270–276
    actual elements, 271–275
    conceptual elements, 271–275
    mechanisms, 275–276
Validation iteration phase, 43, 46
Validation process discipline, 138
Values, 57
Variant behavior sequence, 189
View elements, 31
Visibility, classifier, 213–214
Visibility symbol, 67
Visualizing systems, 2
Volatility, 263–264

W
"White box" description, 38
Words, 13
Work product, 43, 44
Worker, 43
Workflow, 43

World Wide Web, xxii
World Wide Web resource references, 391

X
XML Metadata Interchange (XMI), 9
XP, *see* eXtreme programming

Interaction Diagrams
(Sequence and Collaboration Diagrams)
(Chapter 7)

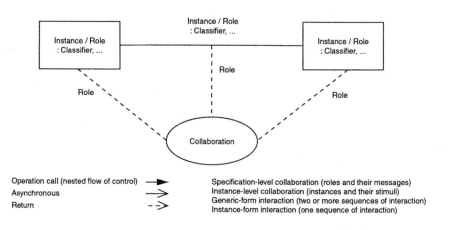

Operation call (nested flow of control) ──▶   Specification-level collaboration (roles and their messages)
Asynchronous   ──>   Instance-level collaboration (instances and their stimuli)
Return   --->   Generic-form interaction (two or more sequences of interaction)
                                             Instance-form interaction (one sequence of interaction)

Sequence Diagrams   Collaboration Diagrams

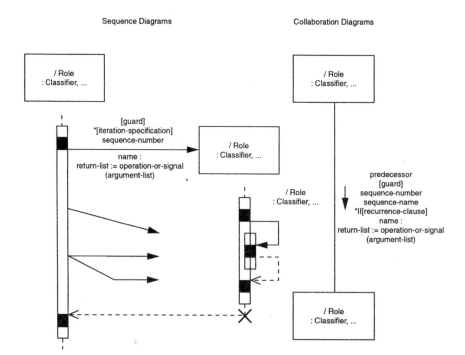